Jeopardy
in the
Courtroom

A SCIENTIFIC ANALYSIS OF CHILDREN'S TESTIMONY

Jeopardy
in the
Courtroom

A SCIENTIFIC ANALYSIS OF CHILDREN'S TESTIMONY

Stephen J. Ceci and Maggie Bruck

American Psychological Association
Washington, DC

First printing, December 1995
Second printing, January 1996
Third printing, December 1996
Fourth printing, August 1999
Fifth printing, November 2000
Sixth printing, October 2002
Seventh printing, December 2003
Eighth printing, April 2005
Ninth printing, April 2007

Published by
American Psychological Association
750 First Street, NE
Washington, DC 20002

Copies may be ordered from
APA Order Department
P.O. Box 92984
Washington, DC 20090-2984

In the UK, Europe, Africa, and the Middle East, copies may be ordered from
American Psychological Association
3 Henrietta Street
Covent Garden, London
WC2E 8LU England

Typeset in Goudy by PRO-Image Corporation, Techna-Type Div., York, PA

Printer: Port City Press, Baltimore, MD
Jacket Designer: Supon Design Group, Washington, DC
Technical/Production Editor: Olin J. Nettles

Library of Congress Cataloging-in-Publication Data
Ceci, Stephen J.
    Jeopardy in the courtroom : a scientific analysis of children's
testimony / Stephen J. Ceci & Maggie Bruck.
        p.   cm.
    Includes bibliographical references and indexes.
    ISBN 1-55798-282-1 (cloth: acid-free paper)
    ISBN 1-55798-632-0 (pbk: acid-free paper)
    1. Children as witnesses—United States.   I. Bruck, Maggie.
    KF9673.C43   1995
    347.73'083—dc20
    [347.30766083]   95-14433
                                                                   CIP

British Cataloguing-in-Publication Data
A CIP record is available from the British Library.

Printed in the United States of America

This book is dedicated to our daughters, Nicole Ceci and Lindsay Wise.

CONTENTS

PREFACE

Each year hundreds of thousands of children in North America become entangled in the legal system. Some are involved in custody and visitation disputes in family courts, others are summoned to appear in civil or juvenile justice proceedings, and still others become involved in criminal cases. Often these children testify about the alleged actions of a parent, teacher, babysitter, relative, or neighbor. And when this happens, the case is often decided on the basis of the relative credibility of the child versus the defendant. Regardless of whether such testimony is made in forensic interviews, during preliminary hearings, or at trial, it may result in life-altering decisions for all involved. Therefore, it is imperative that we better understand the factors, both beneficial and baleful, that influence children's testimony.

In this book, we attempt to describe the complexity of evaluating the accuracy of children's statements, and in so doing we attempt to alert professionals as well as caretakers of children to the need for both common and uncommon sense when interpreting such testimony. To accomplish this goal, we have distilled from the vast corpus of scientific research that part which is most relevant for evaluating and understanding children's statements that are made in the legal arena. Against this scientific backdrop, we shall describe seven actual cases involving child witnesses; we examine some of the investigative methods used in these cases and analyze the factors that may have influenced the accuracy of children's testimony. Some of these cases are used to illustrate the potential for error and misinterpretation when scientific knowledge and common sense are banished from the forensic arena.

At the outset, we wish to acknowledge some of the biases in this book. These biases become immediately evident in our selection of the seven actual cases presented in chapter 2. In six of these cases, there are reasons to be skeptical about the reliability of the children's reports. Why do we focus disproportionately on cases where children's testimony is questionable? Is it because we believe that in the vast majority of cases in which children testify, their testimony is tainted? Our answer to this question is a resounding *no*. We acknowledge the many positive dimensions of children's testimony, their ingenuousness and propensity to speak forthrightly, and their ability to accurately recall distant events. Researchers and parents are aware of such obvious strengths. In this book, however, we have chosen to emphasize the not-so-obvious negative dimensions of children's testimony as a means of increasing the awareness of all actors in the civil and criminal justice systems (attorneys, judges, law guardians, social workers, psychologists, psychiatrists, law enforcement officers) about factors that influence the veracity, durability, and reliability of children's testimony. So, although we do describe children's strengths, we focus disproportionately on their weaknesses, because it is our contention that the latter are less well understood by experts and nonexperts, whereas excellent texts already exist that describe children's strengths (see Myers, 1987a, 1987b for a compendium and analysis of cases in which children's reliability is evident).

We think it is valuable to emphasize that although there are far more documented cases that highlight the weaknesses of children's memories rather than their strengths, the latter type of cases do exist. We believe that this imbalance reflects the fact that much of the time children's statements *are* reliable and credible and in such situations the cases are quickly settled, obviating the need for further investigatory procedures and, hence, for documenting the child's testimony. In contrast, the details of the most contentious cases, those that cast doubt on the accuracy of children's statements, are often brought to public attention because these cases are covered by journalists and legal scholars. When these cases are appealed, transcripts of the original trials are often made available to researchers for scrutiny. So to repeat, although the literature is skewed toward case studies that entail weaknesses, these are probably not the most common types of cases.

Not only is our discussion slanted toward the negative dimensions of children's testimonies, but it also is slanted toward the dissection of cases that involve allegations of sexual abuse, even though sexual abuse cases represent only a minority of the cases that involve child witnesses (neglect hearings and custody disputes are both more frequent). Furthermore, most of the actual sexual abuse cases that we describe are day-care cases in which some of the children make allegations of ritualistic abuse at the hands of their caregivers. Yet these types of cases represent only a small subset of the actual sexual abuse cases. The reader may well wonder why have we sampled our case studies along these lines. We have done so for several reasons. First, the single most important context for children who testify in *criminal* trials is that of sexual abuse; we estimated elsewhere that upwards of 13,000 children testify each year in sexual abuse cases in the United States (Ceci & Bruck, 1993a), and many thousands more give depositions and unsworn statements to law enforcement officials and social workers. If we add to these the large number of civil and family court cases that also include allegations of sexual impropriety involving a child, then the absolute numbers swell considerably. Second, our discussion often centers on day-care cases because, although these may represent only a small proportion of sexual abuse complaints, in absolute numbers they involve a very large number of children (for example, in the infamous McMartin case, 369 children made disclosures of sexual abuse [Sauer, 1993]), and in other day-care cases the number of allegations is also quite large. Also, because of their high level of visibility, day-care cases are often more extensively documented than non-day-care cases, providing researchers with more reliable materials than the less visible cases.

We also focus on cases of sexual abuse in day-care settings because these present the greatest challenge to the application of social science research in the courtroom. That is, although there are some obvious parallels between laboratory studies of children's memories of unusual or surprising events (e.g., witnessing a staged argument) and the ability of child witnesses to accurately recall the details of a witnessed theft or accident, it is not clear how the results of these studies assist in understanding children's allegations of sexual abuse. Indeed, one may ask if this scientific literature has *any* relevance to such cases. The answer is *yes*, otherwise we would not have devoted two years of our professional lives to writing this book. Throughout these pages we will show how this challenge has been met by social scientists, and will describe when science can and cannot assist in understanding real-world problems.

Finally, all of the arguments we make for and against the reliability of children's testimony in sexual abuse cases apply equally to non-sexual-abuse contexts; to make this point, we include among our seven case studies a murder case involving a child witness. Although the unique aspects of sexual victimization can result in differences in children's demeanor and behavior, the underlying mechanisms governing their reports are the same regardless of whether they are couched in terms of acrimonious custody disputes, physical abuse, domestic violence, or sexual abuse. Thus, our focus on sexual abuse cases serves as a window into the more general issues regarding children's testimonial accuracy.

On the most general level, this book is intended for both the nonprofessional and the professional reader who, like the authors, are at times puzzled and disturbed by some children's allegations, wanting to delve beneath them to better understand their source and accuracy. Specifically, this book was written for three audiences. First, it is crafted for the professional who deals with child witnesses; this audience includes, but is not limited to, mental health professionals who assess and/or treat children suspected of sexual abuse, forensic investigators who interview child witnesses, attorneys, and judges. Second, we hope this book will be of interest to our social science colleagues. Although some (but by no means all) of the arguments and data that we present here have appeared in scholarly journals in the last two years, this book provides us with the opportunity to describe many new studies that are not scheduled to appear in scientific journals for another year, and also to discuss in detail the degree to which the scientific research guides our interpretation of life outside of the laboratory. As researchers know all too well, we are prevented from fully exploiting this exercise in the scientific literature because of space limitations imposed by journal editors. Third, this book is designed for the nonprofessional who, like many North Americans, has become captivated by the cases of cultural icons like Michael Jackson, Cardinal Bernadin, Roseanne Barr, and Woody Allen who have become ensnarled in a web of accusations involving childhood sexual abuse.

Our goal in making the social science literature accessible to the nonspecialist was motivated by a set of overlapping forces in our professional lives. As a result of many years of conducting studies in this field and of actively reviewing and synthesizing the scientific literature, we have been overwhelmed in the last few years by requests from the mental health and legal communities for our services as consultants and as expert witnesses. For example, in one year alone we estimated that we jointly received over 600 requests to act as expert witnesses or consultants in cases involving child witnesses. Despite these requests, we rarely agree to be expert witnesses or consultants (between us, we have had only five experiences as an expert witness in a child sex abuse case, and we have declined personal fees in these instances. We have also testified for both sides). Our reason for declining the numerous invitations to enter court as expert witnesses is because we believe that it is easier for us to educate juries, attorneys, and policymakers in our writings than under cross-examination in an adversarial system more geared toward scoring clever debate points than arriving at the truth. This book is our attempt to fulfill this educational role.

This mission has become particularly important in light of two recent court decisions that could have enormous implications for cases involving the child witness. The first decision came down from the Supreme Court of New Jersey in the case of *State v. Michaels* (1994) (which is described in chapter 2 and referred to throughout the book). In *Michaels*, the court ruled that a defendant may request a pretrial "taint hearing" to challenge the adequacy of investigative interviews with child witnesses. As such, the ruling has the potential of excluding child witnesses if they are exposed to highly suggestive interview procedures on the grounds that such procedures could taint their memory and testimony. Regardless of the ultimate wisdom of this decision, it is a warning to those who interview children that if a child is not properly interviewed, his testimony may be excluded regardless of its veracity. This book is intended to alert professionals who deal with children to the possible contaminating factors that may negatively influence the latter's testimony, and to the importance of eliminating these potentially damaging techniques from their practices. Failure to do so may result in a child's testimony being excluded from the courtroom because of interviewer blunders.

The second decision was handed down by the Supreme Court of the United States in the case of *Daubert v. Merrell Dow Pharmaceuticals* (1993) (a case that we discuss in chapter 17). The ultimate thrust of this decision, according to some legal scholars, will be to open the doors to qualifying expert witnesses regardless of their professional reputation, expertise, or scientific knowledge. We fear that this might make a bad situation even worse in this field where advocates on both sides of the bench can be found "shaping" the research to conform to the interests of the side that hired them. At its worst, this is accomplished with a veneer of professionalism, but in a lopsided, partisan manner. The *Daubert* decision may result in the admission of even more of the type of testimony that provides a limited, and at times inaccurate, view of the reliability and suggestibility of children's reports. We hope that the material covered in this book will become a part of the working knowledge of experts who testify in future cases.

To write a book on social science research for nonspecialists, we have tried to avoid jargon and technical constructs whenever possible. Thus, we have abandoned many of the conventions of scientific writing. (For example, to increase the readability of this book, we do not use gender-neutral language, but deliberately use the masculine or feminine forms of pronouns.) We do not pack the text with copious references, we do not provide the details of the theoretical arguments that guide or emerge from the research, and finally, we do not provide a comprehensive review of the literature. We have decided to omit studies that are not central to the understanding of the case studies or that are so poorly designed that there are major problems in the interpretation of the data. For the reader interested in some of these omitted technical details, we supply ample footnotes and an up-to-date reference list that includes our own work, which has been published in scientific journals. Although we present a less complex description of the existing research, we have not short-shrifted the science. Whenever appropriate, we present the details and results of scientific studies. And when appropriate, we critique studies in terms of their designs and interpretations of results. Therefore, our arguments are bolstered by a full consideration of the corpus of scientific research even when we do not regale the reader with all of its minute details.

Finally, a word about the sources of our case studies. The Little Rascals day-care case has been the subject of extensive media coverage. Some of the information in this book was taken from the three excellent documentaries produced and directed by Ofra Bikel for *Frontline* and from the numerous newspaper and magazine articles that have appeared over the last few years. The major source of our information about the Little Rascals case, however, was the actual trial transcripts of *State v. Robert Fulton Kelly, Jr.* (1991–1992) and *State v. Kathryn Dawn Wilson* (1992–1993). One of us (Maggie Bruck) was an expert witness in the former case. We thank Jeffrey Miller, one of the defense attorneys, and Rachel Miller for reading and checking the relevant facts and quotations from this case to ensure their accuracy.

The Michaels case (*State v. Michaels*, 1988) has also captured much media attention. Some of our information is taken from the book by Lisa Manshel (*Nap Time*, 1990) and the many newspaper and magazine articles that have appeared since Dorothy Rabinowitz's (1990) seminal story in *Harper's* magazine. The transcripts of the children's interviews and of the lower court of appeals documents in this case became available to us when we coauthored an amicus brief to the Supreme Court of New Jersey on this case. We thank Robert Rosenthal, the appeals attorney, for reading this manuscript and verifying the information.

The information for the *State v. Fijnje* (1991) case and the *State v. Macias* (1984) case is based on court transcripts and depositions that were made available to one of us (Stephen J. Ceci) who was an expert witness in each of these trials. We thank Juanita Crawford for fact-checking our quotes and the facts in the *Fijnje* case and Doug Robinson for checking the details of the *Macias* case.

The material from Country Walk (*State v. Fuster*, 1985) was taken from Jan Hollingsworth's well-known book about this case, *Unspeakable Acts* (1986), and from Debbie Nathan's (1993a, 1993b) recent articles, as well as from appellate requests submitted to the state by Robert Rosenthal and Arthur Cohen. We relied on official transcripts from this case whenever appropriate. We thank Robert Rosenthal and Debbie Nathan for verifying our accounts of the details of this case.

Our description of the rape at Devil's Dyke, the least detailed of our seven case studies, is based on a series of newspaper articles that appeared in the *London Times* (Horsnell, 1990a, 1990b), as well as on the actual trial transcripts that we purchased.

Throughout this book, we refer to the facts of these cases and when they are available we quote from the trial transcripts and from the investigatory and therapeutic interviews. We have lightly edited these transcripts for dysfluencies and redundancies, but we have never altered the meaning. In addition, to protect the identities of the child witnesses and their families, we have changed their names throughout.

Finally, no undertaking that crosses disciplinary boundaries is possible without the advice and support of many individuals, and this monograph is no exception. We gratefully acknowledge the support of Lucy McGough, Dawn Dekle, John Doris, and Debra Poole, who read preliminary versions of the manuscript and provided numerous and cogent suggestions for improvement. We are also grateful to the excellent help and advice of our editors, Olin J. Nettles and Judy Nemes. Finally, we wish to thank Dort Bigg for his advice and comments. Although the responsibility for what is said throughout these pages is ours alone, without their help and encouragement, we feel that this book would be greatly diminished.

1

INTRODUCTION

An emotional battle is being waged today in our nations' courtrooms, universities, and living rooms. This battle revolves around the credibility of children's testimony, particularly in sexual abuse cases. To listen to one side, you would think that everything that a child tells a social worker or therapist must be believed, no matter how bizarre the allegations, no matter how suggestive or coercive the techniques used to elicit them. The thrust of this side's argument is that because it is difficult for children to reveal the details of their victimization, special techniques must be used to elicit them, such as leading questions, fantasy play, nonverbal props, and various forms of guided imagery. When children subjected to such techniques eventually disclose the details of their abuse, we must believe them because children do not generate false reports of their own sexual victimization.

The other side would have us believe that because young children are more vulnerable to erroneous suggestions and leading questions than are older children and adults, we should always greet their disclosures of abuse with a large dose of skepticism. Child witnesses are depicted by this side as helpless sponges who soak up the interviewers' suggestions and regurgitate these suggestions in court.

If children are as resistant to suggestions or if children are as susceptible to suggestions as the proponents of these opposing camps would have us believe, then decisions about their credibility could be made very easily:

1

Either they should always be believed (save the most egregiously incredible accounts), or they ought never to be believed (except for those rare cases that contain adult eyewitnesses or definitive medical evidence). We believe that these two extreme positions are equally misguided. Anyone who has ever had to make such a decision knows all too well how difficult it can be. A blend of credible and noncredible claims often coexist within a single allegation, rendering the task of deciding the truth quite difficult. Claims that children should almost always be believed exaggerate their strengths and minimize their weaknesses, whereas claims that children's disclosures should be greeted with skepticism minimize their strengths and exaggerate their weaknesses. In our view, such extreme positions about children's credibility are more appropriately categorized under the rubric of "partisan advocacy" than under the heading of "scientifically derived insights."

To illustrate the problem with these two extremes, we cast this argument over children's suggestibility as one that focuses either on the "numerator" (the number of true allegations of abuse *or* the number of false allegations of abuse) or on the "denominator" (the total number of true *and* false allegations of abuse). Those who believe in the ultimate credibility of children often fail to take seriously the number of false allegations in the denominator; that is, they fail to consider the prevalence of false allegations. Similarly, those who defend the position that child witnesses are highly unreliable rarely consider the very large number of cases in the denominator in which child victim-witnesses *are* credible, not to mention the large number of cases of abuse that go unreported.

The numerator/denominator example can be taken one step further in highlighting the weaknesses in the logic of the extremists in this debate. Advocates on one side often claim that it is sometimes necessary to aggressively interview children suspected of sexual abuse in order to obtain reports of their traumatic experiences, whereas advocates on the other side argue that the use of leading questions ineluctably will result in nonabused children making false claims of assault. Both of these arguments fail to consider the combined costs and benefits of passive versus aggressive interviewing practices. For example, before either of these claims can be substantiated, it is important to determine the proportion of abused children who are initially too scared or confused to divulge the details of their victimization, but who will eventually do so if they are questioned more aggressively, as well as the proportion of nonabused children who will eventually disclose false details of abuse if they are aggressively questioned. Thus, the centrists in this battle argue that it is not enough to know that aggressive interviewing techniques will result in reliable disclosures from children who were victimized, but it is also important to determine the risk of using these techniques—that is, the number of nonabused children who will make inaccurate statements under similar conditions. As we will show, these twin dangers need to be considered concurrently.

There is an interesting medical analogy to this battle between the numerators and denominators. Suppose there was a drug that prevented cancer in patients with malignant tumors that are too small to be detected. That is, if the drug were given to these patients, their cancer would be cured. But suppose the same drug created cancer in patients who were cancer-free. Assuming that no reliable method exists for detecting which individuals have cancer and which do not, should this drug be administered to everyone? Probably not—there might be far more cancer-free individuals who would be harmed by administering the drug than there are cancerous individuals who could be cured. Should the drug only be administered to those individuals whose symptoms or histories indicate they are "at risk" (e.g., a 4 out of 5 chance) for having cancer? It depends. Is the diagnostic test for determining the 80% risk status valid? And, if so, is the risk of infecting the 20% who do not have the disease a price we are willing to pay for the chance to treat the 80% who do? These are questions about which reasonable people can and do disagree.

We will argue that the situation regarding children's suggestibility is much like this cancer analogy. Those who focus on the numerators are right to point out that children who have been victimized often do not disclose the details of their victimization easily: If these children are merely asked open-ended questions—questions such as "Is there something you wish to tell me?" or "Can you tell me everything that happened?" or "Can you tell me more?"—many will never disclose the details of their abuse. Unless interviewers pursue these abused children, often across multiple interviews, with a variety of aggressive interviewing techniques, true instances of abuse may go undetected, needed mental health intervention may be undelivered, and these children will remain vulnerable to being revictimized by the perpetrators in their lives. On the other hand, if we pursue children who were not abused in this same aggressive manner, this may result in some nonvictimized children making false disclosures. In later chapters, we shall describe the research basis for this claim. But for now, the point that we wish to make is simply that there seems to be a dilemma between doing all that we can to elicit actual disclosures (i.e., treating cancer) and simultaneously avoiding these very same techniques out of fear that they could lead to false disclosures (i.e., inducing cancer in healthy individuals).

There is a cartoon that appears on the walls of many child protective service workers' offices. In the first panel, a social worker stands blindfolded in front of a firing squad. The caption reads, "Social worker shot for removing child from family too quickly." The next panel shows the same social worker in front of a different firing squad, but with the caption "Social worker shot for removing child from family too slowly." Clearly, the task facing frontline workers who are charged with the protection of children suspected of being abused is a formidable one. If they use their full arsenal of techniques to elicit a disclosure, there is always the risk that it might be false, and the child and family will face serious negative consequences. If they do not pursue disclosures persistently, even aggressively, there is always the risk that they will fail to remove a child from a dangerous situation until it is too late. In this balancing act, it seems as though the options are to cure cancer in some by inducing it in others. Fortunately, there are steps midway between the two approaches that can and should be adhered to when interviewing young children. These are described throughout this book. They are bound to displease extremists on both sides of the debate, as we make the case that the needs of both science and society dictate a middle ground.

Where do we place ourselves in these debates? First, we consider ourselves to be numerator *and* denominator watchers; as both scientists and parents, we think it would be truly awful to ever lose sight of the enormity of child abuse in America today. We recoil at an earlier generation's denial of the magnitude of the problem that exists at all levels of society and at rates that are so high as to call into question some basic assumptions that we hold about ourselves as a people and about the inherently healthy status of the American family. America's children, our own daughters included, deserve no less than our honest appraisal of this problem and our vigorous efforts at protection. Having said this, however, we also do not ignore the possibility of false allegations: We must always temper the incidence of true disclosures with the possibility of false ones. Although there are no reliable data on the frequency of false claims of sexual abuse (existing estimates being problematic for a number of reasons that we shall later describe), a focus on the total number of claims (the denominator) allows us to consider the number of false allegations (the numerator). Thus, although false claims exist, and perhaps in nontrivial numbers, we also believe that, in absolute numbers, the incidence of sexual abuse is very large and must never be minimized.

We do not believe that our position on children's suggestibility can be classified at either extreme on the prosecution-to-defense continuum. That is, although we think that there are data that highlight the potential weaknesses of children's reports, we do not think that these data are so consistent as to categorically discredit children from testifying or even to recommend skepticism upon hearing a child's disclosure. Our position has not been accepted by leading representatives of both extremes of the advocacy spectrum. There have even been times when representatives on each side have tried to thwart the publication of our ideas by organizing letter-writing campaigns to pressure editors against publishing our work. We tell ourselves that because we are attacked by extremists on both sides of the debate, this may indicate that we are doing something right.

In the next 17 chapters of this book we will present the data and arguments that have guided our opinions on these matters. The first five chapters provide the reader with the technical background that is drawn on in the rest of the book. Chapter 2 presents summaries of the seven case histories that will be referred to in the later chapters, as windows through which we may observe the research findings unfold. Chapter 3 provides a discussion and consideration of the available prevalence and incidence statistics on child abuse and on child witnesses in the courtroom. In chapter 4, we provide the reader with a minicourse on some of the psychological terms (such as *memory* and *suggestibility*) that are used in this book. This chapter is the most theoretical in the book; it can probably be skipped without losing the main thread of our argument in the rest of the book. In chapter 5 we provide a historical sketch of the research on children's suggestibility, beginning with the first studies carried out at the turn of the 20th century. In chapter 6 we approach the modern era, and we detail some studies that highlight the strengths of children's memories about being touched when they are interviewed under very controlled and neutral conditions. The next six chapters represent the core of our arguments. We set the stage in chapter 7 by exploring the structure and dynamics of daily conversations between children and adults; we then use this framework to consider the dynamics observed in forensic and therapeutic interviews with children. The degree to which some of the elements used in therapeutic and forensic interviews influence the accuracy of children's reports is considered in chapters 8, 9, 10, and 11, where we review the most recent scientific literature and discuss the implications of the use of certain techniques in the case histories. Chapter 12 continues this format, but it focuses on the use of anatomically detailed dolls, a technique that is quite specific to the interviewing of children suspected of being sexually abused. Chapters 13 and 14 address the highly controversial topic of the recovery of repressed memories of early childhood sexual abuse. Part of this presentation is concerned with how children and adults who *have* been victimized come to report stressful events. The available evidence is critical for understanding the degree to which children deny or forget highly salient or stressful events and for understanding the effects of various interview practices on children's report accuracy. In chapter 15 we take up the important issue concerning age differences in the reliability of reports. Particularly, in this chapter we examine the generalizability of the research findings that often depict young children's performance as inferior in relation to older children's and adults'. We end the chapter with a discussion of some weaknesses of adults' memories. Chapter 16 covers a number of related issues on the psychological and social mechanisms that might account for suggestibility. In chapter 17 of this book we explore the world of professional conduct: how experts testify in court and how professionals treat children. Finally, we conclude in chapter 18 by discussing the generalizability of the social scientific studies discussed in this book, warning against overinterpretation and underinterpretation of the data.

2

CHILDREN AS WITNESSES: SEVEN CASE DESCRIPTIONS

In this chapter we present brief summaries of seven case studies in which children were key witnesses in criminal trials. We chose these cases because, between them, they contain the key elements of the cases we are sent by judges, attorneys, and mental health professionals. For example, child witnesses are either victims of crime or bystanders who observe a crime; some cases involve preschool child witnesses, whereas others involve older children. Sometimes the adults who interview the child attempt to actively explore a number of possible explanations for the child's allegations, whereas some adult interviewers primarily attempt to gather evidence that is supportive of the child's allegations; some children's allegations are spontaneous, but sometimes they emerge only after many forensic or therapeutic sessions. And finally, in an attempt to help the child disclose, some therapists use techniques such as repeated suggestive questioning, visually guided imagery, hypnotic regression, trance inductions, role playing, and self-empowerment training, whereas others do not. In short, the following seven cases were chosen because they provide windows into the world of criminal investigations in which a child is a witness. We start with a brief description of each of these seven cases and then return to them throughout the book, adding more details about each case as it becomes relevant.

As will be seen, juries in some of these cases believed the child, whereas in others they appear not to have done so.

THE SALEM WITCH TRIALS

It may come as a surprise to start off this chapter with a 300-year-old case. We do so not only because it is the earliest recorded instance in American jurisprudence that involved the testimony of child witnesses, but also because it has had long-lasting effects on our attitudes about child witnesses. Some of the elements present in the Salem trials are also present in some of the modern cases involving child witnesses, as we will see later.

Many readers know that during the final decade of the 17th century, a group of children known as the "circle girls" gave testimony in the witch-craft trials of over 20 residents of Salem Village and Salem Farms, Massachusetts. The girls, ages 5 to 16, claimed to have seen the defendants flying on broom sticks, to have witnessed celestial apparitions in the form of speaking animals, and to have observed the defendants instructing insects to fly into the girls' mouths and deposit bent nails and pins in their stomachs that they subsequently vomited during their testimony (Seth, 1969). On the basis of the girls' testimony, 19 defendants were convicted and put to death, and a dozen more were spared execution when they threw themselves on the mercy of the court and admitted their participation in witchcraft. In the aftermath of these executions, some of the child witnesses publicly recanted their testimonies.

Although some commentators have dismissed the Salem trials as irrelevant to modern concerns over the credibility of child witnesses (e.g., Goodman, 1984; Myers, 1994), the children of Salem were subjected to an array of social and cultural forces that at times have been present in modern legal cases, though in reduced form (Ceci, Toglia, & Ross, 1990). To begin with, Salem, at the time leading up to the witch trials, was an emotionally charged community, with accounts of witchcraft common-place. Nearly everyone in 17th century Salem believed in the power of witches. Thus, the court's willingness to accept the children's testimony about flying broomsticks and celestial apparitions was understandable in terms of their shared beliefs. Because of the widespread belief in witchcraft, one was particularly careful to avoid any display of behaviors that resembled those of witches. Therefore, the motivations of some of the child witnesses, whose own behaviors were viewed by some with suspicion, is understandable; their testimony may have been a means of diverting attention from themselves.

The willingness to accept the Salem children's testimony also reflected the cultural zeitgeist regarding children's innocence. This was a time when our colonial ancestors took literally the biblical aphorism "Out of the mouths of babes . . . you have perfected praise." Adults believed that children's innocence enabled them to recognize evils that they themselves could not recognize because of having dwelt in a tainted world. Anyone so evil as to make a pact with the devil (which is what a witch was thought to have done) could be recognized by an innocent child for their vileness. Thus, adults not only "could" accept a child's testimony, they "must" do so because their own lost innocence compromised their ability to recognize evil. This colonial belief in children's ability to see the truth was correctly captured in Arthur Miller's (1953) play *The Crucible* in the skepticism of Judge Danforth:

> Do you know, Mister Proctor, that the entire contention of the state in these trials is that the voice of heaven is speaking through the children? (p. 168)

The adults who interrogated the circle girls used eclectic interviewing techniques. On the one hand, parents and other powerful adults actively encouraged and shaped their children's "recollections" by encouraging them to elaborate their statements, always providing leading questions and positive attention for answers congruent with the charge of witchcraft. Sometimes the children were locked in jail cells for days while they were relentlessly interviewed. On the other hand, adults at times behaved quite rationally in terms of the precautions that they instituted to prevent tainted evidence. For example, several girls vomited bent nails and pins (claimed to be the result of a witch instructing bees to deposit them in their mouths). Villagers removed all nails from the floorboards of the girls' homes, and all pins from their hems, to insure that they were not swallowing these objects purposely. Unfortunately, they did not manage to remove all of them.

Although some of the features surrounding the trials including child witnesses have changed from the days of Salem (for example, we no longer incarcerate child witnesses for days on end), in other ways they have not. Thus, we shall revisit these witch trials later when their lessons for contemporary cases can be unlocked.

THE LITTLE RASCALS DAY CARE CASE

Bob and Betsy Kelly owned and operated the Little Rascals Day Care Center in Edenton, North Carolina. Betsy was primarily responsible for the day-to-day running of Little Rascals while Bob, a licensed plumbing contractor and golf pro, helped out as needed. Set in an idyllic hamlet in northeastern North Carolina, by all appearances Little Rascals was the premiere nursery school for middle-class and upper-middle-class parents to send their preschoolers. All of this changed in the winter of 1989.

In January 1989, a parent of one of the children enrolled at Little Rascals alleged that Bob Kelly had sexually abused her son at the day-care center. This allegation was investigated by Brenda Toppin, an officer with the Edenton Police Department, and by the county's Department of Social Services. On the basis of their interviews with several children enrolled at Little Rascals, they concluded that the allegation was valid.

In February 1989, three additional children made allegations. Soon a wave of panic gripped this small town as parents became more uneasy about whether their own children had also been abused. The local police advised parents to have their children evaluated for abuse, and the police supplied parents with a list of recommended therapists.

Although few children made disclosures when repeatedly questioned by their parents and police officers about suspected abuse, other children would eventually make allegations only after many sessions of therapy. Some of these children took up to 10 months of therapeutic intervention before they began to make allegations.

Eventually, 90 children would make allegations involving physical and sexual abuse, and 85% of these were evaluated and treated by three therapists. Most of the alleged events were claimed to have occurred between September 1988 and December 1988. Although the initial allegations had involved only Bob Kelly, soon they expanded to include dozens of people in the town. Eventually, seven adults were arrested and charged with sexual abuse. These included Betsy Kelly, Dawn Wilson, Robin Byrum, and Shelley Stone, all young women who worked at the day-care center, and Scott Privott, the son of a judge, the president of the country club, and the owner of the local video store. (Privott claimed to have never set foot in the Little Rascals Day Care Center.) Darlene Harris, another of the accused, worked at a Head Start Center that was located several miles from Little Rascals.

The charges against these defendants involved rape, sodomy, and fellatio. Children told of having to perform sexual acts on other children, of having their pictures taken while performing such acts, and of having assorted objects, such as pins and markers, placed into vaginal or anal openings. There were allegations involving "ritualistic" abuse: Betsy and Bob burned a cat with a candle, they murdered babies. Some children claimed to have been tied up, to have been hung upside down from trees, to have been set on fire, and to have been given drugs that made them feel sick and drowsy. Finally, even more improbable claims were made, such as being taken by boat and thrown overboard into a school of circling sharks.

The first of the seven trials, Bob Kelly's, began in August 1991 (*State v. Robert Fulton Kelly, Jr.*, 1991–1992). Twelve children and their parents were among the many witnesses who testified about incidents that allegedly occurred 3 years earlier. These children's memories appear to have been refreshed by their therapy sessions, through meetings with the prosecution, by repeated discussions with their parents about the events, and through attending "court school" to prepare them for their testimony in court. The parents' memories were refreshed through their diaries and through meetings that were conducted by the district attorney's office.

One of the more surprising aspects of this case, and others like it, was the fact that none of the parents of the Little Rascals children had observed anything that caused them to suspect that their children were being abused or tortured during the period of the alleged abuses; there were no reports of unusual incidents from their children. Nor did the parents detect anything unusual when, without notice, they dropped in early to pick up their children from the day care (e.g., to take them to a doctor's appointment). It was only after allegations began to grow that parents also began to remember events or behaviors that were consistent with their child being abused.

Bob Kelly's trial lasted 8 months and was the most expensive criminal proceeding in North Carolina's history. It also was a media sensation, with national newspapers, magazines, and electronic media covering it. PBS's *Frontline* aired three 2-hour specials on this case, winning an Emmy award for its producer, Ofra Bikel (1991, 1993a, 1993b). The media coverage, outside of North Carolina, was decidedly slanted toward the defense. However, despite the media outcry against the state's evidence, the juries returned guilty verdicts across the board: On April 22, 1992, a jury returned "guilty" verdicts on 99 of 100 charges against Bob Kelly, and he was sentenced to serve 12 consecutive life sentences. He would not be eligible for parole during his lifetime. One year later, Dawn Wilson (*State v. Kathryn Dawn Wilson*, 1992–1993) was convicted of five counts of abusing four children; she was sentenced to life imprisonment. In December 1993, Betsy Kelly, who had already spent 2 years in prison awaiting trial, pleaded no contest. After serving 1 year of a 7-year prison sentence, she was released on parole. In June 1994, Scott Privott pleaded no contest to 37 charges involving 16 children. After having served three and a half years in jail before posting bond in June 1993, Privott was placed on probation for 5 years. In short, it appeared as though the first four cases represented a clean sweep for the prosecution. However, on May 2, 1995, the Court of Appeals of North Carolina unanimously reversed the convictions of Bob Kelly and Dawn Wilson. The prosecution has petitioned the North Carolina Supreme Court for a discretionary review. We refer to this case through the book as *Little Rascals*.

THE KELLY MICHAELS CASE

On August 2, 1988, Margaret Kelly Michaels, a 26-year-old nursery school teacher, was convicted of sexually abusing children at the Wee Care Nursery School in Maplewood, New Jersey (*State v. Michaels*, 1988). Kelly

Michaels was said to have licked peanut butter off children's genitals, played the piano while nude, made children drink her urine and eat her feces, and raped and assaulted these children with knives, forks, spoons, and Lego blocks. She was accused of performing these acts during regular school hours over a period of 7 months. During this time, none of the alleged acts were noticed by staff or reported by children to their parents. Nor did any of the parents notice any signs of strange behavior or genital soreness in their children, or smell urine or feces on them when they collected them from school at the end of the day.

The first suspicion that Kelly Michaels abused her charges occurred 4 days after she had left the Wee Care Nursery School to accept a better paying position elsewhere. At that time, a 4-year-old former student of Michaels was having his temperature taken rectally at his pediatrician's office when he said to the nurse, "That's what my teacher does to me at school." When asked to explain, he replied, "Her takes my temperature." That afternoon, the child's mother notified the state's child protective agency.

Two days later, the child was brought to the prosecutor's office, where he inserted his finger into the rectum of an anatomical doll and told the assistant prosecutor that two other boys also had their temperature taken. When questioned, neither of these other boys seemed to know anything about this claim, but one of them indicated that Kelly Michaels had touched his penis. The first child's mother then told a parent member of the school board of her son's disclosures to the pediatrician and assistant prosecutor. This father questioned his son, who told him that Michaels had touched his penis with a spoon.

The Wee Care Nursery School sent out a letter to all parents, informing them of an investigation of a former employee "regarding serious allegations made by a child," and invited a social worker, who codirected a sexual assault unit at a nearby hospital, to make a presentation to the parents. This social worker explained that sexual abuse of children is very common, with one out of three children being victims of an "inappropriate sexual experience" by the time he or she is 18 years old. She encouraged parents to examine their children for genital soreness, nightmares, bed wetting, masturbation, or any noticeable changes in behavior, and to have them examined by pediatricians for injury.

Over the next 2 months, a number of professionals interviewed the children and their families to determine the extent to which the abuse occurred. The most prolific of these interviewers was Lou Fonolleras, an investigator from the Division of Youth and Family Services. Between May 22 and July 8, 1985, he and his coinvestigators conducted approximately 80 interviews with Wee Care children and 19 interviews with Wee Care parents. As was true in the Little Rascals case, many children began to disclose only after they had been interviewed on several occasions by the state's investigators or by their therapists.

Between June and November, three grand juries convened and determined, partly on the basis of the children's testimony, that the case should go to trial. The interviewing of the children did not stop, however. As also was true in the Little Rascals case, one therapist evaluated or treated a large number of the child witnesses. She conducted five group therapy sessions with the Wee Care children and eventually assessed or treated 13 of the 20 child witnesses named in the indictment. The children were also interviewed on multiple occasions by the prosecutors before the Grand Jury hearings, as well as before and during the trial. Finally, before going to trial, the children were interviewed several times by the prosecution's appointed expert, Eileen Treacy.

The trial began two and a half years after the first allegation was made. On the basis of the testimony provided by 19 child witnesses, Kelly Michaels was convicted of 115 counts of sexual abuse against 20 three- to five-year-old children. Sentenced to serve 47 years in prison, Michaels was released on bail after 5 years as a result of the Appeals Court of New Jersey reversing her conviction (State v. Michaels, 1993). The prosecution appealed part of the decision to the Supreme Court of New Jersey; their appeal was denied (State v. Michaels, 1994). The court ruled that if the prosecution decided to retry the case, they must first hold a pretrial taint hearing and show that despite improper interviewing techniques, the statements and testimony of the child witnesses are sufficiently reliable to admit them as witnesses at trial. In December 1994, the prosecution dropped all charges against Michaels. We refer to this case throughout this book as *Michaels*.

THE OLD CUTLER PRESBYTERIAN CASE

In *State v. Fijnje* (1991), Robert Fijnje was accused of sexually abusing a large number of preschool children who attended a church-sponsored day care center in Miami, Florida over a 2-year period. At the time of the alleged abuse, the defendant, a teacher's assistant in the Old Cutler Presbyterian day care, was between 11 and 13 years old.

The initial disclosure came from a 3-year-old child who was in therapy for regressive toileting practices, nightmares, and refusal to attend the church day care. When questioned by her therapist during the initial session as to why she did not want to attend the day care, the young child said that there was a boy who played too roughly, tossing her into the air and catching her. (It was subsequently confirmed by the staff that the defendant did indeed do this, ignoring protests from the children that he was tossing them too high.) Despite an absence of any disclosures of sexual abuse by the child during that session or any physical or corroborative evidence, the therapist appears to have held the hypothesis from the very first session that sexual abuse was at the root of the child's difficulties, because she made her beliefs known after the initial therapy session and soon after she made her first report to the state's Hotline for Abuse.

An official investigation, prompted by the therapist's initial report to the state hotline, produced no reliable evidence to support her suspicions of abuse. However, after approximately 3 more months of therapy, with the assistance of anatomical dolls, the child disclosed the first details of her alleged sexual molestation. Over the course of the following several months, she named a number of other children and adults whom she claimed were present during the abuse.

When notified by the therapist about her daughter's disclosures, her mother proceeded to inform the parents of the other children who were named by her daughter that their children may also have been sexually abused. These parents then enrolled their children in psychotherapy, and after some months in therapy, many of them also disclosed sexual abuse by the defendant, corroborating the first child's report. These children also disclosed some seemingly incredible acts, such as dismembering and eating a human baby, murdering and burying a man, and being driven to distant locations from which they walked back to their day care—alone.

Robert Fijnje was arrested just after turning 14, and he was held in a Dade County youthful offender facility until the end of his trial nearly 2 years later. None of the children testified at this trial; rather, their allegations were relayed to the court via a hearsay exception through their therapists. In Florida, Fijnje would be sentenced to life without parole if he was convicted on any of the criminal charges against him. On May 4, 1991, at the age of 16, Robert Fijnje was acquitted by an eight-member Florida jury on all counts. We refer to this case throughout this book as *Old Cutler*.

THE COUNTRY WALK BABYSITTING SERVICE CASE

Approximately 20 miles southwest of Miami Beach sits a middle-class community known as Country Walk. Francisco "Frank" Fuster Escalona was 36 years old, a small businessman who operated a decorating service out of his house. Iliana Fuster, Frank's 17-year-old wife, operated a day-care facility out of their home, called the Country Walk Babysitting Service.

Around 1983, parents began suspecting that something strange was going on at the Fusters' home because of numerous problems with their children. The case seems to have started when a 3-year-old boy who attended the baby-sitting service told his mother to "kiss my body—Iliana kisses all the babies' bodies." This mother expressed her concern to other parents of children in the Country Walk Babysitting Service. Later, another parent believed her child had been drugged after his first day with Iliana Fuster.

The authorities were notified, and the children were soon interviewed. Two of the main interviewers, Dr. Joseph Braga and Dr. Laurie Braga, became interested in issues related to child protection while designing early childhood education programs for publicly funded inner-city daycare centers. They were contracted by the state as volunteer interviewers of children.

It seems that most children denied abuse in the early interviews but eventually told interviewers about events that had allegedly taken place several years earlier, when they were between the ages of 1 and 5. They claimed that Frank and Iliana kissed their penises, inserted fingers into their rectums, and paraded nude in front of the children. The children also claimed that Frank Fuster videotaped their sexual abuse, although the alleged tapes were never found. Interleaved among the children's plausible allegations were fabulous ones, such as riding on sharks and eating the head of another person. One of the most important pieces of evidence for the prosecution was the finding that Frank Fuster's 6-year-old son by a previous marriage, who lived with the couple, tested positive for gonorrhea of the throat.

In 1986, Frank and Iliana Fuster were tried on multiple counts of child abuse, rape (sexual battery), sodomy, terrorism, and lewdness involving eight children. Only one child testified in open court about these allegations. Another four children testified on closed-circuit television. After nearly 15 months of adamant denials, Iliana Fuster turned state's evidence against her husband and corroborated many of the claims that the children had made against him. Frank Fuster was convicted of 14 counts of sodomy, rape, and abuse and is serving the equivalent of several consecutive life sentences (*State v. Francisco Fuster*, 1985). He will not be eligible for parole until the year 2150, when he turns 201. For her part in the children's abuse, Iliana pleaded guilty to 12 counts of raping, molesting, and terrorizing children and was sentenced to a 10-year term with 10 additional years of probation. In 1989, after serving three and a half years, she was released and deported to Honduras, her homeland.

We had originally included this case because at the time of Frank Fuster's trial there was corroborating evidence to affirm the reliability of the children's allegations, particularly in regard to sexual abuse and to ritualistic sexual abuse. This case thus provided some substantiation to the claim that large numbers of preschool children were being systematically raped and traumatized by perpetrators belonging to satanic cults. We had planned to use this case to argue that even under certain negative circumstances, children could still provide accurate reports of their abuse. However, as we will discuss in later chapters, new evidence has emerged to cast some doubt on the reliability of the corroborating evidence. Thus, this sample case that was originally selected to highlight children's strengths could turn out to be somewhat more ambiguous. We refer to this case throughout this book as *Country Walk*.

THE RAPE ON DEVIL'S DYKE CASE

The four cases we have described each involved multiple allegations of sexual abuse against day-care workers by a number of preschoolers. But there are other circumstances that eventuate in children becoming witnesses about sexual abuse. These cases involve allegations of abuse by a member of the child's family, or by a friend of the family, and in some cases by a stranger. The latter cases require not only that the child describe the alleged events but that she also identify the alleged perpetrator from a lineup, photo parade, or mug book. As the following case shows, sometimes children can be quite accurate in identifying an alleged perpetrator, even after lengthy delays.

On February 4, 1990, a 7-year-old girl named Rachel W., who lived outside Brighton, England, was roller skating past a parked red Ford Cortina with an open trunk. As the girl skated past the parked Cortina, a man suddenly grabbed her from behind and threw her into the trunk and drove off. She was taken to a remote wooded area known as Devil's Dyke, located 14 miles away in East Sussex. It was here that the man transferred Rachel from the trunk to the back seat of the Cortina and raped and attempted to strangle her. She was left for dead in some nearby bushes. After regaining consciousness, the girl staggered down a mud path until she saw some strangers. She was naked and crying and asked, "Are you kidnappers, too?" (Horsnell, 1990a). These strangers took her to the police station.

Rachel told the police how she removed her roller skates while lying in the trunk, so that she could run away when her abductor opened it. Daylight, entering through a crack in the trunk, enabled her to see several items, including a hammer, a chisel, a can of WD-40, a screwdriver, and an orange pen, which she later described to police. She also described her male attacker: He was in his 30s or 40s, dressed in blue, wearing a moustache and a gold watch with a gold strap. On the basis of her description, police arrested Russell Bishop, a 24-year-old unemployed laborer who was a father of three. Bishop, who had been acquitted of assaulting and murdering two 9-year-old girls exactly 3 years earlier, denied that he was guilty of the rape of Rachel at Devil's Dyke and insisted that police were harassing him because of his prior acquittal in the murder case.

Rachel's recollections proved to be uneven. She overestimated the attacker's age but was completely accurate about the items in the trunk of his car, as well about his watch and clothing and moustache. Three days after the attack, Rachel correctly picked Bishop from a lineup without hesitation. After a 5-month investigation that included DNA tests on the semen and saliva samples taken from Rachel, Bishop was brought to trial (*R. v. Russell Bishop*, 1990). Forensic scientists testified that there was only one chance in 80 million that the assailant could be someone other than Bishop (Horsnell, 1990b). He was convicted and sentenced to life imprisonment. We refer to this case throughout the book as *Devil's Dyke*.

THE FREDERICO MARTINEZ MACIAS CASE

Although most of the well-known cases that involve child witnesses concern sexual and physical abuse, children have also served as key witnesses in a wide range of cases, including first-degree murder trials. This final case study is an example.

On January 5, 1984, Frederico "Fred" Macias, a worker in the Old Baltimore Spice Factory in El Paso, Texas, was charged with the armed robbery and murder of an elderly couple, the Haneys. The basis for Macias's arrest was a claim made by a man named Pedro Luevanos, who, when apprehended, was found to possess the decedents' stolen property. Luevanos agreed to plead guilty to armed robbery if the state of Texas would not indict him on first-degree murder. Luevanos told the police that his accomplice in Haney's robbery, Fred Macias, was the actual killer. He claimed that he tried unsuccessfully to talk Macias out of using a machete to slash Haney and his wife to death and that his own role was limited to robbing their home. When arrested, Macias denied being at the murder scene and presented two witnesses to place him elsewhere at the time of the crime.

The law of Texas recognizes that the testimony of an accomplice is inherently suspect, and therefore corroboration is strongly desirable. In the aftermath of Fred Macias's arrest, the state of Texas had only one dubious corroborating witness to back up Luevanos's story. This witness was a fellow inmate of Macias's who received a reduced sentence for his testimony that Macias had told him about his role in the murder.

Another witness was clearly needed, and one was found nearly 6 months later, when a 9-year-old girl named Jennifer F. reported that she had been playing at the defendant's trailer on the afternoon of the murders. Jennifer F. told police that she remembered 6 months earlier when Macias had returned home with blood splattered on his shirt and hands, toting a long BB gun/rifle. Jennifer F. made this revelation just 5 days prior to the start of Macias's trial (*State v. Frederico Martinez Macias*, 1984), when an investigator just happened to be visiting Macias's trailer park and became engaged in casual conversation with the child and her friend. Realizing the potential importance of her story, the police and other law enforcement personnel began a vigorous interrogation of Jennifer F. in the days leading up to the trial.

The decision to put Jennifer F. on the witness stand was made the night before the trial began, and the defense was not informed of her role until 40 minutes prior to the start of the trial. From all accounts, Jennifer F. made a highly effective witness. Although her pretrial statements were riddled with contradictory and implausible claims, by the time of the trial, she managed to provide a coherent story.

Fred Macias was convicted of felonious murder, and under Texas law sentenced to death by lethal injection. Depositions by the foreman of the jury as well as counsel for both sides indicated that Jennifer F. provided the critical testimony that led to Macias's conviction. In a "stay of execution" plea 3 years later, an Appeals Court judge ruled that Fred Macias was entitled to a new trial on the grounds that, among other things, the state of Texas had erred by not allowing the defense's expert witness to testify on children's suggestibility. We refer to this case throughout the book as *Macias*.

SUMMARY

These seven sketches raise a number of intriguing questions about the very essence of human memory, of children's credibility and reliability, and of jurors' ability to discern fact from fiction when evaluating children's reports, especially when the children have been repeatedly interviewed over long periods of time. At times, the details of these cases make us cringe, as we question the very basis of our humanity and treatment of children. For example, if some of the details are taken at face value, it leads to some of the following conclusions. These cases seem to provide persuasive evidence that adults have perpetrated horrendous acts on helpless young children, including ritualistic torture, animal sacrifice, and sexual predation. These cases also appear to show how successfully adults can terrorize entire classrooms of children so that acts of sexual abuse and terrorism can be kept secret or can even be repressed from their memories. Several of these cases appear to show that despite suggestive questioning, children can eventually reveal the true facts of their abuse; one can assume that they are telling the truth because within and across cases, a number of children provide the same facts.

But these very same cases can raise doubts about the accuracy of children's reports. They force us to reconsider some basic notions of memory, of child development, and of motivation. They lead us to ask how the dynamics of a conversation or interview can be so powerful as to lead children to make highly graphic and realistic statements for events that they have never experienced. They lead us to ponder whether children in such situations deliberately lie or whether they are unaware of the inaccuracy of their statements. Some of these cases lead us to ask whether some children may have been aware of the fact that they fabricated events in the early interviews, but that with the passage of time these reports became incorporated into their memories and they came to believe them to be real incidents. Finally, these cases lead us to question if the same factors that can account for the behaviors of young children can also account for similar behaviors in older children and adults.

Although we may not know the answers to these questions for any specific case, in this book we will present the relevant data from social science research along with additional details of the cases that allow us to rationally address these issues. At times, the picture is "mixed," with some research tilting toward support of the accuracy of the children's reports, and other research leaning toward support of the inaccuracy of children's reports. Although no single study is definitive, scientists are more impressed by patterns of data that converge on an interpretation. This book is an attempt to present the pattern in the context of actual case examples.

3

ASSESSING THE SCOPE AND CHARACTERISTICS OF CHILD SEXUAL ABUSE

How widespread is the problem of child sexual abuse? How do children come to disclose the details of their abuse? How common are children's false allegations of sexual abuse? How often do children come to court? For those working in this field, such questions have no easy answers.

In this chapter, we describe the relevant data to address these questions. However, as will be seen, the data are frequently quite difficult to interpret. They may represent underestimates or overestimates, depending on a number of factors. In fact, it may ultimately be impossible to obtain precise answers to these questions. Nevertheless, the available data are important because they allow us to frame the upper and lower boundaries of the problem as well as the issues that must be considered when interpreting the empirical research that will be presented in later chapters.

HOW COMMON IS CHILD SEXUAL ABUSE?

Crime statistics reflecting the sexual abuse of children are of great social concern. These statistics come from two major sources. One is based on an annual tally of child abuse reports for a particular year; the other is based on adults' reports of abusive events that transpired one or more times during their entire childhood. The first source provides estimates of the *incidence* of abuse (the number of new cases reported in a specific time period), whereas the second source provides estimates of *prevalence* (the number of cases in the population accumulated across all time periods).

According to the most recent figures, there were 1.9 million reports of suspected child maltreatment in 1992, involving 2.9 million cases of children below the age of 18. The majority of these were reports of physical neglect (U.S. Department of Health and Human Services, National Center on Child Abuse and Neglect, 1994). Of these 2.9 million cases, approximately 500,000 concerned sexual maltreatment, and of these, 128,556 were "substantiated" or "indicated."[1] Assuming that approximately 66 million Americans are under the age of 18, approximately 1 child in 435 is the victim of a substantiated or indicated sexual abuse report in a given year. This translates to an incidence of childhood sexual abuse of roughly 0.23% for a given year (i.e., 2.3 out of every 1,000 children).

Because this 0.23% incidence estimate is based on "substantiated" and "indicated" reports of child abuse, it may represent an underestimate or an overestimate of the actual number of cases. To determine which it is, we need to consider the meaning of the terms *substantiated* and *indicated*.

Cases are classified as substantiated or indicated on the basis of how consistent the evidence from an investigation is with the allegation of abuse. Often this is a matter of caseworker judgment. Most states use a two-tiered system of classifying cases as either substantiated/founded, on the one hand, or unsubstantiated/unfounded, on the other. Unsubstantiated/unfounded cases include those where there is insufficient evidence to classify the case in the positive category; thus, these cases do not necessarily reflect "false accusations" because many of them may include valid claims of abuse that simply do not rise to the level of evidence needed to pursue an investigation or to prosecute the case in a court of law.

A few states use a three-tiered system for classifying investigations: Intermediate between the *substantiated* and *unsubstantiated* designations is the term *indicated*, which is given to cases in which the agency doing the investigation has "reason to suspect" that abuse occurred, but in which the level of evidence does not rise to the level required for the designation

---

[1]A more precise breakdown of the types of reported maltreatment are provided by the 1991 data: 49% of all reported cases involved neglect, 23% involved physical abuse, 14% involved sexual abuse, and 5% involved emotional abuse (U.S. Department of Health and Human Services, National Center on Child Abuse and Neglect, 1993).

"substantiated." For these reasons it is important not to use the terms *substantiated, indicated,* and *validated* interchangeably.[2]

The accuracy of the incidence rates of substantiated cases has been challenged by a number of commentators (e.g., Besharov, 1991; Finkelhor, Hotaling, Lewis, & Smith, 1990; Wexler, 1992). On the one hand, some claim that these figures may overestimate the extent of child sexual abuse because they may include a number of indicated and substantiated cases that are not valid. Critics like Wexler fear that the low levels of evidence required to designate a case as substantiated may result in innocuous or ambiguous acts being inappropriately designated as abusive. Others, however, argue that these rates may underestimate the incidence of child sexual abuse because many genuine cases of sexual abuse end up being classified as "unsubstantiated," and, more importantly, because significant numbers of cases of actual abuse are never reported to authorities in the first place. It has been estimated, for example, that only 40% of maltreatment cases are reported (Kalichman, 1993; U.S. Department of Health and Human Services, 1988).

A second technique used to estimate the number of sexually abused children involves surveys of adults who are asked about their childhood histories of sexual abuse. Salter (1992) presented a summary of surveys conducted in the 1980s in the United States; 9 surveys sampled men and women from the general population, and 14 surveys sampled men and women from the college population. Averaging across these data, 20% of the women and 8% of the men reported childhood incidents of sexual abuse occurring before the age of 16 years. But these averages mask the highly variable estimates of childhood sexual abuse across the surveys. For women, these estimates range from 6.8% (Siegel, Sorenson, Golding, Burnam, & Stein, 1987, a study not included in Salter's review) to 62% (Wyatt, 1985); for men, they range from 3% to 31% (see Peters, Wyatt, & Finkelhor, 1986). Thus, although in any given year, only 1 in approximately 435 children may be victims of substantiated sexual abuse, over a lifetime, the rate rises to (roughly) 20% for women and 8% for men reporting sexual abuse. A moment's reflection on these numbers reveals that they do not add up. That is, you cannot get from an annual incidence of 1 in 435 (0.23%) to a lifetime prevalence rate of 20%, or 1 in 5—unless

---

[2]It is also important to note that there is much variability among states in the level of evidence required to classify a case as substantiated. At one extreme, some states require only the lowest level of evidence (i.e., "some credible evidence") to substantiate a case. At the other extreme, some states require a far higher level of evidence (i.e., "preponderance of evidence") to substantiate an allegation. Intermediate levels of evidence or idiosyncratic criteria are used by some states (National Center on Child Abuse and Neglect, 1993). Thus, the adoption of a lower level of evidence increases the likelihood that, upon further investigation, the case will be judged substantiated, whereas the adoption of a higher level of evidence raises the odds that a case will be classified as unfounded when it is actually valid.

the average age was 100 years! But these figures *are* reconcilable if one realizes that not all reports of sexual harassment made on surveys come to the attention of state authorities (and thus, they are not incorporated into incidence figures), some being noncriminal instances of verbal or gestural abuse that would not be reported to state hotlines or police, and others being criminal abuse that, for a variety of reasons, does not get reported.

But what about the inconsistent estimates of childhood sexual abuse that have been obtained across studies? There are a number of factors to consider. Foremost is the definition of sexual abuse used in each study. Some studies include only bodily contact, whereas others also include exhibitionism, verbal abuse, and pornography. Studies also differ greatly in the demographic compositions of the samples, with some oversampling college students, others oversampling inner-city adult women, and so forth. Naturally, different ecologies might be associated with different levels of abuse and/or respondents' willingness to report abuse.

In addition, the methods of data collection differ. In some studies, there are face-to-face interviews, in others there are telephone interviews, and in others there are self-administered questionnaires. Although one might guess that the face-to-face interviews produce the most reliable data, there is debate over the relative benefits of using each type of method.

Finally, the number of questions in the interview can influence the rates obtained. Higher prevalence rates of childhood sexual abuse have been obtained in surveys that include a large number of questions about childhood sexual abuse. It is thought that the increased use of questions may cue memory and may also widen the respondent's definition of what is meant by the term *abusive event.*

Although there is some debate over the exact prevalence of child sexual abuse in North America, the existing data lead us to believe that the incidence data most certainly underestimate the number of annual cases of sexual abuse. This is highlighted by the results of a 1985 survey of adults in which 42% of the male respondents and 33% of the female respondents reported that they had never told anyone about their sexual abuse prior to the survey disclosure (Finkelhor et al., 1990).

Another important point to consider is the dramatic rise in the reporting of sex abuse cases over the last two decades. The American Humane Association (1988) estimated a 2,000% increase in reports of sexual abuse between 1976 and 1986.[3] As one example, in the state of Pennsylvania there were 348 substantiated cases of child sexual abuse in 1976; in 1980, there were 868 cases; and in 1986, there were 5,187 cases. Nationally,

---

[3]This increase in the number of sexual abuse claims is roughly paralleled by increases in all types of abuse and maltreatment. Between 1963 and 1986, there was an increase of 1,233%, from 150,000 reports to nearly 2 million reports (Tjaden & Thoennes, 1992). However, sexual abuse reports have increased far faster than other forms of maltreatment between 1976 and 1992.

there were 325,000 claims of child sexual abuse in 1985 versus approximately a half million in 1992. Similar trends have been found in other countries: In both the United Kingdom and Israel, there has been a 14% increase in claims between 1991 and 1992 (Lamb, 1994).

These figures have raised questions about the basis for these increases: Does the rise reflect increases in the rates of overreporting, increases in public sensitivity to the problem, or increases in the actual number of cases of abuse? Our best guess at this point is that the increases over the years reflect broader mandated reporting coupled with increased sensitivity to the pervasiveness of childhood sexual abuse. This view is supported by the following evidence. According to Salter's (1992) review of the various survey studies, there are no consistent differences in prevalence rates between older and younger adults—suggesting that there has not been a dramatic increase in sexual abuse over the last few decades (see Finkelhor et al., 1990, for similar conclusions). Also, even while the rate of *reporting* sexual abuse has skyrocketed, the numbers of cases that are classified as "substantiated" has remained fairly constant or dropped slightly. That is, although there has been a dramatic rise in the raw number of reports, this has been accompanied by an increase in the number of "unsubstantiated" reports, yielding nearly constant numbers of substantiated cases.

The same issues are raised by comparing the rates of reports of sexual abuse across different countries. Figure 3.1 (adapted from Finkelhor's 1994 data) shows that allegations of sexual abuse are far more prevalent in the United States than in most of our industrial partners, often by a factor of 2 to 3. Some have speculated that these differences are real and that the higher rates result from a general societal disinhibition in the United States, reflected in increased acceptance of pornography on television, sexualized behaviors and dress codes, and so on. Others find it hard to believe that the true incidence of abuse is that much higher in the United States. Still others (e.g., Finkelhor, 1994) have speculated that the real rates of abuse in the United States are similar to those of other countries, but that the higher reporting rates reflect a greater awareness or a broader definition of sexual abuse by the American people. Clearly, these arguments are speculative; future research is sorely needed to determine if the United States truly has more sexual abuse than other nations. Barring this research, we are inclined to agree with the view that the real rate of abuse in the United States is roughly comparable to that of most industrialized nations.

To conclude, on the basis of different statistical analyses and extrapolation from both prevalence and incidence studies, some experts estimate that approximately 300,000 children are sexually abused in the United States per year. (This translates to a rate of 0.5%, or 1 in every 200 children.) Regardless of whether the incidence rate is 0.23% (1 in every 435

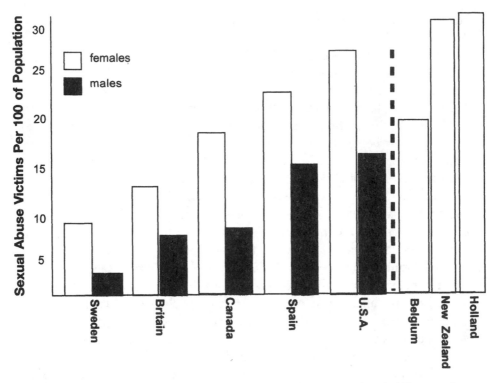

Figure 3.1. Prevalence of sexual abuse per 100 adults in general probability samples for eight countries. Adapted from Finkelhor (1994). (Belgium, New Zealand, and Holland data available for females only.)

children) or 0.5%, these figures reflect an extremely serious societal problem.

SEXUAL ABUSE IN DAY-CARE SETTINGS

Four of the seven case studies presented in chapter 1 involved allegations of sexual abuse in day-care settings, and three of these involved allegations of ritualistic abuse. In the Old Cutler case, some of the parents hired a private investigator to research the possibility that the defendant was part of a nationwide satanic cult that preyed on children. "Evidence" was provided that the defendant wore a pentagon-shaped medallion that could have been used to signify satanic beliefs. Other indicia of witchcraft, such as lit candles and animal sacrifice, were purportedly linked to the alleged abuse. Most dramatically, some of the children claimed to have been forced to kill and eat a live baby. In the Little Rascals case, there were numerous allegations involving ritualistic abuse. Children claimed that they observed animal sacrifices, that they were thrown into a sea of sharks, and that they sat in a circle holding candles. At least one child claimed to have seen one of the defendants dressed up as a witch. One therapist showed the children pictures of masks and other indicia used in cults and asked them if they had seen these before. Furthermore, it seems that the state of North Carolina's belief that child pornography was an important element of this case was the basis for the arrest of Scott Privott, the video store owner who allegedly videotaped the abuse. In Country Walk, the children made allegations that were similar to those made by children in the Old Cutler case as well as in the Little Rascals case.

The children's allegations involving ritualistic abuse are consistent with the beliefs of many professionals who claim that ritualistic abuse often accompanies sexual abuse, particularly in preschoolers. Some of these professionals emphasize satanic activities such as cannibalism, drinking magical liquids, animal sacrifice, and even infant sacrifice. Some assume that accused perpetrators must be members of organized sex rings that abuse children and produce child pornography. Kee MacFarlane, a social worker involved in the McMartin preschool case (*State v. Buckey*, 1990), which was one of the earliest and largest of all sex abuse cases, told Congress, "we're dealing with an organized operation of child predators. . . . The preschool in such cases, serves as a ruse for a larger, unthinkable network of crimes against our children" (Brozan, 1984).

But these are only opinions of professionals. Are there in fact data to support these beliefs? A comprehensive study on the incidence of day-care abuse and ritualistic abuse in day care tends to support these beliefs (Finkelhor, Williams, & Burns, 1988). During a 3-year period, these researchers identified 270 cases of sexual abuse in day-care centers, involving 1,639 victims. Although these figures are alarming, the authors concluded that the risk of sexual abuse for preschool children in day-care centers is less (5.5 victims per 10,000 children) than the risk of intrafamilial abuse for this same age group (8.9 victims per 10,000 children). These authors also assessed the number of cases involving ritualistic abuse. Although only 13% of the cases were judged to involve ritualistic abuse, there were 1,000 children, or nearly two thirds of the child day-care victims, involved in these cases.

What are we to make of these data? We think very little, for two reasons. First, it is clear from reading this study that there were many cases included in the sample where there was no "hard" evidence of childhood sexual abuse. These researchers included cases such as the McMartin preschool and the Kelly Michaels cases in their samples. All of the defendants in the McMartin case were eventually acquitted, and Kelly Michaels's conviction in the Wee Care case was overturned by an appeals court. Although one might argue that perhaps these adults were nevertheless guilty, this is, at best, speculation. For scientific purposes, only validated (not suspected) cases of abuse should be the focus of examination. For these reasons, the Finkelhor et al. (1988) study may tell us more about allegations of childhood sexual abuse in preschools than about the incidence of substantiated cases. Interpreted in this light, the data indicate that reports of abuse in day-care centers are fairly common and worthy of scientific study.

A related and second problem with the Finkelhor et al. (1988) study concerns their estimate of the number of cases of childhood ritualistic abuse. The problem is that to date no physical evidence has been uncovered to substantiate these claims. This conclusion is based on four different sources. Ken Lanning, a special agent for the FBI, has aggressively investigated the allegations of victims of ritualistic abuse and has found no evidence for the portion of those allegations that involve human sacrifice and organized satanic conspiracies (Lanning, 1991). A grand jury in San Diego was recently asked by the San Diego county supervisors to investigate a day-care ritualistic abuse case, much like those described in this book, where the defendant, Dale Akiki, had been acquitted after a 7-month trial. The children in that trial accused the defendant of hanging them upside down from a chandelier, dunking them in toilets, drinking blood, and mutilating and killing animals and a human baby. After reviewing the Akiki case, the grand jury concluded, "There is no justification for further pursuit of the theory of satanic ritual child molestation in the investigation and prosecution of child abuse cases" (San Diego County Grand Jury, 1994).

A study was recently carried out in Great Britain involving 84 cases of reported ritualistic abuse (La Fontaine, 1994). The allegations consisted of human sacrifice, cannibalism, and bestiality together with sexual abuse, torture, and killing children. The author found material evidence to substantiate these claims in only 3 of the 84 cases. However, she concluded that these three cases were not instances of satanism or witchcraft but involved rituals (the use of altars and candles) merely as strategies to achieve sexual abuse. A similar finding was obtained in a recent study conducted in the United States. In a national survey of more than 11,000 mental health and forensic workers, researchers identified more than 12,000 accusations of group cult sexual abuse based on satanic ritual; none of these, however, had ever been substantiated (Goodman, Qin, Bottoms, & Shaver, 1994). However, the researchers did find "evidence for lone perpetrators or very small groups (e.g., two people) who abuse children in ways that include satanic themes" (p. 5). Of course, in any large sample of individuals there will be representatives of every persuasion. For instance, in the population of pedophiles, there will be some Methodists, for example, just as surely as there will be some members of satanic cults. Just because there are some individuals who practice religious or secular rituals in the population of pedophiles does not imply that cult members are pedophiles by virtue of practicing these rituals, any more than it implies that Methodists are pedophiles merely because a few of their sect also happen to be pedophiles. Thus, the surprise is that there have not been more satanic/ritualistic examples reported to authorities, because there are many individuals in the population who call themselves "satanists."

Despite this overwhelming lack of evidence, we expect that a core of professionals will still continue to believe that ritualistic abuse does occur but cannot be uncovered because the perpetrators are so successful in hiding their crimes. Of course, it is possible that these beliefs may eventually be substantiated. But for now, we tentatively conclude that children's allegations involving satanic ritualistic abuse are unfounded.

CHARACTERISTICS OF SEXUALLY ABUSED CHILDREN

To construct a profile of the "typical" sexually abused child, we have relied on a number of studies of the characteristics of children who come to clinical facilities for assessment and treatment of abuse (these are termed "clinical" studies) and of children who make contact with the legal system as a result of their abuse (these are termed "forensic" studies). Although undeniably interesting, each study suffers from particular biases that prevent us from drawing generalizations, as will be seen. On the one hand, data based on children who come into the legal system may be unique in terms of the type of abuse they have suffered, their relationship to the defendant, and a variety of victim and perpetrator characteristics—any one of which may thwart generalizations to all sexually abused children. On the other hand, children sampled through clinical practices may also have unique characteristics that separate them from other abused children whose parents or caretakers do not seek professional assessment and counseling. Finally, these studies tell us nothing about the many children whose abuse goes unreported. Despite their shortcomings, however, these are the best data that we have for beginning to understand the scope of the problem. It is against the backdrop of this caveat that we proceed to discuss the implications of these studies.

Most of the child sexual abuse victims are female (75%–80%). A large proportion of these children are quite young. The results of two clinical samples indicate that between 20% and 31% of sexually abused children are aged 5 years and younger (Sauzier, 1989; Sorensen & Snow, 1991). Reports from individual states reflect similar figures (e.g., the percentage of sexually abused children that are 5 years old or younger is 32% in Texas and 26% in Kentucky; see National Center on Child Abuse and Neglect, 1993). The rates from forensic studies, which include cases that are filed by the district attorney's office, are slightly lower; between 15% and 18% of the sexual abuse cases consist of preschoolers (Goodman, Taub, et al., 1992; Gray, 1993).

Studies of child sexual abuse victims reveal that the offenders are generally known to the children. In one study of preschooler victims, 60% of the abuse was intrafamilial (including mothers' boyfriends), and only 9% was perpetrated by a stranger (Mian, Wehrspann, Klajner-Diamond, Le-Baron, & Winder, 1986). Very similar figures were obtained when a larger age range was included (Sauzier, 1989). The rates from forensic studies differ only slightly from these clinically drawn estimates. In Gray's (1993) study of sexual abuse cases filed in eight jurisdictions, 14% of abuse was perpetrated by a stranger. In a Canadian forensic study (Sas, Hurley, Hatch, Malla, & Dick, 1993), this rate was 9%. Thus, it appears that most of the reported cases of child abuse involve intrafamilial abuse (broadly defined) and that only a small minority involve strangers.

These surveys provide only a gross idea of the nature of the abuse that was reported, because of fairly large inconsistencies across studies, perhaps reflecting differences in the categorization of abuse or the factors peculiar to different samples. For instance, a number of studies indicate that the majority of child sexual abuse does not involve vaginal or anal penetration but instead involves fondling and exhibitionism. In their study of preschoolers, Mian et al. (1986) reported that fondling and exhibitionism occurred in 83% of the cases. Gray's (1993) study of children in the court system revealed that 64% of the cases involved fondling and exhibitionism. Although figures were not given, Sas et al. (1993) reported that fondling was the most frequent act for which defendants were charged. Much lower rates of 10% (Goodman et al., 1992) and 23% (Sauzier, 1989) were reported in one forensic and one clinical study, respectively. The rates for vaginal or penile penetration were similar in three studies: 39% (Goodman, Taub, et al., 1992), 30% (Sas et al., 1993), and 25% (Gray, 1993) and were much lower than the estimate of 65% obtained by Sauzier (1989). Although it is obvious that systematic differences in the way that samples are constituted can lead to distorted estimates, thus diminishing precision, the clinical and forensic samples do provide statistical delineation of the scope of the problem.

NUMBER OF FALSE REPORTS AND ALLEGATIONS OF CHILD SEXUAL ABUSE

The rate of false reports is sometimes mistakenly confused with the number of unsubstantiated or unfounded reports. However, the latter classifications sometimes include reports where there is not enough evidence for a Child Protection Services worker to pursue an investigation all the way through to court action. In other words, with follow-up, some of these unsubstantiated cases may eventually be validated. Thus, the number of false reports is likely to be considerably less than the number of unsubstantiated or unfounded reports. On the other hand, some investigators reserve the designation "false reports" for those cases where there is a deliberate and malicious intent to produce a false allegation. Although such cases should be designated as false reports, these are not the only ones; false reports also occur as a result of both intentional and unintentional coaching, misinterpretation of events, and poor interviewing techniques. As we show below, interpretations of the prevalence data change as a function of one's definition of a false report and one's awareness of the research on interviewing.

In one of the larger and more cited studies, Jones and McGraw (1987) reviewed the disposition of 576 reported cases of child sexual abuse in Denver in one year. Fifty-three percent of these cases were classified as "indicated," 23% were judged "unfounded," and 24% of the cases did not contain enough information to make a clear judgment. Further analyses of the unfounded cases revealed that these could be categorized as either deliberate/malicious attempts to make a false accusation (6% of all cases) or reports made in good faith but that turned out to be wrong (17% of all cases). On the basis of these data, some commentators have concluded that only a small proportion of reports (around 6%) are false.[4] However, this is a misunderstanding of the data because the percentage of false reports is the entire 23%; 6% are deliberate lies, but the other 17% are just as baseless as the lies, even though they may be honest mistakes. And they can do just as much harm.

Other studies have provided lower rates for false allegations. Based on reports from caseworkers, Everson and Boat (1989) estimated that false allegations were more likely to occur when reports came from adolescents (8% were judged to be false) than when they came from children less than 6 years of age (only 2% of these reports were judged to be false). But judging from the criteria that were used to classify reports as false, we feel that these rates may be underestimates. Although we do not have access to the original data, it again seems that "false" reports were those that were judged to be "deliberate and intentional lying." These rates may not include those cases that were originally judged to be substantiated but upon further investigation were found to be the result of subtle adult coaching or other faulty interviewing techniques, either of which could elevate the false-allegation rate.

---

[4]This figure of around 6% has been repeatedly offered in court by expert witnesses. Consider the following testimony given by a clinical psychologist who evaluated the credibility of a 9-year-old boy:

> Attorney: What is your general experience with children in this area?
> Psychologist: General experience is that children don't make up such stories [of anal sex], and the research backs that up. . . . That it's like well under 5% of the cases that it's ever found out not to be true. (*State v. Geyman*, 1986, p. 479)

Many of the studies of false allegations have focused on disputed custody cases, which raises two related issues. First, are rates of reported child sexual abuse elevated in families involved in custody disputes? The answer appears to be yes. Thoennes and Tjaden (1990) counted the number of allegations of child sexual abuse in a large sample of families involved in custodial visitation disputes. In the 9,000 families involved in such disputes, there were 209 allegations of sexual abuse. The authors concluded that the rate of reporting in their sample was six times greater than that observed in the National Incidence Study (National Center on Child Abuse and Neglect, 1988).

The second issue related to custody cases is whether the rates of false allegations are disproportionately high. Some argue that although there are elevated rates of reported abuse in divorced families, this reflects high rates of false accusations that are consequences of the stress of divorce and custodial disputes. Others argue that the elevated rates of reported abuse reflect high rates of sexual abuse in divorced families. This occurs either because once the perpetrator has left the family, some children come forth for the first time to tell of previous abuse or because divorce produces stress and loneliness that lead to child sexual abuse.

Results of studies based on small, select samples of children support the hypothesis that there are high rates of false reports in divorced families. Benedek and Schetky (1985) studied 18 children referred for sexual abuse in custody visitation disputes. Upon evaluation, 10 of the 18 cases were judged to be unfounded. The unfounded cases were instances in which it was the adults who had made the allegations or had deliberately coached the children. On the basis of their review of clinical cases involving allegations of sexual abuse, Paradise, Rostain, and Nathanson (1988) concluded that there were more false allegations among children involved in custodial disputes (33% of the reports were unsubstantiated) than among children not involved in such disputes (5% of these children's reports were unsubstantiated).

Two recent studies have included larger samples, and the authors of both have concluded that their data indicate that false allegations are not disproportionately higher in custody disputes than elsewhere. However, we will argue that these figures in fact show just the opposite.

In the first study, Faller (1991) examined the reports of 136 children of divorced families who were referred to a project on abuse and neglect. On the basis of the child's description of the sexual abuse, and his emotional affect while reporting these details, Faller determined that 65% of the cases were true accounts of abuse. She concluded that sexual abuse did not occur in the remaining 35% of the cases. This is higher than the rate of unsubstantiated cases (23%) reported by Jones and McGraw (1987) in their study of all sexual abuse cases reported in Denver in one year. But we speculate that the 12% difference between the two studies is a conservative estimate of the degree to which false reports are more common in divorced families. The Denver data included custody dispute cases, which for the purpose of the present comparison should be removed from the sample to obtain a pure estimate of the number of unsubstantiated cases in nondivorced families. If this is done, the number of unsubstantiated cases in the Denver comparison study should be reduced and the differences between unsubstantiated cases in divorced versus intact families is increased further.

Returning to Faller's findings, for reasons that we do not understand, Faller did not accept the 35% rate of unsubstantiated cases as a representative figure for the number of false allegations in divorced families. She broke this figure down into three groups: those in which false allegations may have been made (8.8%), those in which false allegations reflect other dynamics besides divorce (11%), and those in which false allegations arose in an atmosphere of acrimony surrounding the divorce (14%). It is this last rate, 14%, that she considered to reflect the number of false allegations in divorced families. Putting her logic aside, this rate is still more than double the number of deliberate or false allegations reported by Jones and McGraw (6%).

Similar results were obtained by Thoennes and Tjaden (1990) in their study of 9,000 families involved in custodial disputes. As already mentioned, these researchers identified cases involving reports of sexual abuse from a sample of families involved in custody disputes. Upon further examination, they concluded that 50% of the reports were likely, 17% were uncertain, and 33% were unlikely (i.e., these were false allegations). Again, these rates are higher than those obtained in the Denver study, suggesting that the rates of false reports are higher among divorced families.

As we argued earlier, and repeat now, we believe that these figures probably underestimate the number of false accusations because in some studies it seems that adult-instigated false allegations and deliberately concocted allegations are the only categories of false allegations considered. But in our view, false allegations should also encompass those cases in which the child's reports reflect the influence of adult interviewers' (including their parents') suggestions. Sometimes, as a result of persistent and suggestive questioning, children's reports may be false. It is not clear that this condition has been fully accounted for in any of the studies cited above, but later in this book we present evidence that such false reports are indeed possible, although we are unsure of their frequency. Having said this, we also feel that it is important not to automatically discount reports that emerge during custodial battles or during divorce disputes. The data from the above studies indicate that as many as 50% of the reports are valid.

THE PROCESS OF DISCLOSURE

What is the process by which children come to make reports of sexual abuse? Professionals know all too well that it can be very difficult to uncover child sexual abuse. According to some models, sexually abused children go through a series of stages in disclosing their abuse. For example, one of the most commonly cited models, Summit's (1983) Child Sexual Abuse Accommodation Syndrome, includes the following stages: secrecy, helplessness, entrapment, disclosure, and retraction. How do these claims stack up against the empirical literature? Below we summarize the results of several studies that, taken together, suggest that such models do not characterize a sizable portion of abused children's disclosure process.

Sorensen and Snow (1991) provided data that are highly supportive of the stages of the disclosure process. They examined 116 cases from a sample of 630 children who had been treated for sexual abuse. For the majority of the children, the disclosures were accidental, and at some point 75% of the children had denied that abuse had occurred. Even after making a disclosure, 22% of the children recanted their previous disclosures.[5]

Data from other studies, however, suggest that at times children more readily tell of their sexual abuse, although it is clear there are some children who may not tell for a long time. Campis, Hebden-Curtis, and DeMaso (1993) reported that the type of disclosure varies as a function of the child's age. A chart review of 72 children who had been seen for suspected sexual abuse revealed that 74% of the preschoolers in the sample made accidental disclosures, whereas all of the older children's disclosures were deliberate. In the Mian et al. (1986) study, 60% of preschoolers who were referred to the sexual abuse team made deliberate disclosures. Thus, it seems that

---

[5]This study is widely cited as evidence that sexually abused children do not immediately disclose their abuse, and often recant after disclosing. The authors studied 630 cases available from their practices and identified 116 cases where there was a guilty plea, a conviction, or medical evidence "highly consistent with sexual abuse." Although one could infer that the remaining 514 cases failed to satisfy these criteria, this is not made entirely clear in the study. In any event, one would also like some assurance that the profiles of the 116 cases the authors studied are similar to the 514 nonincluded cases.

There is also some concern regarding at least one of the authors' objectivity. Her courtroom testimony appears to suggest that she at times believed that the children were abused regardless of what they told her. Consider the following cross-examination of Dr. Snow in *State v. Bullock* (1989):

> Q: But she denied it to you and you just basically told her you had better go talk to somebody else because I don't believe you.
> Snow: It wasn't that I told her that I don't believe her, she got very upset and she felt like she couldn't work with me there. I didn't tell her that she couldn't work with somebody else because I didn't believe her. *I didn't believe any of these kids when they told me it didn't happen.* But [Susan] got upset and I felt she didn't have much rapport with me. . . . (p. 175; emphasis added)

although preschoolers may be prone to making accidental disclosures, the rates of denial are not as high as suggested by Sorenson and Snow.

A closely related issue concerns the degree to which children delay reporting of sexual abuse acts. These rates vary markedly from study to study. For example, in Goodman, Taub, et al.'s (1992) forensic study, 42% of the children had told of their abuse within 48 hours. Compare this with the rates found in Sauzier's (1989) clinical study of children who had been evaluated and subsequently treated for sexual abuse: Only 24% of the children told of the abuse within one week of the event, and 39% of the children never did disclose the abuse but were brought to the attention of professionals because of accidental disclosures. Unfortunately, we simply do not know what percentage of children immediately tell of their abuse and how many never tell. But it is clear that a significant portion of children do tell at some point.

Some experts state that children do not disclose because of explicit threats made by the perpetrators. The available evidence does not support this assertion. In Sauzier's (1989) study, for example, the likelihood of disclosure was unrelated to threats of the offender. When the offender used aggressive methods to gain the child's compliance to keep the secret, children were equally likely to tell about the abuse immediately following the event or to never disclose the abuse. Gray (1993) reported that although 33% of the children in her study were threatened by the perpetrator not to tell, two thirds of these children nevertheless still disclosed.

This picture of the disclosure process may reflect a potential bias in the samples of children in the various studies. Children in forensic samples may be those who readily disclose, whereas children in clinical samples who delay making disclosures may not go through the criminal system as readily; these may be the children for whom it is difficult to extract a report, and thus they are brought by adults for treatment. Finally, these studies provide no information on the number of children or the profiles of children who never disclose.

Some studies are also difficult to interpret because it is not clear how the abuse has been validated. This information is lacking in most of the studies that we reviewed, making it possible that some children do not disclose because there is no abuse to disclose. The criterion of conviction or acceptance of pleas, which is used by some researchers to corroborate abuse, is not always a valid indicator. At times, a guilty perpetrator may be acquitted. And at other times the innocent defendant, unable to cope with the stress and financial burden of going to trial, may plead guilty, sometimes to a lesser charge. Nevertheless, despite these difficulties, the clear message from these data is that there are a number of children who immediately disclose their abuse (either accidentally or deliberately), but there are also a number of children who delay their disclosures for long periods of time. No profile accounts for a sizable portion of these children's behavior.

THE CHILD WITNESS GOES TO COURT

Traditionally, cases of child sexual abuse were handled in family or juvenile courts, which are primarily nonpunitive and have as their foremost goal the protection of the child rather than the punishment of the offender. However, with the increased awareness of the problems experienced by child sexual abuse victims, and with increased recognition of the pervasiveness of abuse, these cases began to turn up in criminal court. Faced with strict evidentiary rules, constitutional protections for defendants, and the frequent lack of physical evidence, there was often only limited success in prosecuting child abuse cases. But by far the largest problem facing the prosecution was the fact that the primary witness was a child. Traditional requirements for corroborating testimony for child witnesses, and the emotional trauma that child witnesses face in the courtroom, presented immense obstacles to obtaining convictions.

In the last decade, there have been a number of proposed and implemented procedures to alleviate these difficulties (see McGough, 1994, for a detailed description and discussion). For example, many jurisdictions have modified their provisions using as a model the *Federal Rules of Evidence*, which minimizes competency hearings for witnesses of all ages, including child witnesses in sexual abuse cases. Devices have also been instituted to reduce trauma for the child in the courtroom. These include providing a child advocate for legal proceedings, permitting a support person to sit with the child during testimony, making structural changes in the courtroom, and adopting alternatives to open court testimony (e.g., videotaped interviews, closing the courtroom, etc.).

There are, however, no reliable national data on the impact of these changes on the number of children who actually end up participating in family court or criminal justice proceedings. Gray's (1993) recent analysis of eight jurisdictions suggests that 3% to 10% of all cases of sexual abuse that are eventually filed with the police result in a trial (similar figures were also produced by Goodman, Taub, et al., 1992). On the basis of the National Center on Child Abuse and Neglect (1993) statistics cited earlier, this would suggest that if all substantiated cases of abuse had been brought to the prosecutor's office in 1991, up to 13,000 children would have testified in sexual abuse trials that year. It is interesting to note that disproportionate numbers of preschool children may end up going to trial. In Gray's (1993) analysis of child witnesses in sexual abuse cases, although only 18% were 5 years old or younger, 41% of all of the cases that ended up in trial involved children of this age. These data point to the importance of focusing on the preschool child in relevant research studies.

When cases do go to trial, conviction rates range from 50% to 75%. In addition, a substantial proportion (between 40% and 60%) of the accused are incarcerated as a result of their convictions or plea bargains (Goodman, Taub, et al., 1992; Gray, 1993; Lipovsky et al., 1992).

Given the very small percentage of cases that actually come to trial, one might reasonably ask what happened to all of the other substantiated cases, which, by law, must be reported to the police and to the district attorney's office. Results of Gray's (1993) and Goodman, Taub, et al.'s (1992) studies reveal that approximately 50% of the cases that reach the district attorney's office are not filed, or the charges are dropped. When cases are filed, 50% to 75% end in either an admission of guilt or a plea bargain. Twenty-three percent of the cases are diverted to alternate forms of treatment.

Although the literature indicates that only a very small percentage of children in sexual abuse cases end up going to trial, the actual incidence of children's involvement in the legal system may be considerably higher than these figures suggest. Even before a case is filed, the child is interviewed by the police and by an investigator at the district attorney's office. The majority of cases that end in plea bargains, or "diversions," still require the child to testify before a grand jury and/or at preliminary hearings, even if the child does not testify in a court trial. Thus, even if a case is eventually dropped, the child witness will often be involved in the legal process, formal and informal, outside the courtroom. Finally, if nonsexual types of abuse and nonabuse cases involving children serving as witnesses are included (e.g., cases of domestic violence, custody disputes, accidents, playground injuries), the estimate of children's participation in the legal system rises considerably. Our educated guess is that the number of children who are annually involved in the legal system exceeds 200,000 per year, but we emphasize that this is only an educated guess.

SUMMARY

By now, some readers may feel lost in a sea of numbers. Why did we cover so many studies? What are the major points to remember while going through this book? We now provide some of the highlights that may be important to consider when reading through the rest of the book.

First, although there are widely varying statistics on the actual number of sexually abused children in this country and in other countries, all estimates reveal that this is a serious problem. Profiles of these children reveal that most are girls, and many are preschool-age children. Preschool-age children also seem to end up in the courtroom at a higher rate than would normally be expected. Many recent courtroom innovations are centered around the needs of this young group of children. For these reasons, researchers have focused much attention on the reliability of young children's testimony.

These data highlight the magnitude of the problem of sexual abuse, but at the same time some of the data indicate that there are also a substantial number of unfounded, unsubstantiated, and false allegations involving sexual abuse. It seems that allegations involving ritualistic abuse are predominantly false. Although there are no precise data, there are hints that false allegations may occur more frequently in disputed custody or bitter divorce battles, notwithstanding arguments to the contrary.

Although some of the data confirm mental health professionals' descriptions of children's process of reluctant disclosure, it is also clear that there are many children who spontaneously report abusive events within a short time of the event. One aspect of these studies that illuminates our understanding of the case studies is the effects of "threats" on children's disclosures patterns. In the case studies, professionals explained the children's failure to disclose their abuse on the grounds that they had been terrorized by their alleged perpetrators. However, the empirical data do not support this pattern of behavior: When children with documented histories of abuse are threatened, they are just as likely to tell of their abuse as when they are not threatened.

4

DEFINING MEMORY
AND SUGGESTIBILITY

The seven case studies that were summarized in chapter 2 highlight two issues that have been the focus of vigorous debate among researchers and advocates alike. The first issue concerns children's ability to accurately recall emotionally charged events over long periods of time. In all but one of these case studies, the children's first attempt to recall occurred many months after the alleged events took place. In the Little Rascals case, for instance, the children were first interviewed about their memories anywhere from 4 weeks to 4 months after Bob Kelly was alleged to have committed his crimes. In the Macias murder case, Jennifer F. was first interviewed 5 months after she alleged to have observed the defendant washing blood off his hands. And in the Old Cutler case, many of the children were first interviewed 6 to 12 months after Bobby Fijnje had allegedly molested them.

Despite an absence of studies during the first 85 years of this century examining children's memories for emotionally charged events, there have recently been a number of such studies. Typically, such studies entail examining children's accounts of events that were traumatic or stressful, such as medical procedures (e.g., genital examinations, visits to the emergency room), witnessing disasters (e.g., the space shuttle *Challenger* explosion,

Hurricane Andrew), or sustaining major injuries. The principal question addressed in this research is whether children accurately remember emotionally salient or stressful events that occurred long ago, or whether they tend to reshape, forget, or repress them. We devote some attention to this question in chapters 13 and 14. To provide a framework for understanding these issues, we outline some current conceptualizations of the processes involved in memory in the first part of this chapter.

The second issue of contention, which is the central focus of this book, concerns the role of suggestibility in children's report accuracy. Are young children any more suggestible than older children and adults? Put bluntly, to what extent might the children in the seven case studies be the victims not of abuse, but of suggestive questioning techniques? Were the interviewers' questions in these case studies phrased in such a way that the children came to incorporate into their reports assumptions contained in the interviewers' questions? In the second part of this chapter we will provide a framework for addressing these issues.

Given the important role that memory plays in understanding suggestibility and also in understanding the nature of the recall of stressful events, we first provide a brief overview of the concepts of this field.

MEMORY

What does it mean to "remember" something? Psychologists who study memory have developed several approaches for thinking about the workings of the human memory system. Despite numerous views on how memory works, a common feature of most models is that memory is a "constructive" rather than a reproductive enterprise. That is, memories are not simply passively recorded by our senses, then stored in their natural form in a brain bin that preserves their initial quality; nor are memories mechanically accessed in their original state at the time of remembering. Rather, because of the constructive nature of memory, reports may be inaccurate because of a number of factors that intrude at the time of the initial recording (encoding) of the event, during the storage of the event, or at the time of the retrieval of the event.

One of the primary factors that affects the quality of memories is our previous knowledge, our assumptions, and our biases about the world. The classic demonstration of this relationship was provided over 60 years ago by Sir Frederick Bartlett of Cambridge University. He demonstrated that when individuals are asked to remember interesting but unusual episodes, they often refashion these so that they make sense to them, given their values and expectations (Bartlett, 1932). For example, adults read a story about North American Indians called "War of the Ghosts" and then were asked to recall the story several times. Bartlett's European subjects changed certain features of the passage that were inconsistent with their prior expectations and understanding. For example, his subjects omitted a supernatural aspect of the story, and recalled canoes as boats. Bartlett's study, and hundreds of demonstrations since then, showed that what one remembers is in part influenced by one's emotional as well as cognitive perspective of the event. Thus, current conceptualizations of memory underscore the fact that it does not resemble a tape recorder or camera—devices that store and retrieve information veridically. Instead, our memory system is an active part of a larger cognitive and social system that constantly interacts with what we know and expect. As long as experiences are in accord with our expectations, there is usually no problem. But when there is a mismatch between what we expect and what we actually experience, it is not uncommon for this to be resolved by the former intruding into our recollection of the latter.

The likelihood that we can remember an event from our past depends on the skill with which we execute a complex set of processes, initially during the event in question, then later at the time of its retrieval. Psychologists who study human memory usually discuss these processes in terms of a flow of information from one stage of the memory system to another. The three main stages of the system are *encoding*, *storage*, and *retrieval*. These are briefly described below. For a more detailed view, the reader should consult any one of a number of excellent treatises on the human memory system (e.g., Baddeley, 1990; Klatzky, 1980; Schneider & Pressley, 1989; Zechmeister & Nyberg, 1982).

Encoding

The first phase of the memory system is called *encoding*. This refers to the process by which a trace of an experience becomes registered in memory. There is selectivity in what gets encoded into the storage system in the first place. In part, this selectivity reflects the limited attentional resources of the human organism; we cannot attend to everything at one time, and as a result we generally only attend to certain aspects of an event and ignore other aspects. Given the limitations of the human cognitive system, not all experienced information is registered (encoded). As an example, a beginning driver may invest her entire attentional capacity to keeping her car in the center of the lane. As a result, she may have no attentional capacity left over to attend to peripheral information such as what songs were played on the radio or what signs were posted along the side of the road. Thus, not everything that is "out there" gets attended to. And nothing gets stored in permanent memory unless it is first attended to.

There are a number of factors that can potentially influence what enters the memory system, and these same factors may also influence how strongly a trace becomes encoded. These include the amount of prior knowledge about the events (usually, the more knowledge, the more easily events are encoded), the interest value or salience of the events, the duration and repetition of the original event, and the stress level at the time of encoding the original event (the debate about how stress may influence encoding is reviewed in chapter 13).

Storage

In the second phase of the memory system, encoded events enter a short-term memory store. Not all of the memories survive the short-term memory's limited storage capacity, but those that do survive enter a long-term memory store. At one time, this stage was assumed to be passive; the contents of an encoded event were thought to be dormant in storage until such time as they were retrieved. This view is almost surely wrong, and we now have some good evidence that encoded information can be transformed, fortified, or lost while it resides in storage (Brainerd, Reyna, Howe, & Kingma, 1990).

The passage of time, the number of times that the event has been re-experienced, and the number and types of intervening experiences, which have also become encoded and stored, can have a strong impact on the strength and organization of the stored information. Thus, memories can increase or decrease in strength as a function of how long they have been stored (usually shorter delays result in better recall) and of the number of times that the original event has been recalled (in some cases, repeated recall strengthens the memory; at other times it weakens it). It is also true that knowledge and expectancies can change the composition of memory during the storage phase, thus transforming the trace to make it more consistent with one's attitudes and expectations. Finally, intervening experiences may at times serve to solidify the initial memory (when these are congruent with the initial trace); at other times these experiences may compete with and interfere with the stored memory if they are inconsistent with the original encoded event.

There have been challenges to some of these general claims. Of importance for our topic is the claim that certain types of memories, specifically those of emotionally arousing events, are not subject to many of the general principles just cited. Some argue that these memories are highly resistant to decay, whereas others argue that there may be repression of memories that are terrifying. These issues will be discussed in chapter 13.

Retrieval

The final step in remembering involves the retrieval of stored information. It is not necessarily the case that there is perfect retrieval of stored memories. In fact, there are times when the contents of the memory system are simply not retrievable. A variety of cognitive as well as social factors influence the retrievability of stored memories, although the nature of their influences is not static: Some of these factors at times enhance recall, whereas at other times the same factors may decrease the accuracy of the recall. We will now consider some of these factors.

The condition of the original memory trace is important; traces that have undergone some decay will be harder to retrieve than those that retain their original strength. In some cases, retrieval of a memory may be facilitated when the conditions for retrieval parallel those of encoding. One of the best examples of this principle is provided by Godden and Baddeley's study of state-dependent learning (1975). Deep-sea divers were asked to learn (encode) lists of words while they were beneath the sea. Their later retrieval of these words was better when they were beneath the sea compared with when they were on land. In recent replications of this work, it has been shown that divers retrieve lists encoded on dry land better when they are put back on dry land, and they retrieve lists encoded under water better when they are put back under water (Martin & Aggleton, 1993).

An extension of this finding is that when an interviewer provides cues that may reinstate the encoding context, accuracy of recall improves. There are various types of cues that can be given. Some involve reminding the subject about parts of the actual event, whereas other types of cues may involve inducing emotional or cognitive states at retrieval that match those present at the time of encoding. Although these techniques may facilitate the recall of actually experienced events, they may promote false recall if an event was never experienced (see chapter 14).

There are also many constructive factors that enter into the retrieval stage. For example, when asked to recall a faded event, we may use our knowledge about what "typically" happens to fill gaps in our memory. A more specific term for this phenomenon is *script-based knowledge*, which refers to our expectations and predictions of how events in the world are sequenced and related to each other. According to Hastie (1981), "The memorability of an event increases when the event is relevant to expectations and beliefs about that event." But as we will discuss in greater detail in chapter 16, the relationship between script-based knowledge and retrieval is not straightforward. If an event is highly congruent with our script-based knowledge, then it is likely to be retrieved. However, if an event is highly incongruent with our script-based knowledge, it is also likely to be retrieved—presumably because of its bizarreness.

Finally, there are a number of higher-level (consciously deployed) factors that influence how well children and adults can recall events. These include a number of intuitively obvious factors, such as the degree to which the individual is motivated to retrieve old memories, the degree to which the individual wishes to cooperate with the examiner, and the degree to which a person understands what is important to recall.

To summarize, what a child or adult "remembers" does not always come directly from storage. Memory is highly "constructive"; we sometimes add, delete, and shape memories of our experiences. These transformations can occur at the encoding, storage, and retrieval stages. Thus, what gets retrieved is rarely a direct match of the original event. We shall return to the mechanisms of the memory system in chapter 13, where we discuss the memory mechanisms underlying highly unusual and stressful events, and in chapter 14, where we provide a developmental perspective on some of the processes just discussed.

Armed with some of the basic concepts of memory, we now turn to a consideration of the term *suggestibility*.

DEFINING SUGGESTIBILITY

Traditionally, suggestibility has been defined as "the extent to which individuals come to accept and subsequently incorporate post-event information into their memory recollections" (Gudjonsson, 1986, p. 195; see also Powers, Andriks, & Loftus, 1979). Although this definition may seem opaque to those unfamiliar with this literature, it contains several important implications. In particular, it implies that (a) suggestibility is an unconscious process (i.e., information is unwittingly incorporated into memory), (b) suggestibility results from information that was supplied after an event as opposed to before it (hence, the term "post-event"), and (c) suggestibility is a memory-based, as opposed to a social, phenomenon. This final point means that suggestions are thought to influence reports via incorporation into the memory system, not through some social pressure to lie or otherwise conform to expectations.

As we will show in chapter 5, early studies of children's suggestibility adhered to this definition. In these early studies, children experienced some event then were exposed to some misleading information that was often embedded in an interviewer's question. For example, children might meet a beardless man in a schoolyard and later be asked, "What color was his beard?" If children reported a color of the beard, then this response reflected their suggestibility.

This traditional conceptualization and demonstration of suggestibility, however, is too restrictive to aid our understanding of the seven case studies and the thousands of others like them. Therefore, we have broadened the definition of suggestibility to encompass what is usually connoted by its lay usage. Hence, we propose that suggestibility refers to the degree to which the encoding, storage, retrieval, and reporting of events can be influenced by a range of internal and external factors. This broader view implies that it is possible to accept information and yet be fully conscious of its divergence from the originally perceived event, as in the case of acquiescence to social demands, lying, or efforts to please loved ones. This broadened definition of suggestibility does not necessarily involve the alteration of the underlying memory; a child may still remember what actually occurred but choose not to report it for motivational reasons. This broader definition also implies that suggestibility can result from the provision of information either before or after an event. In some cases, a child may be given a set of expectancies before the alleged event occurred, and these sensitize the child to subsequent behaviors or events that are consistent with their expectations. Although this can have a salutary effect, by making the child aware of certain behaviors, it can have a deleterious effect when ambiguous behaviors are misinterpreted according to expectations. For example, in the Macias case described in chapter 2, Jennifer F. seems to have been inculcated with the belief, conveyed through her mother, that Frederico Macias was an evil man. Armed with this pre-event expectancy, Jennifer F. may have attributed malign motives to Frederico's behaviors. As one example of this possibility, she subsequently testified during a stay of execution hearing that she may have assumed that chili salsa on Frederico's shirt and hands was blood (he worked in a salsa factory and commonly came home splattered with the red seasoning). We have no way of knowing if her mother's inculcation of negative expectations about the defendant led Jennifer to falsely attribute crime-consistent actions to him, but she herself appears to have subsequently realized this possibility 4 years later during the stay of execution hearing.

Finally, our broader definition implies that suggestibility can result from social as well as cognitive factors. Thus, this broader conceptualization of suggestibility is in accord with both the legal and everyday uses of the term, to connote how easily one is influenced by subtle suggestions, expectations, stereotypes, and leading questions that can unconsciously alter memories, as well as by explicit bribes, threats, and other forms of social inducement that can lead to the conscious alteration of reports without affecting the underlying memory. Using this broadened definition of suggestibility, we can now examine how much children's testimonies reflect their incorporation of information provided before or after the event, whether the effect of the suggestions on their testimony is memory-based or socially based, and whether children consciously or unconsciously process suggestions.

In this book, we examine several issues related to this broadened conceptualization of suggestibility. The first concerns the scope of children's suggestibility; here we explore the parameters of the phenomenon, asking under what circumstances and conditions it might occur. The second issue concerns age differences in suggestibility. Our review of the literature examines the degree to which younger children are more suggestible than older children and the degree to which all children are more suggestible than adults. Before turning to these issues, it is important to emphasize that we do not mean to imply that adults are not suggestible, that their memories are always reliable, or that their testimonies are highly accurate. These statements are clearly false. There is a sizable literature on both the suggestibility (e.g., Belli, 1989; Gudjonsson, 1986; Lindsay, 1990; Loftus, 1979) and the unreliability of adults' memory for highly salient and important events (Neisser, 1982; Ross, 1989).

5

LEGAL AND BEHAVIORAL APPROACHES TO CHILDREN'S SUGGESTIBILITY: 1900–1985

Historically, interest in the accuracy of children's testimony, both by the legal profession and by social scientists, has reflected specific judicial events, changes in the organization of the judicial system, and the social conditions of the era. In our review of the entire corpus of research carried out in the 20th century (see Ceci & Bruck, 1993b), we found that the number of studies conducted in any given decade directly reflected the structure of the legal system at that time, as well as the legal system's view of the contribution of social science research. In this chapter, we describe some of the more important studies carried out in the first 85 years of this century and attempt to couch these in the forensic contexts of their time.

LEGAL VIEWS ON THE ADMISSIBILITY OF CHILDREN'S TESTIMONY

With only one exception (Small, 1896), the first studies on children's suggestibility were conducted in Europe. Suggestibility studies conducted in North America did not occur until the 1920s, and even then there were only a handful of such studies until the mid-1980s. Before discussing some of these studies, it is important to consider why, until quite recently, there was little if any social science research on the reliability of children's testimony in North America and why such research flourished in Europe at the beginning of the century, especially in Germany and in France. We consider three different factors.

First, in America, the Salem witch trials had lasting legal repercussions regarding the credibility of child witnesses. Repeatedly, 19th- and 20th-century legal scholars have cited the excesses of Salem as a basis for their negative views of child witnesses. For the most part, throughout the 300 years following the Salem witch trials, the predominant legal attitude in the United States was one of skepticism when considering the testimony of child witnesses (e.g., see *State v. Morasco*, 571, 1912). In one case, for example, the judge cautioned the jury against the presumption that a 6-year-old's testimony was accurate when he claimed that an itinerant worker had sodomized him:

> I charge you that the testimony of the boy, Robert R___, should be examined with care and caution, for it is manifest that he is but a boy of tender years . . . and children his age are susceptible of impressions that are oftentimes of erroneous character. . . (*State v. Michael*, 1893)

As McGough (1994) pointed out, however, such skeptical rumblings did not convince all jurists of the unreliability of children's testimonial accuracy. One respected jurist, John Wigmore (1940), a pioneer in the rules of evidence governing child witnesses, wrote,

> A rational view of the peculiarities of child nature, and of the daily course of justice in our courts, must lead to the conclusion that the effort to measure the a priori degree of untrustworthiness in children's statements, and to distinguish the point at which they cease to be totally incredible . . . is futile and unprofitable. Recognizing on the one hand the childish disposition to weave romances and to treat imagination for verity, and on the other the rooted ingenuousness of children and their tendency to speak straightforwardly what is on their minds, it must be concluded that the sensible way is to put the child upon the stand and let it tell its story for what it may seem to be worth. (Wigmore, 1940, § 509, 640)

Thus, although Wigmore argued that children's testimony should be admitted into evidence and that the jury be allowed to determine the weight of their story, other jurists argued that children's testimony was so inherently unreliable as to totally disallow them from testifying. In Europe, respected jurists like Lord Goddard expressed such a view, and more recent legal writers have echoed Goddard's skepticism, placing child witnesses in the same category as mental defectives and drug addicts:

> In determining the credibility of a witness and the weight to be accorded it, regard may be had to his age and his mental or physical condition, such as where the witness is a child, is intoxicated, is a narcotics addict, or is insane, or of unsound or feeble mind.[1]

As a result of such jaundiced views, children were only rarely permitted into American, Canadian, or British courts to provide uncorroborated testimony; thus, research on children's suggestibility was largely irrelevant in North America and Great Britain. On the other hand, children's testimony was allowed in some European courtrooms. And, as we shall see, some of the early European research was designed to directly address issues regarding children's testimony in the courtroom.

A second factor that accounts for the research hiatus in North America compared with some European countries involves the difference between adjudication procedures on the two continents. An inquisitorial system of justice prevails in many European countries in which the judge is responsible for calling and questioning witnesses. Because there are often no juries, the European judge is more likely to call on expert witnesses to testify about the competence of witnesses. In the early part of the 20th century, these expert witnesses were often psychologists who carried out experiments to examine the veracity of the children's testimony. In contrast, in an adversarial system, such as the one used in the United States, Canada, and Britain, the use of opposing attorneys and, particularly, cross-examination, as well as a jury, were considered sufficient to evaluate witness credibility.

Finally, little research was carried out in North America on forensic issues, such as children's suggestibility, because of the attitudes of the court concerning social science research. The proper interrelationship between social science and the law, particularly in reference to the development of rules governing the trial process, is a complex area of argument that continues to this day (see Faigman, 1989; Giannelli, 1980; Haney, 1980; Morgan & Maguire, 1937; Weihofen, 1965). In this chapter, we provide a very brief sketch of this debate as it occurred at the turn of the century.

According to Loh (1981), whereas European courts were, at least on occasion, eager consumers of the earliest psychological research on children's suggestibility, studies of both child and adult witnesses were rejected by the American legal profession The earliest and most prominent American jurists believed that psychology had nothing to offer the courts that

---

[1]American Jurisprudence, 1976, p. 670.

was not already intuitively obvious, a view that could still be seen in the early 1960s.[2]

The debate over the forensic value of psychological research was started when a prominent Harvard professor of psychology, Hugo Münsterberg (1907a, 1907b), called upon the courts to replace their untrained intuitions about witness credibility with the findings of scientific psychology. He described some of the European literature bearing on the unreliability of adult witnesses' perceptions and memories, and he also described some of his own studies involving Harvard undergraduates. These studies demonstrated how some students made inaccurate perceptual judgments or how they failed to accurately observe actions or events. Münsterberg concluded that scientific psychology had much to offer the courts because these studies showed that not only were witnesses sometimes fallible, but that systematic individual differences could be detected.[3]

Münsterberg's position was ruthlessly criticized by prominent jurists such as Moore (1907, 1908) and Wigmore (1909) on the grounds that psychology had nothing forensically useful to offer the law. Wigmore claimed that psychological experimentation produced results based on group averages, whereas in a court of law the relevant issue concerns the reliability of a specific witness in a specific situation rather than some hypothetical average. (It should be noted that Wigmore did later soften this stance on the usefulness of scientific psychology.)

In the most vigorous attack on Münsterberg, Moore (1907, 1908) wrote a pair of stinging commentaries, chastising him for his "naivete" and "yellow psychology," stating,

> And if the professor should offer to perpetrate those experiments upon a witness in court . . . the judge would be gifted with the patience of ten Jobs if he succeeded in keeping his temper. Among the legal profession it is familiar learning that experiments are valuable only when the conditions are fairly identical with those attending the occurrence under investigation. If the conditions are substantially dissimilar the experiments are not admissible at all, for the domain of reasoning has been passed and that of pure surmise has been entered. In the first place, the objects or actions to be observed in a class room or court

---

[2]Before he became Supreme Court Chief Justice, Warren Berger argued in 1964 that psychology and psychiatry were "an infant among the family of sciences," and asserted that they "may be claiming too much in relation to what they really understand about the human personality and human behavior" (cited in McGough, 1994, p. 21).

[3]Interestingly, Münsterberg presented a card with a number of dots on it to female students at Radcliffe and male students at Harvard, asking them individually to estimate the number of dots on the card. He found similar errors in their estimates. A week later, he asked them again to estimate the number of dots, this time presenting the card for a longer period and allowing them to influence each other's estimates through discussion. Münsterberg reported that the female students were less likely to change their minds during "deliberations" with other students than were male students, a finding that led him to suggest that women were not suitable as jurors (Hale, 1980). Such views quite appropriately engendered serious concerns among those who were being asked to base judicial policy on psychological findings (Landy, 1992).

room test would probably bear no resemblance to those in actual controversy with their manifold adjuncts of time, place, and circumstance. . . . There is not a scintilla of evidence that (Münsterberg) has ever read a single reported opinion of a judge, or that he has the remotest conception of the processes by which judges are accustomed to arrive at their conclusions. . . . Imagine him (Münsterberg) butting in with his so-called scientific experiments to appraise the testimony of a witness. (Moore, 1907, p. 127)

Münsterberg (1908) rebutted Moore's criticisms with equal force, commenting sarcastically that he

had not known that the jurists of the land were so excellently versed in psychological knowledge. I have attended many a court trial and have read carefully many reports, and have been astonished by the lack of knowledge of mental facts on the part of attorneys and judges. I was continually stumbling over the questions of serious lawyers which could not have been put honestly if those men had a fair understanding of the psychology of memory and attention, of perception and judgment, of feeling and will. And a hundred times have I seen them cease from their efforts where some knowledge of the more modern and subtle psychological methods would have easily carried them forward. I have gone through scores of books on evidence in three languages, and have been astonished at the scarcity of references to the real progress of modern psychological science. I do not see what else I could have done to discover that the courts really know all that the psychologists know—and much more—about the action of the mind. . . . But if it were true for the more modern experimental psychologists that the judges, as Mr. Moore says, "have beaten the psychologists a mile," it would really be a pity that they seem so unwilling to help us in our work. What a cruelty to let us perform thousands and thousands of painstaking experiments on the most subtle points of mental life, while they succeed in knowing it all so much better by common sense and instinct! (p. 145)

Periodically, over the next few decades, some legal theorists expressed the view that psychology had much to offer the courts, and urged that their findings be made available to courts. For example, Gardner (1933) predicted that scientific psychology would eventually be used by courts:

A constant study of the weakness and strength of memory, its reliability in certain particulars and under certain conditions, and the effect of various factors acting upon it, as revealed to us by psychology, will eventually enable us to evaluate properly the testimony of witnesses and thereby render more effective the eternal striving of our courts to approximate absolute justice in each individual case. (p. 409)

Despite these occasional arguments in support of Münsterberg's position, on balance, the day was won by the critics of scientific psychology.

The record indicates that American courts did not cite psychological research or welcome psychologists as expert witnesses until the beginning of the 1950s (see Loh, 1981), and even then psychologists did not testify on witness reliability but in the areas of mental disorders, pretrial publicity, and civil rights.

It is against this backdrop that we provide examples of the research on the suggestibility of children. For simplicity, we divide the 85-year span into three separate periods. The review that we present here is not exhaustive, and the interested reader is referred to our more detailed papers in this area (see Ceci & Bruck, 1993b; Ceci, Leichtman, & Bruck, 1995). We have elected to highlight those studies that are emblematic of the era rather than rehash the comprehensive reviews we have published elsewhere.

EARLY EUROPEAN RESEARCH: 1900–1914

During this period, there were a number of studies on the suggestibility of children and adults. Because only one of these was published in English (Pear & Wyatt, 1914), Anglophones have had to rely on reviews of this research for its details (see Whipple, 1909, 1911, 1912, 1913, for the most influential of these reviews). This is unfortunate because we have found through our own readings of some of the original articles that the studies were extremely creative and thought-provoking, even in 1995, and that the reviews of this work omitted many of the important details. In this section, we describe the work of four pioneers in this area: Binet, Varendonck, Stern, and Lipmann. Although there were many others whom we shall not describe here, these four pioneers had the most profound influence on subsequent psychological research.

Alfred Binet

Binet, a French developmental psychologist, is best known as the father of the IQ test. Although he is less known for his work in the field of suggestibility, his data continue to stand up well in the modern forum. In 1900, Alfred Binet published *La Suggestibilité*, in which he reported a series of studies on the suggestibility of school children between 7 and 14 years of age. Here, he maintained that suggestibility reflected the operation of two broad classes of factors.

The first class of factors concerns the influence of a prominent thought ("autosuggestion") that develops within the individual and is not the result of another's influence. Binet believed that auto-suggestions paralyze a child's critical thought processes, and he attempted to construct experimental situations in which suggestions came from the subject himself. The best known of these tasks involved showing children a series of lines of progressively greater lengths. In one case, five lines of increasing length were presented, and these were followed by a series of "target" lines that were of the same length as the longest (final) line of the series (see Figure 5.1). After the child was shown each line, she was asked to reproduce it on paper as faithfully as possible. Children tended to be swayed by suggestion, which in this case was the expectation of ever-increasing lines; that is, the children's reproductions of the target line were systematically too long because they inferred that it was longer than the line that had preceded it.

Binet questioned his subjects after the study to determine why they had drawn the target lines so long, and found that many children knew that the lines they had drawn were incorrect, and were able to redraw them more accurately on demand. Binet claimed that this ability showed that following the experiment, children could escape the influence of the auto-suggestion and regain control of themselves.

Binet realized, however, that suggestibility, even in this very simple situation, could not be attributed to a single factor. One of his daughters provided some of the impetus for this realization. When Binet gave her the line test just described, she quickly became suspicious that the stimuli were equal, but because of emotional or motivational mechanisms she continued to adhere to the "directing idea" of increasingly longer lines. Observations such as these led Binet to postulate a second set of factors that were external to the child and that reflected mental obedience to another person. In one test of external forces, Binet examined the effects of the examiner's language on children's responses. Children studied five objects for 10 seconds. Some children were told to write down everything they saw, whereas others were asked questions about the objects. For example, one of the objects was a button glued onto a poster board. Some children

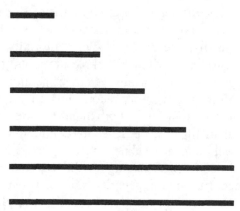

Figure 5.1. Binet's (1900) line experiment to measure the suggestibility of children.

were asked simple direct questions about the button (e.g., "How is the button attached to the board?"), whereas other children were asked either mildly leading questions (e.g., "Wasn't the button attached by a thread?") or highly misleading and suggestive questions (e.g., "What was the color of the thread that attached the button to the board?"). There were several major findings of this study. First, free recall (which was prompted by the request to "write down everything you saw") resulted in the most accurate statements, whereas highly misleading questions resulted in the least accurate statements. This was the first demonstration of a pattern of results that was to be repeatedly replicated throughout the rest of this century. Second, the children's answers to the questions were characterized by an exactness and confidence, regardless of their accuracy level. This, too, was to prove a highly consistent finding throughout the century. Third, when the children were later asked if they had made any mistakes, unlike Binet's previous studies, they did not correct their inaccurate responses to misleading questions. Binet concluded that children's erroneous responses reflected gaps in their memories, which they reasonably attempted to fill in order to please the experimenter. However, once an erroneous response was given, Binet surmised, it became incorporated into their memory.

Another element of external influences in suggestibility concerns the child's willingness to imitate the group response. Binet showed a group of three children the same objects described in the previous study. They were then asked a series of misleading questions. The children were told to call out the answer to each question as quickly as possible. Much to his surprise, Binet found that children who responded second and third were most likely to give the same answer as the first respondent, even if the answer was inaccurate. Thus, Binet concluded that the group is more suggestible than the individual. Until recently, this work was one of the few studies in this century that examined the important effects of peer influences on children's suggestibility.

Binet was prescient in a number of different ways. First, he was a forerunner of modern considerations of the basis of suggestibility. He distinguished between errors of reporting that are the result of actual memory changes versus those that are due to social conformity, arguing that the latter manifestations of suggestibility include attempts to please powerful adult authority figures and do not always reflect genuine incorporation of the false suggestion into the memory record. His unique position was that suggestibility was a combination of both memory and social forces. This position was radical in his day, because the common view was that suggestibility was a psychological weakness that stemmed from internal constitutional factors. In contrast, Binet argued that suggestibility was a normal psychological process that was largely dependent on external factors.

Second, Binet's work was methodologically exemplary, and thus the methods that he developed to examine internal and external forces were adopted or elaborated by researchers during the next 90 years. For example, the perceptual tasks he developed to examine internal forces were commonly used through the 1960s (e.g., Hurlock, 1930; McConnell, 1963; Messerschmidt, 1933; Otis, 1924; Sherman, 1925). His categorization of questions along a continuum ranging from neutral (free recall) to highly misleading has subsequently been used by most researchers in the field.

Finally, Binet attempted to apply his research to the courtroom context. He recommended to French judges that they take responsibility for obtaining reliable testimony from children, and he cautioned them about the dangers of forcing their own questions into a child's memory. Unfortunately, Binet met with great disappointment in his efforts to apply his research directly to the courtroom. According to Cunningham (1988a, 1988b) he bemoaned the fact that his work was never used in French courts. Furthermore, he had hoped to extend his research purview from laboratory studies on schoolchildren's suggestibility to more naturalistic research in the courtroom, by analyzing the transcripts of criminal cases; but he was prevented from doing so by the authorities. Binet's unfulfilled dream of applying his research to the courtroom was taken up by other European researchers such as Varendonck and Stern.

J. Varendonck

Varendonck, a Belgian psychologist, conducted a number of interesting studies on young children's testimony. These studies were primarily motivated by a trial involving allegations by several children that a young girl named Cecile was murdered by a local man. Varendonck, who was an expert witness in this trial, provided the following details (Varendonck, 1911). Two of Cecile's friends, who had played with her on the day of her murder, were awakened that night by Cecile's mother, inquiring after her whereabouts. One of the children, Louise, replied that she did not know; after leaving Cecile, she had returned home, had dinner, and gone to bed. Still later that night, Louise led the police to the spot where the children had played, not far from where Cecile's body was found. She was the fourth murder victim in a small town within a period of a month. After much suggestive questioning, Louise stated that a tall dark man with a dark moustache had coaxed Cecile to follow him. The next day, the two children were questioned again, and during this interrogation they altered their original testimony. After further questioning, which involved suggestions of the names of potential murderers, one of the children said the name of the man was "Jan." One month later, an anonymous letter was received by the police accusing one of the town members (who was the father of one of the playmates) of the murder. On further questioning by powerful authority figures, Louise provided additional details about the murder.

The prosecution's case at the trial centered on the testimony of the two children. On the basis of the details of the case, Varendonck was convinced of the defendant's innocence. He quickly conducted a series of studies with the specific intent of demonstrating the unreliability of children's testimony.

In one study, 7-year-old children were asked about the color of a teacher's beard. Sixteen of 18 children provided a response, whereas only 2 said they did not know. The teacher in question did not have a beard (Varendonck, 1911). In another demonstration, a teacher from an adjoining classroom came into Varendonck's classroom and, without removing his hat, talked in an agitated fashion for approximately 5 minutes. (Keeping one's hat on when entering a room was uncommon because it was a sign of rudeness in that day's society.) After this teacher had left the classroom, the children were then asked in which hand that teacher had held his hat. Only 3 of the 27 students claimed that the hat was not in his hand. In another demonstration, Varendonck asked the children in his class to name and describe the person who had approached him in the school yard that morning. In fact, although there was no such person, most of the children fell sway to the suggestion, with 17 out of 22 giving a name for the person, the color of his clothes, and other details. Varendonck claimed that the types of questions that he used during this procedure were parallel to those that the examining magistrate had used with one of the child witnesses in the murder case.

On the basis of his demonstrations, Varendonck drew the conclusion that the two children's statements to the police were false, the result of suggestions provided by influential adults. He carefully documented how the children changed their testimonies between the first and second interrogations, and how other social factors (e.g., repeated questioning by powerful adult figures) conspired to produce their testimony. Varendonck concluded that children could not observe accurately and that their suggestibility was inexhaustible. He maintained that children would believe anything that adults wanted them to. Varendonck's work is noteworthy because his empirical data were frequently used in courts to cast doubt on the testimony of child witnesses. With almost unbridled and unquestioning exuberance, his American translator summarized this research as follows:

> The presentation of his testimony reached the jury and induced a verdict of "not guilty." The psychology of testimony has, therefore, found its way formally into the court room and saved a man's life. (Whipple, 1912, p. 268)

William Stern

Stern (1910), a German psychologist, developed two types of testimony experiments that still are in use today. In the first paradigm, subjects were shown a picture and asked to study it for a short period of time. Immediately after its presentation, they were asked to recall what they had seen in the picture. They were then asked a series of questions, some of which requested information that was in the picture, whereas other questions were misleading—such questions requested information about nonexistent objects. In one developmental study that included children between the ages of 7 and 18, free recall produced the fewest errors, whereas misleading questions produced the most errors (Stern, 1910). Although younger children were the most suggestible, Stern found that even the 18-year-olds were occasionally misled by the suggestible questions.

The second paradigm that Stern developed was called the "reality" experiment. This grew out of Stern's desire to mimic situations that were closer to real life. In these real-life experiments, naive subjects observed staged incidents. In a typical experiment, an argument occurred during a seminar between two students, one of whom drew a revolver. The other students in the class were then questioned about the scenario. Although Stern did not report any developmental data, this paradigm is described here because it was adapted by many future researchers to study the reliability of adult and child witnesses' memory of events (e.g., King & Yuille, 1987; Loftus, 1979; Marin, Holmes, Guth, & Kovac, 1979; Peters, 1991).

Although there are few empirical data available in English on Stern's developmental studies, he did make the following observations, which continue to be important issues of study. He warned against repeatedly questioning subjects about the same event, and he claimed that a subject's original verbal answers are better remembered than the actual events themselves. Stern also talked about the "force" that questions may have in determining answers. He claimed that many children answer questions because they view them as imperatives. Stern strongly stated that in many cases the questioner, by virtue of the nature of the questions asked, is responsible for the unreliable testimony of witnesses. As we shall see, this has also become a current line of research in this field.

O. Lipmann

The work of Lipmann, a German psychologist, is of interest because many of his hypotheses are the focus of modern research. Lipmann began by asking why children's reports were less reliable than those of adults. He concluded that these age differences reflect, in part, attentional factors in the encoding of the stimuli. Children pay attention to different attributes of stimuli than do adults; children do not have fewer memories than adults, but different kinds of memories. Lipmann stated that these attentional factors, as well as social factors, accounted for children's greater suggestibility. That is, children may be questioned by adults, who have great authority over them, about events that are neither essential nor salient to the child. In these circumstances, the child will attempt to compliantly revise his memory, making his report consistent with the question. "If the respected person who is questioning me expects such an answer then it must be the right one" (Lipmann, 1911, p. 253). Thus, rather than simply answering "I do not know", the child accepts any material that comes to mind to fill in these gaps, whether it is imaginary or real. Eventually, everything that is imagined becomes real. That is, the child fails to differentiate fantasy from reality. Modern researchers would return to the issue of the young child's ability to separate the sources of their information, including whether it was imagined or perceived (Foley & Johnson, 1985; Foley, Johnson, & Raye, 1983; Johnson, Hashtroudi, & Lindsay, 1993; Lindsay, Johnson, & Kwon, 1991). And modern researchers would also return to the idea that children have different perceptions (or scripts) of the world than adults and that these can also affect the nature of their memories (Hudson & Nelson, 1986).

Summary of Research During the Early European Period (1900–1914)

There are three important elements of the early European work on children's suggestibility that deserve mention. The first was an attempt to draw explicit parallels between the experimental contexts and the proceedings in a court of law. All of the European researchers during this early period were interested in applications of children's memory research to the legal system. The second noteworthy feature of this early research was its attempt to provide multifactorial explanations involving cognitive factors (related to children's encoding, storage, and retrieval of events) as well as social factors (related to children's compliance with authority figures or with group pressures). Finally, this early work foreshadowed a large number of findings that were to appear in the modern literature, such as the idea that repeated questioning is detrimental, that questions are interpreted as "imperatives" by young children, requiring answers even if none are available, that free recall produces fewer errors than yes/no questioning, that a witness's confidence is often unrelated to accuracy, that fantasy–reality distinctions are problematic for very young children, and that even adults are suggestible to some degree.

THE DRY MIDDLE YEARS: 1915–1963

Following the spate of European research around the turn of the century, there were only 16 studies published during the next half century in the United States, Canada, and England. Most of these were carried out in the 1920s and 1930s, and for the most part, they are marked by their unoriginality and failure to go beyond the work of their European predecessor. A major focus of these studies was to examine the relationships of age, intelligence, and gender to suggestibility, or to study the correlations among different suggestibility measures, most of which were adaptations of tasks devised by Binet, Varendonck, and Stern. Children's suggestibility was usually assessed by asking them to write answers to written questions in a testlike atmosphere. The tasks, however, seem to provide little information that may be of forensic value. For example, Otis (1924) devised a test to measure children's ability to rely on their own judgments. For some items, children were shown three words with a circle under each. Two of the circles contained the word directly above them, and the third circle was empty. Children were told to write a word in the third circle. If they wrote the word directly above it, this was counted as a suggestible response. Other questions assessed the influence of external forces. For example, children were shown a picture with a slight resemblance to a horse and were asked, "This figure looks like a race horse. Do you not think so?" (see figure 5.2).

Two consistent findings emerged from this set of studies. First, there is an important relationship between age and suggestibility: Children were

YES   NO

Figure 5.2. An example from Otis's (1924) test of children's ability to rely on their own judgments.

more suggestible than adults, and younger children were more suggestible than older children. Second, there was a negative correlation between suggestibility and IQ, with those possessing lower IQs being less able to resist suggestion. However, because many of these suggestibility measures were paper-and-pencil tests, the correlations may reflect the fact that the younger or poorer students had more difficulty dealing with written materials, or keeping their attention focused during long written tasks, than with the suggestibility of the experimental manipulations.

In contrast with the earlier European studies, the studies conducted by American researchers during the 1924–1963 period were not couched in legally relevant terms. For reasons stated at the beginning of this chapter, there was never any mention of the applicability of these findings to the issue of children's courtroom testimony.

One is also struck by the simplicity of the methodology. Because all of the studies involved giving groups of children paper-and-pencil tests, there was no opportunity to directly observe the questioner's influence on the child, nor how children would react when questioned individually. And, as would be forcefully argued throughout the rest of the century, the results of these types of demonstrations of suggestibility may have little relevance for actual court cases in which children testify.

In summary, a reading of the early and middle period literatures indicates that a consensus was building that children were especially prone to suggestive influences. This was reflected in Burtt's (1948) description of child witnesses as

> dangerously vulnerable to coaching and erroneous leading questions: Suggestion is especially apt to play a role in the testimony of children because they are more suggestible than adults. (p. 307)

ENTERING THE MODERN ERA: 1964 to the 1980s

At the end of the 1970s, there was a small resurgence of studies on children's suggestibility. These studies started to show a paradigmatic shift in several ways. First, subjects now viewed a film or participated in a staged incident, and this was followed by the provision of some misleading information. The effects of the misleading information were assessed in an interview that took place hours, days, weeks, or months later. Thus, for the first time, some developmental studies began to provide a glimpse of the long-term effects of providing misinformation. It is also true that, using this approach, the handful of studies produced at the beginning of the 1980s showed an inconsistent pattern of results not found in earlier work. Sometimes children were found to be more suggestible than adults (e.g., Cohen & Harnick, 1980), whereas in other studies no age differences were noted (e.g., Marin, Holmes, Guth, & Kovac, 1979).

As will be seen in the next chapter, because of pressures from the judicial system, social scientists began to attack this area with a renewed vigor and with different and more satisfactory scientific methods. Inconsistent results were less common than inconsistent interpretations of results. But with additional studies, a unified interpretation of the data began to emerge.

6

THE RECENT PAST: CHANGES IN LEGAL AND BEHAVIORAL APPROACHES

In the 1980s, there was a resurgence of interest among developmental researchers in the reliability of children's reports. Whereas some researchers continued in the tradition of earlier ones, examining the effect of misleading questions on children's reports, other researchers broke new ground by expanding the traditional parameters of suggestibility research, and thus in spirit have come closer to our expanded definition, proposed in chapter 3. We will discuss some of these experiments in this chapter and the next five chapters. There have also been other areas of study directly relevant to the child witness. For example, since 1985, a number of studies have been conducted on children's interactions with anatomically detailed dolls, on children's memories of highly stressful events, including personally embarrassing ones, and on children's abilities to deliberately deceive (or lie). We discuss some of these experiments in chapters 12, 13, and 16. Researchers have also examined more general questions, such as adults' judgments of the credibility of child witnesses and jurors' reactions to a number of courtroom modifications. Although a small part of this work is discussed in chapter 17, the interested reader is referred to recent reviews by Leippe and Romanczyk (1989); Luus, Wells, and Turtle (in press); and Ross, Dunning, Toglia, and Ceci (1990) (see also Goodman, Bottoms, Herscovici, & Shaver, 1989; Leippe, Manion, & Romanczyk, 1992; Wells, Turtle, & Luus, 1989).

SOCIAL SCIENTISTS' RENEWED INTEREST IN THE CHILD WITNESS

For the most part, the increased number of studies and the exploration of new areas in child development were more motivated by social and judicial concerns than by theoretical ones. We identify four interrelated factors that account for this dramatic upsurge in the empirical work.

First, beginning in the middle of the 1970s, there was a broadening of the admissibility of expert psychological testimony related to the eyewitness accuracy of adults (see Loftus, 1986). Certainly, this transition was not a smooth one—it was opposed not only by various members of the legal community, but also by some respected members of the psychological research community (see Elliott, 1993; McCloskey & Egeth, 1983). As was the case earlier in the century, jurists and a vocal minority of social scientists argued against, and at times refused to admit, the testimony of expert witnesses on the grounds that the testimony was within the realm of knowledge possessed by the average juror, that the testimony might confuse the juror, that the testimony was more prejudicial than probative, that the content of the testimony was inaccurate, or that the admission of expert testimony consumed too much court time. It was also argued that the admission of expert testimony would lead to a battle of the experts in the courtroom, thus diminishing jurists' opinion of behavioral science research. Despite this continued debate concerning the admissibility of expert testimony (which we revisit in chapter 17), after a long period of being ignored or rejected by judicial policymakers, social science research has come to be viewed, at least on occasion, as relevant to the legal system. Although some judges still refuse to admit into evidence the testimony of psychologists, more and more appear to be willing to do so.[1]

A second stimulus for the increase in research on children's suggestibility was the sociopolitical zeitgeist of the late 1960s that spurred social scientists to apply their scientific training to socially relevant issues, particularly those issues concerning vulnerable populations, such as children's rights and the protection of minors.

---

[1] We make this assertion strictly on the basis of our personal experiences (i.e., being asked repeatedly to serve as expert witnesses), in addition to our conversations with judges when we have conducted judicial training seminars in the United States and Canada. It is our impression that many social scientists are now entering courtrooms and giving testimony in child-related cases. Unfortunately, no national data exist to bolster this impression.

The third and undoubtedly the biggest stimulus for the explosion of research on children's suggestibility is a result of the changes in the court system regarding the treatment of child witnesses (e.g., McGough, 1994). As a result of society's reaction to the dramatic increases in child abuse, and particularly its reaction to the ineffective prosecution of child abuse cases, the legal systems in many countries (including Australia, Canada, the United States, and the United Kingdom) have been forced to change some of their rules concerning the admissibility and treatment of child witnesses.

For example, until recently, courts of law in all English-speaking countries were reluctant to accept the uncorroborated statements of child witnesses (Chadbourn, 1978). This reluctance was reflected in competency hearings, corroboration requirements, and cautionary instructions that some judges gave to juries concerning the risk of convictions based solely on the testimony of child witnesses (Andrews, 1964; Cohen, 1975). For example, Lord Goddard, a respected British jurist, expressed incomprehension at the prosecution's attempt to support its case with the uncorroborated testimony of a 5-year-old witness who claimed she had been imprisoned and sexually assaulted:

> The jury could not attach any value to the evidence of a child of five. It is ridiculous to suppose that they could . . . in any circumstances to call a little child of the age of five is most undesirable, and I hope it will not occur again. (R. v. Wallwork, 1958)

During the 1980s, all but a few jurisdictions dropped their corroboration requirement for children in sexual abuse cases, a crime that by its nature often lacks corroboration. Many states in the United States, modeling their procedures after the *Federal Rules of Evidence*, now allow children to testify regardless of the nature of the crime, permitting the jury to determine how much weight to give to the child's testimony. In Canada, with the adoption of Bill C-15, the court can now convict on the basis of a child's unsworn testimony. In England, children over 3 years of age are now admitted as witnesses in the courtroom and may provide unsworn corroborated testimony in sexual abuse cases.

As more and more children have been admitted as witnesses in the courtroom, legal procedures have been modified. For example, some courts have instituted shield laws that permit a child witness to testify either behind a one-way screen or over closed-circuit television, to occlude the child's view of the defendant but not the defendant's view of the child (e.g., *Coy v. Iowa*, 1988; *Maryland v. Craig*, 1990). Hearsay exceptions are also allowed, whereby therapists, pediatricians, and others are permitted under certain circumstances to describe what children have said to them.

And, most recently, there has been experimentation with mandated videotaping of interviews (Child Victim Witness Investigative Pilot Projects, 1994). These measures serve to assist child witnesses who otherwise might be "psychologically unavailable" to testify in open court (McGough, 1994; Montoya, 1992, 1993).

Interestingly, the modifications in the judicial system regarding the treatment of child witnesses were brought about by social pressures and by the presumption that courtroom modifications will increase testimonial accuracy (Harvard Law Review Notes, 1985; Montoya, 1992) rather than by a consideration of the social science data. As a result, jurists and social scientists continue to raise fundamental questions about whether these changes actually facilitate the accuracy of children's testimony or result in more reliable judgments of a case by fact finders (Montoya, 1992, 1993).[2]

Because of this uncertainty, social scientists and health care professionals have been frequently called to court to testify about the reliability of statements of child witnesses. Until quite recently, it would have been fair to say that even well-read professionals would have had to base their testimony on speculation. One major problem in the interpretation of the literature was the fact that until the 1980s most studies of children's suggestibility focused on school-age children and adolescents; there was not a single study during the first 80 years of this century that included preschoolers. This void made it difficult if not impossible to evaluate the testimonies of preschool witnesses, who were increasingly becoming participants in the legal system (see chapter 3 on the prevalence of preschoolers in criminal proceedings). As will be seen, this void has begun to be filled; in the last decade, many studies of children's suggestibility have included preschoolers.

However, the predominant problem that the expert faced in interpreting the existing literature was that it was difficult to make any generalizations from the scientific literature to the courtroom because the studies of children's suggestibility bore so little resemblance to the situations that

---

[2]Few scientific data addressing these issues are yet available, although some data on the costs and benefits of courtroom innovations on children's courtroom behavior have been gathered (Batterman-Faunce & Goodman, 1993; Flin, 1993). What is needed is evidence showing that children who experience an emotional, painful, and/or embarrassing bodily event (e.g., a genital catheterization) can provide more accurate descriptions of the event when they are asked to do so behind a one-way screen or in a videotaped interview than when they have to provide such testimony before an open forum. And conversely, it is important to show that when children have been coached or suggestively interviewed that their descriptions of the alleged event are equally deceiving in both the open forum and videotaped procedures. To date, no satisfactory evidence exists. In light of claims that many of the new courtroom modifications challenge the constitutional rights of defendants to confront their accusers (*Coy v. Iowa*, 1988; *Maryland v. Craig*, 1990), it is important to determine whether such modifications do, in fact, facilitate the accuracy of children's testimony (Montoya, 1993).

brought children to court. For example, although the consistent finding in this older literature is that younger children are more suggestible than older children or than adults, this conclusion is based on examinations of the influence of one or two misleading questions or suggestions on children's memories of details about neutral events (e.g., stories, slides, movies, or objects). As a result, some researchers have questioned the usefulness of these results in the evaluation of the testimony of a child who makes allegations of sexual abuse or of other potentially distressing events. Perhaps there is no generalization that can be made from the research context to this real-world context of abuse, a point that was made by some in the research community itself:

> Most research on children as eyewitnesses has relied on situations that are very different from the personal involvement and trauma of sexual abuse. Researchers have used brief stories, films, videotapes, or slides to simulate a witnessed event. A few have used actual staged events, but these events—for example, an argument between two adults over the scheduling of a room, or a man tending plants—are also qualitatively different from incidents of child abuse. The children are typically bystanders to the events, there is no bodily contact between the child and adult, and it is seldom even known whether the events hold much interest for the children. Of even more importance . . ., the questions the children are asked often focus on peripheral details of the incident like what the confederate was wearing, rather than on the main actions that occurred, or more to the point, whether sexual actions were committed. (Goodman & Clarke-Stewart, 1991, pp. 92–93)

◆ ◆ ◆

> Finally a word of caution is in order for those who would try to generalize the present findings to cases of children who testify about their experiences in courts of law either as victims or witnesses. There are notable differences between such cases and the present set of experiments. Children in these experiments were presented short vignettes in an affectively neutral context by unfamiliar adults. In court cases, however, the events about which children testify are often of a repetitive nature, for example, sexual molestation, in an emotionally charged context and perpetrated by a familiar person, often a family member. Researchers are still a long way from understanding and predicting child witness behavior. (Ceci, Ross, & Toglia, 1987)

In the remainder of this chapter we will discuss a relatively new line of research that has attempted to address these criticisms. This line of study asks the question, "Are children so suggestible that they will make inaccurate statements about very important or salient events, especially those involving their own bodies?"

ASKING CHILDREN QUESTIONS ABOUT SALIENT EVENTS, ACTIONS, AND THEIR BODIES

Modern researchers face the challenge of developing paradigms that allow for the study of children's reports when the child is a participant rather than a bystander, where there is some bodily contact between the child and the adult, and where the events hold some interest for the child. In developing these new methodologies, researchers have also realized the importance of questioning children about the main actions that occurred during these events rather than about details of peripheral incidents or objects such as the color of the experimenter's beard. The ultimate challenge has been to incorporate questions that ask whether or not sexual actions occurred during these events, but to do so in an ethically permissible manner, one that parents of the children would feel comfortable about.

Some investigators have conducted studies in which children are brought into a university laboratory to participate in some interesting event with a confederate. At some later point, these children are questioned about what happened during the event. Typically, children are first asked open-ended questions; they are asked to tell as much as they can remember about what happened when they came to the laboratory. Then children are asked more direct questions that may require yes/no answers or one-word answers (e.g., "Did the man show you a picture?"). Some of these questions are misleading (e.g., "The man showed you the picture, didn't he?" or " What color was the frame around the picture," when in fact no picture had been shown). There is an additional feature to some of these studies. The interviewer asks children a number of questions termed *abuse-related*. These are questions that if answered in the affirmative could lead to suspicions of child abuse, for example, "Did the man take off your clothes?" (this would be classified as a direct abuse question), or "He took off your clothes, didn't he?" (this would be classified as a misleading abuse question).

As an example of this approach, Rudy and Goodman (1991) sought to determine whether there were differences in the accuracy of children's reports if they were participants in an event as opposed to merely being bystanders. Pairs of 4-year-old and 7-year-old children were left in a trailer with an unfamiliar adult. One child played a game with the adult that involved being dressed in a clown's costume and being lifted and photographed (i.e., the child was a participant), whereas the other child was encouraged to carefully observe this interchange (i.e., the child was a bystander). Approximately 10 days later, both children were brought back to the laboratory and individually questioned about the events. They were first asked some open-ended questions and then 58 specific questions about the event. As described above, these questions were classified as either direct or misleading, and some were classified as abuse-related. Surprisingly, there were few differences between participants' and bystanders' responses.[3] As might be expected, the older children were more accurate than the younger children. Older children's responses were more accurate than those of the younger children for all types of questions except misleading abuse questions; for these latter questions, there were no age differences in accuracy. A more detailed analysis of the incorrect answers to the misleading abuse questions revealed only one false report of abuse; a 4-year-old bystander falsely claimed that he and the participant had been spanked. Thus, Rudy and Goodman demonstrated that 4-year-olds are more suggestible than 7-year-olds; however, the important finding of this paper is that there were no age differences in suggestibility when misleading abuse questions were examined separately. This finding has commonly been used to support the position that although there may be age differences in suggestibility, and although children in general may be misled, these conclusions do not apply to suggestions concerning sexual abuse.

A second study by Saywitz and her colleagues (Saywitz, Goodman, Nicholas, & Moan, 1991) takes this paradigm one step further. Here, they examined 5- and 7-year-old girls' reports of an earlier visit to their pediatrician. During their pediatric visit, half of each age group had a scoliosis exam (for curvature of the spine) and half had a genital exam. Children were tested between 1 and 4 weeks following their exam. As in the previous study, children were asked misleading and direct questions that were abuse- or nonabuse-related. The older children's answers to the misleading non-abuse questions and to the direct abuse questions were more accurate than those of the younger children. However, there was essentially no age differences for the misleading abuse questions (e.g., "How many times did the

---

[3]It should be noted that our interpretation differs from the conclusion offered by Rudy and Goodman (1991), who claimed that participation in an event made children more resistant to suggestion about that event and that sometimes the effects of participation were more evident for young children. These authors noted, "As predicted, participation in a real-life event heightened the children's resistance to suggestion. On misleading action questions, participants were less suggestible than bystanders. On misleading questions concerning the confederate's appearance, 4-year old participants were less suggestible than 4-year old bystanders, and an age difference appeared only for bystander witnesses. This pattern indicates that participation can strengthen resistance to suggestion and that at least at times, the effects are especially evident for young children" (p. 534).

What Rudy and Goodman fail to consider in this discussion is that the effect of participation is no longer significant for one set of questions, once "don't know" answers are included in the data. In effect, only one of the four analyses of misleading questions yielded a significant benefit for participation. When only the misleading abuse questions were considered (a fifth analysis), participation did not strengthen resistance to suggestion. Additionally, the analyses of the non-misleading questions as well as the free recall data failed to reveal any advantage for participation. Thus, it would seem that these authors' conclusion needs moderating in view of the actual pattern of results.

We have gone into this amount of detail, and do so for other frequently cited studies, because the conclusions offered by the authors do not correspond with our own analyses of the raw data. This is an important point especially in the field of forensic psychology. Often, legal jurists and expert witnesses simply rely on authors' summaries of papers without understanding the empirical basis for their conclusions.

doctor kiss you?"), with few children at either age giving incorrect responses. The 7-year-old children never made a false report of abuse, and this occurred only three times (out of a possible 215 opportunities) for the 5-year-olds. Again, this result supports the statement that children cannot be easily misled into making false statements about sexual abuse. (Note that some other results of this study are discussed in greater detail in chapter 12.)

These authors stressed the importance of specific patterns of results in this study. They concluded that when children's inaccurate reports are examined, they involve mainly *omission* errors (i.e., failing to include information in their reports) rather than *commission* errors (i.e., including false events in their reports). Most children in the genital examination condition did not disclose genital contact unless specifically asked, "Did the doctor touch you here?" In the scoliosis condition, when children were asked this question, the incidence of false reports (commission errors) was only 1%:

> Obtaining accurate testimony about sexual abuse from young children is a complex task. Part of the complexity rests in the fact that there are dangers as well as benefits in the use of leading questions with children. The benefits appear in the finding in the studies by Goodman and associates that leading questions were often necessary to elicit information from children about actual events they had experienced (genital touching). . . . The children in the studies by Goodman and associates were generally accurate in reporting specific and personal things that had happened to them. If these results can be generalized to investigations of abuse, they suggest that normal children are unlikely to make up details of sexual acts when nothing abusive happened. They suggest that children will not easily yield to an interviewer's suggestion that something sexual occurred when in fact it did not, especially if non-intimidating interviewers ask questions children can comprehend. (Goodman & Clarke-Stewart, 1991, pp. 102–103)

In general, we agree with the summary of the above work that "children will not easily yield to an interviewer's suggestion that something sexual occurred when in fact it did not," although we feel that these authors have overestimated the degree to which "children will not easily yield." It seems that this claim is based on children's responses to misleading abuse questions. In the trailer study, children's correct answers to the misleading abuse questions ranged from 88% to 94%. In the genital–scoliosis study, the rates were even higher, ranging from 96% to 99%. However, children were more inaccurate when asked abuse questions that were not misleading. When children were directly asked questions about potentially abusive events, the accuracy rates in the trailer study ranged from 82% to 90%. In the genital–scoliosis study, the accuracy rates were even lower, ranging from 77% to 87%. Thus, although it is fair to say that the overwhelming majority of the answers to abuse questions were accurate, there were still a sizable number of inaccurate answers to questions such as "Did [the man in the trailer] kiss you?" or "Did you take your clothes off?" It is not quite clear why children responded more accurately to the misleading than to the direct questions. Perhaps the content of the misleading questions made them more difficult to accept, or perhaps there were some subtle verbal or nonverbal cues in the phrasing of the questions that alerted children to the fact that the misleading questions were in fact misleading. For these reasons, we think it is more instructive to focus on the children's responses to the nonleading questions; when one examines these, one sees that some children are not uniformly accurate in their responses to questions about abuse, a conclusion supported by other studies as well.

Three studies by Ornstein and his colleagues provide additional information on the accuracy of children's recall of events involving bodily touching (see Ornstein, Shapiro, Clubb, & Follmer, in press, for a summary). These studies, which focused on children's recall of their visits to a pediatrician, examined the rate at which memories fade over different periods of delay and the degree to which children include nonoccurring events as part of their reports of their visits.

In these three studies, the children ranged from 3 to 7 years old. Following their yearly medical examination, most of the children were immediately interviewed and then reinterviewed at varying time intervals, ranging from 1 to 12 weeks. In each interview, the children were first asked open-ended questions (e.g., "Can you tell me what happened when you went to the doctor?") and then were asked more specific yes/no questions (e.g., "Did he look in your nose?"). Children were also asked "strange" questions about events that never happen at a doctor's office (e.g., "Did the Doctor cut your hair?") or about silly actions that if responded to affirmatively might be interpreted as sexual (e.g., "Did the nurse lick your knee?"). The common element of all of these questions is that they involve actions on the child's body.

There are several important findings of these three studies. First, there were significant age differences in children's immediate and delayed recall, with the 3-year-old children performing the poorest on all types of questions. The 3-year-olds were particularly noteworthy for the lack of information that they provided to the open-ended questions, thus forcing the interviewer to ask a large number of specific yes/no questions in order to obtain a full report about the visit. Second, as the delay intervals increased, there was notable forgetting among the youngest children; they were increasingly inaccurate when questioned following delays of 1, 3, 6, and 12 weeks. Seven-year-olds did not show impairment until a delay of between 6 and 12 weeks after the medical examination. A third important finding is that the accuracy of children's answers to the strange and silly questions also varied as a function of age and delay interval. As before, younger children gave more inaccurate responses to these questions than older children, and in some cases these scores became more inaccurate at various delays. In one of the studies (Gordon, Ornstein, Clubb, Nida, & Baker-Ward, 1991), the 3-year-old children's responses to these "silly" questions (e.g., "Did the nurse lick your knee?") were at chance levels of accuracy when questioned 12 weeks after their examination. Older children's responses to silly questions remained highly consistent and accurate across delays and studies (error rates averaging about 10% for silly questions). Older children's relatively stable performance may reflect their well-formed notions (or in technical terms, *scripts*) of probable and improbable events that occur during pediatric visits, leading them to automatically reject the latter without even checking their memories for these events.

Results of the Goodman and Ornstein studies reflect how accurately children report salient events, which may include bodily contact, when they are asked to give reports immediately following the events or up to a 3-month delay. The children were fairly, but not entirely, accurate about a number of salient events that involved bodily touching. Furthermore, their accuracy increased as a function of age (with preschoolers being most inaccurate) and as a function of the delay between the interview and the actual event. Ornstein's data indicate that when accuracy drops off, it is not merely the case that children forget and therefore make errors of omission, but they also make errors of commission. Children, especially the younger children, reported events that never happened, and these reported nonevents included not only acts that could conceivably occur in a doctor's office, but also acts that would not occur in the doctor's office and that have sexual connotations, at least to some adults.

It is also interesting to note that both Ornstein and Goodman have commented on the behaviors of children when they are asked misleading or silly questions. In defense of the position that children cannot be easily led to make false allegations about "sexual" events, they note that the children often laughed at these questions, refusing to take them seriously. We might add that similar responses have also been noted in some of the case studies described in chapter 2 when the children were first interviewed and asked misleading questions. As the following examples from our cases show, at times their answers to some of the interviewers' "abuse questions" seem playful, and at times they seem horrified that an adult would even ask such questions. The first example comes from the testimony of one of the mothers in the Little Rascals case:

> Mother: I asked him, "Has Mr. Bob ever touched your pee-bug,"
>   "Has Mr. Bob ever touched your hiney," "Has he ever put
>   his finger in your hiney." I was using very specific questioning.

Attorney: And what were his responses?

Mother: He thought it was funny. He was laughing at me when we were just talking in general. . . . He was so young. He wasn't even three years old.

In the following interview, the interviewer is trying to get a child from the Michaels case to demonstrate on the dolls the alleged abuse. The child is given a wooden spoon and hits the legs of the doll.

Interviewer: Where else are you hitting, on the legs.

Child: On the bottom. . . .

Interviewer: Did anything happen back here? (laughter) Huh? (laughter)

Child: She doesn't hurt and do this.

Interviewer: Stick a crayon in her butt?

Child: Yeah. (laughter)

Interviewer: Oh, how does that feel. How does a crayon in your butt feel?

Child: (laughter)

In the Michaels case, one of the parents testified at trial about the disclosure made by the parent's child: "Kelly puts a penis on her nose and she looked like a penis head. It was funny" (child giggles).

Finally, the following example, also from the Michaels case, shows a child's horror at the content of the interviewers' questions:

Interviewer: Did she drink the pee pee?

Child: Please that sounds just crazy. I don't remember about that. Really don't.

The Ornstein and Goodman data reflect how accurately children respond to direct questions and to misleading questions, which mainly require yes or no answers. The misleading questions in these studies were embedded in an unemotional, neutral interview that contained a host of other types of questions, so that the interview was not tilted toward having the child respond in only one way. These are the types of questions that one might ask children when they provide no information to more general open-ended questions. These are the optimal conditions under which children should be interviewed, and as we will argue throughout this book, when testimony is obtained in this way, we can have the most faith in the accuracy of children's statements.

However, the Goodman and Ornstein studies are not informative about the accuracy of children's statements when the latter are obtained by more aggressive interview methods such as those that are sometimes used with actual child witnesses. The children in these research studies were not repeatedly interviewed about alleged abusive events, questions were not repeated within interviews, nor were there threats or inducements to have the children reply in a certain way. The interviewers in these studies were very supportive and neutral. In contrast, in many cases, children are questioned by anxious parents, by therapists, and by legal officials. Consequently, child witnesses may be more likely to comply with the suggestions of their interviewers than in analogous experimental situations, where interviewers are generally less important or less imposing to the child subjects. It is also true that when children come to court, they are frequently questioned months or even years after the occurrence of an event (as opposed to the shorter delays that are common in most experimental studies). Although the effect of delay on children's reports has been examined in some previous studies, these effects may be increased when paired with some of the suggestive interview techniques just described.

To summarize, the studies that we have reviewed do not shed light on how a web of motives, threats, and inducements (which might act independently as subtle forms of suggestion and interact with more explicit forms of suggestion) might tilt the odds one way or another in terms of obtaining accurate reports from a child. Thus, although many of the experimental studies that we have reviewed up to this point may be immensely important in revealing the underlying mechanisms of suggestibility and of children's memory, they may underestimate the potency of suggestive techniques in actual cases. Because important elements are missing from these studies, it makes it difficult to generalize these results to many forensic situations. It is this concern that has motivated another group of modern researchers to look more closely at the structure of conversations and interviews between children and adults and to examine the effects of various interviewing practices on the accuracy of children's reports. The next seven chapters, which form the core of this book, are devoted to an analysis of these issues.

7

THE ARCHITECTURE OF
INTERVIEWS WITH CHILDREN

Because the testimony of child witnesses is elicited in interviews, it is crucial to understand the architecture of interviews or conversations between children and adults in order to evaluate the source as well as the reliability of child witnesses' statements. In this chapter, we briefly outline a set of practices and assumptions exhibited by adults who are responsible for eliciting information from young children. We defer until subsequent chapters the detailed scientific evidence for the claims we make here, as we also defer until later chapters examples of the baleful effects of some of these practices.

How do children first come to report forensically significant events, such as sexual abuse or witnessing a crime? As we have already described in chapter 3, some children make spontaneous disclosures; they deliberately and quickly tell adults of an incident. In other cases, children may accidentally refer to an event during a conversation with an adult. For example,

> When a 3-year old began to masturbate vigorously, her mother told her to stop. The child protested, "But my daddy puts his finger in there."

or

> While a 3-year old was having her hair washed her mother asked her to "plug her holes" (referring to her ears). The child placed her finger

in her vaginal opening. She then spoke of the man who had touched her "secret holes" by putting something in and out. She was told not to tell anyone or he would kill her. (Campis, Hebden-Curtis & DeMaso, 1993, p. 922)

In other cases, children do not spontaneously make accidental or deliberate disclosures. Rather, an adult has a suspicion that an event may have occurred, even though the child has not affirmed it. For example, on the basis of the child's affect or play during therapy sessions, the therapist may come to suspect that the child was a participant or victim in a stressful event. Or sometimes a parent's suspicion that their child was involved in some negative event may be based on statements made by the child's friends.

Whether children make spontaneous or accidental disclosures, or whether adults have a suspicion that the child has experienced some event, the next step involves interviewing the child about the alleged or suspected event to determine what, if anything, happened. Sometimes interviewers do not have sufficient information following the initial questioning period to make a determination; as a result, there may be a series of interviews, sometimes with different interviewers, before a decision can be reached.

Although interviews may be highly structured, they need not be. An interview, at minimum, is a verbal interaction between at least two people in which one of the participants (the interviewer) has the goal of obtaining specific information from one of the participants (the interviewee). As such, interviews are a particular type of conversation that can be carried out by a wide variety of professionals and nonprofessionals, such as child protection workers, police officers, mental health professionals, attorneys, parents, and teachers.

As we discuss below, obtaining accurate information concerning forensically important events in interviews with children is not a straightforward process; it can be impeded by three types of factors. The first concerns the general linguistic problem of obtaining detailed information from children who are unaccustomed to providing elaborate verbal narratives about their experiences. The second concerns the cognitive problem that arises when children are asked to recall events that happened long before the interview; as a result, the child may have problems remembering the information. Finally, reporting information about stressful, embarrassing, or painful events may be very difficult, especially for the young child. Thus, the interviewer is sometimes limited by the linguistic, cognitive, motivational, and emotional characteristics of the child. Next, we discuss these problems in greater detail and describe some techniques that interviewers use to deal with them. First we deal with everyday adult–child conversations, and then we focus on forensic and therapeutic interviews with children.

ADULTS' EVERYDAY CONVERSATIONS WITH CHILDREN

Obtaining detailed and accurate accounts from children about events that may have happened weeks, months, or even years ago can be a difficult task. Adults encounter this difficulty whether they ask children about everyday neutral events, special pleasant events, or stressful events in which the child was a participant or a victim. For example, when parents ask their young children about what happened at school or at their friend's birthday party, they typically receive answers such as "nothing" or "we played." These noninformative responses to open-ended questions are very common among young children, as parents can attest (see Pillemer & White, 1989). In order to obtain more detailed information, adults must structure the conversation and guide the child into providing responses. Analyses of adult–child conversations reveal the following strategies that adults use to obtain information from children.

On the most general level, the adults ask many questions. These questions serve as probes or prompts to assist the child in reporting the appropriate information (see Fivush, 1993, for a review). More specifically, adults attempt to structure the interaction around their knowledge (or their script) of the topic. So when adults question a child about a birthday party, they may begin with a very general question ("What happened at John's party?"), but after receiving no information, they may immediately begin to ask very specific and often leading questions that reflect their knowledge or script of what generally happens at birthday parties (e.g., "What kind of cake did they have?" "What games did you play?" "What did you do after the gifts were opened?"). When the adult does not receive a satisfactory answer, she may repeat the question. To ensure that the interaction continues, the adult may reward children for their responses, making comments like "Wow, that is really funny" or "That is so interesting, and what happened next?" When children go off-topic and make unrelated remarks, adults frequently try to pull them back into the topic by ignoring the unrelated comments or promising to talk about them at a later time. This often has the intended effect of extinguishing the child's production of extraneous remarks and focusing on the topic at hand.

Of course, when the adult does not have full knowledge of the actual events or a script for those events, she may have difficulty interpreting a child's statements and come to make an inaccurate assessment of the actual event. For example, consider the following dialogue between a mother and her 4-year-old child:

Mother: So tell me about his crayon.

Child: It's a special crayon.

Mother: Ya.

Child: And sparks.

Mother: What do you mean sparks?

Child: Sparks come out of the crayon.

Mother: When you draw, you mean?

Child: Yes.

Mother: Oh, wow. You mean like fire sparks?

Child: Ya sparks.

The child, who was a subject in one of our experiments, was trying to tell his mother about a crayon that has "sparkles." Having never seen this type of crayon before, the mother inaccurately concluded that the crayon burns a hole in the paper.

One might also argue that when adults have to structure conversations with plenty of questions and prompts, the child merely has to answer in ways that are consistent with the beliefs of the adult questioner, or that the child's answers simply mirror the information that is contained in the adult's questions. Although some investigators of everyday parent–child conversations dispute this interpretation (e.g., Fivush, Hamond, Harsch, Singer, & Wolf, 1991), arguing that children incorporate very little of adults' questions into their subsequent recall, there is also other evidence to suggest that children's responses to adults' questions may sometimes reflect what the child thinks the adult wants to hear, rather than what the child actually thinks. This line of research emphasizes the fact that although children may not provide an abundant amount of information during their conversations with adults, they generally are cooperative and compliant participants in verbal interactions. As a result, when questioned by adults, children sometimes attempt to make their answers consistent with what they see as the desire of the questioner, rather than consistent with their knowledge of the event (e.g., Ervin-Tripp, 1978; Read & Cherry, 1978). Furthermore, from an early age, children perceive their adult conversational partners as cooperative, truthful, and not deceptive (Garvey, 1984; Nelson & Gruendel, 1979; Romaine, 1984). Thus, children place more faith in the credibility of adults' statements than in those of their peers (e.g., Ackerman, 1983; Sonnenschein & Whitehurst, 1980).

Another reflection of children's attempts to be cooperative partners in interactions with adults is their attempt to provide answers to adults' questions even when the questions are bizarre. When asked nonsensical questions such as "Is milk bigger than water?" or "Is red heavier than yellow?," most 5- and 7-year-olds will reply "yes" or "no"; they only rarely respond "I don't know" (Hughes & Grieve, 1980). These data suggest that children perceive adults as cooperative conversational partners who ask honest and logical questions that must have real answers.

Another finding that reflects children's attempts to be cooperative conversational partners is that when they are asked the same question more than once, they often change their answers. They appear to interpret the repeated question as "I must not have given the correct response the first time, therefore to comply and be a good conversational partner, I must try to provide new information" (e.g., Gelman, Meck, & Merkin, 1986; Rose & Blank, 1974). For example, in one study, young children saw a videotape of a puppet being given a test by an adult interviewer (Siegal, Waters, & Dinwiddy, 1988). After the puppet had responded to the interviewers' questions, the children were asked if the puppet had answered to please the interviewer or because that was what the puppet really thought was the true answer. When the interviewer repeated the question and the puppet changed its answer, many children said that the puppet did so to please the interviewer. This reveals a desire among preschoolers to conform to what they think an interviewer wants to hear. Even very young children appear to be sensitive to this need to please adult interviewers.

The above discussion points out some of the difficulties that adults may encounter when they engage very young children in everyday conversations and when they attempt to assess the accuracy of the children's statements. As we will see, the same issues occur in magnified form in the case of conversations with young children around forensically important topics.

ADULTS' CONVERSATIONS WITH CHILDREN ABOUT FORENSICALLY RELEVANT EVENTS

Some of the elements that characterize adult–child conversations about daily events or about neutral laboratory tasks also characterize adult–child conversations about topics with potential legal implications. But sometimes because of the urgency or seriousness of forensic interviews, the intensity of many of the characteristics of such interviews increase greatly. This may pose a serious reliability risk when coupled with some special techniques that are used by professional interviewers.

A major dimension along which interviews can be characterized is that of "interviewer bias." Interviewer bias characterizes those interviews where interviewers have *a priori* beliefs about the occurrence of certain events and, as a result, mold the interview to elicit statements from the interviewee that are consistent with these prior beliefs.

One of the hallmarks of interviewer bias is the single-minded attempt to gather only confirmatory evidence and to avoid all avenues that may produce negative or inconsistent evidence. Thus, while gathering evidence to support his hypothesis, an interviewer may fail to gather any evidence that could potentially disconfirm his hypothesis. The interviewer does not challenge the child who provides abuse-consistent evidence by saying things like, "You're kidding me, aren't you?" or "Did that really happen?" The interviewer does not ask questions that might provide alternate explanations for the allegations (e.g., "Did your mommy and daddy tell you that this happened, or did you see it happen?"). And the interviewer does not ask the child about events that are inconsistent with his hypothesis (e.g., "Who else besides your teacher touched your private parts? Did your mommy touch them, too?"). When children provide inconsistent or bizarre evidence, it is either ignored or interpreted within the framework of the interviewer's initial hypothesis. In short, interviewer bias can be found wherever an interviewer thinks he knows the answers before the child divulges them.

From a theoretical standpoint, Dawes (1992) has argued that the failure to remain open to alternative hypotheses that are believable (on the basis of our prior knowledge) can pose serious risks to obtaining a scientifically adequate answer. This point is just as true for forensic investigators and therapists as it is for scientists. Failure to test an alternative to a pet hunch can lead interviewers to ignore inconsistent evidence and to shape the contents of the interview to be consistent with their own beliefs. In chapter 8, we review the relevant scientific literature on interviewer bias, and then explore the extent to which interviewer bias characterized the interviews with the children in some of our sample cases.

Interviewer bias influences the entire architecture of interviews and is revealed through a number of different component features that are highly suggestive. For example, to obtain confirmation of their suspicions, interviewers may not ask children "open-ended" questions, but resort to a barrage of very specific questions, many of which are repeated or leading. When interviewers do not obtain information that is consistent with their suspicions, they may repeatedly interview children until they do obtain such information. Thus, children are sometimes interviewed over a prolonged period of time, and reinterviewed on many occasions about the same set of events. For example, in five of our sample case studies, many of the children were officially interviewed at least six or more times by police, social workers, and attorneys before coming to trial. No one knows how many unofficial interviews were conducted by parents, neighbors, and therapists. These estimates are consistent with the findings of two experts who testified before the Attorney General's Task Force on Family Violence that found that child victims of intrafamilial violence are subjected to at least a dozen investigative interviews before legal proceedings can be resolved (see Whitcomb, 1992). In part, some of these repeated interviews are due to administrative factors; but it is also true, as we will show, that some children are repeatedly interviewed until they provide the desired testimony. In chapter 9, we discuss social science research on the influence of repeated questioning on children's testimony and discuss the degree to which repeated questioning may have influenced the testimony of the children in our cases histories.

"Stereotype inducement" is another strategy that is commonly used in these interviews with children—one reflecting the bias of the interviewer. Here the interviewer gives the child information about some characteristic of the suspected perpetrator. For example, children may be told that a person who is suspected of some crime "is bad" or "does bad things." In chapter 10, we discuss this topic more thoroughly, drawing on the scientific literature and actual case examples for illustrations.

Interviewer biases are reflected in the atmosphere of the interview. Sometimes, interviewers provide much encouragement during the interview in order to put the children at ease and to provide a highly supportive environment. Such encouraging statements, however, can quickly lose their impartial tone when a biased interviewer selectively reinforces children's responses by positively acknowledging statements (e.g., through the use of vigorous head nodding, smiling, and statements such as "Wow, that's great!") that are consistent with the interviewer's beliefs or hypotheses, or by ignoring other statements that do not support the interviewer's beliefs. Some interviewers who feel an urgency and responsibility to obtain the desired disclosure may even use threats and bribes. To obtain full compliance and cooperation from child witnesses, interviewers often tell them that they are helpers in an important legal investigation, and sometimes they tell children that their friends have helped or already told and that they should also tell. In chapter 11, we provide results of experimental studies that have examined how such interviewing procedures can affect the accuracy of children's statements. We then consider the degree to which such interviewing procedures were used in some of our case histories.

There are other characteristics or techniques that are specific to interviews between professionals and children. One of these involves the use of anatomically detailed dolls in investigations of sexual abuse. Children may be given these dolls and asked to reenact the alleged or suspected sexual molestation. It is thought that these props facilitate reports of sexual abuse for children with limited language skills, for children who feel shame and embarrassment, and for children with poor memories of the abusive incident. In chapter 12, we shall examine the relevant empirical literature on anatomically detailed dolls and attempt to relate these data to the use of the dolls in some of our case studies.

Another professional technique involves "guided imagery" or "memory work." Interviewers sometimes ask children first to try to remember or pretend if a certain event occurred and then to create a mental picture of the event and to think about its details. We delve into this technique in chapter 14 in our discussion of the recovery of repressed memories.

Because our description of the architecture of interviews is based on our review of hundreds of transcripts that have been made available to us by judges, attorneys, parents, law enforcement agencies, and medical and mental health professionals, it should be accepted with two caveats. First, the materials we have reviewed may not be representative of many of the interviews carried out with children in forensic or therapeutic situations. Interviews come to our attention because they contain components that might be considered to be suggestive in one way or another and that have the potential to lead the child astray. Therefore, when we say "typical" of interviews, we really mean "typical of the interviews that we have been sent." Undoubtedly, there exist many interviews that do not contain these components. This said, some recent studies reveal the pervasiveness of some interviewing styles. Warren and her colleagues (see McGough & Warren, 1994) have analyzed the child sexual abuse investigative interviews conducted by Child Protective Services professionals in the state of Tennessee. These interviewers spent little if any time asking children open-ended questions; 90% of all questions were highly specific, requiring one-word answers (see Lamb et al., in press, for similar results for trained Israeli "youth" investigators).

A second caveat is that our descriptions are not based on a quantitative analysis of all of the interviews we have reviewed. That is, we do not provide the number of times that each type of element occurs in an interview. However, the different components that we have used to describe these interviews exist across a wide range of interviews that we have reviewed. Throughout this book, we will present some of these descriptive data.

The above caveats notwithstanding, it is clear that professionals do use these techniques and they defend these practices, particularly in investigations of sexual abuse, on a number of related grounds. First, there is a large clinical literature that documents the difficulty of extracting reports from sexually abused children. Often, these youngsters feel shame, guilt, embarrassment, or terror about disclosing their abuse, and as a result, a number of sexually abused children delay making disclosures (see chapter 3). Many professional interviewers argue for the necessity of using a variety of tools that, although potentially suggestive in nature, are crucial for digging out reports of sexual abuse, particularly when the child has alleged to have been threatened not to tell of their abuse.

When criticized for the use of biased interview techniques that reflect the search for evidence that is consistent with suspicions of sexual abuse and that avoid the search for evidence that is inconsistent with such suspicions, some professionals defend their practices on the basis of the patterns of disclosures commonly found in sexually abused children. As we have seen in chapter 3, there are a few studies that suggest that it is common for children first to deny sexual abuse, then to disclose sexual abuse, and then, because of fear or guilt, to recant their allegations. Because of this pattern, these professionals claim that it is important to fully support children's reports of sexual abuse when they occur; any challenge to their reports may drive the children back into denial.

Professional interviewers also support the use of their techniques on the basis of some of the research on children's suggestibility and memory. One interpretation of this literature is that although it may be possible to influence children to fabricate reports of unimportant details, children cannot be influenced to "lie" about sexual abuse. Some professionals go even further, stating that children do not lie about sexual abuse (Faller, 1984; Melton, 1985; Sgroi, 1982; Veitch & Gentile, 1992). It is claimed that identifying oneself as the victim of abuse is not socially desirable, and that therefore one can always trust the accuracy of children's disclosures of abuse regardless of the interviewing procedures that have been used.

Furthermore, analyses of children's reports of actual events reveal that although they often fail to recall a number of details, what they do recall is highly accurate. According to some studies, when children make mistakes it is because they omit details, not because they add or fabricate details (see Ceci & Bruck, 1993b). This research has assured professionals that when children do report sexual abuse, there is no need to question their accuracy, no matter how suggestive the interviewing procedures.

Finally, some interview techniques are defended on the grounds that they are necessary to revive children's memories of events that occurred in the distant past. In many investigations, the alleged events are said to have occurred not days or weeks ago, but months or years ago. Sometimes, 5-year-old children are asked about events that allegedly occurred when they were 2 or 3 years old. A number of the techniques are thought to help them organize and cue their recall of events that have been forgotten.

Some of these assumptions about the inherent accuracy of children's statements have been given scientific credibility by modern developmental psychologists who have found that children, especially very young children, have much higher levels of cognitive competence than was revealed by previous studies. The "competent infant" or "competent child" view suggests that, when given the appropriate social, environmental, and cognitive supports, young children's memories are often accurate (e.g., Bauer, Hertsgaard, & Dow, 1994; Fivush, 1993; Hudson, 1990; Hudson & Nelson, 1986; Leichtman, 1994).

We hope that it is clear from the above discussion that the use of the interviewing techniques described in this chapter is well-intentioned. Interviewers use them because they are concerned about the welfare of the child and want to be assured of their future protection They use them to make children feel comfortable in the interview and to try to extract details of potentially dangerous situations. These techniques are not consciously used to deceive children, nor are they used with the aim of producing inaccurate reports that are consistent with the interviewers' beliefs. No interviewer sets out to deliberately elicit a false report; no interviewer sets out with the intention of tainting a child's memory.[1]

Although the road to disclosures may be paved with good intentions, the contents of its structures are now being challenged on empirical grounds. The next part of this book examines how different components of biased interviews influence the accuracy of children's statements. The research literature that we will describe indicates that when interviews with young children contain a number of suggestive features or strategies, the accuracy of their reports can be compromised—sometimes significantly. This literature cannot be dismissed on the grounds that the events being recalled are neutral or uninteresting and, as a result, are of little relevance to forensic situations. Rather, much of this literature is forensically important: Some studies concern salient events involving the children's own bodies—events that are painful or embarrassing. These studies challenge the conventional wisdom that when children are inaccurate in their reporting about such events, it is because they fail to report some events (i.e., "errors of omission") and not because they fabricate events out of whole cloth ("errors of commission"). This newer research indicates that under certain conditions, children also make commission errors about non-experienced events involving their own bodies. Some of these newer studies also demonstrate the far-reaching influences of the use of some suggestive interviewing techniques on the accuracy and credibility of children's reports. In these newer studies, children do not simply parrot statements made by the interviewer, but rather construct highly elaborate, coherent, and believable autobiographical narratives that happen to be highly inaccurate. Although we do not want to convey the impression that this is an inevitable consequence of the use of suggestive techniques (it is not), it does occur in research studies often enough to engender concern about its possible occurrence in actual field situations.

Researchers have a major advantage over forensic interviewers. Because of the designs of their studies, they can determine the accuracy of their subjects' reports with some certainty because they control the events that are experienced. In the real world, unless there is a corroborating eyewitness, a confession, or some definitive physical evidence, interviewers have a much more difficult task trying to assess the accuracy of a child's report. This is particularly true in cases of sexual abuse, a private crime for which there is rarely any physical evidence, eyewitness report, or spontaneous confession. Because of the difficulty of making such decisions, interviewers need the very best tools for eliciting reports from children. Our

---

[1]We do not include in this assertion the small percentage of documented cases in which adults purposely coached children to give false statements (see Jones & McGraw, 1987, chapter 2). One such case example is provided by Terr (1994) in her book *Unchained Memories*.

argument is that the accuracy of a child's report decreases when the child is interviewed in highly leading and suggestive ways by interviewers who are uninterested in testing alternative hypotheses; such interviews may tarnish the evidence to such a degree that markers of the truth may be buried forever. Presently, there is no scientifically acceptable test or procedure that allows one to determine whether allegations that emerge under such circumstances are accurate or are merely a product of the suggestive interviewing procedures. When children have been subjected to relentlessly suggestive interviews over long periods of time, there is no "Pinocchio Test" (i.e., their noses do not grow longer when they are inaccurate).

Much of what research has discovered about interviewing child witnesses runs counter to our natural impulses. An implication of some of the newer research is that effective interviewers must, at times, suppress the natural instincts and strategies that they commonly use in conversations with children. And yet it is crucial to preserve enough of these natural instincts to make the conversation flow freely. This is indeed a difficult job, as even the best-trained research assistant knows. Thus, in addition to offering criticisms of how not to interview young children, we will, when research warrants, include discussions about how to best interview them.

8

THE ROLE OF INTERVIEWER BIAS

We now turn to the field of social science research to ask whether there is evidence that interviewer biases can, in fact, influence a child's or adult's behavior in a significant manner. The answer is yes. The topic of "interviewer bias" or "experimenter bias" has been researched throughout the century.

One of the earliest studies was reported by Rice (1929). He studied 12 experienced interviewers from various social service agencies in New York City who were assigned to interview approximately 2,000 homeless men to ascertain the causes of their destitution. Rice was struck by how some of the interviewers' beliefs influenced the contents of the reports they obtained from the homeless men. The most obvious example of this came in the case of two interviewers who differed in their social orientations, one being known by co-workers as a "socialist," the other as an ardent "prohibitionist." Rice found that the socialist was nearly three times more likely to report that the men's destitution was due to industrial causes beyond their control (e.g., layoffs, plant closings, seasonal labor), whereas the prohibitionist was nearly three times more likely to report that the basis of the men's destitution was alcohol or drug related. Not only were the findings of these two interviewers consistent with their "pet" hypotheses about the causes of societal dissolution, but the homeless men themselves seem to have incorporated the interviewers' biases into their own explanations of their homelessness. Rice viewed this as an example of interviewer bias acting as a suggestive form of questioning. In fact, although this analysis was conducted 65 years ago, his conclusion is thoroughly modern in terms of its explanatory construct, namely suggestibility due to interviewer bias.

Since Rice's study, there have been hundreds of other demonstrations of the influences of interviewer biases. One reason that this topic has received so much attention is because of its implications for conducting both therapy and reliable scientific studies. Thus, a number of studies were designed to examine whether an experimenter might influence the subjects' performance in a such a way that their behaviors would be consistent with the hypotheses of the study (see Rosenthal, 1985; Rosenthal & Rubin, 1978, for reviews). The results of a number of studies indicate that when experimenters or interviewers are aware of the hypothesis of a study, they unconsciously or unintentionally alter the way they test subjects, resulting in performance consistent with the hypothesis of the study. Often the biases are observed in subtle ways, such as a slight nuance, a smile, a nod of the head, the tone of voice, or the phrasing of a question.

Expectations and biases affect how situations are encoded and subsequently remembered. Generally, expectancy-consistent results are more likely to be remembered: The number of confirming cases are overestimated (Chapman, 1967), and these confirming cases are more easily recalled (Crocker, 1981). Prior expectations (or biases) may also work on incongruent information in such a way as to transform it so that it fits into one's existing beliefs (Crocker, 1981).

Perhaps the best-known studies on expectations or experimenter bias are those that examine the role of teacher expectations on student outcome. The first and most cited of these studies, "Pygmalion in the Classroom," was conducted by Robert Rosenthal in 1968. The following is a brief description.

At the beginning of the school year, all of the children in one elementary school were given a nonverbal intelligence test. The teachers were told that this test predicts intellectual blooming, and they were given a list of the children in their class whose scores indicated that they would show surprising gains in the next 8 months. In reality, however, children on the list were chosen randomly from the class. Thus, the teachers were misled into believing that the randomly selected children had performed exceptionally well, when in fact, as a group, they performed at the same level as their classmates who were not on the list. Eight months later, when all the children in the school were given another intelligence test, the selected children made greater gains than the children who were not on the list. These results and many others like them demonstrate that if teachers have low expectations about their students, the students will perform poorly academically, and if teachers have high expectations for their students, these students will excel. These expectations are transmitted through differential treatment of students: Teachers pay more attention to high-expectancy students, providing them with more emotional support and more favorable feedback (see Jussim, 1986, for a review).

Although this line of work highlights the importance of interpersonal expectancy effects, the results do not directly indicate whether interviewers with specific biases or beliefs can influence children's responses to an interviewer's questions. The question that we address next is the following: To what extent will children eventually make statements consistent with a biased interviewer's beliefs? We describe three recent studies that have examined this issue.

THE EFFECTS OF INTERVIEWER BIAS ON THE ACCURACY OF CHILDREN'S REPORTS

Simon Says

In the first study, preschoolers played a game similar to "Simon Says" (Ceci, Leichtman, & White, in press). One month later, they were interviewed by a trained social worker. Before the interview, the social worker was given a one-page report containing two types of information about the play episode: accurate information and erroneous information. For example, if the event involved one child touching his own stomach and then touching another child's nose, the social worker would be correctly told that the child touched his own stomach but incorrectly told that he touched the other child's toe. The interviewer was not told that some of the information in the report was inaccurate. She was merely told that these actions *might* have occurred during the play episode. She was asked to conduct an interview to determine what each child could recall about the original play episode.

The information provided on the one-page sheet influenced the social worker's hypothesis (or beliefs) about what had transpired, and powerfully influenced the dynamics of the interview, with the social worker eventually shaping some of the children's reports to be consistent with her hypothesis, even when it was inaccurate. When the social worker was accurately informed, the children correctly recalled 93% of all events. However, when she was misinformed, 34% of the 3- to 4-year-olds and 18% of the 5- to 6-year-olds corroborated one or more events that the interviewer falsely believed had occurred. Interestingly, the children seemed to become more credible as their interviews unfolded. Many children initially stated details of the false events inconsistently or reluctantly, but as the interviewer persisted in asking leading questions that were consistent with her false hypothesis, a significant number of these children abandoned their contradictions and hesitancy and endorsed the interviewer's erroneous hypothesis.

During these interviews, the social worker kept notes about the children's reports. Two months later, these notes were given to another interviewer, who reinterviewed the children about the original play episode. As can be seen in Figure 8.1, the children continued to give inaccurate reports, and their frequency increased somewhat from the previous session. It seems that the social worker's notes influenced the beliefs and the hypotheses of the second interviewer, who not only got the children to continue to assent to erroneous statements that were consistent with her hypotheses (e.g., some falsely claimed that their knees were licked and that marbles were inserted in their ears), but the children did so with increasing confidence. If we had continued to reinterview the children in this study, each time passing along the notes of the prior interviewer to a new interviewer, there is no telling how far astray the children might have gone.

In sum, when interviewers' hypotheses are correct, children's recall is highly accurate, with few errors of omission or commission. However, when interviewers' hypotheses are incorrect, they elicit a substantial amount of inaccurate information, especially from the youngest preschoolers.

A Class Visit

Similar findings were reported from Australia by Pettit, Fegan and Howie (1990). These investigators examined how interviewers' beliefs about a certain event affect their style of questioning children and the accuracy of children's subsequent reports. Two actors, posing as park rangers, visited the classes of preschool children to ask them to help a bird find

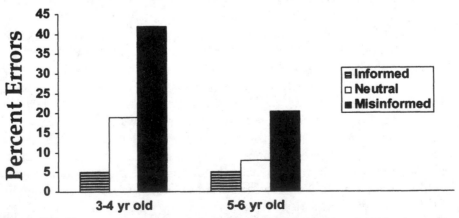

Figure 8.1. Three-month interview (adapted from Ceci, Leichtman, & White, in press).

a nest for her eggs. During the presentation, one of the rangers accidentally knocked over a cake perched on top of a piano. When the cake fell and shattered on the floor, there was an abrupt silence and a halt to all activities. Two weeks later, all of the children were questioned about the event.

Interviewers' beliefs about the event were manipulated in the following manner. Some interviewers were provided with full, accurate knowledge of the event, whereas others were given inaccurate information (i.e., false beliefs). Finally, some interviewers were given no information about the event. The interviewers were told to question each child until they found out what happened, and they were also asked to avoid the use of leading questions.

Despite the warning to avoid leading questions, 30% of all interviewers' questions could be characterized as leading, and half of these were misleading. Interviewers with inaccurate knowledge (false beliefs) asked four to five times as many misleading questions as the other interviewers. Overall, children agreed with 41% of the misleading questions, and those interviewed by the misled interviewers gave the most inaccurate information. Thus, when an interviewer's belief was contrary to what the child actually experienced, the interview was characterized by an overabundance of misleading questions, which, in turn, resulted in children providing highly inaccurate information.

Chester the Molester/Chester the Cleaner

Clarke-Stewart, Thompson, and Lepore (1989; see also Goodman & Clarke-Stewart, 1991) conducted a study in which 5- and 6-year-olds viewed a staged event that could be construed as either abusive or innocent. Some children interacted with a confederate named "Chester" as he cleaned some dolls and other toys in a playroom. Other children interacted with Chester as he handled the dolls roughly and in a mildly abusive manner. Chester's dialogue reinforced the idea that he was either cleaning the doll (e.g., "This doll is dirty, I had better clean it") or playing with it in a rough, suggestive manner (e.g., "I like to play with dolls. I like to spray them in the face with water").

The children were questioned about this event several times on the same day, by different interviewers who differed in their interpretations of the event. The interviewer was (a) "accusatory" in tone (suggesting that the janitor had been inappropriately playing with the toys instead of working), (b) "exculpatory" in tone (suggesting that the janitor was just cleaning the toys and not playing), or (c) "neutral" and nonsuggestive in tone. In the first two types of interviews, the questions changed from mildly to strongly suggestive as the interview progressed.

Following the first interview, all children were asked to tell in their own words what they had witnessed. They were then asked some factual questions (e.g., "Did the janitor wipe the doll's face?") and some interpretive questions regarding the janitor's activities (e.g., "Was the janitor doing his job or was he just being bad?"). Then, each child was interrogated by a second interviewer who either reinforced or contradicted the first interviewer's tone. Finally, the children were asked by their parents to recount what the janitor had done.

When questioned by a neutral interviewer, or by an interviewer whose interpretation was consistent with the activity viewed by the child, the children's accounts were both factually correct and consistent with the janitor's script. However, when the interviewer contradicted the activity viewed by the child, those children's stories quickly conformed to the suggestions or beliefs of the interviewer. By the end of the first interview, 75% of these children's remarks were consistent with the interviewer's point of view, and 90% answered the interpretive questions in agreement with her point of view, as opposed to what actually happened.

Children changed their stories from the first to second interviews only if the two interviewers differed in their interpretation of the events. Thus, when the second interviewer contradicted the first interviewer, the majority of children then fit their stories to the suggestions of the second interviewer. If the interviewer's interpretation was consistent across two interviews, but inconsistent with what the child had observed, the suggestions planted in the first session were quickly taken up and mentioned by the children in the second session. Moreover, when questioned by their parents, the children's answers were consistent with the interviewers' biases. Finally, although the effects of the interviewers' interpretations were most observable in children's responses to the interpretive questions about what the janitor had done, 20% of the children also made errors on the factual questions in the direction suggested by the biased interpretation, even though no suggestions had been given regarding these particular details.

Summary

These three studies provide important evidence that interviewers' biases and beliefs about an event can influence the conduct of their interviews and influence the accuracy of the children's testimony. The data highlight both the benefits and dangers of having only one hypothesis about an event. When the hypothesis is correct, it results in very high levels of accurate recall by young children (e.g., 93% in Ceci et al., in press), but when the hypothesis is incorrect, it can lead to high levels of inaccurate recall. Thus, we see rather graphically an instantiation of the cancer drug metaphor we described in chapter 1. The message from these studies is that interviewers should follow the same principles as scientific investigators. They should arrive at the truth by ruling out rival hypotheses—particularly, the most reasonable rivals—and by attempting to falsify their favored hypothesis (Ceci & Bronfenbrenner, 1991; Dawes, 1992). This is what scientists mean when they endorse "proof by disproof" as the best means of ascertaining the truth.

PRACTICAL LIMITS OF FALSIFICATION

It might be argued that these criteria are too rigid for interviewers involved in child abuse cases. These professionals need to act quickly to protect the child from further abuse. The requirement that they test a number of relevant alternate hypotheses is unreasonable under these constraints. Furthermore, the requirement that these interviewers not be biased by previous information concerning the allegations may be detrimental to the protection of the child; unless a worker has all the background information, he or she may fail to detect some important or relevant information told by the child.

Although we are sympathetic to these constraints, we believe that the risks associated with confirmatory bias are too great to be swayed by these arguments. Although it may not be possible to "blind" interviewers from all information about the case that could lead to the formation of expectancies, they should be told only as much as necessary, and allowed to form and test their own hypotheses on the basis of their investigations. In well-worked fields of scholarship, if scientists do not attempt to disconfirm their hypothesis, other scientists can be counted on to do the job for them—sometimes with embarrassing candor and detail. Unfortunately, in clinical and forensic interviews, it is not always the case that others can be counted on to test alternative hypotheses if front-line professionals fail to do so. Interviewers need training in how to entertain two or more competing hypotheses simultaneously, without conveying disbelief or skepticism to the child. This is not as difficult as it may sound, and competent interviewers probably already do this without being aware they are doing it.

We believe that the evolution of many of the mass-allegation day-care cases, as well as some other cases involving sexual abuse, stem from this phenomenon of interviewer's bias. Sometimes these initial biases unfold in therapy sessions in which the therapist pursues a single hypothesis about the basis of the child's difficulties (for a review of the evidence that therapists rarely test alternatives, and fall prey to illusory correlations and confirmatory biases, see Alloy & Tabachnik, 1984; Brehm & Smith, 1986; Kayne & Alloy, 1988). Following sustained periods of therapy, some children make disclosures that are then pursued in multiple interviews by law enforcement and Child Protective Service workers. At other times, the interviewer bias is rooted in the investigative process by officers of the court who initially interview children. And finally, some allegations grow out of interviews conducted by parents who are convinced that abuse took place and who relentlessly pursue a single hunch in conversations with their children. In the rest of the chapter, we will examine case studies for examples of confirmatory biases in the interviewing process.

CONFIRMATORY BIAS: EXAMPLES FROM CASES

Before turning to our case histories, we provide an example from another case in which an adult was accused by his children of ritualistic sexual abuse. We do this because some of the procedures for interviewing children in this case closely parallel the procedures in the experimental studies described above where the interviewer is provided with "false information."

In this case, Mr. P. was convicted of various acts of ritualistic sexual abuse against his children. One of the grounds for appeal was that the children's therapist, Dr. L., was the source of all of the allegations. One of the bases of this claim was that police officers became suspicious about some of the allegations of Mr. P.'s children because they were so similar (and at times identical) to those made by other children involved in independent sexual abuse cases. One thing that all of these children had in common was that Dr. L. was their therapist. To test these suspicions, one police officer selected a highly unbelievable claim and told Dr. L. that it was important that such information be present in the children's statements. According to this officer's testimony, after Dr. L. was deliberately fed this false information, she reported that it appeared in the children's statements.

Examples of interviewers' biases, blind pursuit of a single hypothesis, and failure to test alternate, equally believable explanations of the children's behavior characterize many aspects of the Little Rascals case. It appears from our reading of the materials from this case that many of the investigators in the Little Rascals case were poised to find allegations of sexual abuse. The seeds of this case may have been sown in the spring of 1988, months before the first allegations of child sexual abuse had been made. At a 3-day conference in the Outer Banks town of Kill Devil Hills, law enforcement and social service workers convened to learn about the dangers of child molesters operating day-care facilities. The seminar was co-sponsored by a counseling group and assisted by Judy Abbott, a social worker who would become one of the most active therapists for the child victims in this case. The featured speaker was Ann Burgess, editor of the book *Child Pornography and Sex Rings* (1984). Also attending this conference were H. P. Williams who would co-prosecute the case, and Brenda Toppin, the Edenton police officer who was the first to interview most of the children in the case and to advise the parents of their abuse.

The first allegation was made by Karl B., whose mother was a friend of Brenda Toppin. Prior to the allegations, Mrs. B had voiced concern over her 3-year-old son's nightmares and bedwetting and his reticence to go to day care. Toppin urged her friend to question her son about what was going on. During this time, in response to his mother's questions, Karl told his mother that he had been playing a "doctor" game with a child across the street. Mrs. B again called Toppin, asking how to question her child about these concerns. After a few days of further questioning, Karl claimed that Mr. Bob played doctor with other children, but not with Karl. According to the available evidence, it seems that the "doctor" game incident with the child across the street was never mentioned during the investigation. It was never a topic of questions for the child. Karl was only questioned about the "doctor" games that Mr. Bob played. The failure to probe the child about playing doctor with his friend across the street may reflect the interviewers' bias that there was abuse in the day-care center, hence their predisposition to neglect any evidence that the allegations could be explained by other hypotheses

A few weeks after making his first allegation, Karl B. was interviewed by a psychiatric nurse who provided therapy to many children in the case. After a 15-minute interview, she made the diagnosis that Karl was suffering from posttraumatic stress disorder (PTSD) as a result of sexual abuse in the day-care center. There is no indication from this therapist's notes that she considered the facts that Karl had played "doctor" with a friend across the street, that his mother and father were away from home for major portions of the day because of their careers, or that prior interrogations might be the basis of his PTSD. She did not consider that the family was considering a move. And finally, she did not consider that there was much sibling rivalry, involving aggression with his younger brother. Furthermore, there was no attempt on the part of this therapist to elicit details of the alleged abuse. Given the history of this child, a variety of hypotheses that could have been raised concerning his nightmares and reticence to go to school do not appear to have been seriously entertained. Sexual abuse at the day-care center might be very low on the list of a skilled child therapist's hypotheses in trying to understand the symptoms of this child. Nevertheless, this therapist and Officer Toppin both concluded that sexual abuse had occurred.

It seems that this failure to test equally, and sometimes more, plausible alternate hypotheses characterized many of the professional interviewers in this case. For example, one of the children, Lisa, was brought for evaluation of abuse to Dr. M., another therapist for a number of children in this case. During the first few appointments, Lisa denied that any abuse had occurred. According to her parents, she was disappointed that the day-care center closed. She missed her friends and she missed her teacher (whom she later accused of abuse). When her parents asked her about what happened at the center, she consistently replied, "Mr. Bob is nice." These very state-ments were the reason that her parents brought her for evaluation: They were suspicious about the consistent positive remarks about Mr. Bob. They suspected that Lisa may have been abused. After several sessions, Dr. M. showed Lisa an anatomically correct doll and asked her where she had been "touched by someone at the day-care." Even though she had not yet made any allegations about sexual touching at the day-care center, Lisa now claimed that Mr. Bob had touched her buttocks. Two months after this interview, a baby sister was born. Almost one year after the first eval-uation, when Lisa asked her mother why men have penises, her mother explained how babies were born. This 5-and-a-half-year-old child's interest in reproduction sparked subsequent discussions with her grandmother and with Dr. M. Using an anatomically detailed doll, Dr. M. showed Lisa how babies descend the birth canal. Then the following entry was made in the therapist's notes:

> She said Mr. Bob's penis went into Miss Dawn's privates. Then she added "There was one thing my mom forgot to tell you—A long, long time ago, Mr. Bob sticked his penis in my vagina." . . .
>
> This is the first time that has given any indication of penile pene-tration although her recent interest in making babies and penises and sperm may have been a way of leading up to this disclosure.

It is true that Dr. M. used the word "may" in the last sentence, but it is more surprising that she does not entertain other plausible hypotheses, for example, that this child had been in therapy for a year in which one focus had been "bad touching"; that a baby sister had been born; and that Lisa was very interested in the reproductive process. Her recent interest in babies may have been a way of leading up to the disclosure, but it is just as probable that her disclosure was a result of intensive therapy and sex education. Of course, if one's primary hypothesis is that the child was really abused, this alternative hypothesis might not be seriously entertained.

One important factor that might explain why the children's allega-tions were never seriously questioned by therapists is that the interviews were conducted by a small group of intertwined, committed therapists. Brenda Toppin, the police officer, gave the name of one therapist to the first set of parents whose children had made allegations. When the number of suspected child victims grew, a few more names were added to the list. Parents were urged to take their children to one of these professionals for evaluation and treatment. Four therapists treated over 90 children in this case; they were reimbursed by the state of North Carolina, and they kept in contact with Toppin and with the district attorney's office about new developments. Parents who wanted to seek outside opinions were severely discouraged from doing so. One mother, who had moved out of Edenton shortly after the initial allegations were investigated, spoke at trial of this effort:

Mother: Sometime in April of '89, right after we moved, I got a couple of phone calls. The first phone call I got was from Brenda Toppin at my work. She said that she was concerned that with my moving away that I hadn't kept in touch and wasn't aware of the ongoing investigation. She would like to urge that I have my son evaluated. There was a lot more to the case than they had originally realized. . . . I thanked her, and the conversation was over in a few minutes. She was nice. . . . She did inform me that there was some organization I could contact, victim's assistance, and some different places I could call, district attorney's office to get referrals for help.

Attorney: Referrals for what?

Mother: To have my son evaluated.

Attorney: Was that the end of the matter at that point?

Mother: After Brenda Toppin called me, Judy Abbott [Note: Judy Abbott was one of the therapists.] phoned me. . . . I didn't know who she was. I had never met her. . . . I told her that I was aware of what was going on. I told her that I had been keeping in touch, that I still had friends in Edenton and family. I told her I was not interested in complying with her request. I told her that I was not interested in bringing my son back to Elizabeth City to one of their group therapists. I wasn't interested in participating in any parent meetings or sessions. I told her that I felt very comfortable that my son was fine. He was not showing any problems and never had. I told her that should it become necessary to have him evaluated I wanted to take him to an independent evaluation where they had no knowledge of Edenton or this case, that I felt like that would be more fair. . . .

I had asked her why I couldn't take my son to my own independent physician. I didn't understand why it was so imperative that I only see the doctors and therapists that were working on this particular case. I also didn't understand why the only way there would be any payments made through this victims assistance program would be only if I went to their doctors and came back to Edenton. . . . It was a long conversation. It was real upsetting. . . .

It started out with her being very friendly, very supportive, wanting me to know how much she was concerned about myself and how well she knew my family and that she was just worried about us having moved and not being given the proper attention. When I was insistent about wanting to stay uninvolved and my feeling that my son

was fine, I felt very intimidated. She was very forceful.
. . . I was concerned at the end of the conversation that
should I not follow her suggestions that I might be found
to be an unfit mother. . . .

I felt very threatened that they might be able to
speak with my son against my wishes. . . . At the end of
conversation I thanked her and said I didn't want to speak
with her anymore.

Attorney: Now after that conversation did Ms. Abbott contact you
any further?

Mother: No. She contacted my family, not me.

The Little Rascals case is characterized by the number of allegations
involving ritualistic abuse that may have arisen as a result of interviewer
bias. It does not seem that the children made any spontaneous allegations
concerning ritualistic abuse, but rather that such allegations unfolded in
response to a therapist's probes that may have been based on the premise
that when sexual abuse takes place in day-care centers it is sometimes
associated with ritualistic abuse. For example, one of the therapists showed
her child clients pictures of satanic symbols (according to one mother,
these were sometimes left in the waiting room) in an effort to uncover
evidence of devil worship. Although some of the children claimed to have
seen these before, these symbols are easily confused with other objects that
most children could encounter (e.g., Halloween masks).

Similar examples of interview bias can be found in the Country Walk
case. The initial interviews were carried out by a husband-and-wife team,
who had strong beliefs about the protection of young children in day-care
settings. The following excerpts from one child's interview reflect these
interviewers' pursuit of a single hypothesis that abuse had occurred that
involved feeding children poison or drugs and playing games while in the
nude. This passage suggests a reluctance to consider alternative explanations for the purported events.

Interviewer: [W]hen they gave you the stuff to drink, did you feel
dizzy? [Note that drinks were not mentioned previously
in the interview.]

Child: No, but I feel bad. . . . I would be dead. [The child then
says that the kids gave him the drink that made him be
dead and describes the drink.]

Interviewer: When you had the drink and you were dead were some
of the other children doing some stuff? Were they playing games and stuff when you were dead?

Child: They were sitting on me.

Interviewer: . . . Did they have their clothes on or off?

Child:	Off.
Interviewer:	Did Frank and Iliana have their clothes off?
Child:	Only some of the kids . . . I didn't.
Interviewer:	I understand that but some of the kids had their clothes off?
Child:	Yes.
Interviewer:	[D]id some of the kids touch each other's private parts?
Child:	(shaking head no)
Interviewer:	Did you see any of the other children go in the room with Frank and Iliana?
Child:	. . . What did they do?
Interviewer:	I don't know. I wasn't there. I am just asking did they ever go into the bedroom by themselves?
Child:	Yes.
Interviewer:	Did they take their clothes off? . . . [D]id any of the children when they played games sometimes and Frank and Iliana would tell them like the boys to touch the girl's vaginas or do something like that?
Child:	(nodding in the negative)
Interviewer:	You were dead, oh [from the "drink"] . . . If you had been alive, do you think you would have seen that? . . . Maybe it did happen.

Note that the investigator rather than the child first introduced the topic of "drink" into the interview. This could reflect the investigator's belief that the children were being drugged. Furthermore, this investigator did not ask the child to explain what happened or what it meant to be "dead." Instead, the investigator asked a series of specific questions about abusive behavior that the child might have seen "if you had been alive."

Examples of interviewers' biases, blind pursuit of a single hypothesis, and failure to test alternate, equally believable explanations of the children's behavior appear rife in the interviews conducted in the Michaels case. These biases seem apparent when interviewers' persistently maintained one line of inquiry even when children consistently denied that the hypothesized events occurred. Interviewer biases are also revealed by a failure to follow up some of the children's inconsistent or bizarre statements when doing so might undermine the interviewer's primary hypothesis.

The following dialogue between the interviewer and Child A during an early investigatory interview is illustrative of an interviewer's failure to seriously consider any evidence that was contrary to her primary beliefs.

Interviewer: Do you think that Kelly was not good when she was hurting you all?

Child A: Wasn't hurting me. I like her.

Interviewer: I can't hear you, you got to look at me when you talk to me. Now when Kelly was bothering kids in the music room . . .

Child A: I got socks off . . .

Interviewer: Did she make anybody else take their clothes off in the music room?

Child A: No.

Interviewer: Yes?

Child A: No . . .

Interviewer: Did Kelly ever make you kiss her on the butt?

Child A: No.

Interviewer: Did Kelly ever say—I'll tell you what. When did Kelly say these words? Piss, shit, sugar?

Child A: Piss, shit, sugar?

Interviewer: Yeah, when did she say that, what did you have to do in order for her to say that?

Child A: I didn't say that.

Interviewer: I know, she said it, but what did you have to do?

The interviewers had developed the belief that Kelly Michaels had abused the children with various utensils and also that part of the abuse involved smearing peanut butter on their bodies. In this next example, the investigator pursues these hypotheses with a child who was given an anatomically correct doll and some utensils.

Interviewer: Okay, I really need your help on this. Did you have to do anything to her with this stuff?

Child B: Okay. Where's the big knife at. Show me where's the big knife at.

Interviewer: Pretend this is the big knife because we don't have a big knife.

Child B: This is a big one.

Interviewer: Okay, what did you have to do with that? What did you have to . . .

Child B: No . . . take the peanut—put the peanut butter . . .

Interviewer:	You put what's that, what did you put there?
Child B:	I put jelly right here.
Interviewer:	Jelly?
Child B:	And I put jelly on her mouth and on the eyes.
Interviewer:	You put jelly on her eyes and her vagina and her mouth?
Child B:	On her back, on her socks.
Interviewer:	And did you have to put anything else down there?
Child B:	Right there, right here and right here and here.
Interviewer:	You put peanut butter all over? And where else did you put the peanut butter?
Child B:	And jelly.
Interviewer:	And jelly?
Child B:	And we squeezed orange on her.
Interviewer:	And you had to squeeze an orange on her?
Child B:	Put orange juice on her.
Interviewer:	And did anybody—how did everybody take it off? How did she make you take it off?
Child B:	No. Lick her all up, eat her all up and lick her all up.
Interviewer:	You had to lick her all up?
Child B:	And eat her all up.
Interviewer:	Yeah? What did it taste like?
Child B:	Yucky.
Interviewer:	So she made you eat the peanut butter and jelly and the orange juice off of the vagina too?
Child B:	Yeah.
Interviewer:	Was that scary or funny?
Child B:	Funny, funny and scary.

We see from these examples that when children's responses contain discrepant, inconsistent, incomprehensible, or no information, the investigators seemed to consider these responses to be consistent with the fact that abuse had taken place, or else they chose to ignore these statements. We are struck by the inconsistencies and the bizarre statements made by the children in response to the interviewers' questions. Most adults interacting with children in these situations would try to figure out just what the child was thinking about or why the child might be so confused to make such statements. Yet this did not appear to happen. The children were not reined in (e.g., instructed to describe only things that really happened), nor were they asked commonsense questions such as "Did this happen to you or are you just pretending that it happened to you?" or "Did you see this happen or did someone tell you that it happened?" Children were rarely challenged about their statements ("This really didn't happen, did it?"). Competent investigative interviewers would have at least asked themselves how it was possible for all of these alleged acts, some of which were very painful, to occur without the other day-care workers' or parents' knowledge. The hypothesis that these alleged acts were the products of suggestive interviewing techniques or of children's imagination seems not to have been seriously considered.

Our statements concerning the possible preconceived biases of the interviewers in the Michaels case are not based on conjecture, but on these interviewers' stated beliefs. For example, Dr. Susan Esquilin, a child therapist who presided over two heavily attended parent meetings when allegations were first made, who conducted five group therapy sessions with the Wee Care children, and who eventually assessed or treated 13 of the 20 child witnesses, stated that her goal was to induce the children to discuss sexual abuse. In the first group therapy session, she told the children that they were assembled together because of some of the things that had happened at Wee Care with Michaels. On the basis of courtroom testimony, it seems that at least three children made allegations after their contacts with Esquilin.

Lou Fonolleras was the most prolific of all the interviewers in the case. An investigator from the Division of Youth and Family Services, he conducted approximately 80 interviews with Wee Care children and 19 interviews with Wee Care parents, between May 22 and July 8, 1985. At trial, Fonolleras described his interviewing techniques as follows: "The interview process is in essence the beginning of the healing process." To rationalize his use of persistent questions with the children, he stated, "Because it is my professional and ethical responsibility to alleviate whatever anxiety has arisen as a result of what happened to them." As we shall see in chapter 11, one of Fonolleras's major interview techniques was to tell the children about other children's allegations. He thought that this technique was appropriate for "children who needed some reassurance . . . [that] they were not alone." Finally, one other detail is of importance in understanding the bias and pursuit of a single hypothesis in Fonolleras's interviews. He reported that he himself had been abused as a child. And in at least one recorded interview he uses this to lead the child's testimony. Of course, having been abused may sensitize the interviewer to the dynamics of abuse (extreme reluctance by some children to report, need for emotional support, etc.), but it might also engender a form of advocacy in the guise of aggressive investigatory interviewing. It was only after their interviews with Fonolleras that most of the children (at least 13 of them) began making allegations to their parents; before the Fonolleras interviews, these children had not reported any abusive episodes to their parents.

Eileen Treacy, an expert for the prosecution, also interviewed most of these children several times between November 1986 and February 1987. At trial, she testified on her interviewing techniques, "So you open the interview in an effort to disempower Kelly of these super powers that she allegedly has or that the kids thought she had and also to let the children know that telling about these things was okay and they would be safe." This statement seems to reflect Treacy's view of the case and her role in it. It appears that she saw little if any need for investigatory procedures because these children were clearly abused.

Finally, we do not limit our consideration of interviews to those held between children and legal and therapeutic professionals, but also extend these to conversations between parents and their children. Although we do not have any recordings or descriptions of the structures of these conversations, parents were soon instilled with the belief that abuse had taken place. Two weeks after the first allegation in the Michaels case, Peg Foster, a sex abuse consultant, told the parents at a school meeting that three children had been abused, and urged them to discover whether their own children had been abused. These parents, as well as parents in many of the other day-care cases, received phone calls from other parents who related the newest disclosures made by some of the children; a parent might be told that their child was named in the most recent disclosure and to question the child about this event. At least some of the parents aggressively questioned their children throughout all parts of the investigation, right up to the trial itself.

Some parents of the child witnesses may have raised alternative hypotheses, but these were suppressed by the dominant claim that Michaels had abused the children. For example, one mother recounted at trial that her child made the following statement: "Kelly [Michaels] puts a penis in my nose and she looked like a penis head. It was funny (child giggles)."

This mother goes on to relate how different the child's affect was during this disclosure than during a previous allegation about the child's own father. This child had told the child's mother and baby-sitter that the father had pinched the child's "thighs" and legs. And when describing these alleged behaviors by the father, the child cried. Nevertheless, the mother had enough confidence in her child's allegations about Kelly to allow the child to testify at trial.

We conclude this chapter with an excerpt of a child's trial testimony in the Little Rascals case. Throughout the trial, the two prosecuting attorneys repeatedly pursued their hunches without an apparent desire to test an alternate theory. This resulted in a rather spectacular false admission by

6-year-old Andy, who had been a 3-year-old at the time of the alleged sexual abuse by Bob Kelly.

Prosecutor: Do you remember a time where you ever had to do anything to Mr. Bob's hiney with your mouth?

Andy: No, ma'am.

Prosecutor: Do you remember telling Dr. Betty that one time you had to lick Mr. Bob's hiney? Did that happen? Did you ever have to do that, that you didn't want to do it?

Andy: Yes, ma'am.

Andy's assent to the prosecutor's question was an admission of an uncharged crime. In reality, the prosecutor had made a mistake, thinking that the charge was that Andy sodomized Bob Kelly, rather than the other way around. The state dropped this charge after it realized that Andy admitted to the wrong charge. This ought to have sensitized the prosecution to the very real dangers of pursuing a single hypothesis in the relentless manner we have described, but unfortunately, it did not appear to have done so.

Academics are often accused by the mass media of ignoring the way research findings get translated into the real world, the insinuation being that they use the research findings to discredit children who have truly been abused. Both of us have observed instances of this happening, and it is repugnant; in fact, we have written courts to complain that a defense expert witness's testimony was not in accord with the full corpus of scientific research. But there is another side that is equally repugnant, namely, that in the real world, false accusations are sometimes made as a result of the very interviewing violations that we have been describing in these pages. Bob Kelly was sentenced to serve 12 consecutive life sentences because of what the children in Edenton, North Carolina claimed he did to them. Perhaps he is guilty and the children were completely correct; or perhaps the children were correct about the gist of the allegations although they may have made some errors concerning the details of their abuse. But it is also possible that the children were largely or even completely wrong, and that as a result the Little Rascals defendants were unjustly accused. Certainly, the admission by Andy of a noncharged crime is living proof that pursuit of a single hypothesis is a risky business. Even if one were to argue that Andy's assent to the prosecutor's question was true even if it had not been charged, there is still the nagging feeling that Andy might have been just as easily led to admit to other uncharged crimes, involving innocent people.

If the type of interviewing that we described in this chapter is widespread, it raises some real concerns. We have already shown, and will show again in greater detail, that researchers are beginning to understand that even milder versions of such interview techniques can increase the risk of eliciting false reports, especially if they are conducted repeatedly and over long delay intervals. In the next three chapters, we examine some interviewing strategies that commonly reflect the presence of an interviewer bias.

9

THE EFFECTS OF REPEATED QUESTIONING

REPEATING QUESTIONS ACROSS INTERVIEWS

When children are witnesses to or victims of a crime, they must tell and retell their story many times, to many different people. Although some authorities estimate that the average child witness may be questioned up to 12 times during the course of an investigation (Whitcomb, 1992), this figure may actually be an underestimate if one considers the number of times that parents, friends, and mental health professionals may question these children, "off the record." The vast majority of the children in our case studies were certainly interviewed on many, many occasions before testifying in court. And the bulk of the questioning was "off the record," conducted in the privacy of children's homes and therapists' offices, and not electronically preserved. Although we do not have transcriptions of these repeated interviews, we do know, because of therapists' notes and parents' depositions, that they took place.

There are different purposes for reinterviewing children. The first is purely administrative: Given the legal structure of our society, a witness may have to tell his story to a number of different parties in a legal dispute. A second reason is to provide the witness with ample opportunity to reveal all details of the alleged event: Perhaps additional details and more complete reports will emerge upon second or third tellings; perhaps the use of certain interviewing techniques will facilitate this process by providing an emotionally and cognitively supportive climate that allows the unblocking of memories or that conveys to the victim a sense that it is safe to tell her story. Finally, as new case-related information becomes known, it may become necessary to reinterview the witness about newly emerging issues that were unanticipated at the time of the earlier interview. For any or all of these reasons, it may become necessary to reinterview a witness.

What theoretical or empirical support is there that repeated interviewing does, in fact, improve the accuracy of reports? On the basis of a large tradition of memory research, it has been argued that repeated interviewing is itself a form of rehearsal that prevents memories from decaying over a period of time. According to this argument, it is important for the witness to repeatedly recall the details of the event so that they will not be forgotten. The literature also indicates that the formation of a memory (i.e., consolidation) is facilitated when the first recall takes place soon after the target event. Finally, a number of laboratory studies indicate that when given multiple opportunities to recall previously memorized materials, subjects often remember additional details during each session, the so-called "hyperamnesia" effect.

When the studies are taken outside of the memory laboratories and into more naturalistic settings (where subjects recall a series of events or an episode), some of these findings are replicated. Specifically, when asked for free recall, both children and adults remember new items with additional interviews, thereby providing additional information for their original descriptions (see Fivush, 1993; Poole & White, 1995; Warren & Lane, 1995, for detailed reviews). Thus, repeated interviewing of a child is associated with beneficial effects.

Unfortunately, for several different reasons, repeated interviewing is also associated with baleful effects. First, as interviews are repeated, so is the length of time between the original event and the interview; this allows for weakening of the original memory trace, and as a result of this weakening, more intrusions are able to infiltrate the memory system. In fact, although as we mentioned above, when asked for free recall, both children and adults remember more with additional interviews, it is also true that their reports become more inaccurate over time (i.e., they recall both more accurate and more inaccurate details over repeated trials). Some recent data by Poole and White (1993) suggest that this decline in accuracy over a long delay may be most apparent in children. These researchers retested children and adults 2 years after their initial observation and recall of a staged event. Children (who at the time of follow-up testing were between the ages of 6 and 10 years) provided many more inaccurate details in response to open-ended questions, compared with adults. The children's responses to direct yes/no questions were at chance when interviewed again 2 years following the event. Finally, 21% of the children confused which actors performed certain actions 2 years earlier; such errors were never made by adult subjects.

Thus far in our discussion of the effects of repeated interviews, we have assumed that each repeated interview is neutral (nonsuggestive) in tone: They only require the witness to tell in his or her own words everything that happened. But as we have already seen, and will see later, this is not the tone of many forensic interviews with children. In these interviews, there are many examples of misleading information. This raises the possibility that repeated interviews that contain misleading information may ultimately result in impaired and inaccurate recall of events.

We have conducted one study that highlights the deleterious effects of repeating misinformation across interviews in young children's reports (Bruck, Ceci, Francoeur, & Barr, 1995). These effects are particularly pernicious because not only can the repeated misinformation become directly incorporated into the children's subsequent reports (they use the interviewers' words in their inaccurate statements), but it can also lead to fabrications or inaccuracies that, although not directly mirroring the content of the misleading information or questions, are inferences based on the misinformation. The following is an example of this.

The children in our study visited their pediatrician when they were 5 years old. During that visit, a male pediatrician gave each child a physical examination, an oral polio vaccine, and an inoculation. During that same visit, a female research assistant talked to the child about a poster on the wall, read the child a story, and gave the child some treats.

Approximately one year later, the children were reinterviewed four times over a period of 1 month. During the first three interviews, some children were falsely reminded that the male pediatrician showed them the poster, gave them treats, and read them a story and that the female research assistant gave them the inoculation and the oral vaccine. Other children were given no misinformation about the actors of these events. During the fourth and final interview, when asked to recall what happened during the original medical visit, children who were not given any misleading information gave highly accurate final reports. They correctly recalled which events were performed by the male pediatrician and by the female research assistant. In contrast, the misled children were very inaccurate; not only did they incorporate the misleading suggestions into their reports, with more than half of the children falling sway to these suggestions (e.g., claiming that the female assistant inoculated them rather than the male pediatrician), but 38% of these children also included nonsuggested but inaccurate events in their reports. They falsely reported that the female research assistant had checked their ears and nose. These statements are inferences that are consistent with the erroneous suggestion that the research assistant had administered the shot: She therefore must have been the doctor, and therefore she carried out procedures commonly performed by doctors. None of the control children made such inaccurate inferences. Thus, young children use suggestions in highly productive ways to reconstruct and at times distort reality (see the Chester study by Clarke-Stewart et al. (1989) in chapter 8, and the Sam Stone study by Leichtman & Ceci (in press) in chapter 10, for similar results).

Multiple suggestive interviews may have deleterious effects on reporting not only because of their quantity but also because with each additional suggestive interview the delay between the original event and the child's report of it increases. Sometimes these two variables are inseparable. As we have seen in some of our case histories, it was not only that the children were subjected to repeated interviews, but there was also a long delay between the alleged event and the final interviews. This raises the following question: Is the effect of misinformation less deleterious if it is provided in an interview that occurs soon after an event compared with an interview that occurs long after an event? Perhaps when events are fresh, it is harder to be swayed by suggestions than when the memories for the event have faded. A number of studies with adults and children confirm this pattern (Belli, Windschitl, McCarthy, & Winfrey, 1992; Loftus, Miller, & Burns, 1978; Zaragoza & Lane, 1994).

The pediatrician study just described also illustrates the differential impacts of providing misinformation immediately after an event compared with many months later. In the first phase of this study, we examined the effect of giving different types of feedback to 5-year-old children immediately following their inoculation. Children were given pain-affirming feedback (emphasizing that the shot hurt), pain-denying feedback (emphasizing that the shot did not hurt), or neutral feedback (the shot is over). One week later, when we interviewed these children about their visit, they did not differ in their reports concerning how much the shot hurt or how much they cried.

These results indicate that the children in this study could not be easily influenced to make inaccurate reports concerning significant and stressful procedures involving their own bodies—when their memory for the inoculation was still relatively fresh. The pattern of results changed dramatically when we provided the same children similar feedback during multiple interviews 1 year after the inoculation. Thus, during the three interviews when the children were given no information or misinformation about the pediatrician and the research assistant, we also provided them with feedback about how much they had cried in the pediatrician's office 1 year previously. During these three interviews, they were given either additional pain-denying or neutral feedback. At the fourth and final interview, children who were given pain-denying feedback reported that they cried less and that the shot hurt less than did the children given neutral feedback. These results indicate that suggestive interviewing procedures can influence children's reports about stressful events involving their own bodies, when they are provided long after the event takes place and when they are provided on multiple occasions.

Other researchers have examined the effects of sequencing suggestive and neutral interviews, asking whether early neutral interviews protect against the potential detrimental effects of later suggestive ones. Warren and Lane (1995) found that neutral interviews that occur immediately after an event protect adults from the effects of future suggestive interviews. Under the same conditions, children were also protected, although to a lesser extent. Furthermore, these researchers also found that children who were subjected to two suggestive interviews reported many more suggested details in their free recall reports than did children subjected to only a single suggestive interview.

Taken together, these results suggest that the highest ratio of accurate-to-inaccurate testimony is obtained in the first interview. As the delay between the event and the interview increases and/or as the number of misleading interviews increase, the chance for serious misreporting also appears to increase. Thus, if an initial interview is neutral, it seems to have the effect of reinforcing the memory, perhaps by providing a rehearsal. As a consequence, subsequent interviews that are suggestive result in less alteration than might be the case if the initial interview was either suggestive or absent.

Faced with this evidence, how do we interpret the children's testimonies from the case studies? Unfortunately, we face a real barrier in this exercise. This is because for some of the cases (Michaels, Little Rascals, and Old Cutler), we do not have records of any of the initial interviews with the children. Thus, we cannot ascertain the degree to which the allegations that emerged in later taped investigatory interviews are consistent with the first reports made by these children, or the degree to which they may reflect the earlier implantation of suggestions. We also do not have verbatim records of the conversations that the children had with their parents; it is possible that some of the allegations that occurred in these later investigatory interviews reflect suggestions incorporated from earlier conversations with parents who were urged by other parents and professionals to look for signs of abuse in their children. Some analyses of the existing information suggest that children did initially deny abuse.

In the Country Walk case, where with one exception all of the first and subsequent investigative interviews were videotaped, all but one child initially denied abuse. Unfortunately, the first interview with this child was not videotaped; it was conducted at night in the prosecutor's office. The next day, when he was interviewed by the Bragas, he provided a graphic description of abuse. For the other children, it took many interviews with parents and professionals to elicit reports of abuse. We provide the example of one of the child witnesses, J. L., a 5-year-old.

In her first videotaped interview, J. L. appears cheerful and confident in stating that she knows of no wrongdoings by the Fusters. At various points during the interview, she says she knows that they are in jail because her mother told her and because she saw the news on TV. In this interview, she goes on to say,

> Because they didn't do anything bad to me. . . . And I would tell my mom and if they said it was a secret, I would say, "I wouldn't do it," but I would trick them. . . .

Five months later, she was reinterviewed by Dr. Laurie Braga. Partly in response to the interviewer's leading questions, J. L. accused the Fusters of taking off their clothes in front of children, terrorizing them with a knife, filming them, and playing games while naked. When Braga says to the child, "you didn't tell for a long time. How come, were you scared?," the child replies, "I think I was too young."

Some of this child's testimony during this taped interview raises the possibility that she may have been under pressure at home to generate accusations. For example, when she is asked if she has had bad dreams about what has happened, she answers, "No, but my mom has a dream about my grandma and my grandma tells what happened in my mom's dream."

In the Little Rascals case, there are no electronic recordings of the initial interviews with the children. On the basis of the available evidence, it seems that many children denied during initial interviews that anything sexual had happened. Some of the children talked about hitting or spanking in the day-care center, but they mainly made these claims about other children (in the next chapter, on stereotype induction, we will address these reports of hitting in more detail). The only child who made any statements that may have been indicative of abuse was Carl P. But this was not the first time that Carl had been questioned. His mother had been questioning him since at least the beginning of December; initially, he had denied any wrongdoing at the center, although he later said that Mr. Bob had played "doctor" with some of his friends, but not with him. During Officer Toppin's 2-hour interview, when Carl was asked to show on the doll how Mr. Bob played "doctor," he inserted his finger in the doll's anus and pulled on the doll's penis (the interpretation of these behaviors is covered in chapter 12). After demonstrations on the doll, the investigators asked him to show on his own body "what playing doctor was." According to Toppin's trial testimony, Carl grabbed his penis "and took his hand like he was inserting his finger in his rectum. . . ." But when asked "how Mr. Bob played doctor," he replied, "I don't think he does it anymore." According to Toppin's recollections of this unrecorded interview, Carl initially stated that this happened only to two of his friends, but not to him; later in the interview, he also said it happened to him. None of the other children made similar claims in their first interviews.

Parents in the Little Rascals case also interviewed their children. When the first allegations became public, many parents refused to believe them; they remained loyal to the Kellys. However, as more and more children made allegations, even the faithful began to have their doubts. Some parents admitted to relentlessly questioning their children until they finally gave sway and admitted to abuse. According to some parents, this process took more than 10 months. The testimony of one of the mothers illustrates how some of these children may have been questioned at home, prior to any of the investigative interviews, and how allegations of sexual abuse may emerge when young children are repeatedly questioned by their parents.

Mother: First time I questioned him, we were laying on my bed and I was just, you know, "Do you like Mr. Bob," "Do you like Ms. Betsy," um, "Has Mr. Bob ever done anything bad to you," "Has Mr. Bob ever spanked you," and as we were talking I got more specific with him; I asked him, "Had Mr. Bob ever touched his privates," I didn't feel like he really knew what his privates were called that, and so I asked him has Mr. Bob ever touched your pee-bug," "Has Mr. Bob ever touched your hiney," "Has he ever put his finger in your hiney." I was using very specific questioning.

Attorney: And what were his responses?

Mother: He thought it was funny. He was laughing at me when we were just talking in general. . . . He was so young. He wasn't even three years old then.

Attorney: Was that the only time you questioned him?

Mother: No, it went on. When I was asking him that first time if Mr. Bob had ever spanked him he kept on saying, "No," and I kept on asking him, "Has he ever touched your pee-bug," and finally he took his hand and he slapped it on his privates like that (indicating), and he said, "He did that." And I asked him about a rope, did anybody ever tie him up with a rope, . . . and he said, "No." And then he said they played a bonkey game, at the day care. And I said, "Well, who do you play the bonkey game with?" And he played the bonkey game with Anthony and Mr. Bob, and, um, they used a rope when they played the game. So I got a tie belt out of the dresser drawer, and, you know, I told him to show me how he was tied up with that rope. And he tied it around his feet with the rope. And when I relayed this conversation to Sally (her best friend), then there was a lot of concern. Sally felt like I needed to and listening to the rumors and all, I did proceed to question him further.

[Attorney then asks why she asked him about the rope and being tied up.]

Mother: I don't know. Everything I was getting I was getting from Eleanor (parent of nonindicting child), but I couldn't tell you for sure that I heard that from her. I don't know. I heard it from somebody. . . .

Attorney: Now, tell me how that developed that you began to get statements from him that raised a question in your mind of sexual abuse.

Mother: Dick was being questioned a lot from that first time on (i.e., the end of January), quite often. And then that last week then it was probably a few hours every day thing. And on that Friday (the end of April), I got a response out of him. . . . Um, he told me that Mr. Bob had put his penis in his mouth and peed on him

Attorney: Now, are those things that he just came up with on his own?

Mother: No, sir, he did not.

Attorney: How did he come up with those kind of statements?

Mother: Because I asked him . . . he had been hearing it at least once a week since I first started questioning him and then that last week he was hearing it every day.

Attorney: Now, the questions you asked him about . . . whether or not Bob had put [his] penis in his mouth and peed on him and that kind of thing, was that part of the information you had been receiving as types of allegations that had been made?

Mother: Yes. . . .

Attorney: Now, up to this point in your questioning of Dick you said that you had been fairly specific in your statements to him about asking him whether or not Bob did this or whether or not Bob did that; did you name specific acts to him?

Mother: Yes, sir. "Did Bob put his finger in your hiney," things like that, yes, sir, I did.

Attorney: And did some of the time you get no answer to those questions?

Mother: It was "no" the majority of the time, . . . most of the time he didn't know what I was talking about.

[After this child assented to his mother's question, she called Brenda Toppin, the police officer, to make a report.]

Attorney: Did you tell her (Officer Brenda Toppin) that basically you had just gotten answers in response to your questions, yes or no type answers? Or did you relate it as a story coming from Dick?

Mother: As a story coming from Dick. . . . I don't really think I told her anything he was asked. I just told her the major part of what he said, that Mr. Bob had put his penis in Dick's mouth and had peed on him right there.

Attorney: Now, in spite of the fact that Mrs. Toppin told you that he had made no statement to her about sexual abuse at that time, did she offer any opinion to you as to whether or not Dick had been abused?

Mother: I asked her if she thought Dick had been abused, and she said, "On the record I can't tell you; off the record, I would say yes," and there's a whole lot more to come.
[According to this mother, Officer Toppin interviewed Dick in the evening. After the interview, Toppin told the mother that although Dick had not make any allegations of a sexual nature, she felt that he would feel more comfortable with his mother in the room. When the mother asked him questions, Dick did not assent to allegations of sexual abuse.]

The above testimony from the Little Rascals case makes clear the lack of information available to the court about the style and frequency of the nonrecorded interviews. Because none of the original law enforcement or therapeutic interviews appear to have been taped (or if they had been, none reached the courtroom), it is impossible to evaluate their suggestiveness. All that is known for sure is that although the children initially denied the abuse, they eventually admitted to it—usually after many months and intervening interviews.

Similarly, there is also scanty information concerning the style and frequency of the interviews in the Michaels case. Importantly, to our knowledge, there are no electronically preserved copies of the initial interviews with the children, nor with their parents. Several weeks into the interviewing of the children, the prosecutor's office decided that the investigators should audiotape their interviews. The team began to record those children who had not fully divulged their disclosures. Although there are some examples of taped interviews in which there seem to be few leading questions and in which the child gave a coherent report of abuse, these were not the initial interviews, and thus it is impossible to evaluate their validity without knowing about the details of the prior interviews. If in the first interview a child had been subjected to the same techniques evident in most of the taped interviews, concerns over the validity of that child's statements might be warranted.

The allegations made by the Michaels children continued to unfold after the investigatory interviews, some of them not emerging until 2 years later. This is unsurprising because the children were interviewed many times after the initial investigatory interviews. They were interviewed prior to their appearance before the grand jury, they were questioned by therapists, and they were questioned by members of the prosecutors' office leading up to trial. Perhaps some of the most suggestive interviews in the Wee Care case were conducted by Eileen Treacy, a state-appointed expert who interviewed most of the child witnesses on at least two occasions before the trial. As we argued earlier, repeated suggestive interviews may have their most profound effect after a long delay between the alleged events and the interviews. Treacy's interviews occurred 2 years after the alleged events. The following give a flavor of the interactions of some of these interviews:

Treacy: Let me ask you this: Did she touch boys, did she touch girls, did she touch dogs?

Child A: She touched boys and girls. . . .

Treacy: Did she touch them with telephones? Did she touch them with spoons? What kinda spoons?

Child A: Teaspoons. . . .

Treacy: Can you make a mark where she hurt you? . . . Make a mark. Just show me where Kelly hurt you. Then I can show that to the judge. . . .

Treacy: Tell me about 7C. What happened to 7C?

Child A: I don't know.

Treacy: 7C told me about some of the stuff that happened to you.

Child A: (no response)

Treacy: She cares about you. Some of the kids told me that things happened with knives at Wee Care. Do you remember anything like that? . . .

Treacy: I see and did the kids want Kelly to do that peanut butter stuff?

Child A: I didn't even think that there was a peanut butter. . . .

Treacy: Well what about licking the peanut butter?

Child A: There wasn't anything about peanut butter. . . .

Treacy: Some of the kids told me that things happened with knives. Do you remember anything like that?

Child A: No
            [Although the child professes no knowledge of utensil abuse, at trial this child testified to numerous abuse allegations.]

Treacy: . . . Well what about that cat game?

Child A: Cat game?

Treacy: Where everybody went like this, "Meow, Meow."

Child A: I don't think that I was there that day.
            [Although the child professes no knowledge of the Cat game, at trial she described a cat game in which all the children were naked and licking each other.]

After some questioning, Treacy gets the following child to say that Kelly's private parts were the same as little girls':

Treacy: Did Kelly have hair?

Child B: Nah, I know 'cause it's grown ups . . . I know about that.

Treacy: So I guess that means you saw her private parts huh? Did Kelly ask the kids to look at her private parts, or to kiss her private part or . . .

Child B: I didn't really do that. . . . I didn't even do it . . .

Treacy: But she made you.

Child B: She made me. She made me. . . . But I couldn't do it. . . . So I didn't even really do it. I didn't do it. . . .

Treacy: Did it smell good?

Child B: shhh

Treacy: Her private parts?

Child B: I don't know.

Treacy: Did it taste good? Did it taste like chocolate?

Child B: Ha, ha. No, I didn't even do it. . . .

Treacy: You Wee Care kids seem so scared of her.

Child B: I wasn't. I'm not even. . . .

Treacy: But while you were there, were you real scared?

Child B: I don't know.

Treacy: What was so frightening about her, B., what was so scary about her?

Child B: I don't know. Why don't you ask her? . . .

Treacy: Did she drink the pee pee?

Child B: Please that sounds just crazy. I don't remember about that. Really don't.

In the Old Cutler case, most of the disclosures were made to parents and therapists. And for the most part, there are few transcripts of these. However, the parents' depositions and the few audio recordings of therapy sessions indicate that the children were subjected to the same types of suggestive interviewing procedures that occurred in the previous cases. The following are excerpts taken from testimony in the cases:

Attorney: Now when you questioned your daughter in August of '89, she told you that essentially nothing had happened?

Mother: She said she didn't remember, it was so long ago. "I don't remember, mommy."

Attorney: Then when you questioned her this second time, do you recall what you asked her?

Mother: I asked her again. "Did anything happen while you were at the church?" She said she didn't remember it was so long ago. Then I had told her . . . that Bobby Fijnje was in jail and that he couldn't hurt anyone anymore. Then I asked her if he had ever pulled his pants down, exposed himself, take his pee-pee out and she said, "Yes."

Attorney: Why did you ask her if he had pulled his pants down, had you heard anything about that occurring?

Mother: Well, I had just heard from the news media that it was a sexual abuse and that seemed like a logical place to start.

A consideration of the research findings suggests that if the children had not been abused, this magnitude of repeated suggestive interviewing could have the effect of planting and cementing false reports. On the basis of our own work with children of this age, we are fairly confident that if we were to interview a random sample of day-care children, and to use the same suggestive techniques used by some of the interviewers in our case studies, we could bring a subset of our subjects to assent to abuse-related themes. Most of the children would not assent immediately. But gradually some allegations would probably emerge as suggestions were repeated.

Although we have reason to fear the cumulative effects of such sug-gestive questioning, insinuations, and atmosphere of accusations, it is also clear from the transcripts of the case studies that we should not assume that children will inevitably succumb to leading questions the first time they are asked. Some children are remarkably resistant, as was Child B above. We have seen many children hold out against suggestive—even intensely pressurized—questioning for long periods. But we also have seen many instances of children assenting to the suggestions, especially after repeated attempts over long intervals and if reinforced by parents and therapists.

REPEATING QUESTIONS WITHIN INTERVIEWS

The previous section documented some of the potential hazards of multiple suggestions *across* interviews for children's reports. A related concern is the degree to which repeating a question *within* an interview can taint a child's report (see Ceci & Bruck, 1993b; Poole & White, 1995; Warren & Lane, 1995, for descriptions of many studies). When interviewing children, adults frequently repeat a question because the child's first response may not provide enough information. In forensic interviews, questions may be repeated to check the consistency of a child's reports. Sometimes, interviewers' repetition of questions signals their biases: They seem to keep asking a child the same question until they receive the answer they are expecting.

A number of studies, from different domains, demonstrate that when young children are asked the same question more than once within an interview, they change their answer. In some studies, it is the youngest children who are most likely to change their answers. We provide some brief descriptions of these studies.

Poole and White (1991) examined the effects of repeated questioning within and across sessions (and thus this study also speaks to some of the issues raised in the previous section). Adults, as well as 4-, 6-, and 8-year-olds, witnessed an ambiguous event. Half of the subjects were interviewed immediately after the event as well as 1 week later. The remaining subjects were interviewed only once—one week after the event. Within each session, all questions were asked three times. Repeated *open-ended* questions (e.g., "What did the man look like?"), both within and across sessions, had little effect, positive or negative, on children's or adults' responses. However, on repeated *yes/no* questions (e.g., "Did the man hurt Melanie?"), 4-year-olds were most likely to change their responses, both within and across sessions. Also, when children were asked a specific question about a detail for which they had no information (e.g., "What did the man do for a living?"), many answered with sheer speculations. Furthermore, both children and adults used fewer qualifiers with repeated questions (they omitted phrases such as "it might have been") and consequently sounded more confident about their statements. These findings illustrate the danger of repeatedly asking specific questions: Children will often cooperate by guessing, but after several repetitions, their uncertainty is no longer apparent.

Thus, the major finding of this study is that repeated questioning may affect very young children's responses to specific questions. Whereas repeating *open-ended* questions may merely signal a request for additional information, repeating specific questions that have a limited pool of responses (yes/no) may signal to young children that their first response was unacceptable to the interviewer. This finding is important because young children tend to give limited responses to open-ended questions, and interviewers therefore often resort to specific questions to elicit additional information. To confirm a child's answer, interviewers frequently repeat the question.

Although Poole and White did not use leading questions, their repeated use of yes/no questions can be viewed as a subtle form of suggestion. As noted above, simply repeating a yes/no question could have the effect of suggesting to children that the interviewer is unsatisfied with their initial answer. However, there are other studies that have directly addressed the issue of what happens when leading questions are repeated within an interview.

Cassel and Bjorklund (in press) questioned children and adults about a videotaped event they had viewed 1 week earlier. The subjects were asked leading questions. If they did not fall sway to the lead, they were asked a more suggestive follow-up question. Kindergarten children were most affected by this manipulation. As expected, compared with adults and older children, they were most inaccurate in answering the first misleading questions; but also when the second more suggestive question was asked, they were more likely than older subjects to change their answers and to incorporate the suggested answer into their second responses.

These findings demonstrate that younger children are more prone to change their answers when asked the same question within a session. They are sensitive to the question repetition and seem to reason that the interviewer is requesting additional or new information: "The first answer I gave must be wrong, that is why they are asking me the question again. Therefore, I should change my answer." At other times, children may change their answer to please the adult who is questioning them; they appear to reason that "the adult must not have liked the first answer I gave so I will try another answer." Some have argued that children's answers may change because the interviewer's previous suggestions become incorporated into their memories. For example, children are given a list of items to study, and later their memory for these items is tested by asking them to respond "yes" to previously studied items and "no" to new items that were not on the study list. This procedure increases the rate of false positives on a later test; that is, the children say that the "no" items from the memory test were on the original study list (Brainerd & Reyna, 1994). Furthermore, there is some evidence that these false recognition responses are as stable, and sometimes more stable, as true responses (Brainerd, Reyna, & Brandes,

1994). This last explanation may have more power when applied to repeating misinformation across interviews (when there is some time allowed for the misinformation to be incorporated into memory), rather than when the repetition occurs within an interview.

There are, unfortunately, numerous examples of the risks of question repetition in the actual case studies presented. Perhaps the most dramatic can be seen in the Little Rascals children, who frequently changed their answers on the witness stand upon being re-asked a question by the prosecutor. For example, one child was asked the following:

Prosecutor: Did you have to lay on top of Bridget?

Bobby: Yes.

Prosecutor: And when you were laying on top of Bridget, where was your private?

Bobby: I forgot.

Prosecutor: Do you remember telling Miss Judy that you had to put your private next to her private? Did you have to do that, Bobby?

Bobby: No Sir.

Prosecutor: What did you say?

Bobby: No Sir.

Prosecutor: Did you say No or Yes?

Bobby: Yes Sir.

It is anyone's guess how many times Bobby might have switched his answers in response to the prosecutor's repetitions. A similar example is seen in the Michaels case at the grand jury hearing:

Prosecutor: Did she touch you with a spoon?

Child: No.

Prosecutor: "No?" OK. Did you like it when she touched you with the spoon?

Child: No.

Prosecutor: "No?" Why not?

Child: I don't know.

Prosecutor: You don't know?

Child: No.

Prosecutor: What did you say to Kelly when she touched you?

Child: I don't like that.

The Michaels investigatory interviews also provide numerous examples of questions frequently repeated after a child denied abuse or when the child's answer was inconsistent with an interviewer's beliefs. Although there are instances when the children tenaciously rejected the interviewer's persistent suggestive questions, the children often changed their answers to ones that were consistent with sexual abuse, upon repetition of the interviewer's question. Consider the following example:

Interviewer: When Kelly kissed you, did she ever put her tongue in your mouth?

Child: No.

Interviewer: Did she ever make you put her tongue in her mouth?

Child: No.

Interviewer: Did you ever have to kiss her vagina?

Child: No.

Interviewer: Which of the kids had to kiss her vagina?

Child: What's this?

Interviewer: No that's my toy, my radio box. . . . Which kids had to kiss her vagina?

Child: Me.

The following example, which is taken from the Country Walk case, illustrates how repeated questions sometimes serve to confuse children and lead them into making inconsistent statements. The following interaction between a child and one of the investigatory interviewers occurred after what would later be transcribed as 40 pages of questioning that included numerous questions about "bad touching." Up to this point, the child had denied any knowledge of the occurrence of untoward behavior or sexual abuse at the school.

Child: I wonder if they played ring around the rosy with no clothes on.

Interviewer: Do you think they did? . . . Do you think maybe so?

Child: (nodding in the affirmative.)

Interviewer: Do you know ring around the rosy and they all fall down? Do you know what they would do then?

Child: They would just fall down.

Interviewer: And anything else?

Child: I wonder if they played or (inaudible) no clothes on.

Interviewer:	I don't know. I wonder if they did play duck, duck, goose with no clothes on. I wonder what they would do, you know, like if you go duck, duck, goose and you would tag somebody, is that what you call it? You touch somebody?
Child:	No.
Interviewer:	I wonder if they did, if they would like touch each other in their private parts. Do you think?
Child:	(shaking head in the negative)
Interviewer:	No? You don't think so? If they did, you think that they probably played it with their clothes off?
Child:	Off?
Interviewer:	Off. What do you think they would do with their clothes off?
Child:	Play games.

When one listens to the actual tapes of this interview, the confusion on the part of the child as to what actually happened is apparent, as is the way the investigator may have encouraged speculation on the part of the child by acting confused and "wondering" about possible activities. By repeating the same question, the interviewer eventually elicited from the child statements of playing games while naked. These statements then become part of the fabric of the child's interview (see Chapter 14 for an explanation of a "source misattribution" that can result in this type of situation). In later interviews, some children may be confronted with their prior statements and asked to confirm them, or, as we will see later, these statements may be presented to other children (e.g., "Your friends have already told me. . . .") as part of the application of peer pressure.

Some of the interviews with Jennifer F. in the Macias case illustrate how repetitive questioning can at times influence the reports of older children. The following excerpts are taken from the trial testimony of this 9-year-old child. She frequently incorporated the interviewer's suggestions immediately, not requiring repeated or prolonged questioning to alter her reports:

Interviewer:	What kind of shirt was Mr. Macias wearing?
Jennifer:	It was a blue shirt.
Interviewer:	Was it a solid blue shirt?
Jennifer:	Yes, that's what it was. Solid blue.
Interviewer:	Are you sure it didn't have a check pattern on it, like a cowboy shirt?

Jennifer: Yes, that's it. It had a large check on it. . . .

♦ ♦ ♦

Interviewer: What time was it?

Jennifer: It was nearly dark, around 6 o'clock, I guess.

Interviewer: Are you sure it was nearly dark or was it in the afternoon?

Jennifer: Yeah, I guess it was around 2 or 3 o'clock.
[Jennifer changed the time of day that she alleged to have observed Macias return home. Her initial report was inconsistent with the prosecution's thesis.]

♦ ♦ ♦

[Jennifer had previously told police investigators that the weapon she observed with Macias in his trailer was a rifle/gun. She went on to describe it as longish, like a BB gun, but not a BB gun. At trial, as the following excerpt shows, it was necessary for the prosecutor to address this seeming inconsistency, because the weapon that they were trying to link with Macias was either a machete or a small-caliber pistol.]

Prosecutor: Can you tell the ladies and gentlemen of the jury what kind of gun he (Macias) had?

Jennifer: It was like a BB gun, but it wasn't a BB gun.

Prosecutor: Jennifer, I'll show you what's been marked State's Exhibit 6, and ask you if the gun he had looked like this. [The prosecutor showed her a small handgun.]

Jennifer: Yes. [It looked like this.]

Prosecutor: And did it look a lot like this or exactly like this?

Jennifer: It looked like that.

Prosecutor: I believe you described the gun once as a rifle/gun?

Jennifer: Yeah, but it was not a rifle gun.

Prosecutor: Do you know what a rifle is?

Jennifer: It's like a long gun, but it isn't. I think it's a long gun.

Prosecutor: Is this what you meant when you say a rifle/gun?

Jennifer: Yes.

Prosecutor: Because of the long barrel?

Jennifer: Yes.

Prosecutor:	Is this the gun or is it like the gun that Fred was carrying that day?
Jennifer:	Yes.
Prosecutor:	Is there any question in your mind about that?
Jennifer:	No.

As can be seen, Jennifer F. repeatedly incorporated leading questions directly into her testimony. There was no need for the customary "marination phase," wherein a suggestion must be given time to seep into the child's report. Jennifer F. readily picked up on the prosecutor's insinuations and added them to her testimony as she went along, including changes that were crucial to the prosecution's case. One would have thought that Jennifer's erratic testimony would be transparent to the jury (she did this a lot), but the following statement from the foreman of the jury shows just the opposite:

> During the trial, the testimony of Jennifer F., the little girl, had a great impact and proved crucial for the prosecution. Her testimony was given considerable weight by the jury and was important in our deliberations.

To summarize, repeated interviews and repeating questions within interviews may decrease the accuracy of children's reports and increase the risk of taint when these are conducted by biased interviewers. These techniques allow an avenue for the introjection of misinformation that, if repeated enough times, may become incorporated by the child. As well, these techniques may signal to the child the bias of the interviewer so that the child eventually learns how to answer the questions to provide the information that she thinks the interviewer wishes to hear.

10

STEREOTYPE INDUCTION: A SUGGESTIVE INTERVIEWING TECHNIQUE

As we have argued in chapter 7, suggestions do not necessarily have to be in the form of an explicit (mis)leading question such as "Show me how she touched your bottom" in order for them to take their toll on preschoolers' testimonial accuracy. There are a number of powerful suggestive interview techniques that are more subtle than leading questions. One such technique is the induction of stereotypes. In the present context, we use stereotype induction to refer to the attempt on the part of an interviewer to transmit to a child a negative characterization of an individual or an event, whether it be true or false. Telling children that the suspect "does bad things" or "tries to scare children" is an example of negative stereotype induction.

The use of stereotype induction in interviews is one of the more blatant reflections of the interviewer's bias; she is telling the child how powerful adult authority figures, as well as their peers, characterize the defendant. Interviewers, however, often justify their use of such techniques on the grounds that they provide a hospitable and supportive environment for the child to tell about the abuse. Lou Fonolleras, the most prolific interviewer of the Michaels children, explained,

He [i.e., the child being interviewed] saw that there was an adult horrified and reacting angrily toward his discussion of the penis, vagina, and that he felt guilty. Then he felt a little better about giving details.

Notwithstanding the assumption that a stereotype induction makes a child feel better about disclosing details, a review of the scientific literature indicates that stereotype induction can have a very powerful negative effect on the accuracy of children's subsequent reports. Some naive children may eventually begin to incorporate the interviewers' stereotypes into their own reports.

We have already reviewed a number of these studies. For example, children's reports of what the janitor "Chester" was doing in their classroom was dependent on the interviewer's stereotype of Chester. When interviewers induced a positive stereotype (e.g., Chester was depicted as doing a good job cleaning the classroom), many children came to report the event in that manner, regardless of what Chester had actually done. Similarly, when the interviewer induced a negative stereotype (e.g., Chester was fooling around), many children came to report the event according to this view regardless of Chester's actual behavior (Clarke-Stewart et al., 1989). The two studies that we report below provide further evidence of the powerful effects of stereotype induction on children's reports.

THE INCRIMINATION OF DALE

In the first study (Lepore & Sesco, 1994), children ranging in age from 4 to 6 years played some games with a man called "Dale." Dale played with some of the toys in a researcher's testing room, and he also asked the child to help him take off his sweater. Later, an interviewer asked the child to tell her everything that happened when Dale was in the room. For half of the children, the interviewer maintained a neutral stance whenever they recalled an action. For the remaining children, the interviewer reinterpreted each of the child's responses in an incriminating way by stating, "He wasn't supposed to do or say that. That was bad. What else did he do?" (Note the conceptual similarity between these statements and the content of the Fonolleras quote presented above; both types of statements could be argued to make children feel better about reporting someone's misdeeds.) Thus, in this incriminating condition, a negative stereotype was induced: "Dale does bad things." At the conclusion of these incriminating procedures, the children were asked three highly suggestive/misleading questions ("Didn't he take off some of your clothes, too?" "Other kids have told me that he kissed them, didn't he do that to you?" and "He touched you and he wasn't supposed to do that, was he?"). All children were then asked a series of direct questions, requiring yes or no answers, about what had happened with Dale.

Children in the incriminating condition gave many more inaccurate responses to the direct yes/no questions than did children in the neutral condition; this was largely because these children made errors on items related to "bad" actions that had been suggested to them by the interviewer. Interestingly, a third of the children in the incriminating condition embellished their incorrect responses to these questions, and the embellished responses were always in the direction of the incriminating suggestions. The question that elicited the most frequent embellishments was "Did Dale ever touch other kids at the school?" Embellishments to this question included information about who Dale touched (e.g., "He touched Jason, he touched Tori, and he touched Molly"), where he touched them (e.g., "He touched them on their legs"), how he touched them (e.g., ". . . and some he kissed . . . on the lips"), and how he took their clothes off ("Yes, my shoes and my socks and my pants. But not my shirt"). When they were reinterviewed one week later, children in the incriminating stereotype condition continued to answer the yes/no questions inaccurately, and they continued to embellish their answers.

Finally, the incriminating condition had a very powerful effect on children's interpretations of Dale's character and actions. In comparison with children in the neutral interview condition, children in the incriminating interview condition were more likely to spontaneously make negative statements about Dale (e.g., "The guy came in and did some bad things") and to agree that Dale intended during the play session to be bad, be mean, fool around, and not do his job.

SAM STONE, THE KLUTZ

The second study also demonstrates the powerful effects of a stereotype induction when it is paired with repeated suggestive questioning. A stranger named "Sam Stone" visited preschoolers (ages 3 to 6 years) in their classroom for 2 minutes in their day-care center (see Leichtman & Ceci, in press). During this visit, he merely said, "Hello," walked around the room, then said, "Goodbye," and left. He did not touch, tear, throw, or break anything. Following Sam Stone's visit, the children were asked for details about the visit on four different occasions over a 10-week period. During these four occasions, the interviewer refrained from using suggestive questions. She simply encouraged the children to describe Sam Stone's visit in as much detail as possible. One month following the fourth interview, the children were interviewed a fifth time by a new interviewer who asked about two "nonevents" that involved Sam doing something to a teddy bear and a book. In reality, Sam Stone never touched either one. When asked in the fifth interview, "Did Sam Stone do anything to a book or a teddy bear?" most children rightfully replied, "No." As seen in Figure 10.1, only

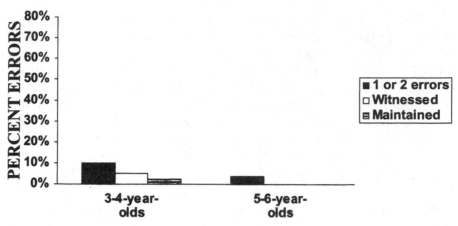

Figure 10.1. Control group in the Sam Stone Study: no negative stereotypes and no erroneous suggestions.

10% of the youngest (3- to 4-year-old) children's answers contained claims that Sam Stone did anything to a book or teddy bear. When asked if they actually saw him do anything to the book or teddy bear, as opposed to "thinking they saw him do something" or "hearing he did something," now only 5% of their answers contained claims that anything occurred. Finally, when these 5% were gently challenged ("You didn't really see him do anything to the book/the teddy bear, did you?"), only 2.5% still insisted on the reality of the fictional event. None of the older (5- to 6-year-old) children claimed to have actually seen Sam Stone do either of the fictional events. These children's responses can be regarded as a control against which to measure the effects of stereotype induction paired with repeated questioning.

A second group of preschoolers were presented with a stereotype of Sam Stone before he ever visited their school. Each week, beginning a month prior to Sam Stone's visit, these children were told a new Sam Stone story, in which he was depicted as very clumsy. For example

> You'll never guess who visited me last night. [pause] That's right. Sam Stone! And guess what he did this time? He asked to borrow my Barbie and when he was carrying her down the stairs, he tripped and fell and broke her arm. That Sam Stone is always getting into accidents and breaking things!

These inductions were so successful that the children would commonly offer their own version of a story's ending before the experimenter finished telling it.

The day after Sam Stone's visit, the children were shown a ripped book (the same one that they were reading when Sam Stone came to visit) and a soiled teddy bear (that had not been in the room during Sam Stone's visit). They were asked if they knew how the book had been ripped and the teddy bear soiled. Very few children claimed to have seen Sam Stone do these things, but one fourth of them said that *perhaps* he had done it—a statement that is reasonable, given the stereotype induction they received prior to his visit.

Following Sam Stone's visit, these children were given four suggestive interviews over a 10-week period. Each suggestive interview contained two erroneous suggestions, one having to do with ripping a book and the other with soiling a teddy bear (e.g., "Remember that time Sam Stone visited your classroom and spilled chocolate on that white teddy bear? Did he do it on purpose or was it an accident?" and "When Sam Stone ripped that book, was he being silly or was he angry?"). Thus, children in this condition got a double "whammy": They were subjected to a negative stereotype and a series of suggestive questions.

One month later, when a new interviewer probed about these events ("Did anything happen to a book?" "Did anything happen to a teddy bear?"), 72% of the youngest preschoolers claimed that Sam Stone did one or both misdeeds, a figure that dropped to 44% when asked if they actually *saw* him do these things. Importantly, 21% continued to insist that they saw him do these things, even when gently challenged. The older preschoolers, although more accurate, still included some children (11%) who insisted they saw him do the misdeeds, as can be seen in Figure 10.2.

What was most surprising about these children's reports was the number of false perceptual details, as well as nonverbal gestures, that they provided to embellish their stories of these nonevents. For example, children used their hands to show how Sam had purportedly thrown the teddy bear up in the air; some children reported seeing Sam in the playground, on his way to the store to buy chocolate ice cream, or in the bathroom soaking

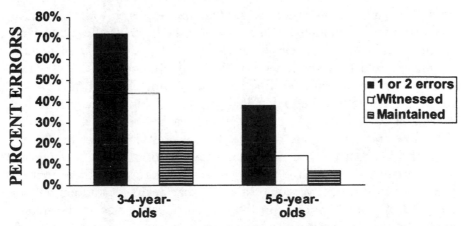

Figure 10.2. The double whammy in the Sam Stone Study: negative stereotypes and erroneous suggestions.

the teddy bear in water before smearing it with a crayon. Some children claimed there was more than one Sam Stone. And one child provided every parent's favorite false detail: This child claimed that Sam had come to his house to trash his room.

Some might criticize the Sam Stone results on the grounds that the effects of stereotype induction are exaggerated because of focusing on the fact that 72% of the youngest children claimed that Sam had done at least one of the misdeeds; after all, one might argue, when the children were really challenged, only 21% of the youngest children and only 11% of the older children continued to hold onto their previous claims. This is a good point, and one that should not be overlooked.

There are two points to consider. First, no weight should be given to the precise percentages in this or in any other study because the rate of false responding can be elevated or depressed; by making the experimental manipulations more or less intense (e.g., by increasing the number of suggestive questions or the length of the delay interval), we can make this number go up or down. Second, if children in the forensic arena are interviewed the same way our subjects were, the stereotype induction may ultimately influence only a small proportion of the youngest children. But how many times are children in the forensic arena interviewed the same way as the children in this study? If children will change a false answer to a true one when the interviewer challenges them a single time ("This didn't really happen, did it?"), perhaps they can likewise be induced to change a true answer to a false one if they are challenged repeatedly, as was true of the Little Rascals child in a previous chapter (see p. 104) when he changed his answer to assent to the noncharged offense. In our case examples, there are numerous examples of children retracting previous allegations that seem to be discounted by the interviewers.

Zeke, one of the Little Rascals children, adamantly denied sexual abuse to his mother, his father, and his therapist. It was only after 3 months of therapy and questioning by his parents that he began to allege that some of the day-care staff had sexually abused him. Approximately 14 months later, Zeke told his father that Mr. Bob had not touched the children. When his father asked if Mr. Bob had touched the children in the bathroom and at naptime, he said, "Well just a little bit." Although he had previously made claims about his day-care teacher sexually abusing him, Zeke now claimed that she was nice. He told his father that he did not remember her touching the children and he did not remember making any such allegations. According to the father's memory, Zeke then abruptly tried to change the conversation. It seems that Zeke's recantation was interpreted by the professionals in this case as merely a sign of the trauma of abuse and therefore it could be ignored.

At the trial of Kelly Michaels, one of the Michaels children's therapists made the following statement about one child's allegations during a therapy session:

> [The child] said that Kelly had pooped and that pee pee had trickled down [the child's] legs onto the gym floor, and then [the child] said, "But it really isn't true."

And another child told Eileen Treacy,

> Yeah but . . . I don't even know, when I go to Sara's [i.e., one of the prosecutors, Sara McCardle], um Sara that's here? Well even when I go there 'cause I don't know and she keeps asking me and asking me, but I don't know. I don't even know anything 'cause I wasn't in her class.

But these retractions frequently are explained away by invoking the children's fright and their use of denial to defend against it, when making a true disclosure. Although it is certainly possible that denial is at work to protect against negative emotions associated with true disclosures, it is also possible that children's retractions of earlier claims reflect their desire to set the record straight. Although this last explanation might seem most consistent with the Sam Stone data, perhaps a naive observer, who did not know what the children had actually seen during Sam Stone's visit, might interpret their later retractions of previous claims in terms of the first mechanism—denial of the truth. The point is that science provides no certain answers to this dilemma, and prudence dictates that we be clear and consistent in invoking mechanisms that have little compelling evidentiary basis. We cannot simply pick and choose when to accept a retraction as real and when to deny that it is real.

Critics of the Sam Stone study also wonder about its forensic relevance. After all, what is the significance of the event in the Sam Stone study? We agree that the 2-minute visit of Sam to the classroom is not a significant event. We even go a step further: There really was *no* event. Some of the children came to tell elaborate stories about an event that never happened. We think it important to make the following distinction: Children's reports can be unreliable because they confuse, omit, or blend details when recounting an actual event. But they can also be unreliable because they fabricate an entire episode or sequence of events within a larger episode. The latter most clearly occurred in the Sam Stone study. This is an important point because it demonstrates that children's inaccurate reports or allegations do not always reflect a confusion of events and details of an experience, but may at times reflect the creation of an entire experience in which the child did not participate.

In summary, we have reviewed three studies (Chester, Dale, and Sam Stone) that focused on the effects of stereotype induction. These studies varied in their procedures, and yet the results are quite consistent, with all showing negative effects of pairing stereotype induction with suggestive questioning.[1] These effects are apparent regardless of whether the child is interviewed one time (as was true in the Dale study) or over the period of several months (as was true in the Sam Stone study). The negative effects are apparent whether the stereotype induction took place before an event (Sam Stone) or after an event (Chester, Dale). Both situations have their forensic analogues. For example, some children may come to misinterpret an event as negative on the basis of postevent negative stereotypes that were conveyed to them by interviewers, as seen in some of the transcripts we have already presented, whereas others may misinterpret an event on the basis of pre-event incriminating statements that parents have made about a certain person. In the Macias case, for instance, before Jennifer was ever questioned by the police, she was given a negative stereotype about Macias by her mother. She was told not to go near him because he was a jailbird and not to be trusted. Apparently, Jennifer's mother heard stories to the effect that Macias had called her a whore. Consequently, Jennifer told the court that she was afraid of Macias. In other cases, there may be no misinterpretation or reinterpretation of an event, but children may come to fabricate an entire event on the basis of acquired stereotypes. Our sample cases provide numerous examples of this situation.

According to some commentators, the allegations of sexual abuse in the Little Rascals case may reflect a much earlier induction of a stereotype that "Mr. Bob does bad things." The following facts have been well documented. In the fall of 1988, several months before the first allegation of sexual abuse, a 4-year-old attending Little Rascals told his mother that he had been slapped by Bob Kelly. Upon hearing this, the mother recalled, "My life crumbled. Life would never be the same." She went to Bob and Betsy Kelly demanding an apology. Betsy would not apologize, and according to one of the parents, "[She] had a crying fit." The mother went back to the day-care center for a second time looking for an apology, which she did not receive. She removed her child from the center, and her husband told Betsy that they were going to start talking about the slapping to others. And they did seem to do this. The first allegation of sexual abuse was reported by another mother soon after she had been told of the slapping incident. The stereotype-induction interpretation of this allegation is that parents had been asking their children whether Mr. Bob had spanked them just as he had spanked one of their classmates. It is possible that the children had developed a stereotype that Mr. Bob did bad things and that this

---

[1]The Sam Stone study also examined the effect of providing only stereotype induction. Although there is a negative effect, it is not as great as when it is paired with suggestive questioning. For further technical details, the readers should consult Leichtman and Ceci (in press).

stereotype was sufficient to allow the allegations to emerge with additional types of prompts.

We do not know how many children had been questioned by their parents about being slapped at the day-care center, but it is interesting that when children were first interviewed by authorities, some of them reported hitting in the center, although few reported that the hitting happened to them. Other children who were initially silent often began their disclosures with incidents of "hitting" or of "spanking." Only after many therapeutic interviews did the allegations become sexual in nature. Of course, this is one interpretation, and it could be very wrong.

The Michaels interviews are also rife with examples of stereotype induction. On the basis of analyses of the existing interviews, the investigators told 15 of the 34 interviewed children that Michaels was in jail because she had done bad things. They told the children that they needed their help to keep Michaels in jail. They also promoted the children's fear of Michaels by asking leading questions about whether Michaels had threatened them or their families if they were to tell on her. Sometimes the investigators suggested that she had claimed to have supernatural powers ("Did she ever tell you that she had any powers, secret powers, like she could see through walls or anything like that?"). The investigators constantly told the children that they were now safe and could talk, because Michaels was in jail.

It is interesting that, despite these statements, many of the children did not completely incorporate the suggested stereotypes of Michaels. Sixteen of the 34 children never said they were afraid of her. In fact, there were some children who continued to insist that they liked Michaels, amid allegations of her terroristic acts. For example, one child said, "I feel bad because she is still in jail. Because she was my best friend." One parent told the grand jury that his child loved Michaels "to this day."

Although some children claimed that Michaels was bad, their claims were uncompelling. For example, in one of the few examples we have of two transcribed interviews for the same child, we see that in the first of the transcribed interviews (which was not the initial interview), the child was repeatedly asked about bad things that Michaels did. She denied that Michaels did anything bad to her. In the next (transcribed) interview, the following exchange took place:

Interviewer: Was Kelly [Michaels] a good girl or a bad girl?

Child: She was a bad girl.

Interviewer: She was a bad girl. Were there any other teachers who were bad?

Child: No.

Interviewer: Kelly was the only bad girl? What did Kelly do that made her a bad girl?

Child: She readed.

Interviewer: She what?

Child: She readed and she came to me and I said no, no, no.

Interviewer: Did she hurt you?

Child: I hurted her.

Interviewer: How did you hurt her?

Child: Because I didn't want to write and she write and I said no, no, no, no and I hit her.

When other children made statements that Michaels was bad, it is impossible to tell whether these statements reflect the fact that Michaels actually did bad things or whether these reports reflect the children's adoption of the interviewers' suggested stereotypes of Michaels, an indeterminacy exacerbated by the general absence of recorded initial interviews.

In the Country Walk case, interviewers used various approaches to tell the children that Frank and Iliana Fuster were bad and that bad things happened at the Country Walk house. In the following example, the stereotype that Frank and Iliana are strangers to be feared was provided to the child by her mother.

Child: I am afraid of them [Frank and Iliana] now because my mom told me that they are strangers.

Interviewer: Were you afraid of them before?

Child: (nodding in the negative)

Interviewer: No? You only . . . how many times did you go?

Child: Two but they acted . . . they acted like they were nice. . . . They acted like they were good people. . . .

Interviewer: Does it worry you they acted like they were good and now people tell you they were bad? Does that worry you? Does that worry you, that maybe some other people aren't good (inaudible)?

Child: Does that worry you?

Interviewer: It doesn't worry me because I am a grown-up but I want you to know that your mom and dad will protect you. They will make sure. They will protect you so you don't need to worry.

In the next example, the investigator embellished the mother's stereotype induction by discussing the fact that Frank Fuster was in jail.

Interviewer: How do you feel about Frank being in jail? . . . Does it make you sad or are you glad or what?

Child: I am glad.

Interviewer: You are glad? How Come?

Child: (inaudible)

Interviewer: Did you think he was bad before?

Child: (eventually nods in the negative) . . .

Interviewer: What is it that makes you think that he's bad?

Child: My mom told me.

To summarize, stereotype induction is a technique that is used by interviewers to help frightened or ashamed children disclose the details of their abuse or of a witnessed event. However, as evidenced by the scientific literature, the use of this technique, particularly in the hands of biased interviewers, may seriously tarnish the accuracy of children's reports.

11

OTHER SUGGESTIVE INTERVIEWING TECHNIQUES

In this chapter, we describe some additional components of suggestive interviewing techniques. Although we have divided these into distinct categories, in reality, some of these components often overlap. Examples taken from the case studies often entail more than one component. Nevertheless, for clarity, we have attempted to keep these distinctions separate when possible. At the end of this chapter, we present a fairly long section of a forensic interview in order to summarize the different aspects of biased interviewing techniques that have been discussed in chapters 9, 10, and 11.

EMOTIONAL TONE OF THE INTERVIEW

Interviewers of children place particular importance on building rapport with their young clients so that they feel relaxed and unthreatened. To achieve this goal, they may spend time talking or playing with the child before beginning the actual interview or test; during this time, an interviewer may ask the child to talk about school or after-school activities. Ideally, interviewers attempt to provide a supportive atmosphere by acting positively toward the child, paying attention to and taking seriously the child's answers.

Few would criticize such techniques whether they be used with children or adults. Goodman and her colleagues (Goodman, Bottoms, Schwartz-Kenney, & Rudy, 1991) demonstrated some of the benefits of these techniques on young children's recall of a stressful event. In this study, 4- and 7-year-old children were questioned about a previous visit to a medical clinic where they had received an inoculation. Half of the children were interviewed in a supportive environment: At the beginning of the interview they were given cookies and juice. The interviewer was warm and friendly; she smiled a lot and gave the child considerable but random praise (i.e., praise was not contingent on the child providing any specific information), such as "You're doing a great job" or "You've got a great memory." The other children were not treated as warmly. They were not given juice or cookies, and the interviewer was more distant, occasionally responding "OK" or "alright." Children who were interviewed under the supportive conditions made fewer incorrect statements when asked to tell in their own words what had happened during their inoculation visit. In addition, supportive interviews diminished children's inaccurate answers to misleading questions in some instances. The authors suggested that providing children with a warm interviewing environment increases their resistance to suggestion because it decreases their feelings of intimidation, allowing them to counter the interviewer's false suggestions.

Few would disagree with the recommendations that forensic interviewers create a supportive environment for the child. A problem arises, however, if interviewers presume that they are establishing a supportive relationship when in reality they are setting a very different emotional tone through the use of implicit or explicit threats, bribes, and rewards. For example, in forensic contexts, in order to obtain information from child witnesses, interviewers sometimes make some of the following statements: "We know something bad happened," "It isn't good to let people touch you," "You'll feel better once you tell," or "Don't be afraid to tell." They make these statements to help the child reveal facts that they may be too frightened or embarrassed to disclose.

However, these "supportive statements" may create reliability risks because in some contexts they may be ambiguous. That is, these statements may in fact create an accusatory tone (which reflects the interviewer's bias) and a context that promotes false disclosures. In some studies, when some of these so-called "supportive statements" were used, children were more likely to fabricate reports of past events even in cases when they had no memory of any event occurring, as will be seen below. In some cases, these fabrications were sexual in nature (see review in Ceci & Bruck, 1993b).

In one study that was conducted 4 years after children had played with an unfamiliar research assistant for 5 minutes, Goodman and her colleagues asked these same children to recall the original experience, and then asked them a series of questions, including abuse-related suggestive questions about the event (Goodman, Wilson, Hazan, & Reed, 1989; also described in Goodman & Clarke-Stewart, 1991). At this time, the researchers created what they described as "an atmosphere of accusation" by telling the children that they were to be questioned about an important event and by saying such things as "Are you afraid to tell? You'll feel better once you've told." Although few children had any memory of the original event from 4 years earlier, they were not always very accurate when answering questions that suggested abuse. Five out of the 15 children agreed with the interviewer's erroneously suggestive question that they had been hugged or kissed by the research assistant, 2 of the 15 agreed that they had had their picture taken in the bathroom, and 1 child agreed that she had been given a bath. The important conclusion of this study is that children may begin to give incorrect information to misleading questions about events for which they have no memory, if the interviewer creates an atmosphere (emotional tone) of accusation. These forms of emotional atmospherics are conceptually similar to the negative stereotype inductions we discussed in the preceding chapter.

In most of our sample cases, an atmosphere of accusation was created by telling children that the defendants were in jail and by then telling them that they were safe and that it was OK to tell. This is exemplified by a mother's statement in the Old Cutler case:

Mother: Then I told her Bobby is in jail, that he wouldn't be hurting anyone else ever again. He is in jail now. There was a long hesitation and I asked her again, "Did he ever pull his pants down?" She said "yes." [The mother explained that her child felt safe enough to tell since Bobby was in jail.]

Similar examples are found in the Little Rascals case. The following statements were provided by mothers of the child witnesses at Bob Kelly's trial:

Attorney: How did you reassure him that he was safe from Shelly Stone?

Mother: Well Shelly was not in jail. He knew some other people were but she wasn't. So we explained to him that she couldn't see any of the children; that he was safe; that he didn't have to worry about seeing Ms. Shelly; that she couldn't hurt him; and that the others in jail couldn't get out and hurt him either. I think he probably lumped her in the category even though he had never said anything negative about her; he knew that she was still involved with all the group of people or the others that he knew about.

Attorney: So you feel he lumped her into that group . . . of day care people?

Mother: And was concerned about his safety. She's not in jail, you know she's out, she might be able to come and get me.

Attorney: Had he expressed that concern to you at that point in time?

Mother: Not about her.

Attorney: Okay. He had not made any reference to her coming and getting him or being afraid of her at that point in time?

Mother: No.

◆ ◆ ◆

Mother: Sometimes I would tell him that he was safe, that Bob was in jail that people couldn't get out of jail, that that was a brick house and Bob couldn't get out of there. Once I went past and I just said "Ha-ha-ha, Mr. Bob's in jail." I don't know if I said it more for me or for him.

◆ ◆ ◆

Attorney: Prior to June the 16th when you're telling her about jail, she had not raised any issue about jail, had she?

Mother: June 14th. No I don't believe that she had.

Attorney: That's right. . . . And the issue of jail was raised by you, is that right?

Mother: That's right.

Attorney: And she asked you what a jail looked like and you told her it was like a cage; is that right?

Mother: That's right.

Attorney: Okay. And you told her that Bob was in jail because kids were telling their moms what Bob did to them; is that right?

Mother: She asked me why is he in jail and I said, "Remember I told you children were telling their moms what he did to them and . . . those are not things that are supposed to happen at a day care."

Attorney: Okay. And she told you she hated Mr. Bob and you said you hated him too?

◆ ◆ ◆

Attorney: Okay. And then when was the first time that Sabina talked about jail to your knowledge?

Mother: The first time that she mentioned jail was on July 11th when she started having bad dreams about Bob putting her in jail.

Similarly, the interviewers in the Michaels case often created an atmosphere of conspiracy and tried to enlist the children's cooperation. For example,

Investigator: The police want to keep her in jail. The police put her in jail. Because she was hurting you, you know. That's why I really need your help, especially you older kids, you six years old and kindergartners because you can talk better than the little kids and you can show things a little clearer on the dolls and if you help us out we can take you on a little tour of the jail and you will be helping to keep her in jail longer so that she doesn't hurt anybody else. Not to mention that you'll also feel a lot better once you start.

◆ ◆ ◆

Investigator: Do you feel a little bit more safer? Uh, or do you feel more nervous? Good. Cause that's how we want you to feel. Kelly's not going to be able to hurt any of you guys again. And that's why you're helping us the way you have been which you have been doing real good by the way, it's only going to help us keep her in jail longer. So she doesn't hurt anybody anymore. How do you feel about that?

Child: Good.

◆ ◆ ◆

Investigator: Your mommy tells me that you guys are interested in busting this case wide open with us, is that right?

Although investigators may have intended these statements to be "supportive," they cross the boundary into the category of "accusations."

It is also important not to confuse statements that provide a supportive emotional context with statements that selectively reinforce specific responses. There are many studies in the social science literature showing that reinforcing children for certain behaviors, regardless of the quality of the behaviors, increases the frequency of these types of behaviors, whereas ignoring or punishing certain behaviors decreases their occurrence. For example, if a child is told, "You are a really good boy" after he makes certain kinds of responses, the child will tend to increase these types of responses and to decrease other responses that are not reinforced. When interviewers are overly supportive of children, the children tend to produce many inaccurate as well as many accurate details (e.g., Geiselman, Saywitz, & Bornstein, 1990). Certainly, there appears to be some trade-off in the effect of positive and neutral support on the accuracy of children's reports.

The two following examples demonstrate how positive and negative statements were used in the interviews with children in the Michaels case:

Fonolleras: And where else do you think a little girl might get hit with a wooden spoon or did you get hit with the wooden spoon? On the a . . .

Child: Arm.

Fonolleras: On the arm? OK and who's doing the hitting? Who did the hitting?

Child: The wooden spoon.

Fonolleras: The wooden spoon, but who was holding the wooden spoon?

Child: Me.

Fonolleras: OK, but we're talking about the kids being hurt in school, all right, right, who were we talking about before?
[At this point, the child does not provide the desired answer, and Fonolleras continues to ask questions.]

Fonolleras: Which was the teacher that we're talking about that was hurting kids? The person we were talking about earlier, remember?

Child: Kelly.

Fonolleras: Right. OK, now you've been very helpful. . . .

The following excerpt is an interview with another child in the same case.:

Fonolleras: Do you want to show me what Kelly did to Cindy with the big wooden spoon? . . . Where is that?

Child: A belly button.

Fonolleras: The belly button, and where else did she put the wooden spoon, where else did she put the wooden spoon, what else did she do with it? Did she do anything else with the wooden spoon, no, did she do anything to any part of your body with it? So she just put that in your bellybutton and did you have your clothes on or off?

Child: Off.

Fonolleras: What room was it in, was that in the nap room or the music room?

Child: At home.

Fonolleras: At home, Kelly wasn't at your home. Was it in the nap room or the room with the big black piano or the bathroom, do you remember which room, which room was it in?

Child: The bathroom.

Fonolleras: The bathroom, OK. . . .

Sometimes interviewers' use of selective reinforcement becomes so intense that statements that are intended to be rewarding seem more like "bribes" and statements that are intended to be mildly discouraging seem more like "threats."[1] Although the quality and quantity of positive support and reinforcement provided in many of the research studies exemplify good interviewing techniques that most interviewers would use, the types of "encouraging" statements made by some of the investigators in the Michaels case could be viewed as unacceptable examples of how children should be encouraged in an interview:

McGrath: Do you want to sit on my lap? Come here. I am so proud of you. I love big girls like you that tell me what happened. That aren't afraid and I can protect you.

[After a few minutes, he continues.]

    Because that is my job to protect cute, little beautiful little girls, God bless you just like you. OK. You got such pretty eyes. You are going to grow to be a beautiful young lady. I'm jealous, I'm too old for you.

In the interviews with children in the Michaels case, there are also numerous examples of bribes. Some children were given police badges in exchange for their incriminating statements. Sometimes, the bribes took the form of promises to terminate the interviews ("You're hungry? OK. You tell me why you want to hit the Sally doll and I'll give you something to eat"). Some uncooperative children were berated ("Don't be a baby. You're acting like a nursery school kid").

These statements on the part of the Michaels interviewers seem to reflect their biases and their attempts to get children to admit abuse. They sometimes rewarded the children when they produced abuse-consistent responses, but ignored or even berated them when they produced abuse-inconsistent responses. As we saw in the Goodman et al. study, the problem

---

[1]The examples provided in the following texts reflect how interviewers use threats and bribes to elicit information from children who do not disclose. There is also the situation when perpetrators may use threats for the opposite purpose—to silence their victims. There have been a few studies that have examined the effectiveness of such threats in a laboratory setting. Peters (1990) staged an event in which children between 5 and 9 years of age saw a "thief" come into the testing room and steal a book. The "thief" told the child not to tell. When later questioned about the event by a parent, only 5% of the children disclosed the theft if the thief was also present. If the thief left the room, however, 67% of the children told about the theft (see McGough, 1994, for a review of other studies).

with such statements is that they may have deleterious effects on the subsequent accuracy of young children's reports.

Similar types of examples can be found in some of the interviews with the Country Walk children. The investigators sometimes created an "accusatorial atmosphere"; that is, they were highly supportive of statements of abuse and equally critical of statements contrary to a theory of abuse. In addition to the investigators casting such an accusatory aura, parents were enlisted into service:

> Mother to daughter: Tell [one of the investigators] one little thing, then I will give you the necklace.

In addition to offering children tangible rewards, parents used other reinforcement techniques to get their children to tell about things that had happened at the day-care center. The following incident, taken from the Little Rascals case, occurred after one family's first visit to the therapist. Up to that time, the child had not made any allegations of sexual abuse despite much concern and questioning by his parents.

> Mother: For some reason that night I got very upset. And I was very frustrated from the standpoint that I felt like my son should be able to come to me if there was a problem and tell me about it, that he should not have some sort of secret or some adult that I really didn't know that well should have a secret with him that he wouldn't be able to tell me about. Because I felt like he and I were close enough that we could talk. And so I got very upset that night, and I cried in front of him that night. And he realized I was crying and looked at me and asked me why I was crying. And I said because he couldn't talk to me about Mr. Bob. And then he looked at me and said, "I'll talk to you, mommy, but you talk."
>
> And about that time he was getting a little sleepy and he said that he had seen Mr. Bob's wee-wee—that's what he calls it—and he said Mr. Bob had touched his wee-wee and his bottom. . . .

A parent might not interpret this behavior as a "bribe," but one could construe this mother's crying as an emotional bribe that the child accepts to protect his mother, or, along the same lines, the mother's crying could be classified as a negative reinforcer that leads the child to assent in order to terminate discomfort.

THE EFFECTS OF PEER PRESSURE OR INTERACTION ON CHILDREN'S REPORTS

The effects of letting children know that their friends have "already told" is a much less investigated area in the field of children's testimonial research. Certainly, the common wisdom is that a child will go along with a peer group; but will a child provide an inaccurate response just so she can be one of the crowd? The results of three studies suggest that the answer is yes.

First, Binet (1900) found that children will change their answers to be consistent with those of their peer group even when it is clear that the answer is inaccurate. Second, in the Pettit et al. (1990) study in which park rangers visited preschoolers' classrooms (described in chapter 8), there were seven children who were absent from their classrooms when the target event (the cake falling off the piano) occurred. Yet when questioned 2 weeks later, six of these children indicated that they had been present. One presumes that these six children gave false reports so that they would feel like they were part of the same group as their friends who did participate. Importantly, this study shows how the peer group's actual experiences in an event can lead nonparticipants to fabricate reports of the event.

Finally, Pynoos and Nader (1989) studied people's recollections of a sniper attack. On February 24, 1984, from a second-story window across the street, a sniper shot repeated rounds of ammunition at children on an elementary school playground. Scores of children were pinned under gunfire, many were injured, and one child and a passerby were killed. Roughly 10% of the student body, 113 children, were interviewed 6 to 16 weeks later. Each child was asked to freely recall the experience and then to respond to specific questions. Some of those children who were interviewed were not at the school during the shooting, including those already on the way home or on vacation. Yet even the nonwitnesses had "memories":

> One girl initially said that she was at the school gate nearest the sniper when the shooting began. In truth she was not only out of the line of fire, she was half a block away. A boy who had been away on vacation said that he had been on his way to the school, had seen someone lying on the ground, had heard the shots, and then turned back. In actuality, a police barricade prevented anyone from approaching the block around the school. (p. 238)

One assumes that children heard about the event from their peers who were present during the sniper attack and that they incorporated these reports into their own memories.

The Country Walk investigators tried to get the children to disclose by telling them what other children allegedly reported. Sometimes, the investigators told the children that they could help their friends by telling about abuse at Country Walk. The following are some examples:

Interviewer: Some of the children don't understand. They are afraid. Some children said that they were acting like monsters and they wore these masks and they scared them.

Child: Is that true?

Interviewer:	I am not sure but some of the children said so and I believe the children because I don't think children make up stories like that. Do you?
Child:	Which children?
Interviewer:	Well Douglas and some of the other children.
Child:	. . . But some of them are bigger than me and did they tell you that they were naked or anything like that?
Interviewer:	Yes.
Child:	What did they say?
Interviewer:	They said that they played games with Frank and Iliana and some of the littler children and everybody took off their clothes and they played games and people touched each other's private parts.
Child:	That's true.
Interviewer:	Is it true?
Child:	Yes but Douglas (inaudible) the other children said it, so Douglas might be right. . . .
Interviewer:	You thought maybe if Douglas said it, . . . maybe it wasn't right?
Child:	It was true because the other children said it.

◆ ◆ ◆

Child:	Do you know what [Frank] did?
Interviewer:	Well I am not sure because I am not like a policeman or something like that. So I am not sure but would you like me to tell you what Douglas said?
Child:	(nodding)
Interviewer:	. . . Okay, Douglas said—he took the dolls and he kind of talked a little and he showed me and one of the things is that he took all the clothes off the dolls.
Child:	Why?
Interviewer:	Well, he said that the children played a game like—one of the games he said they would play was ring around the rosy.
Child:	With no clothes on?
Interviewer:	With no clothes on.

◆ ◆ ◆

Interviewer:	And your sister said that Iliana used to spank the children, did she do that?

Child: No, she didn't spank me.

Interviewer: What about the other children? Did she spank them?

Child: No.

Interviewer: How come your sister said that?

Child: I didn't.

Similar techniques were frequently used by the Michaels investigators, who frequently told the children that their friends had already told:

Interviewer: All the other friends I talked to told me everything that happened. Randy told me. Charlie told me, Connie told me. . . . And now it's your turn to tell. You don't want to be left out, do you?

◆ ◆ ◆

Interviewer: Boy, I'd hate having to tell your friends that you didn't want to help them (in response to a child who did not disclose).

◆ ◆ ◆

Interviewer: All your friends that I mentioned before were telling us that Kelly, the teacher we are talking about, was doing something they didn't like very much. She was bothering them in kind of a private way and they were all pretty brave and they told us everything, and we were wondering if you could help us out too, doing the same thing.

◆ ◆ ◆

Interviewer: I will get you the badge if you help us get this information . . . like all your other friends did.

This last example from the Michaels case shows how children may sometimes change their responses when provided with information that their friends have already told:

Interviewer: Did you ever see bleeding in her vagina?

Child: Umm hmmm.

Interviewer: . . . Did you ever see her take anything out her vagina with blood on it? Did you ever see anything like that? You did?

Child: Nooo.

Interviewer: Well, he said yes.

Child: No, really! No.

Interviewer: Come on, seriously.

Child: Really! No. . . . You're gross.

Interviewer: Well, that's gross, but other kids are telling me that they saw her pull something out, and I'm wondering if you saw her bleeding from her vagina like that.

Child: Ooooh yes.

Children were also interviewed together in some of the case studies, presumably as a way of getting one or both children to disclose. For example, on one occasion only, one of the Little Rascals children, Mary, was brought into the same therapy session as her friend. Mary had attended Little Rascals and was seeing another therapist. Apparently, Mary was not disclosing and was brought as a guest into this session so that her friend could open her up once she saw how other children spoke to their therapists about abuse. In this session, the therapist tried to elicit allegations about some of the day-care workers.

There are some examples that suggest that the children in some of our sample cases did talk to each other about the allegations, or perhaps parents merely told their children about other children's allegations. The two following examples are taken from the Michaels interviews:

Interviewer: Do you know what [Kelly] did?

Child: She wasn't supposed to touch somebody's body. If you want to touch somebody, touch your own.

Interviewer: How do you know about her touching private parts? Is that something you saw or heard?

Child: Max told me.

◆ ◆ ◆

Interviewer: When you and the other kids were upstairs in the music room, was she wearing clothes then?

Child: I saw clothes on, but the other kids didn't.

Interviewer: Oh how do you know that?

Child: Because my mommy told me that.

Perhaps children do eventually decide what is the truth on the basis of statements of their peers; this hypothesis is raised by the following trial testimony of one of the Little Rascals child witnesses:

Child: He touched kids. I just know it because if he's touched everybody else and everyone else has been up here then I kind of know that they've been touched.

Attorney: Okay. Did somebody tell you that?

Child: No sir: It's just that everybody has been up here and I think they have been telling the truth.

The Little Rascals children seemed to have talked to each other about the abuse. Sometimes siblings questioned siblings to get them to provide incriminating evidence. Steve, a 3-year-old child, had only attended the day-care five times and had only admitted to spanking when questioned by the authorities. His mother had accepted that this was all that had happened until Steve had become terrified when watching something on television. When questioned by his mother, Steve brought up the name of Mr. Bob and then he ran off. Also present during this "interview" was Steve's 11-year-old brother, Bruce. According to the mother, the following interactions ensued:

We spent about 30 minutes asking Steve questions while he changed the subject and ran around back and forth . . . he had told us that he couldn't tell us anything, that he had a secret. I said to him something like, Steve, what did Mr. Bob say to you to make you keep a secret. . . . He didn't say anything then. I asked him what would happen if he told the secret, and he said that Mr. Bob would keep on spanking. . . . And I had already said that some of his friends were telling the secret and it was okay and that kind of thing.

We were trying to get him to really open up. And Bruce took the afghan off the couch, and he said let's get in here and you can tell your brother the secret and no one can hear. I guess when you are 3, maybe that will work, and he tried it but it wouldn't work, he wouldn't tell Bruce anything.

In our sample cases, there were times where it seems that therapists deliberately used one sibling to "open another sibling up." Sometimes, siblings who were treated by two different therapists sat in on their brother's therapy session. And not surprisingly, a disclosure by one sibling might be followed by the same disclosure at a later date by another sibling.

One might argue that there is some scientific evidence to support the practice of using peers to elicit disclosures from children who have something to disclose. In a recent study, 7- and 10-year-olds witnessed a staged classroom incident and were later asked to recall its details (Moston & Engelberg, 1992). As is customary in such studies, younger children recalled less information about the incident and were more susceptible to suggestive questioning than were the 10-year-olds. However, when these 7-year-olds were allowed to discuss the incident with a friend who accompanied them to the interview, age differences were significantly reduced. The presence of a friend at the interview created a favorable emotional environment that resulted in more accurate and less suggestible reports for the youngest children. But these data are relevant only if the children do have something to disclose. Otherwise, such practices may taint their reports.

THE EFFECTS OF BEING INTERVIEWED BY ADULTS WITH HIGH STATUS

Young children are sensitive to the status and power of their interviewers and as a result are especially likely to comply with the implicit and explicit agenda of such interviewers (see Ceci et al., 1987, for experimental evidence). If their account is questioned, for example, children may defer to the challenges of the more senior interviewer. To some extent, the child's recognition of this power differential may be one of the most important causes of their increased suggestibility. Children are more likely to believe adults than other children, and they are more willing to go along with the wishes of adults and to incorporate adults' beliefs into their reports. This fact has been recognized by researchers since the turn of the century and has been demonstrated in many studies (see Ceci & Bruck, 1993b, for a review). For example, children are less open to suggestive influences when the suggestions are planted by their peers than when they are planted by adults (Ceci et al., 1987).

However, children may also be sensitive to status and power differentials among adults. This is a particularly important issue for the testimony of child witnesses who are interviewed by police officers, judges, and medical personnel.

The children in the Michaels case were interviewed by law enforcement agents or by social workers who made reference to their connection to law enforcement agents. The children were explicitly made aware of the status of their interviewers by such comments as the following:

Interviewer: I'm a policeman, if you were a bad girl, I would punish you wouldn't I? Police can punish bad people.

◆ ◆ ◆

Interviewer: After we finish here, depending on how much you guys help me today, I'm going to introduce you to one of the men who arrested Kelly and put her in jail. . . . Remind me before you leave today, I want to introduce you to the policeman who arrested her. So that he can show you his handcuffs, his badge and he can tell you how hard it is to break out of jail.

A similar example is taken from one of the only surviving taped interviews of a Little Rascals child witness:

Prosecutor: Do you know who put him [Mr. Bob] in jail?

Child: The police.

Prosecutor: Right. Did you know that the police work for me? That I tell the police what to do?

Child: Yeah.

Prosecutor: So Mr. Kevin and Ms. Brenda came to me and asked if we should put Mr. Bob in jail and I said let's put Mr. Bob in jail. Why is he in jail, Jed? Do you know?

A recent study by Tobey and Goodman (1992) suggests that interviews by high-status adults who make such statements may have negative effects on the accuracy of children's reports. In this study, 4-year-old children played a game with a research assistant who was called a "baby-sitter." Eleven days later, the children returned to the laboratory. Half of the children met a police officer who said,

I am very concerned that something bad might have happened the last time that you were here. I think that the baby-sitter you saw here last time might have done some bad things and I am trying to find out what happened the last time you were here when you played with the baby-sitter. We need your help. My partner is going to come in now and ask you some questions about what happened. (p. 783)

A research assistant dressed up as a police officer then questioned these children. Half of the children never met the police officer; they were questioned only by a neutral interviewer about what happened with the baby-sitter. When the children were asked to tell everything they could remember, the children in the police condition gave fewer accurate statements and more inaccurate statements than the children in the neutral condition. Two of the 13 children in the police condition seemed to be decisively misled by the suggestion that the baby-sitter had done something bad. One girl said to her mother, "I think the baby-sitter had a gun and was going to kill me." Later, in her free recall, the same child said, "That man he might try to do something bad to me . . . really bad, yes siree." The second child inaccurately reported his ideas of what something bad might be by saying, "I fell down, I got lost, I got hurt on my legs, and I cut my ears."

Goodman (1993) summarized these findings as follows:

One should be concerned not only with the actual questions but also with the context of the interview. An accusatory or intimidating context leads to increased errors in children's reports. (p. 15)

It is important to further explore the potential effects of these "accusatory" contexts. It seems that children may become very excited that they are part of an investigation, thus bringing many of their fantasies into reality. In some of our sample cases, the children were given badges, they were taken to the jails housing the accused, and they were rewarded by their parents and therapists for telling things that would keep these bad people in jail. One mother in the Little Rascals case told of the ritual by which her son would often make new allegations. New claims might first be told to his therapist, and he would then insist on telling Brenda Toppin, the police officer. Sometimes, Toppin would come to the house to hear the new charges; other times, the child would be taken to the police station.

> Mother: She [Brenda] told me to ask Ken where he wanted her to meet, at the police station or at her house or at our house. I couldn't get up with Brenda right away, and I talked to her about 4:30 from work when Ken was at home and she said to call her back at 7. I called her back at 7 and she wasn't home. . . . Ken was very desperate to see her. He said he had to tell her about this. And so he would not rest about it. And I said, okay, we'll ride around to see if we see her car, and we did. But we couldn't, so we went back home and got up with her on the phone.

Some might argue that these measures are important to assist children in divulging all the horrors of their abuse. We have both had experiences where there was fairly good documentation that abuse occurred, but where the child victim refused to acknowledge it until such techniques were used. On the other hand, one might also argue that providing children with all of these props encourages the evolution of false allegations. Certainly, the empirical literature and the case analyses are consistent with this interpretation, though much more research is needed on this important issue before we can be certain.

Another feature of some of the interviews in the sample case studies was that there was often more than one adult questioner present in the interview. For example, both Joseph and Laurie Braga co-interviewed a number of child witnesses in the Country Walk case, and sometimes, there were two or even three adults present in the interviews of the Michaels children. One might argue that this could be a safeguard to ensure that the child tells the truth—especially if one of the adults is the child's parent. Or one might reason, as the Michaels investigators did, that it was necessary to have a second interviewer for emotional support and also to have a witness for the child's disclosures. However, it also seems that additional adults may tilt the odds toward false disclosures for two reasons. First, the presence of extra adults, all of whom share the same beliefs about what may have transpired, may induce a child to join them. Second, extra adults multiply the number of questions that the child is asked about the same theme: "Tell us how you were sexually abused." And these increased questions may increase children's willingness to defer to the adults' agenda rather than to their own memories of whether an event actually occurred.

In the following example from the Michaels case, a preschooler is interviewed by social worker Fonolleras and Detective Mastroangelo:

Fonolleras: What little girls did she do that to?

Child: (names a child)

Fonolleras: Who?

Child: (repeats)

Fonolleras: Really.

Mastroangelo: You want to show us again what she did with the fork?

Fonolleras: Show us again what you just showed us.

Mastroangelo: She put the fork where?

Child: The vagina.

Mastroangelo: OK, whose vagina?

Child: um . . .

Mastroangelo: Do you know? Who, honey?

Child: Down there.

Fonolleras: OK but who's this little girl?

Child: Huh?

SUMMARY: COMPONENTS OF BIASED INTERVIEWING TECHNIQUES

In wrapping up this chapter, we present a long excerpt from one interview. This excerpt contains many components that are indicative of the kinds of interview biases that we have been discussing in the last three chapters. The interviewer is Lou Fonolleras, and he is interviewing one of the children in the Michaels case. Occasionally, a police detective joins in the interview. Intermittently, we annotate the interview with commentary:

Fonolleras: We have gotten a lot of other kids to help us since I last saw you.

Child: No. I don't have to.

Fonolleras: Oh, come on. Did we tell you she is in jail?

Child: Yes. My mother already told me.

Comment: The interviewer's bias regarding the defendant's guilt, as well as stereotype induction, is apparent. The interviewer insinuates that because Kelly Michaels is now in jail that the child need not be afraid of her. Note that it is not clear that this child was ever afraid. Also note the use of peer pressure (a lot of other kids have already "helped").

Fonolleras: Well, we can get out of here real quick if you just tell me what you told me last time.

Comment: The interviewer fails to test an alternative hypothesis; rather, through the use of a bribe, he desires the child to reaffirm on tape what the interviewer recalls from an earlier interview.

Child: I forgot.

Fonolleras: No you didn't, I know you didn't.

Child: I did, I did.

Fonolleras: No, come on.

Child: I forgot. . . .

Fonolleras: I thought we were friends last time.

Child: I'm not your friend any more.

Fonolleras: How come?

Child: Because I hate you.

Fonolleras: Is it because we are talking about stuff you don't want to talk about? What are you, a monster now? Huh? . . .

Comment: This provides an example of interviewing that borders on being coercive. There is little respect for the child's wish not to discuss this matter.

Fonolleras: We talked to a few more of your buddies—we talked to everybody now. And everyone told me about the nap room, and the bathroom stuff, and the music room stuff, and the choir stuff, and the peanut butter stuff, and everything and nothing surprises me any more.

Comment: Again, no alternative hypothesis is being tested. This is also an example of utilization of peer pressure. The interviewer essentially tells the child that his friends already disclosed about the defendant and that the child should do the same.

Child:	I hate you.
Fonolleras:	No you don't. . . . You just don't like talking about this, but you don't hate me.
Child:	Yes, I do hate you.
Fonolleras:	. . . . We can finish this real fast if you just show me real fast what you showed me last time.
Child:	No.
Fonolleras:	I will let you play my tape recorder. . . . Come on, do you want to help us out? Do you want to help us keep her in jail, huh? . . . Tell me what happens when (names four children). Tell me what happened to them. Come on. . . . I need your help again, buddy. Come on.
Child:	No.
Fonolleras:	You told us everything once before. Do you want to un-dress my dolly? . . .
Child:	I want my mother.
Fonolleras:	Let's get done with this real quick so we could go to Kings to get popsicles. . . .

Comment: In this example, the interviewer comes close to bribing the child for a disclosure, by implying that the aversive interview can be terminated as soon as the child repeats what he said earlier. Popsicles and playing with a tape recorder are offered as rewards.

Fonolleras:	Did Kelly ever tell you she could get out of jail?
Police:	She could never get out.
Child:	I know that.
Police:	Cause I got her. . . . She is very afraid of me. She is so scared of me.
Fonolleras:	She cries when she sees him (indicating the police de-tective) because she is so scared. . . . What happened to (another child) with the wooden spoon? If you don't re-member in words, maybe you can show me.

Comment: Here we see examples of using statements of two authoritative adults, one of whom is a policeman, and the failure to test the hypothesis that the defendant did not do what the interviewers believed she did.

Child:	I forgot what happened, too.
Fonolleras:	You remember. You told your mommy about everything, about the music room, and the nap room. And all the

stuff. You want to help her stay in jail, don't you? So she doesn't bother you any more. . . . Mommy told me that you had a picture of yourself in your room and there was blood on your penis. . . . Who hurt you?

Child: Kelly, I told you.

Fonolleras: Kelly? So, your penis was bleeding, oh. Your penis was bleeding. Tell me something else: Was your hiney bleeding, too?

Child: No.

Comment: The child never says to this investigator that his penis was bleeding. The investigator provides this misleading information to the child.

Fonolleras: Did (defendant) bleed, too?

Child: No.

Fonolleras: Are you sure she didn't bleed?

Child: Yes. . . . I saw her penis, too.

Fonolleras: Show me on the Kelly doll . . . you saw that? Oh.

Child: She doodied on me. . . . She peed on us.

Fonolleras: . . . Did she pee on you or did you have to pee on her?

Child: She peed on me.

Fonolleras: . . . Who peed on her, you and who else?

Child: (Child names a male friend.)

Fonolleras: Didn't his penis bleed?

Child: Yes.

Fonolleras: It did? What made it bleed? What was she doing?

Child: She was bleeding.

Fonolleras: She was bleeding in her penis? Did you have to put your penis in her penis? Yes or No?

Child: Yeah. . . . And I peed in her penis.

Fonolleras: What was that like? What did it feel like?

Child: Like a shot.

Fonolleras: Did (friend) have to put his penis in her penis, too?

Child: Yes, at the same time.

Fonolleras: At the same time? How did you do that?

Child: We chopped our penises off.

Fonolleras: So, she was bleeding in her penis and you had your penis and your friend's inside her penis.

Child: At the same time.

Comment: This is another example of interviewer bias. When the child says something that is not part of the interviewer's hypothesis (in this case, that the children chopped off their penises), the interviewer ignores it. Furthermore, we see that the child does not begin to make allegations until after much initial resistance. Previous research indicates that when children want an interview to end, they often increase the quantity of false statements (Pettit et al., 1990). Here, one worries about the child's initial denial about blood and his subsequent incorporation of blood into his narrative.

At this point, the child and interviewer began discussing a stream of events in which the child alleged that the defendant urinated in his mouth and that he urinated in her mouth; he and others were made to walk in her urine and slide on the classroom floor in her urine.

Nowhere in this interview, or in numerous others by this and many other professionals, could we find any evidence that an alternative hypothesis was being tested. Specifically, there was no attempt by this interviewer to try to get the child to assent to an incompatible hypothesis (e.g., one in which the child's pediatrician put his penis in the child's mouth, or where the sheriff made him drink his urine, or that he was just teasing about the defendant bleeding). As can be seen, there was no attempt to encourage the child to deny that any of this happened. Although it is not possible to know how much of what the child reported is factually accurate, there is a certain suspiciousness about his disclosures—and this is even more troubling in the interviews of some of his classmates. This is partly due to the heavy-handed use of coercive tactics ("If you tell me real quick, we can go get popsicles") and a refusal to believe that the child has forgotten or has a legitimate motive for not wanting to repeat an earlier remark he allegedly made to his mother (e.g., the child may realize that the former statement is false, made to please a loved one in the secrecy of his home).

In countless interviews, in countless cases, there is a similar absence of incredulity on the part of the interviewer that may reflect a confusion between taking everything the child says seriously versus believing everything the child says. As parents, we have seen how easily our own children and their friends lapse into scatological humor with the slightest encouragement from an adult. One wonders if the interviewers (the parents among them included) realized this about some children.

12

THE PROS AND (MOSTLY) CONS OF USING ANATOMICALLY DETAILED DOLLS

Diagnosing sexual abuse in children is a complicated and difficult process. Often there are no witnesses or medical evidence to confirm or disconfirm a child's claim or a parent's suspicion. To further complicate matters, there is no syndrome or constellation of behaviors, such as depression, anxiety, or nightmares, that are diagnostic of sexual abuse (Kendall-Tackett, Williams, & Finkelhor, 1993). That is, there is much overlap in the behavioral symptoms shown by abused and nonabused children. Furthermore, there are also a significant number of asymptomatic abused children; aggregating data across a number of studies, Kendall-Tackett et al. (1993) calculated that approximately one third of child victims have no symptoms. Because of these diagnostic difficulties (i.e., the frequent absence of witnesses, medical evidence, and symptoms), professionals have developed a number of assessment tools. Anatomically detailed dolls are one such tool, and they have been used by professional interviewers in the United States since the 1970s (Koocher et al., in press).

One rationale for the use of anatomical dolls is that they allow children to manipulate objects reminiscent of a critical event, thereby cuing recall and overcoming language and memory problems. A second and more important rationale is that they overcome motivational problems such as embarrassment and shyness; children may feel more comfortable enacting abusive events using the dolls than verbally recounting the details of such events. The dolls are also used as projective tests; some professionals claim that if a child actively avoids these dolls, shows distress when they are undressed, or shows unusual interest or preoccupation with the dolls' genitalia, these behaviors are consistent with the hypothesis that the child has been abused (Mason, 1991). If any one of these assumptions were well-founded, anatomically detailed dolls clearly could be valuable in the detection and treatment of sexually abused children.

Anatomically detailed dolls are frequently used to assess children for sexual abuse by child therapists, police, child protection workers, and attorneys. The rate of doll use in some jurisdictions may be as high as 90%, as indicated by recent surveys (Boat & Everson, 1988; Conte, Sorenson, Fogarty, & Rosa, 1991). Some states allow children to use anatomically detailed dolls during their courtroom testimony. For example, Alabama has a statute that allows children under the age of 10 to use anatomically correct dolls to facilitate their courtroom testimony (see McGough, 1994).

Although there are no available national figures, expert testimony of mental health professionals as to whether a child has been sexually abused is sometimes based on doll-centered assessments. In Mason's (1991) analysis of 122 appellate court cases that involved challenges to expert witness testimony about child sexual abuse, 21% of the challenges specifically concerned the expert's use of anatomical dolls.

SKEPTICISM OVER DOLL-CENTERED INTERVIEWS

Despite the widespread use of anatomically detailed dolls in therapeutic and forensic settings, some researchers and professionals have expressed skepticism about their usefulness as diagnostic tools. Two related arguments have been made against their use. The first is that the dolls are suggestive. According to this claim, the dolls, by their very nature, may encourage the child to engage in sexual play even if the child has not been sexually abused (e.g., Terr, 1988a). For instance, a child may insert a finger into a doll's genitalia simply because of its novelty or because it is there inviting the child to act on it. (For example, if one presents a preschooler with a doughnut, it should not be surprising to find that the hole "invites" the child's finger to be inserted.)

A related criticism of the dolls is that it is impossible to make any firm judgments about children's past abuse on the basis of their play with these dolls, as no normative data exist on how abused and nonabused children play with the dolls in a standardized test setting. Such data are lacking mainly because of the fact that there are no standard guidelines for doll-centered assessments (e.g., when during the interview the dolls should be introduced; how many dolls should be introduced at one time; whether the dolls should be presented in dressed, undressed, or semidressed formats; what the interviewer should say when she introduces the dolls; etc.). Sometimes interviewers explicitly ask children to show what happened in the alleged abusive situation. Other times, interviewers may leave children to play freely with the dolls. And at other times, interviewers use the dolls to obtain the child's terms for body parts and may subsequently invite the child to point to the doll's parts when discussing sexual acts. Finally, there are no standard recommendations for the frequency with which the dolls should be used; some investigators use the dolls repeatedly across interviews with the same children who are thought to be victims of sexual abuse, whereas others may only use them in one interview with a given child. In the Old Cutler case, some therapists used the dolls frequently in their weekly therapy sessions with the children, whereas others had the dolls (undressed) in their offices during all sessions:

> Therapist: The dolls were part of the treatment sessions as much as the children wanted to use them. Sometimes they would be—they would use them in the sessions, sometimes they would not want to play with them. I would say it was about 40% of the time after that initial interviewing process did we use the dolls.

◆ ◆ ◆

> Therapist: Then I asked her to help me clarify what it is that she had told me happened, to use the dolls to describe it, but the dolls had been in the room from the time she first came here to see me and . . . I'm not saying that she undressed them every time, but she used to bathe them, and I think, for the most part, she took their clothes off most of the time.

Any person can obtain a set of dolls if they can afford to purchase them (approximately $250 for a set of four dolls). When we ordered a set of these dolls for our research, described later, the only information to arrive in the package was a five-page unannotated bibliography of the research literature and clinical articles in the area. There were no suggested procedures for their use, nor caveats about their potential misuse. Consistent with this experience are the results of surveys carried out at the end of the 1980s indicating that few professionals had received formal training in the use of anatomically detailed dolls (Boat & Everson, 1988). A few years later, a survey of Boston-area mental health professionals and forensic interviewers who used dolls showed that this situation had improved (Kendall-Tackett & Watson, 1992). In this study, 97% of those surveyed had received some training in the use of the dolls. However, because the Boston area contains so many universities, medical schools, and hospitals, which encourage and provide training, these figures may greatly overestimate the number of trained professionals outside of the Boston area. Furthermore, it is difficult to judge the quality of the training that these professionals received: This training could include a number of different activities such as reviewing written or taped instructions (which presumably arrive with the dolls) or attending workshops or professional meetings. The training is only as good as the qualifications and experience of the instructors—which cannot be ascertained from the details of the study.

Because of these concerns, the use of anatomically detailed dolls for the purposes of providing legal evidence has been banned in a few juris-dictions until further scientific data can be produced to attest to their validity. The American Psychological Association's (APA's) Council of Representatives formally adopted the following statement on the use of anatomically detailed dolls in forensic evaluations:

> Anatomically detailed dolls are widely used in conducting assessments in cases of alleged child sexual abuse. In general, such dolls may be useful in helping children to communicate when their language skills or emotional concerns preclude direct verbal responses. These dolls may also be useful communication props to help older children who may have difficulty expressing themselves verbally on sexual topics. . . . These dolls are available from a variety of vendors and are readily sold to anyone who wishes to purchase them. The design, detail, and nature of the dolls vary considerably across manufacturers. Neither the dolls, nor their use, are standardized or accompanied by normative data. There are currently no uniform standards for conducting inter-views with the dolls. . . . We urge continued research in quest of more and better data regarding the stimulus properties of such dolls and normative behavior of abused and non-abused children. (statement is-sued by the APA Council of Representatives, February 8, 1991, p. 1; cited in Koocher et al., in press)

At the present time, there are at least 20 studies that address concerns related to the use of anatomically detailed dolls. In the next part of this chapter, we describe and critique the scientific basis of this literature. And then we attempt to generalize these findings to actual forensic and thera-peutic interviews that we have taken from the case materials.

RESEARCH ON ANATOMICALLY DETAILED DOLLS

We describe three related areas of study that address the following three issues: (a) Do abused children interact with the dolls differently than do nonabused children? (b) How do normal children interact with the dolls? and (c) How accurately do children use dolls to report events? (See

Berry & Skinner, 1993; Ceci & Bruck, 1993b; Wolfner, Faust, & Dawes, 1993, for detailed reviews of these studies.)

Comparisons of Abused and Nonabused Children's Play With Anatomically Detailed Dolls

At the time of this writing, there are at least eight studies that compare abused and nonabused children's interactions with anatomically detailed dolls. The specific details of the methods vary among studies, but they contain some of the following components: First, children play freely with a set of dolls (there is always at least one male and one female doll). Then the children are shown the dolls' "special" body parts and are asked to name them; in some cases, the interviewer leaves the room to allow the child to play with the dolls. In some studies, the number of times that the children play with the dolls in sexually suggestive or explicit ways is counted; in other studies, raters view the children's doll play and then classify children as "abused" or "not abused" on the basis of how the child positions the dolls, how she touches them, and so forth.

The results of these studies are inconsistent, with three of them (August & Forman, 1989; Jampole & Weber, 1987; White, Strom, Santili, & Halpin, 1986) providing support for the diagnostic utility of anatomically correct dolls. In these studies, children with known or suspected histories of abuse played with the dolls differently than children with no histories of abuse: These target children were more likely to enact a sexual activity with the dolls, to make more reference to the dolls' private parts, to show more avoidance of the dolls, and generally to demonstrate "suspicious" behaviors in their doll play. Although doll play discriminated statistically between the two groups in these three studies, it is important to note that it was not a perfect indicator of which children were abused. Some children in the abused group did not show distinctive behaviors; in other cases, children in the nonabused group were mistaken for abused children. Thus, although the abused children did, on average, engage in more sexual acts with the dolls, there were many exceptions.

On the other hand, the results of five other studies indicate that there are no reliable differences in the doll play of children referred for sexual abuse and nonabused children. In two of these studies, both groups of children showed low and equal rates of sexually explicit behaviors with the dolls (Cohn, 1991; Kenyon-Jump, Burnette, & Robertson, 1991). In two other studies, highly trained professionals could not accurately differentiate abused from nonabused children on the basis of a doll-centered assessment conducted by an experienced child psychiatrist (Realmuto, Jensen, & Wescoe, 1990; Realmuto & Wescoe, 1992). In the fifth study, abused and non-abused preschoolers both showed the same high levels of sexual and aggressive behavior with the dolls (McIver, Wakefield, & Underwager, 1989).

(It is important to point out that this last report has been criticized for the failure to differentiate between explicit sexual behavior and aggressive behavior.)

There are a variety of factors that may account for the inconsistent results and that also limit the interpretation of these studies. These include variability in the delays between the disclosure of abuse and the experimental interview, the length of the interview sessions, the use of different procedures for eliciting doll play, and the failure to "blind" the interviewer (or, in some cases, the raters) to the abuse status of the child. Although each of these are potentially important, we dwell on only two factors.

First, in most of the studies, children "suspected" of being abused were compared with children "not suspected" of abuse. As there was rarely any validation of group membership, it is likely that some of the children were misclassified; that is, some children who were assigned to the "abused" group may not have been abused, whereas some who were assigned to the nonabused group may have been abused. The failure to include children with verified abuse may result in an *underestimate* of the diagnostic utility of the dolls because truly abused children who are misassigned to the nonabused group would behave more like their nonabused peers; conversely, nonabused children misassigned to the abused group would behave like their abused peers.

The second important factor that limits the interpretation of the results of these studies concerns differences in the abused and nonabused samples' experiences with the dolls, in particular, and with being interviewed about sexual abuse, in general. In many of the studies that have demonstrated differences in the doll play of abused and nonabused children, those in the abused sample had received prior evaluations for sexual abuse. If in these pre-experimental interviews children suspected of abuse were asked about sexual abuse, if they were shown drawings of human figures and asked to show where they were touched, and/or if they were encouraged by their parents, law enforcement officials, and social workers to discuss sexual themes freely prior to the experimental interview, any one of these experiences could culminate in sexualized behavior in doll-centered interviews regardless of whether the child had been sexually abused. In contrast, the children in the nonabused samples in the literature described above had their first experience with dolls in the experimental setting, and would presumably not have been involved in any previous interviews that might have encouraged the discussion of sexual themes. Thus, the existing data on the diagnostic utility of the dolls are difficult to interpret because abused and nonabused subjects were not equated in terms of their prior experiences with all sexual-related activities, particularly the encouragement to discuss sexual themes or the exploration of the dolls' genitalia. Perhaps if the nonabused children had received doll-based interviews before they participated in the experiment, they would have interacted with the dolls similarly to the abused children. This failure to equate for prior experiences of abused and nonabused children may have resulted in an *overestimate* of the diagnostic utility of the dolls.

In summary, the failure of any single study to control for the variables we have discussed greatly reduces the interpretation and generalizability of its results. The ideal study would be one in which all children experienced their first interviews and first interactions with the dolls in the experimental setting. Ideally, there should be three groups of children: children referred for assessment of sexual abuse who, on the basis of assessments not involving the use of the dolls, are eventually diagnosed as "sexually abused"; children referred for assessment of sexual abuse who, on the basis of assessments not involving the use of the dolls, are eventually judged not to have been sexually abused; and nonabused children with no suspicion of abuse. However, because of the difficulties in obtaining valid corroborating information about sexual abuse that would meet scientific standards, other lines of study have had to be undertaken to investigate the diagnostic utility of the dolls.

Normative Studies of Nonabused Children's Play With Anatomically Detailed Dolls

This line of study represents an attempt to provide more details on how children who are not suspected of being abused play with anatomical dolls. The general format of these studies involves watching the child play with the dolls in an unstructured free-play situation, then showing the child the dolls' private parts (sometimes the child is asked to name the body parts), and then leaving the child to play with the doll alone.

One general finding from these studies is that when children not suspected of abuse are given the dolls to play with, few, if any, demonstrate explicit sexual activity (e.g., Gabriel, 1985; Glaser & Collins, 1989; Herbert, Grams, & Goranson, 1987; Sivan, Schor, Koeppl, & Noble, 1988). However, there are many children who show reticence or avoidance of the dolls (Glaser & Collins, 1989) or, at the other extreme, overt interest in the genitalia of anatomically detailed dolls (Gabriel, 1985). For example, Herbert et al. (1987) conducted doll-centered interviews with 14 preschool children. The interviewer asked each child if anyone had touched their genitalia, and then these researchers followed up with more specific questions. None of the children used the dolls to demonstrate sexual intercourse. However, 50% of the children did insert their finger in the opening for the vagina or anus, and most stroked or tugged the penis or used it as a handle to swing the dolls. Also, most children indicated their wish to terminate the interview before it was finished.

Everson and Boat (1990) asked whether children between the ages of 2 and 6 years old would use the dolls to show suggestive intercourse positioning or explicit intercourse positioning. They observed over 200 children who first played with dolls in the presence of an interviewer who asked the child to show what the dolls could do; then the child played with the dolls alone. None of the 2-year-olds showed suggestive or clear intercourse positioning. A small but significant proportion of the older children did show suggestive positioning, especially in the interviewer-present condition (perhaps this was because the children were instructed to show what the dolls could do together). Ten percent, 9%, and 18% of the 3-, 4-, and 5-year-olds, respectively, demonstrated suggestive positioning. When the interviewer left the room, the children were more likely to demonstrate clear intercourse positioning; these rates varied from 3% for the 3-year-olds to 12% for the 5-year-olds. When the data were further analyzed in terms of race, social class, and gender, only Black boys from lower social class backgrounds showed clear intercourse positioning in the interviewer-present condition (27% of the cases). When children played with the dolls alone, the highest rates of explicit sexual play occurred for Black boys and girls from lower social class backgrounds. On the basis of these data, Everson and Boat concluded that explicit sexual play with anatomical dolls is an uncommon occurrence among nonabused children; higher rates of such behavior are associated with demographic characteristics such as age, socioeconomic status, race, and gender. However, as the authors cautioned, "because of small cell sizes, these results must be considered to be only exploratory in nature, but they suggest the existence of demographic pockets in our society in which the exposure of preschool-aged children to the mechanics of sexual intercourse is commonplace"(p. 742).

As mentioned earlier, one concern that has been raised in relation to the use of anatomically detailed dolls is their potential suggestive influences on children's subsequent behavior. That is, perhaps after doll-centered interviews, nonabused children display highly sexualized behavior that may be misconstrued as symptomatic of abuse. To determine if their subjects' initial exposure to the anatomical dolls had any long-lasting influences, Boat, Everson, and Holland (1990) interviewed a subsample of mothers of the 3-, 4-, and 5-year-old children who had played with the dolls 2 weeks previously in the Everson and Boat (1990) study just described. None of the mothers of 5-year-old children reported any noticeable behaviors that may have been related to the doll play. However, 37% of mothers of 3-, and 4-year-old children reported that there were behavioral sequelae to the doll play; their children showed increased sexual interests that involved talking or asking about sexual parts. In addition, 50% of the mothers of this age group believed that their children's behaviors were more sexually focused. However, the authors considered these to be benign behaviors that would not lead to a later interpretation or question of sexual abuse. Nevertheless, these data do indicate that after one exposure to the dolls, preschool children's behaviors are noticeably different as viewed by their mothers. It is also true that, as the authors pointed out, the mothers in this study had a point of reference: the previous doll interviews with their children. Thus, when the children showed behaviors with sexual connotations, these did not raise any suspicions in the parents. But suppose that the child was involved in an investigation of sexual abuse and that after a doll-centered interview, the child showed heightened awareness of body parts and an increased focus on sexual matters. In this hypothetical case, the same behaviors that were of little concern to the mothers in the Everson and Boat study might now raise some alarm and suspicion of sexual abuse in parents whose children are undergoing doll-centered investigative interviews. It is possible that months later some parents, when attempting to recall past symptoms associated with abuse, might misidentify the source of such behavior.

To summarize, the results of these normative studies suggest a number of conclusions. First, both avoidance of the dolls *and* preoccupation with the dolls' genitalia is fairly common among nonabused samples; thus, these behaviors cannot be considered as diagnostic of sexual abuse. Second, the results of these studies indicate that normal children show very low rates of sexually explicit behavior when playing with anatomically detailed dolls for the first time. Everson and Boat (1990) estimated that less than 2% of the children in all of the normative studies showed sexually explicit behavior; variations in rate may be explained by demographic factors. And third, after a single exposure to the dolls, a significant proportion of 3- and 4-year-olds exhibit increased interest in sexual play and the discussion of sexual themes. This last conclusion brings us full circle to our earlier caution about the effects of prior interviews: In those studies that have compared abused children's doll play with the doll play of nonabused children, any differences could be due to the former group's prior exposure to the dolls (during actual investigations) rather than to the dolls' diagnostic validity. Even nonabused children exhibit heightened sexual interest following a single doll experience (Boat et al., 1990).

Effects of Anatomical and Nonanatomical Dolls on Children's Reports

Because the studies discussed in the previous section did not ask children to use the dolls to depict a previously experienced event, the results do not reflect how accurately children report events through the use of the dolls, and they do not reflect the degree to which dolls may increase the accuracy of children's reports over what would be obtained without the dolls. This, in fact, is the crucial issue in evaluating the usefulness of dolls in interviews. If young children cannot use dolls accurately to depict certain events, then there is little justification for using them in forensic or therapeutic interviews, because the children's demonstrations with the dolls, whatever they may be, would have to be viewed with caution. In this section, we describe a number of recent studies that examined non-abused children's accuracy when they were asked to use dolls to enact previously experienced events that had been staged or observed by the experimenter. The advantage of these studies is that the examiner knew the details of what was being investigated, and could therefore precisely determine the degree to which dolls influence the accuracy of children's reports.

Goodman and Aman (1990) questioned 3- and 5-year-old children 1 week after the children had played games with a male experimenter. Children were asked to provide general information about their recollection of the event, and they were also asked straightforward as well as misleading questions, some of which related to sexual abuse (e.g., "Did he touch your private parts?"). The children answered these questions in one of the four following interview conditions: (a) anatomical dolls, (b) regular dolls (with no anatomical details), (c) regular dolls that the child could see but not touch, and (d) no dolls. The children with access to the dolls were encouraged to use the dolls to show what happened. Goodman and Aman found that the children's recall of events and answers to all questions were similar across all conditions, with 5-year-olds consistently giving more detailed and accurate reports than 3-year-olds. Thus, in this study, anatomical dolls did not promote inaccurate reports of sexual events among nonabused children. It is important to note, however, that the dolls did not facilitate accurate memory of this neutral event either, suggesting that the mnemonic value of the dolls may be limited. Furthermore, the fact that the 3-year-olds did not show any benefit from the use of the dolls suggests that one of the premises for the use of the dolls may be faulty. One would expect that given their more limited verbal competence, the 3-year-olds would have benefited from the dolls to a greater extent than the older children. But this was not the case.

A study by Ornstein and his colleagues (Gordon et al., 1993) raises further doubts about the usefulness of dolls to obtain accurate reports from young children. Three- and 5-year-old children were asked to report the details of a medical check-up; some children were questioned verbally with no props, whereas other children were questioned verbally with the use of a doll (the dolls were not anatomically detailed). These researchers found that the dolls provided "some" assistance to the older children in their recall; however, for the 3-year-olds, the provision of the dolls actually lowered recall in certain instances.

Perhaps anatomically detailed dolls enhance children's reports of embarrassing events of a sexual nature. One of the purported benefits of the dolls is to provide children with a tool that will allow them to overcome their shyness and embarrassment concerning sexual matters. To address this issue, Saywitz et al. (1991) asked children to recall a doctor's visit, where they had received either a genital examination or a scoliosis examination (some of the details of this study were discussed in chapter 6). In the scoliosis condition, the doctor did not touch the children's genitalia and buttocks, but he did touch the children's genitalia and buttocks in the genital condition. When the children were asked for a verbal report of their genital examination, 78% of the children who had received a genital examination failed to disclose that the doctor had touched their genitals ("omission" errors). When given the opportunity to provide the same information with the dolls ("show me with the dolls what happened"), 83% of the children failed to disclose genital touching. However, when the experimenter pointed to the genitalia of the doll and asked a direct question ("Did the doctor touch you here?"), only 14% of the responses were incorrect denials. The figures were similar when children were asked about anal touching: 89% of the children failed to mention anal touching in free recall and in demonstration with the dolls, but when asked a direct question with the aid of the doll, 69% of the children correctly disclosed. Children who received a scoliosis examination with no genital touching never made a false report in the verbal free-recall or doll-enactment conditions. However, 2.86% of the children falsely affirmed vaginal touch and 5.56% falsely affirmed anal touch when the experimenter pointed to the genital or anal region of the doll and asked, "Did the doctor touch you here?"

Thus, the scoliosis examination results indicate that regardless of interviewing technique, children rarely if ever make false reports about genital touching unless they are asked direct questions with the dolls. The genital examination results, however, indicate that many children will not divulge potentially embarrassing material unless the interviewer uses direct questions with the dolls. What remains unknown from this study is whether it is possible to have obtained the same result without the use of the dolls but merely through the use of a direct verbal question ("Did the doctor touch your privates?").

The results of these three experiments do not support the notion that dolls enhance the recall of the youngest children. These results are also in conflict with our common intuitions that because young children play with dolls (or other pretend animals) in such elaborate and creative ways, they therefore should be able to transfer these play skills to an interview situation. The work of Judy DeLoache, a developmental psychologist at the University of Illinois, suggests that these intuitions are wrong. Specifically, her work attacks the notion that very young children can treat a doll as though it is a model of themselves. DeLoache's findings demonstrate that children under the age of 3 years have great difficulty in dealing with three-dimensional symbolic representations. For example, when young children watch an experimenter place a toy under a chair in a room, they cannot find a smaller version of the toy in an exact small-scale model of the room—that is, they cannot find the toy under the small chair. Deloache suggests that young children have difficulty finding the toy in the model because they do not understand the relationships between the symbol (i.e., the small-scale model) and the actual object. This work suggests that perhaps young children might have difficulty using a doll to enact real-life events because to be successful, they must treat the doll as a symbol of themselves. The task is even more difficult in doll-centered interviews because the dolls are not exact replicas of the real object (the child).

A recent study by DeLoache and Marzolf (in press) reveals how difficult it is for young children to accurately use dolls as symbolic objects. These experimenters used dolls to interview 2-, 3-, and 4-year-old children about a play session they had just experienced in which a male experimenter played Simon Says and placed stickers on different parts of the children's clothed bodies. The dolls did not help the children report their experiences in a subsequent interview. The younger children, in particular, gave fuller and more accurate accounts of where they had been touched without the dolls than they did with the dolls. When asked to place stickers on the doll in the same places that stickers had been placed on their own bodies, the younger children were not very successful. Indeed, many of them did not seem to realize that they were supposed to treat the doll as a representation of themselves. Furthermore, several children rejected the suggestion that they "pretend that this doll is you." This last finding is important because a reluctance to play with dolls in forensic or therapeutic interview sessions is sometimes taken as a possible indicant of abuse (see Mason, 1991). Generally, these results indicate that very young children may not have the cognitive sophistication to use a doll to represent their own experiences. Hence, the use of dolls with this age group may actually impede or distort accurate communication, rather than facilitate and clarify it.

We recently completed a study that shares some similarities with the studies already described in this section but that also goes beyond them in a number of ways. In our study (Bruck, Ceci, Francoeur, & Renick, 1995), 3-year-old children visited their doctor for a routine medical examination. Half of these children received a genital examination where the pediatrician gently touched their buttocks and genitals. The other half of the children were not touched in these areas. Immediately after the examination, an experimenter pointed to the genitalia or buttocks of an anatomically detailed doll and asked the child, "Did the doctor touch you here?" Only 47% of the children who received the genital exam correctly answered yes, a figure approximating that obtained by others for errors of omission (i.e., saying no when something really did happen). On the other hand, 50% of the children who did *not* receive a genital exam incorrectly answered yes to this question (i.e., 50% of these children falsely reported touching or made "errors of commission"). When the children were simply asked to "show on the doll" how the doctor had touched their buttocks or genitalia, accuracy did not improve. Now only 25% of the children who had received genital examinations correctly showed how the pediatrician had touched their genitals and buttocks. Accuracy decreased in part because a significant number of female subjects inserted their fingers into the anal or genital cavities of the dolls—something that the pediatrician never did. When the children who did not receive a genital examination were asked to show on the doll how the doctor had touched their genitals and buttocks, only 50% of the children correctly showed no touching; 50% of the children who did not receive genital examinations falsely showed either genital or anal touching when given the dolls.

Our findings indicate that a substantial proportion of 3-year-old children are inaccurate when reporting how and where they were touched, even when the touching occurred within 5 minutes of the interview. Children who were not touched demonstrated on the dolls that they *were* touched, and children who were touched either refused to admit that they were touched or, at the other extreme, showed penetration when none had occurred. The use of the dolls seems to increase this type of inaccurate reporting in 3-year-old children.

The interview procedures in our study also elicited a number of other behaviors that adults might interpret as sexual. When the children were given a stethoscope and asked to show what the doctor did with it, some children incorrectly showed on their own bodies that he used the instrument to examine their genitals. The children were also shown a small spoon and asked whether the doctor had used it (the doctor had not used a spoon). A number of the children were inaccurate, stating that he had given them medicine with it. When the children were asked, "How might he use this spoon?" (this was a question asked of some of the children in the Michaels case; chapter 2), a small but significant number of them (18%) inserted the spoon into the doll's genital or anal openings or hit the doll's genitals with it.

We believe that these "sexualized" behaviors do not reflect 3-year-old children's sexual knowledge or experiences, but rather two other factors. First, the types of questions and props used in an interview (asking children to name body parts, including genitals, showing children anatomically detailed dolls, and asking children to manipulate these dolls) may lead 3-year-olds to think that it is not only permissible but expected to respond to the interviewers' questions using these same terms. Second, perhaps the children insert fingers or objects into the dolls' openings for the same reasons they would insert a finger into the hole of a doughnut; it is there, it is something to manipulate, it "affords" this activity.

The results of this study are somewhat startling because they show that 3-year-old children are not particularly accurate in giving details of bodily touches for an event that happened 5 minutes prior to an interview.

Furthermore, many of these children made verbal or nonverbal reports of genital touching or digital penetration even though none occurred. The use of the dolls increased this inaccuracy mainly because of false reporting of genital touching or digital penetration. These findings stand in stark contrast to those obtained by Saywitz et al. (1991), who found that not a single 5-year-old exhibited such errors of commission. The major explanatory factor appears to be differences in the ages of the children tested. Unlike the 5-year-olds in the Saywitz et al. study, 3-year-old children may be highly inaccurate when using the dolls to report bodily touches; their inaccuracy when demonstrating on the dolls may merely reflect their poor accuracy in reporting bodily touches.[1] But, as we have already noted, it is precisely the younger children for whom the dolls are claimed to be needed to lessen embarrassment and surmount their linguistic limitations. By the time children are 5 years old (the age of the children in the Saywitz et al. study), there appears to be little advantage to doll use, because their verbal skills are sufficient to express their experiences.

ANATOMICAL DOLLS IN FORENSIC CONTEXTS: THE BRIDGE BETWEEN RESEARCH AND PRACTICE

In the previous section, we discussed over 20 experimental studies that examined children's interactions with dolls. Although the data, taken together, do not present persuasive evidence for the value of dolls in forensic and therapeutic settings, there are small pockets of data that would appear to provide some support for the validity of doll-centered interviews. Specifically, the results of the studies that examined the doll play of abused versus nonabused children provide the most support for the use of dolls in forensic and therapeutic interviews. However, we feel that these types of studies are not very relevant to the issue of the diagnostic utility of anatomically detailed dolls because those interviewing procedures bear little relationship to the procedures used in actual interviews with children suspected of sexual abuse. In the latter situation, children are rarely observed for over an hour in a free play situation, nor are these children merely asked to undress a doll and name its body parts. Rather, children are asked direct, leading, and misleading questions about abuse with the dolls, and they are often asked to reenact alleged abusive experiences. Often, when children do not respond to the interviewer's questions, they are repeated or rephrased.[2]

---

[1]Our ongoing work indicates that the problems persist even with 4-year-olds (Bruck, Ceci, & Francoeur, 1995).

[2]This assertion is based on our reviews of many videotapes of doll-based interviews that have been conducted by mental health professionals both in the sample cases and elsewhere.

As one example of the dubious generalizability of the studies in question, consider the following example from the Little Rascals day-care case. Mrs. F. was the mother of one of the suspected abuse victims, and her testimony concerned the police officer's first interview with her son Fred. She eavesdropped on the doll-centered interview from an adjacent room, and testified as to what she heard through the wall:

> Mrs. F.: She (the female officer) asked Fred what he liked to play with. He went and got some of his He-Man guys, and he said that those were what he wanted to play with. After a few minutes of the playing back and forth she said she had dolls with her. And he said, no, he preferred playing with his. And she said, you know, she had some she wanted him to see.
>
> I couldn't see what was going on, but at some point the dolls came out. I remember clearly her saying, "You do realize the difference between little boys and little girls, and little boys have a penis and little girls have opening here," and that's when my husband and I looked at each other and got real upset, and realized for the first time that . . . we were talking about some type of sexual abuse here. My husband wanted to stop the interview right then. I asked him just to hang on and let's see what Fred has to say.
>
> She asked him about pretending and did he know how to pretend, and he said "yes." . . . She asked him to pretend that this doll was Mr. Bob and this (other) doll was him. I remember him at one point saying, "I don't want to be the girl doll." He kept getting his toys back out. I don't think he was very attentive. He didn't like playing with her toys. . . . At some point, and I'm not sure how, because it was difficult sometimes to hear her because she was speaking softly, she demonstrated something, I'm surmising because she said, "Have you ever seen anyone do this," and "Have you ever seen this?" Um, at one point he said, "That's gross." I'm not sure what he saw, but that was his reply.
>
> Attorney: Had your son ever been exposed to that type of anatomical doll prior to this occasion?
>
> Mrs. F.: No, but after she left he understood intercourse. He asked me why anybody would want to do that which I think was inappropriate for someone that age. He thought it was pretty disgusting, and thanks to their interview at that young age he was well versed in what it was.

A number of the procedures used in this interview are absent in the experimental studies described in the first part of this chapter. First, the child was asked to pretend that the dolls represented the defendant and himself. Asking the child to pretend may have overridden the understanding that he should be telling the truth, because he was given permission to pretend. Next, this child was given instruction on the sexual parts of the doll. Finally, it seemed that the interviewer manipulated the dolls into sexually explicit positions. In this one case, it does not appear that these suggestive techniques were associated with the child making allegations of sexual abuse. In fact, this one child appeared to react negatively to the whole interview. However, it is still possible that a nonabused child who was interviewed in this manner might be easily coaxed into pretense play that mimics the sexual demonstrations of the interviewer, especially if he were to be interviewed a second time. In other words, maybe little Fred might react differently the second time he is interviewed with the dolls, not because they are valid diagnostic tools, but rather because he has become bored with doing the ordinary things with them and begins to explore their cavities. This is the essence of one of the criticisms of doll studies that we raised in the first part of this chapter.

In our materials, there are numerous other examples of a disjunction or mismatch between research procedures and clinical practices that further caution us against drawing generalizations from the research literature to clinical or forensic practice. The examples provided by Mrs. F. are far from unique. Adults manipulated dolls in a number of sessions we reviewed. Sometimes parents were co-opted into this role. For example, another parent in the Little Rascals case described a therapy session involving her young daughter; her daughter's therapist, Ms. J.; and herself:

Mother: And I asked her, "Does this doll look like Mr. Bob?"
And she said, "Sort of."
And then she was standing near me, and Ms. J. was over there because this had turned into such a spontaneous thing. She didn't have a tape going to record the session; she was over there trying to write down what was being said.
And Ms. J. asked me to ask her—she was mouthing it—if Mr. Bob's penis was soft or hard.
And I did. I said, "Was Mr. Bob's penis soft or hard?"
And she said, "It was soft." And I said, "How do you know?"
She said, "Because I had to touch it."
And then I said—she [Ms. J.] asked me to ask her what position his penis was in. All of this was very embarrassing. And I said, "Barbara, was Mr. Bob's penis like this," holding it up (indicating), "Or was it like this?" holding it down (indicating), "Or was it like this?" (holding it straight out). So Ms. J. handed—gave me or instructed me. I'm not, you know, sure exactly how we got the doll, gave me the female adult anatomical doll and I undressed the doll and I said, "Barbara, does this doll look like somebody you've seen?"

In another interview in the same case, an experienced child interviewer showed a videotape to the jury of a doll-assessment interview that she conducted with one of the child witnesses. This interviewer, like Barbara's mother, undressed the dolls before the child had a chance to respond whether she was dressed or undressed. Then the interviewer pointed to various parts of the doll's anatomy and asked the child questions of a sexual nature. Our research on 3-year-old children's interactions with anatomical dolls suggests that children may supply answers about how they think they were dressed or how they think things looked by simply looking at the doll and reporting what they see on the doll (Bruck, Ceci, Francoeur, & Renick, 1995). For example, in our study, we had the children take the socks off the doll, and then we asked them whether their socks were on or off during their pediatric examination. In all cases, the children replied that their socks were off during the examination. We suspect that they took their cues for this inaccurate answer by looking at the doll. Of course, none of their socks were off during the pediatric examination.

In the Little Rascals case, dolls also were used in many therapeutic and investigative sessions with the children. In one memorable example, after Sue had been in therapy for a number of months, she was interviewed with the dolls three times in one week. Interviews were carried out with her therapist and the investigating police officer, and the final interview was conducted by another mental health professional at a university hospital unit that specialized in the assessment of sexually abused children. The latter interview was videotaped and presented as evidence by the prosecution. Note the following interaction at the beginning of this interview:

Interviewer: I've got some special dolls here; they're special because they have all their body parts. Have you ever seen dolls like this before, that have all their body parts?

Sue: (shakes her head no)

It is not clear whether this highly trained interviewer had reviewed the record of this child and had known that this child had been subjected to many doll-centered interviews. Certainly, given the publicity of this case, she at least might have suspected that there had been previous interviews. Even several years later, when she took the stand, this interviewer did not qualify her remarks about her interpretation of this interview, given her knowledge that this child had had multiple previous interviews with the dolls.

We keep coming back to this issue of the effect of multiple prior interviews with dolls on children's reports. On the one hand, we admit that our conjectures are not backed by any definitive empirical data. On the other hand, on the basis of the literature that documents the effects of repeated suggestive interviews on children's reports, we predict that there should be effects of repeated interviews with dolls, especially when there is a suggestive component. One case study of a normal nonabused child also leads us to predict that perhaps repeated nonsuggestive interviews with dolls will result in tainted reports. We now describe this pilot study (Bruck, Ceci, Francoeur, & Renick, 1995).

A three-and-a-half-year-old nonabused girl was examined by a pediatrician. She was not given a genital examination. Immediately after the examination, when interviewed by the experimenter, she correctly said that the doctor had not touched her genitals or buttocks. Furthermore, when shown an anatomically detailed doll and told to show how the doctor had touched her genitals and buttocks, she correctly stated that he had not touched her. Three days later, the same child was given an anatomically detailed doll and asked to show all the things that the doctor had done in her previous visit. This time, she inserted a stick into the vagina of the doll and said that this had happened at the doctor's office. However, upon further questioning, she said that the doctor had not done this. Three days later, the child was asked to use the anatomically detailed doll to show her father everything that had happened at the examination. This time, she hammered a stick into the doll's vagina and then inserted a toy earscope into the doll's anus. When asked if this really happened, she said, "Yes it did." When her father and the experimenter both tried to debrief her with such statements as "Your doctor doesn't do those things to little girls. You were just fooling. We know he didn't do those things," the 3-year-old tenaciously clung to her claims that she had just demonstrated on the doll.

Thus, repeated exposure to the doll, with minimal suggestions, resulted in highly sexualized play for this 3-year-old subject. Although this pilot observation calls for more systematic research on the influence of repeated exposure to anatomically detailed dolls in interviews with sexual themes, the dramatic and startling results of this one subject show the potential suggestiveness of anatomical dolls with nonabused 3-year-olds. And even though it is a single example, it vividly negates extremist claims that the dolls cannot lead to such behaviors.

There are further examples of how the conditions in which children are interviewed in research studies diverge from those conditions present in actual forensic interviews. In the Michaels case, anatomically detailed dolls were shown to the children before they said anything about abuse in 20 of the 39 interviews. In 17 of these interviews, silverware was given to the children and they were asked questions such as the following:

Interviewer: Did Kelly ever do anything to you with a knife that hurt you or bad things to you with a knife?

Child: No.

Interviewer: Did she ever do bad things or hurt you with a spoon?

Child: No.

Interviewer: Did she ever do bad things or hurt you with a knife?

Child: No.

Interviewer: Okay. What about a wooden spoon?

Child: No.

Four children were asked to speculate about how silverware could have been used. The following are examples:

Interviewer: Why don't you show me how you think a little girl can be hurt by the fork?

◆ ◆ ◆

Interviewer: Why don't you show me what Kelly did with the big wooden spoon?

Often the children resisted these suggestions, but sometimes after much repetition, a child might respond by poking the silverware into the doll's genitalia or buttocks, as is shown in the following:

Interviewer: I mean she was hitting little girls with the wooden spoon, how else would she have done that?

Child: (indicates the arm)

Interviewer: And where else?

Child: Here . . . pimples.

Interviewer: Like the chest, right? Where's that hitting now?

Child: Back.

Interviewer: (After a few more unsuccessful tries, the interviewer changes to a fork.) How do you think Kelly used this fork to hurt little girls? Why don't you show me . . . Where did you put the fork? (after 8 probes of the type "where else?") Is there anywhere else that she put the fork . . . okay . . . where's that?

Child: The bottom.

The information from these interviews contributed to the interviewers' conclusion that the children had been abused and that the abuse involved the use of utensils. In our own study of 3-year-olds' reports of their medical check-ups, we found a small proportion of children who quickly inserted the spoon into one of the doll's openings or hit the doll's genitals with it. (Apparently, we were more successful than the interviewers in the Kelly Michaels case because the latter rarely if ever got children to make a sexualized report when first asked how one might use a spoon.)

Other examples of practices used with the children in doll-centered interviews involved having the interviewer name the dolls after the defendant (some of the transcribed interviews in the Michaels case reveal investigators naming a doll Kelly rather than allowing the child to do so) and then berate them (the symbolic dolls) for alleged abuses against the children; assuming the role of fantasy characters in doll play; and creating a persistent atmosphere of accusation. Perhaps one of the most salient features of some of these interviews is that the dolls provided the interviewers with opportunities to ask persistent questions involving sexual themes that went beyond the knowledge and experience of the child interviewees. The following is taken from the Michaels case:

> Interviewer: Did Kelly and Brenda [another teacher] do anything to each other? . . . What did Kelly and Brenda do to each other? . . . Did they kiss? . . . Huh? Nobody can hear us. What did Kelly and Brenda do to each other? What? They kissed? Is that what you're showing me? I can't hear you. They kissed?

We have presented a number of examples of how clinical practices diverge from experimental presentations of anatomically detailed dolls. We did this for two reasons. First, as we have argued earlier, this disjunction between research and practice makes it difficult if not impossible to draw any generalizations from children's doll play in highly sanitized experimental settings to how abused or nonabused children might interact with dolls in actual forensic and therapeutic situations. As seen, the latter settings are often imbued with fantasy play, accusatory atmospherics, and persistent discussions of sexual themes, whereas experimental settings are not.

Second, as we have pointed out elsewhere, practitioners frequently seem to be unaware of the available research results and, as a result, misinterpret children's doll play. For example, in a recent survey of what professionals consider normal behavior with anatomical dolls, only 16% of mental health and law professionals felt that avoidance of the dolls was normal, and 80% rated digital penetration as abnormal (Kendall-Tackett, 1991). However, the existing data consistently indicate that these types of behaviors are common among nonabused children. One might argue that perhaps Kendall-Tackett's data are specific to this one sample of professionals, who may have had limited training. However, these were the same professionals who, according to Kendall-Tackett & Watson (1992), had received extensive training in the use of the dolls. This underscores our earlier point that the amount of training received by an interviewer may not be an indicator of the competence of the interviewer, particularly if the trainers are unaware of the research literature.

As an example of how children's interactions with the dolls seems to have been misinterpreted by professionals who are unaware of the research, we turn once more to the Little Rascals case and review some of the trial testimony of Brenda Toppin, the police officer who, along with a social worker, conducted the first interviews with the children involved in the case. According to Toppin's testimony, she had received 80 hours of advanced training in sexual abuse investigations, and this training included how to interview children and how to use anatomically correct dolls. According to Toppin's testimony at trial, the dolls were used in five of the initial interviews with the children who testified in court. Here are her descriptions of these interactions with the preschoolers:

Child 1

Toppin: He pulled the pants down. I do not recall if he took them completely off, but he did pull them down. He took the underpants down. I always tell the kids that these are special tools and they have all their body parts. And that's usually all I tell them. And he took the little penis and he pulled it like this (indicating), and he turned the doll over and he put the finger in the anus like that (indicating).

Child 2

Toppin: And I was just observing, not really trying to get anything out of him with that, and he just started playing with the doll. And he killed the doll. The doll fell off the building. He shot the doll. Anything negative that could happen to the doll happened to the doll. I had asked him who the doll was, and he told me that the doll was Mr. Bob. Mr. Bob was ugly. He hated Mr. Bob and Miss Betsy.

Attorney: At any time did he take any of the clothes off of any dolls?

Toppin: No.

Attorney: Did he do anything sexual with any of the dolls?

Toppin: No.

Child 3

Toppin: Well, after we got into the interview, we let Nat use the dolls. And he showed us that Mr. Bob touched Jim all over with his pants down. He said that Mr. Bob spanks Jim because he does not go to sleep and then he puts him in the ugly chair. And then he shows on him—a doll that Mr. Bob puts his finger, Mr. Bob's finger, in Jim's rectum and spanks his peenie or—what his term he uses for penis. And when asked if Mr. Bob did this to him—after he had shown us that Mr. Bob did this to Jim, we asked him, you know, if it ever happened to him. He said, "Well, not really. Almost." And then says, "No, not me."

Child 4

[Note: This child was not given anatomically detailed dolls. However, she did have one of her own dolls present during the interview.]

Toppin: And during this time Jill had a doll and she was sitting on the sofa and during the time that we were asking her about the doctor, she just took the doll—just repeatedly hitting the back of the sofa with the doll. Nothing she really said, it was just her actions. She said she didn't like talking about nap time, when she got into nap time.

Child 5

Toppin: After some time had passed and Brett was not going to talk with me, I asked him that if I showed him my special dolls if he would show me. And he showed me that Mr. Bob had pulled his pants down and slacks and his underwear and spanked him on the bottom.

Before discussing the content of these reports, several points must be made about their accuracy. First, we do not know whether these were the only five children who were given dolls during the initial interviews; it is possible that many more children were given dolls, but that only those that showed some unusual behavior were mentioned. Mrs. F., whose description of her own child's doll play was presented earlier, claimed that Officer Toppin did use anatomically detailed dolls in the initial interview with her son; however, there is no mention of doll play in Officer Toppin's report of this interview. Second, Toppin's official report and testimony may be inaccurate because they are based on notes taken during the interview, and these notes were later destroyed. One indication of this is Mrs. F.'s claim that the official written report of her son's interview contained many inaccuracies. For example, the written report stated that her son said, "He (Mr. Bob) never checked butts or dingalings, just knees." At trial, the mother commented, "I'm sorry, my son has never used that word 'dingaling' ever. That word has never been used in my house. My son says wee-wee and pee-pee until he learned the proper words. I've never heard that word used. I don't know where it came from. Maybe some other child used it." We mention this because it seems likely that Officer Toppin's recollections are inaccurate in places—a problem that befalls all of us who try to recall verbatim details from sketchy notes made months earlier. As we have argued throughout this book, memory is highly constructive, and no one is impervious to making serious errors under similar conditions. We shall return to this point in chapter 15 when we discuss the arguments for and against videotaping of interviews.

Even if one assumes that Officer Toppin's testimony is accurate, there is little in the children's first interactions with the dolls to indicate sexual abuse. The children played with the dolls aggressively and sometimes poked their fingers into their openings. However, as was already seen from the research reviewed earlier, all of these behaviors can be found among non-abused children. The fact that the children played with the dolls aggressively may reflect physical abuse, but it may also reflect the effects of 4 months of prior questioning and suspicion about hitting in the day-care center (see chapter 10 for a discussion of this theory). The important point, however, is that according to Officer Toppin, this group of children who were suspected of abuse did not engage in sexually explicit play with the dolls in the first interview. Two different conclusions can be drawn from these observations. On the one hand, if the children were abused, the dolls are not useful tools to help the interviewer extract accurate reports of abuse. On the other hand, if the dolls *are* a useful diagnostic instrument, one might conclude that these children were *not* abused. In this latter case, the interviewer's misinterpretation of the children's interactions with the dolls could form the basis of erroneous allegations of sexual abuse.

CONCLUSIONS

On the basis of the literature reviewed in this chapter, what conclusions can one reach about the feasibility of using anatomically detailed dolls in sexual abuse interviews with very young children? Remember that there are two related issues at stake. The first is the degree to which the dolls are a good diagnostic tool and can reliably differentiate abused from nonabused children. The second, and related, issue is the degree to which the dolls are suggestive and lead to inaccurate reports of abuse either in the initial interview or in subsequent interviews. Different answers to these questions have been expressed by professionals in the field.

At one pole is the opinion that the current research indicates that the dolls are not suggestive. Although this view does not seem to reflect the many factors we have discussed in this chapter, it was espoused in a recent review of the literature by two respected doll researchers:

> The most common criticism of anatomical dolls, that they are suggestive and overly stimulating to sexually naive, young children, is not supported by the available literature. To the contrary, a growing body of research is beginning to raise serious doubts about the validity of this argument against the dolls. In addition, this criticism has only moderate applicability to the use of dolls as demonstrations aids, their most frequently advocated use. Evaluators can be confident in their continued informed use of anatomical dolls in sexual abuse evaluations.

Neither a review of the relevant empirical data nor an examination of the major criticisms leads to the conclusion that anatomical dolls are unsuitable for use, while clinical and research experience suggest that they are a valuable tool. (Everson & Boat, 1994, p. 126)

This point of view is consistent with the APA's concluding remarks in their statement on dolls quoted in the first part of this chapter:

Neither the dolls nor their use are standardized or accompanied by normative data. . . . We urge continued research in quest of more and better data regarding the stimulus properties of such dolls and normative behavior of abused and nonabused children. . . . Nevertheless, doll-centered assessment of children, when used as part of a psychological evaluation and interpreted by experienced and competent examiners, may be the best available practical solution for a pressing and frequent clinical problem. (American Psychological Association, 1992)

The APA's policy position seems contradictory in noting, first, that there are no standardized methods for doll interviews or normative data on nonabused or abused children's doll play, but then in asserting that experienced interviewers may nevertheless find doll-centered assessment the best available method for evaluating children suspected of sexual abuse. Even if one assumes (a) that experienced examiners can avoid making false inferences from children's doll play and (b) that such doll play can provide important clinical insights not obtainable from other sources, the APA should nevertheless codify this expert knowledge in such a way that researchers can accurately assess the incremental validity of doll-based assessments.[3]

A second position reflects our own view. Simply put, we conclude that there is no available scientific evidence that supports the clinical or forensic diagnosis of abuse made primarily on the basis of a very young child's interaction with anatomical dolls (see Berry & Skinner, 1993; Wolfner et al., 1993, for similar conclusions). In part, this position is based on the grounds that an assessment tool should only be used if it provides reliable additional information. There is no evidence that the dolls do this; in fact, in some cases, the dolls seem to impede children's reporting, and

---

[3]By incremental validity we mean the following: Suppose that an evaluator has access to multiple sources of information in trying to determine whether a child was abused (medical test results, child's verbal statement, defendant's psychological profile, child's doll play, parent's report of abrupt behavior change, etc.). The question to be asked is the following: What unique benefit does each source of information provide in the determination of abuse? In statistical terms, the question becomes "What is the incremental validity of each source of information?" A correlation between some behavioral indicator and abuse does not necessarily provide justification for the diagnostic validity of the indicator because it may be correlated with other sources of information, too, such that it provides no independent prediction of abuse. In fact, when this is the case, the use of such information can actually lead to misplaced confidence in an abuse determination because we tend to think that we have uncovered more signs of abuse than we have. In actuality, we may simply have uncovered a chained set of signs that always co-occur (see Ceci & Loftus, 1994, for examples).

in some cases, the dolls appear to lead to false judgments about the status of abused and nonabused children.

Certainly, it could be argued that the appropriate research has not yet been done and, therefore, that such a strong position as the one just stated is premature. As empiricists, we accept the possibility that future research may, in principle, provide support for the use of dolls.[4] But in practice, it is not clear that research can ever be carried out that will generalize to clinical forensic contexts, because for ethical reasons nonabused children cannot be subjected to the sorts of practices seen in many of the case studies (i.e., naming a doll after the defendant, berating the doll for alleged transgressions, assuming the role of fantasy characters in doll play, creating an atmosphere of accusation, persistently interviewing the child with dolls within a short time span, demonstrating suggestive acts with the dolls, encouraging children to discuss sexual themes while in the presence of the dolls, encouraging parents to prompt their children to discuss sexual themes).

Furthermore, we do not find the APA argument persuasive that anatomical dolls are important tools when used by competent clinicians. How are we to define "competent"? How many courses should the clinician take to become experienced in sexual abuse training? What are the qualifications of the trainer of such courses to become certified? What standards do we use to classify some clinicians as "competent" to distinguish them from others? And how can we tell when a competent clinician makes a correct determination? There is too much disagreement in the field about these important matters to be lulled into believing that the entire matter can be solved by such wishful thinking. Finally, we question the claim that trained workers are able to use the dolls in an accurate and sensitive manner. When we have presented workshops and medical grand rounds to those with experience in interviewing children suspected of sexual abuse, we receive very mixed and yet very confident statements about the status of

---

[4]Recently, the APA commissioned a new task force to update its 1991 position. In recognition of some of the difficulties that we have discussed in this chapter, the task force reached the following ambivalent and intellectually unsatisfying conclusion:

> In summary, research to date mainly supports use of AD [anatomically detailed] dolls as a communication or memory aid for children 5 years or older, albeit with a certain risk of contributing to some children's errors if misleading questions are employed. Interestingly, it seems that many children beyond the preschool years are unlikely to make commission errors to abuse inquiries, at least under the conditions examined in the above studies. Greater caution is needed when preschool children are interviewed with AD dolls because of these younger children's greater tendency toward suggestibility and difficulties with symbolic representation. Further research that includes preschool children will provide important clues about interviewing children ages 4 and under with AD dolls. Although findings to date indicate that young preschoolers are more prone than older children to false report in a leading AD doll-aided interview, these results do not rule out AD dolls' potential usefulness in forensic investigations involving young children (Koocher et al., in press).

the 3-year-old children in our anatomical doll study. Although we always begin our presentations by telling the audience that these children do not have any known histories of abuse, nevertheless, there are always a number of professionals who argue this point with us after seeing the children interact sexually with the dolls. Although we cannot rule out that some of these children may have had some prior sexual experience, we find it difficult to believe that there were so many children with histories of previous abuse in this one pediatric sample of 3-year-olds. There are also comments on the other side; some professionals tell us with great confidence that anyone could tell that these children were *not* abused—their affect is "telling," their language is a "give-away," and so on. Later, we will review evidence showing that experienced clinicians are unable to agree with each other about abuse determinations when presented the identical data. So how can we expect the doll's validity to be settled by leaving it to "competent clinicians"? We can't.

In conclusion, we feel at this point that there has been sufficient concern raised in the literature, and enough evidence of potential misuse, without sufficiently counterbalanced evidence to the contrary, to urge that dolls not be used diagnostically, at least not with very young children. Of course, some skilled professionals will decry the loss of a valuable tool without which many children will go undiagnosed and be forced to continue living in an abusive situation. On the other hand, we have reviewed enough studies that demonstrate that *this* tool has the potential for serious misuse, including misdiagnosis, which could result in removing nonabused children from their homes, the implantation of false memories in therapy, and the imprisonment of innocent adults. Both conditions are horrific, and our goal should be to find techniques that minimize both consequences, not to support a technique that guards against one type of error at the expense of increasing the other. To do otherwise is akin to giving the cancer pill to all people, irrespective of their cancer status.

13

THE EVIDENCE FOR DELAYED RECALL OF CHILDHOOD SEXUAL ABUSE

In some of our sample case histories, children did not report abuse immediately; rather, there was a long interval between the alleged events and their reports. Several explanations have been given for such delays. Some professionals claim that the children were so frightened or terrorized by the alleged perpetrator that they purposefully did not divulge details of their abuse. Other experts maintain that because of the traumatic nature of the events, the children avoided thinking about them; the memories of the events became "blocked" or "repressed" (e.g., Kelley, Brant, & Waterman, 1993). These memories are termed "repressed" because they are assumed to have split off from conscious awareness because of their threatening nature. The children were eventually able to recover parts of their memories, it was claimed, because of the supportive interviewing and therapeutic techniques used.

This concept of "blocking" and subsequently "unblocking" repressed traumatic memories has currently found its way into the courtrooms and the media in the form of adults' recovery of "repressed memories" of childhood sexual abuse. Some adults claim to have recovered detailed memories of abuse in infancy. Armed with their newly unearthed memories, many of these adults have brought criminal or civil charges against their alleged perpetrators for crimes that were claimed to have occurred decades earlier. These claims are not going unchallenged; indeed, they have spurred heated debates in the legal, scientific, and therapeutic communities about the validity of these delayed memories.

Because our understanding of the basis of children's delayed recalls of traumatic memories is based largely on the literature involving adults' delayed recall, we will devote this chapter to exploring the clinical and scientific evidence for adults' ability to uncover childhood memories of traumatic events. In the next chapter, we will examine the evidence for the claim that some of the memories that are uncovered are false, the result of suggestive interviewing techniques.

THE PHENOMENON

Those readers who occasionally glance at the weekly tabloids while waiting in the supermarket checkout line are no doubt aware of the many celebrities who claim to have been sexually abused as young children. Of course, this is to be expected because celebrities live in a society where child abuse frequently occurs (see chapter 3). What makes these celebrities' accounts so interesting, however, is the professed absence of any memory of the childhood abuse until they entered therapy for some complaint unrelated to sexual abuse, such as depression, eating disorders, marital distress, or job-related anxieties. Although many do not recover their memories in therapy, the majority do.

A well-known case is Roseanne Barr's claim to have recovered a memory of being abused by her mother when she was 6 months old. This memory was uncovered during therapy, along with memories of subsequent abuse by her parents. Her story has been told in national magazines, on television talk shows, and on news magazines (CBS's 60 Minutes, April 17, 1994). Joining Roseanne Barr are a legion of glitterati, including a former Miss America, several popular singers, a talk show host, and elected officials.

In the most typical repressed memory case, a "memory" of childhood abuse surfaces for the first time in therapy or in a support group for survivors of childhood incest. As already mentioned, clients may have sought therapy for any number of problems that are not uniquely associated with early sexual abuse (e.g., depression is associated with hundreds of psychological problems, including, in some cases, sexual abuse). After weeks or months of therapy, clients make a startling "discovery": Someone sexually assaulted them when they were young—perhaps someone trusted, such as a parent, uncle, sibling, baby-sitter, or neighbor.

Proponents of the validity of these uncovered memories point to the consistency of the picture; the sexual abuse memory fits with the client's larger symptom package. For example, the client's long-standing fear of dental procedures may be linked to forced oral copulation; gastrointestinal problems may be tied to early penetration. Some argue that even if there is no verbal memory of early abuse, there can be valid "behavioral memories of trauma that remain quite accurate and true to the events that stimulated them" (Terr, 1988b, p. 96). Hence, a child may repeatedly tear out her hair at a location similar to where she witnessed someone's head crushed by a rock, despite her inability to consciously connect these two events (Terr, 1994). Hence, it is sometimes claimed that, even if we are no longer aware of early abuse, "the body keeps score." Occasionally, the client's memory of early abuse can be verified (e.g., the perpetrator may confess; a sibling may independently reveal a similar abuse experience). However, such corroboration is the exception, not the rule. Usually, it comes down to "she says/he says."

The best-known "repressed memory" case involved Eileen Franklin-Lipsker, a housewife in Los Angeles. One day, she looked at her 5-year-old daughter, Jessica, and noticed her hair and eyes. This momentary image triggered what was alleged to be a repressed memory, the face of a childhood friend who, she claimed, was murdered in her presence:

> The look in Jessica's eyes —her very blue eyes that were so much like Susie's—took Eileen back to a look of betrayal in the eyes of Susie Nason almost 20 years earlier. From then on, there were fragments. The first one she talked about to Kirk Barrett, her therapist, was the long silver ring. The ring was on Susie Nason's bloody hand and it was smashed. Then Eileen had an image of riding in a van, and then there was a mattress, and a lavender sweater. . . . The images were frightening. Little Susie Nason had been only 8 when she was murdered by an assailant who was never found. Eileen told Kirk Barrett that she couldn't believe that the images were coming into her mind and she didn't understand what they meant. It was 3 or 4 sessions later that her father (George Franklin) was there—in her memory. As she eventually testified: "I remembered looking into Susie's eyes and I saw the silhouette of my father with his hands raised up above his head with a rock in them. . . . It was something that was completely, to my recollection, unknown to me, and it frightened me." (Edmiston, 1990, p. 229)

Franklin-Lipsker's "memory" of witnessing her friend's rape and murder by her father has been chronicled by MacLean (1993), who has pointed out significant discrepancies in her account and in the timing of her self-revelations. Regardless of the veracity of her claims, however, they set in motion a landmark case in which her father, George Franklin, was tried for the 20-year-old murder of her girlhood friend. He was convicted of murder in the first degree and given a life sentence.[1]

During the last 3 years there have been many similar cases (Oldenberg, 1991), and it is now common to read about repressed memories dating back to toddlerhood. In February 1995, an Illinois court began hearing a case involving a murder that occurred 27 years ago. The state's case is based on the recovered memory of a 30-year-old woman, Connie Sievak, who now recalls seeing her father participate in the slaughter, disemboweling, and burning of Hattie Barnes. Sievak, who was only 3 years old at the time, claims to have recovered her memory of the grisly murder after she began seeing a psychotherapist (Fisher, 1994). Similar claims are also being made by children. For example, in Albion, New York, an 8-year-old boy claimed to have uncovered a "memory" of witnessing his father murder his mother with a baseball bat when he was 23 months old. In Cincinnati, Ohio, a preadolescent girl described her "memory" of the way she had murdered her 14-month-old cousin when she was only 3 years old. According to the girl, she had committed the murder in retaliation for the murder of her own mother by her cousin's mother (i.e., her maternal aunt).[2]

Although there have been cases of alleged repressed memories of witnessing murders, robberies, and other crimes, the most frequent allegation concerns repressed memories of childhood sexual abuse. According to advocacy organizations, there are thousands of such claims each year in the United States, and they are increasingly finding their way into civil and criminal courts.

THE CONTROVERSY

Is it possible to repress something that is as personally significant as sexual abuse, and to regain access to the memory of it months, years, or decades later? A large number of clinical researchers and therapists argue that it is indeed possible, that such "discoveries" that surface in therapy

---

[1]In 1993, the California Court of Appeals upheld the conviction, and the California Supreme Court declined to hear George Franklin's appeal. Recently, however, the conviction was overthrown on the grounds that the contents of Eileen's recovered memories were part of the public record and consequently could have emanated from newspapers instead of her memory.

[2]This is a fascinating example of "back-propogation," where the preteen used current psychological motives to explain an earlier childhood action. It is unlikely that a 3-year-old child would make the following inferential chain: (a) *My aunt killed my mother*; (b) *I hate her for doing that*; (c) *she loves her own children*; (d) *so therefore, I will avenge my mother's murder by murdering one of her children, which will make her sad.* It is difficult to imagine 3-year-olds reasoning this way, although it is perhaps possible. Far more usual is for a child this age to dislike someone yet nevertheless like their children very much, seeing no causal connection between child and parent. But it is alluring for an adult or adolescent to invoke adult motives to retrofit childhood behaviors. To paraphrase George Vaillant (1977), there is a tendency for caterpillars to develop into adult butterflies and then to imagine that they had always been butterflies, only smaller ones. If we want to know what motivated the 3-year-old, we need to study the caterpillar, not its adolescent "butterfly" incarnation.

and support groups are legitimate memories that reflect the mind's unburdening of its deep, dark, ego-threatening secrets. Proponents of the validity of repressed memory draw on ample anecdotal accounts of clients whose discoveries of allegedly repressed memories were verified or seemingly verified (e.g., Terr, 1994).

Therapists use a number of techniques that purportedly assist survivors of childhood sexual abuse to make contact with their lost memories of abuse. These techniques include age regression, body memory interpretation, hypersuggestive questioning, guided visualization, dream interpretation, and sodium amytal interviews. In addition, a number of therapists have published self-help books to aid suspected victims uncover their repressed memories of childhood abuse through such techniques as concentrating on and embellishing a focal event from childhood (e.g., Bass & Davis, 1990; Fredrickson, 1992). The position taken in the recent edition of the *Diagnostic and Statistical Manual* of the American Psychiatric Association (1994), that cognitive and affective dissociations are common sequelae of sexual abuse, has provided legitimacy to such therapeutic probing of dormant memories that lay behind the client's presenting problems.

But there are a number of critics of this approach who argue that these "memories" are false, that they are little more than the residue of the fertile imagination of a highly suggestible client in the hands of a therapist who relentlessly uses suggestive techniques to create false memories. These critics point out that convincing verification of such memories is quite rare. This position is gaining strength in America's courtrooms. In May 1994, a California court awarded $500,000 to Gary Ramona, who had been accused by his adult daughter of sexually abusing her during childhood. Ramona's attorneys argued successfully that his daughter, who sought therapy because of bulimia, was the victim of false suggestions by her therapist, who convinced her that 70% to 80% of bulimics were sexually abused as children. After being subjected to suggestive techniques (e.g., sodium amytal, a short-acting barbiturate that reduces inhibition), Ramona's daughter became convinced that she recovered repressed memories of abuse. Many similar cases can be found throughout the United States, and we anticipate that it will get worse before it gets better.

Who can we believe in this debate? This is a complex problem that has already garnered the attention of four international scientific bodies, which have issued task force reports (the American Psychological Association's, the American Medical Association's, the American Psychiatric Association's, and the British Psychological Association's). The three American reports are decidedly more skeptical of the validity of repressed memories that are unearthed in therapy then is the British report. Nevertheless, all four of these reports contain an acknowledgment that it is possible to regain contact with long-lost childhood experiences that one has not thought about for decades.

CLARIFYING THE CONCEPTS

To understand why the task force reports emphasize these opposite possibilities, it is critical to distinguish among the five related but different concepts of *forgetting, suppression, repression, dissociation,* and *infantile amnesia.* Media and therapeutic accounts rarely distinguish among these terms and, judging from many scholarly accounts of delayed recall, researchers sometimes mingle them as well.

Forgetting

Forgetting is a normal developmental process. Unlike a computer's internal memory, the human memory system does not store information by laying down tracks of data and then retrieving them in a mechanical fashion. As we outlined in chapter 3, human memory is an imperfect device. Very little of our experience is preserved in a perfect or pristine condition. Rather, only a portion of the available information is stored, and only a portion of what is stored is subsequently retrieved. Memory is also highly constructive in nature; our current beliefs, expectations, and knowledge shape what is stored, what is recalled, and how our recall is interpreted. Memory is highly selective; unimportant or incongruous details are often ignored or reinterpreted.

Sometimes we "recall" information that was never stored but that is inferred on the basis of our knowledge of scripts, stereotypes, or semantic knowledge (e.g., see Ceci & Bruck 1993b; the Sam Stone study in chapter 10). For example, when children are told a story about their favorite television characters, they are able to correctly describe the details of the story immediately after listening to it, even if the portrayal of characters in the story is inconsistent with children's knowledge (e.g., instead of the hero being described as strong, he is described as weak). If, however, they are tested several weeks later when their memories for the story have faded, they are more likely to insist that the hero in the story had been portrayed as strong—just as he usually is on television (Ceci, Caves, & Howe, 1981). The tendency to make inferential leaps, especially when memory is weakened by time and by repeated suggestions, is common among all children, but especially preschoolers.

Similar errors are also made by adults. What is interesting about many such errors is that they sometimes concern very important events. Individuals of all ages become very confident about their memories regardless of whether they are accurate or inaccurate (Ceci, 1994). For example, the Boston Red Sox hitting phenom, Tony Conigliaro, was nearly killed by a fast ball thrown by pitcher Jack Hamilton of the California Angels. A decade later, upon Conigliaro's untimely death, Hamilton reconstructed that fateful pitch as follows:

It was like the 6th inning when it happened. I think the score was 2–1, and he [Conigliaro] was the 8th hitter in their batting order. With the pitcher up next, I had no reason to throw at him.

I tried to go see him in the hospital late that afternoon or early that evening but they were just letting his family in. (Anderson, 1990, p. B-9)

Both of these "recollections" are wrong. But they are more than wrong, for they represent a reconstruction that allowed Jack Hamilton to maintain his belief that he did not deliberately throw at Conigliaro's head. To begin with, it was only the fourth inning, and there were two outs and no one on base: the perfect occasion for a brush-back pitch. Second, Conigliaro was batting sixth, followed by Rico Petricelli. Conigliaro had already amassed 20 homers and 67 RBIs that season, so he represented a real threat. Third, it was an evening game, so Hamilton, who may want to imagine that he tried to visit the hospital immediately after the game, actually did not go there until the following afternoon (Anderson, 1990).

Hamilton has said that he thinks about that fateful day a lot and has had to learn to live with it.[3] Yet for all of his professed ruminations, he seems to have got the story wrong, not only in its peripheral details, but in its gist, its core truths. He has constructed an account that permits him to view himself as a more benign player than he may have been that day.

Thus, the memory system is organic; it assimilates events into pre-existing knowledge or belief systems, sometimes adding and at other times deleting information to better fit the extant knowledge. And when the original memory trace has faded because of the passage of time or the occurrence of interfering suggestions, as is especially true of very young children's memory, the organic or constructive nature of memory becomes even more important.

Given the organicity of the human memory system, it is to be expected that childhood events will be remembered with some distortions, if they are remembered at all. In fact, all experiences—no matter how emotionally salient—are susceptible to distortion, although for the most part highly salient events seem to be very well remembered. Survivors of death camps, of natural disasters, and of serious accidents all appear to have distorted aspects of their experiences, including such forensically significant aspects as the identity of an individual who gouged out their eye while in prison (Wagenaar & Groeneweg, 1990), the context of their internment (Langer, 1991), or what they were doing at the time of the *Challenger* space shuttle explosion (Neisser & Harsch, 1992).

---

[3]Hamilton has reason to think about that fateful game when he nearly killed Conigliaro, for his own career ended as a consequence of it. Fans booed and threw things at him so persistently that he retired at the end of that season.

Suppression

When we say that we suppressed an experience, we mean that we have consciously elected not to dwell on it because it is too unpleasant, embarrassing, or threatening. After a while, of course, we may lose contact with the memory of the unpleasant experience as a result of not thinking about it. But the memory can usually resurface if a hint or reminder is given. Thus, suppression may start out as a conscious form of avoidance, then develop into genuinely forgotten memories that may or may not be accessible with cues.

Repression

The concept of repression has a long history, dating back more than a century to Janet and, later, Freud. According to Freud, repression was at the core of the defensive organization; it occluded memories of societally conflictual or ego-threatening experiences from conscious awareness. Although he was inconsistent in his use of the term *repression*, Freud wrote that the purging from awareness of memories, desires, and thoughts could be a conscious or unconscious means of avoiding threatening memories. The earliest oedipal conflicts were assumed to be unconsciously repressed, unavailable to later probing.

In contrast with suppression, repression is an automatic and unconscious process, as most clinical anecdotes illustrate. For example, Van der Kolk and Van der Hart (1991) described the case history of a 56-year-old woman who appeared to have completely repressed being trapped in the great Boston fire of 1941 that killed nearly 100 patrons of a club. Several decades later, she began acting strangely, setting off fire alarms, asking if anyone was saved, and so forth. In the course of therapy, she was led to discover her repressed memory of having sought refuge during the fire in the club's walk-in freezer. In such clinical accounts of repressed memory, it is evident that the client is not consciously suppressing an unpleasant memory. Rather, the memory lies buried beneath consciousness, perhaps causing symptoms that are otherwise hard to explain, such as setting off fire alarms.

Ofshe and Watters (1993), however, have argued that the sudden discovery of a memory of early abuse during therapy requires a much stronger form of repression than that originally conceived by Freud. Specifically, they argue that a type of

> robust repression . . . [is required] to cause the knowledge of an event to disappear entirely from awareness, perhaps only minutes after it happened. (p. 6)

In fact, it does appear that in the discussion of "repressed memory," many experts are referring to this strong form of repression, one in which events get submerged in the unconscious and are later exhumed in their pristine or veridical form. Such repression is referred to as "fierce," "robust," or "total."

This refashioned concept of repression allows for new conceptualizations about memory loss and retrieval, both of which have been questioned by memory researchers. This form of repression has been used to explain a retroactive erasure of salient memories, such as the case of a child who is initially aware of repeated episodes of abuse (e.g., 50 molestation incidents over a period of 3 years) but who subsequently loses all memory for these incidents (after, say, the 51st one). Some experts have provided more definitive boundaries for the conditions of retroactive erasure. For example, Terr has claimed that memories become repressed or dissociated primarily when there have been multiple traumatic experiences, as opposed to only one or two (Terr, 1988a, 1994).[4] Memory researchers, who have challenged these descriptions, ask the following: What type of mechanism can account for such retroactive erasure? How can experiences be accessible and then made inaccessible as a function of additional experiences? Retroactive forgetting mechanisms, such as repression, would not seem productive candidates to explain this type of erasure.

This form of repression also allows for the view that when repressed memories are uncovered, they can be described in "Sleeping Beauty" terms; that is, the memories are seen as preserved in their pristine state, not subject to the usual processes of decay, alteration, and interference that influence ordinary (i.e., nonrepressed) memories. Again, memory researchers ask what kind of mechanism can explain this "time capsule" effect?

In reply to some of these challenges, trauma theorists have argued that repressed memories work differently from ordinary memories because persistent trauma results in long-term structural changes in the brain structures that subserve memory processing. (For full details of this line of argumentation, the interested reader should consult Van der Kolk, in press.) Some have claimed that repressed memories are "special" because they are stored in a special place in the brain. To understand the flavor of this argument, we must first provide the following very simplified view of the neurophysiology of repression.

All experiences that get stored result in some alteration of the connections among brain cells, called *synapses*. This is done by either potentiating or depressing the cellular activity through the release or inhibition

---

[4]As Pendergrast (1994) pointed out, the empirical basis of the claim that multiple traumatic experiences are more likely to be repressed than a single traumatic experience is problematic. To our knowledge, there is no scientifically compelling evidence for making this distinction, although perhaps such evidence will become available some day.

of chemicals known as *neurotransmitters*. Fearful experiences result in the release of *noradrenaline*, a neurotransmitter linked to arousal and alertness, in a brain structure known as the *amygdala*, which connects the visceral brain stem to the prefrontal cortex, hence tying the sensorimotor areas to the autonomic nervous system. The amygdala stores unconscious, emotionally charged memories. Some have likened these "amygdala memories" to what we have been calling repressed memories, whereas others have provided evidence for other mechanisms. Although highly interesting, these observations were based largely on rodent footshock experiments (see LeDoux, 1994). If they can be generalized to the human brain, they would provide a means of understanding how some experiences could result in learning and remembering that bypass conscious awareness altogether (see Kandel & Kandel, 1994).[5]

Thus, repression is an automatic process that is not conscious; that is, we do not elect to repress material, it happens indeliberately. A repressed memory is not usually easily elicited by a cue or hint the way that a suppressed memory is. Finally, some claim that the content of a repressed memory is stored in a special place in the brain where its exact form can be recovered without distortion decades later. Perhaps such conjectures will receive convincing empirical support some day, but presently they are speculations that have no greater claim to scientific validation than the opposite claim that repression does not exist.

Dissociation

Recently, in response to criticisms of repression, proponents of memory recovery have shifted to "dissociation" as their construct of choice (Alpert, Brown, & Cortois, in press; Spence, 1994). Dissociation refers to a disconnection between one form of memory and another (Yates & Nasby, 1993). For example, various types of information in memory (feelings, thoughts, actions) may not be integrated, and as a result the individual may express out-of-body feelings, self-induced trance states, and inappropriate affect. In other words, the memory of a thought is split off from the memory of its emotional content, resulting in robot-like enactments of events that are devoid of emotional valence. Various types of dissociative

---

[5]Such models, however, do not adequately explain the phenomenon that we described earlier, namely, the retroactive erasure of an existing conscious memory. Some evidence, although contradictory, would seem to suggest that for complex events (which for a rodent in a footshock experiment means simply that two lights rather than a single light co-appear with an aversive shock), the higher, usually conscious, cortical processes "serve to interpret stimuli when they become more intricate." However, other evidence suggests that damage to the region between the older and newer cortex may prevent the expression of an already stored emotional memory in rats (LeDoux, 1994, p. 54). Although fascinating and potentially of great importance, this work is still far from providing convincing evidence of how repression of emotional memories might work in humans.

states have been identified, including "multiple personality disorder," "psychogenic amnesia," "fugue states," and "depersonalization." Many believe that these states arise out of a rupture in the modulation and integration of knowledge about the self across different states of consciousness (see Alpert et al., in press).

It is claimed that dissociation results most commonly from trauma, and particularly sexual-abuse-related trauma. For example, Chu and Dill (1990) observed greater dissociative symptomatology (e.g., trance states, emotionless memories) in female patients who had been victims of childhood sexual abuse than among those who had not suffered sexual abuse. Adult survivors of sexual abuse are nearly always said to be exhibiting dissociations (see Van der Kolk, in press).

According to Alpert et al. (in press), dissociation differs from repression in that dissociated memories may fluctuate in and out of consciousness, whereas repressed memories are deeply buried in the unconscious. Furthermore, dissociated memories are associated with traumatic events; they do not result from the blockading of unacceptable impulses or fantasies. And unlike repression, dissociation does not require acceptance of a psychodynamic model and its attendant theoretical implications.

In sum, it is hypothesized that a traumatic event triggers a dissociative state that can result in a failure to integrate various types of self-knowledge (e.g., emotion and memory). It is further hypothesized that a particularly potent traumatic event is sexual abuse. Unlike forgetting, dissociation implies that the original encoded event is inaccessible because it is associated with highly charged negative affect. Some commentators have argued that dissociation is simply a pseudonym for repression and that regardless of the term used there is little empirical support for such a construct (Holmes, 1994).

Infantile Amnesia

Infantile amnesia refers to the near-total eclipse of memories from the first few years of life. For example, some of us can remember our birthday party when we were 7 years old, but few can remember a party when we were only 2 or 3 years old.

Scientists are not in complete agreement as to when this period of infantile amnesia ends. Some claim that it is impossible to retrieve memories from the first 4 or even 5 years of life (indeed, Freud and others thought that it was impossible to recall memories from the first 7 years), and others set the end of this period around 2 years of age for some types of memories and 3 or 4 years of age for others (e.g., for a review, see Howe & Courage, 1993; Loftus, 1992; Usher & Neisser, 1993). Thus, although it might be possible for a small proportion of adults to recall that their mother went to the hospital to give birth to a younger sibling when they were 2 years old, it is extremely unlikely that one could recall most types of experiences from this epoch.

We will briefly summarize some of the explanations that have been provided to account for this phenomenon of infantile amnesia. The simplest explanation is that the mental architecture of the 2-year-old is so different from that of the older child and adult that the original memories are simply not retrievable. The mental architecture used by adults to encode and access memories involves interpretive/semantic analyses that are qualitatively different from the sensorimotor analyses used by the infant to encode events into storage. To provide a very simple example, a toddler may have been touched on the genitals by his uncle, but because a 16-month-old does not have the concept of "bad touching," this experience may not be salient enough to be encoded, or if it is encoded, it will simply be encoded in its sensory form. It seems unlikely that with development, sensorimotor memories are automatically converted (recoded) into elaborated interpretive/semantic memories. Perhaps it is possible, as adults, to retrieve aspects of a sensory image from infancy and then to consciously and willfully recode it in light of its adult meaning.

Others have argued that the emergence of autobiographical memory, around the end of the period of infantile amnesia, is a function of the child's increasing cognitive and language skills (Nelson, 1988, 1993; Sugar, 1992). The advent of language prepares children to talk about, organize, and represent personally experienced events. These structures and processes are clearly important foundations of adultlike autobiographical memory.

Finally, others have emphasized the primary role of the emergence of self-concept during the toddler years.[6] As Howe and Courage (1993) have argued, the emergence of a sense of self (or self-concept) is fundamental to the development of autobiographical memory; once a child has some sense of himself as a referent around which personally experienced events can be organized, the period of infantile amnesia ends.

Does this mean that it is impossible to resurrect and reinterpret images from early childhood? Couldn't an adult retrieve the sensory details of a childhood event that may not have been interpreted beyond its bare sensory details (e.g., the vision of a finger inserted into one's anus; the visceral reaction accompanying its penetration), and later import these into

---

[6]A well-known demonstration of the emergence of self-concept is found in many developmental psychology textbooks: Lipstick is smeared on the nose of an 8-month-old, and she is then held in front of a mirror. Although the 8-month-old will smile at the clownish image in the mirror, she will not attempt to wipe her nose or otherwise remove the lipstick. Some, although not all, researchers interpret this to indicate that the infant lacks a sense of self. She does not wipe her nose, because the image in the mirror is not recognized as herself. Thus, the argument goes, how can an early memory about one's self be recovered if at the time it was originally experienced the infant did not even possess a sense of self? In short, there can be no autobiographical memory before there exists an "auto."

her cognitive system for interpretation? Researchers are still a long way from answering such questions.

Fortunately, however, it is possible to inform the debate over repressed memories without having complete knowledge about these issues. This is because even if it proves to be possible to interpret early abusive events that were not originally interpreted by the child as abusive, it would present the following conundrum: Namely, how can this event be the source of an adult patient's intrapsychic conflict if it was not interpreted as assaultive when it originally occurred? In other words, if this memory is a recovered memory, its intepretation postdates the patient's symptoms and therefore cannot account for the onset of those same symptoms, which may have brought the patient into therapy. And why are other seemingly assaultive events not associated with similar forms of adult intrapsychic conflict? Infant circumcisions, which represent early painful genital experiences, are not commonly recalled in therapy, nor are the insertion of anal suppositories, genital catheterizations, and other invasive medical procedures from the first few years of life. So why should sexual events such as genital touching, anal insertions, and vaginal penetrations, but not nonsexual events such as vaginal catheterizations, be uncovered in therapy? Of course, the answer is that both clients and therapists may probe for memories of sexual events, not of societally sanctioned ones. However, if memories of circumcisions, anal suppositories, and catheterizations were probed, would these be recalled if they occurred within the first 2 years of life? We doubt it; there is nothing in the developmental literature that leads us to think otherwise. In our own research, we commonly find that children are unable to recall medical procedures one year after they were subjected to them.

To argue that societally sanctioned events (e.g., circumcisions) are qualitatively different from unsanctioned events like sexual abuse is to ignore the way they are construed by the infant or young child. Indeed, one might well imagine that the young child feels betrayed by a loved one who delivers him to a medical team and leaves the room while the team engages in painful genital procedures like a catheterization. To a 2-year-old child, such painful genital procedures might be every bit as anxiety-provoking as sexual experiences. Furthermore, the concept surrounding what is and is not "sanctioned" is messy; if one wants to dismiss medical trauma on the grounds that a trusted loved one approved of it, then similar sanctioning of incest exists. From an infant's or toddler's perspective, being delivered by a loved one to an abusive molester or a legitimate doctor may be indistinguishable.

To carry our argument one step further, if emotionally charged events are most likely to be recovered, it is surprising that there are so many recovered memories of infant childhood sexual abuse. This is because the vast majority of reported child sexual abuse from infancy and early childhood does not involve penetration, but fondling, oral copulation, exhibitionism, pornography, and so forth—acts that may not be interpreted as assaultive by the infant or very young child.

Some readers may challenge the construct of infantile amnesia by claiming that they vividly remember a very early childhood event, perhaps one that occurred during the first year of life. There is some "anecdata" that such memories may exist from the second year of life. For example, Sugar (1992) described three case studies of trauma memories from the first 2 years of life. In one, an adult allegedly recalled an anxiety-producing image from the age of 18 months, of her mother standing next to some material on the floor, which her mother later confirmed was the aftermath of a miscarriage.

How are we to account for such recollective experiences? Many researchers argue that these may not be actual recollections but rather the product of "back-propagation." That is, perhaps we can actually retrieve the original perceptual image, and even though we were unable to interpret it at the time of its occurrence (e.g., the meaning of the miscarriage), we can now as adults reinterpret the image in light of adult understanding (i.e., back-propagation). Again, it is worth noting that we have no scientific data that this can occur; we mention it more as a hypothesis in need of validation than as a statement of fact.

It is also possible that memories of early childhood events are the result of post-event rehearsal with family members. For example, you may remember getting carsick on the way to your grandmother's house at age 3, having an awful temper tantrum at the supermarket at age 2, or witnessing a red blob on the floor of the bathroom when you were 18 months old, not because you can actually gain access to the original encoding of these experiences and their contexts, but because you subsequently heard about them from family members and you mentally created images based on these retellings. These images may come to take on a vividness that is easily mistaken for a memory of the original event.

Sometimes, a family's understanding of an event may be incorrect, leading to the creation of a false memory in its children through subsequent retellings. Jean Piaget, the great developmental psychologist, told the story of his false memory of an early abduction attempt:

> One of my first memories would date, if it were true, from my second year. I can still see, most clearly, the following scene, in which I believed until I was about fifteen. I was sitting in my pram, which my nurse was pushing in the Champs Elysées, when a man tried to kidnap me. I was held in by the strap fastened round me while my nurse bravely tried to stand between me and the thief. She received various scratches, and I can still see vaguely those on her face. . . . When I was about fifteen, my parents received a letter from my former nurse . . . she wanted to confess her past faults, and in particular to return

the watch she had been given as a reward. . . . She had made up the whole story. . . . I, therefore, must have heard, as a child, the account of this story, which my parents believed, and projected into the past in the form of a visual memory. (Piaget, 1945/1962)

As Piaget's example illustrates, it is possible to create a vivid but false memory through family retellings. It also illustrates how easy it is to underestimate the power of suggestions, image inductions, and stereotypes in forming vivid but untrue images of our past. All of us are prone to these types of confusions. When push comes to shove, there is no substitute for corroboration of our memories, no matter how vivid they may seem to us.

FROM THEORY TO RESEARCH

Armed with the concepts of *forgetting, suppression, repression, dissociation*, and *infantile amnesia* and the theoretical framework detailed above, we can now ask how common it is for adults to "repress" memories of childhood sexual abuse. At the time of this writing (1995), there are four retrospective surveys that have been offered in support of the validity of repressed memories. Each of these surveys involves adults who were asked to recall abusive episodes from their past. Although there were adults in each study who claimed to have experienced sexual abuse during childhood but who had lost contact with the memory of their victimization for long periods of time, there was a very wide range of rates of alleged repression across the four studies.

In the earliest of these studies, 53 women who attended a 12-week group therapy program for incest survivors were asked if there were periods in their life when they lost contact with the memory of their abuse (Herman & Schatzow, 1987). There was a great deal of memory impairment in this group: 64% of the clients had some degree of memory impairment, and 26% revealed severe memory impairment.[7]

These findings were echoed in a much larger survey conducted by Briere and Conte (1993). They reviewed data on 450 patients in therapy for reported incidents of childhood sexual abuse. Over half of this sample (59%) reported that at some point, they had lost contact with this experience. Factors leading to lost memories of abuse were age of onset of the abuse and amount of abuse: The earlier it occurred, the less it could be recalled, and the more persistent the abuse, the less it could be recalled.

---

[7]This study has been criticized on the grounds that impairment was poorly defined by the researchers, was not specific to sexual abuse, and was assessed by memory-recovery therapists. The most damaging criticism is that part of the criteria for a severe memory impairment was the recovery of repressed memories during the therapy, thus resulting in a circularity (see Lindsay & Read, 1994). Similar interpretive problems characterize the study by Briere and Conte (1993).

In the third survey (Williams, 1994), 129 adult women with documented histories of childhood or adolescent sexual abuse were interviewed to determine if they remembered this abuse. Thirty-eight percent of the women appeared to have no memory of their childhood abuse, or else were unwilling to report it. Because the majority of these women were willing to discuss other sexual themes with the researchers, it was concluded that their memory lapses were not the result of some form of embarrassment or unwillingness to report, but were due to truly lost memories.

Finally, Loftus, Polansky, and Fullilove (1994) interviewed 100 female clients at a substance abuse clinic. Of these, 55% reported childhood sexual abuse. Of those reporting abuse, 19% reported that they had forgotten the incident(s) at some point during their life.

The rates of repression of childhood sexual abuse vary considerably among these four different surveys; they range from a low of 19% to a high of 64%. The basis for the different values across the four studies is not readily apparent, because two of them comprised mainly middle-class White female samples (Briere & Conte, 1993; Herman & Schatzow, 1987), and the other two comprised predominantly inner-city African American women.

Although these four studies differ in their rates of "repression," three of them tend to find statistical associations between memory lapses and both earlier onset of the abuse and its violent nature: That is, generally speaking, the earlier the abuse occurred during childhood, the more likely it was that the adult claimed to have lost contact with the memory of it. Similarly, the more violent the abuse, the more likely it was repressed from conscious memory.[8] Finally, some researchers also reported that the more repetitive the abuse, the more likely repression occurred. Thus, adults were more likely to remember their abuse when it was nonviolent and nonrepetitive. The exception to these claims is the Loftus et al. (1994) survey, where violent, early, repetitive abuse was no more likely to be forgotten than other forms of abuse.

Aside from differences in outcomes, all four of these retrospective surveys make it abundantly clear that it is common for adult survivors of childhood sexual abuse to report periods during which they did not remember or think about their abuse. The question is not whether this happens, but whether this is due to repression or to some other less esoteric mechanism like forgetting, suppression, or infantile amnesia. As we already noted, repression entails special memory mechanisms. For example, the notion that the "repressed" memory is split off from conscious brain structures and is retrievable in veridical form decades later is unlike the notion

---

[8]Actually, one of the two studies that purported to show a link between the violent nature of the abuse and its repression (Williams, 1994) appears to have been based on an error (reversal of the sign of a correlation). Thus, only one of four studies reports this link.

that ordinary nontraumatic memories are susceptible to decay and alteration.

We believe that the key to understanding the results of these studies lies in understanding how the respondents interpreted the survey questions. We now look a bit more closely at this issue.

In the Briere and Conte (1993) survey, for instance, the wording of the critical question that indicated repressed memory was as follows:

> During the period of time when the first forced sexual experience happened and your 18th birthday was there ever a time when you could not remember the forced sexual experience?

And in the Loftus et al. (1994) study, the critical repressed memory question, number 3, was worded as follows:

> People differ in terms of how they remember their abuse. Which of the following experiences best characterizes your memory? 1) Some people have always remembered their abuse throughout their lives, even if they never talked about it. 2) Some people have remembered parts of their abuse their whole lives, while not remembering all of it. 3) Some people forget the abuse for a period of time, and only later have the memory return.

It seems possible that many adults who were abused may never have lost contact with their abuse experiences, but nevertheless may have answered the Briere and Conte question and the Loftus et al. question positively because they thought they were being asked if there were long stretches of their life when they did not think about the abuse, perhaps because of its upsetting nature, or even because their minds had moved on to other things.

Certainly, crime victims report doing something like this; that is, following victimization, it is common to avoid thinking about the unpleasant, often traumatic experience. Returning veterans from combat zones frequently report that they engage in various forms of deliberate blockading of combat memories. Of most pertinence to the present discussion are the results of a longitudinal study where formerly incarcerated delinquents were questioned at age 15 and then again at age 24 about sexual and physical abuse (Femina, Yeager, & Lewis, 1990). Although there were a number of discrepant reports between these two periods, none of these discrepancies reflected amnesia for the abuse. When abuse was initially not reported or was minimized, but disclosed later, the subjects said that they had done this for social or personal reasons, not because they had initially failed to remember the abuse. For example, when asked why she had not reported sexual abuse in the follow-up interview, one female subject burst into tears, saying, "I didn't say it 'cuz I wanted to forget. I wanted it to be private. I only cry when I think about it" (p. 229).

In the four retrospective surveys, the wording of the questions prevents us from confidently determining the number of women who meet our criteria for "repressed" memories of abuse. To more accurately determine the number of adults with repressed memories, a question is needed such as "Was there ever a time when you would have honestly denied that you had been abused as a child if someone asked you, only to subsequently discover that you had, in fact, been abused?" We suspect that if such a question were added to surveys, the number of respondents giving evidence of repressed memory would decline. This does not mean that they would disappear altogether, however, but merely that they would decrease in frequency. As we have seen, there are many competing explanations of memory failure. We think that it is highly likely that individuals who have experienced severe trauma may later be unable to recollect certain aspects of their experiences—either because the information was never encoded into memory in the first place, or because they find it too upsetting or disjointed to deal with.

Before we leave this literature, there are several other points to be considered in evaluating the rates of repressed memories reported by the survey participants. First, for some respondents, it seems that the abuse may have taken place at a very early age; as a result, it may not be recalled because of infantile amnesia. This is particularly relevant for the Williams (1994) study, in which the researchers selected their subjects on the basis of hospital records documenting abuse. (However, it should be noted that even when Williams segregated older cases, there was still a substantial number of women who failed to remember their abuse.) Second, for two of the studies (Briere & Conte, 1993; Herman & Schatzow, 1987) that included patients in therapy groups, there is no systematic corroboration of the subjects' abuse. Thus, it is not clear whether subjects report not remembering the abuse because of true memory loss or because it never occurred but was seeded by suggestive therapeutic practices.

Finally, one might ask the following: If adults forget details of previous abusive experiences, what evidence is there that abused children also block out, forget, or suppress memories of their previous experiences? Although the figures may not be as high as that found in the adult population, one would expect that similar mechanisms would be at work. Interestingly, although some of the child therapists in our case studies indicated that the children needed time to unblock their memories of earlier abuse, we have failed to find any empirical studies on the correlates of childhood sexual abuse among children where amnesia for the event is listed as a symptom (for reviews see Beitchman, Zucker, Hood, DaCosta, & Akman, 1991; Kendall-Tackett et al., 1993). Thus, it seems that if there is any loss of contact with memories of abuse, it must happen after childhood.

UNUSUAL PHENOMENA IN THE MEMORY FIELD

There are some other areas in memory research that may help inform the debate on repressed memories. These areas of study are important because they address some common intuitions or raise questions that we have about memory.

The first issue concerns whether frightening stressful events are recalled more elaborately and more accurately than other types of events. Results from several different types of studies indicate that memory for stressful experiences, which do not include sexual abuse, fall prey to the same forces that influence the evolution of memory for less stressful or neutral events.

Some of this evidence is based on studies of "flashbulb" memories that were conducted to account for our common intuition that there are certain events that we will never forget, such as where and whom we were with when we learned of the assassination of President John F. Kennedy or of the space shuttle *Challenger* explosion. Special neural memory mechanisms that permanently imprint details for certain events have been invoked to account for the subjective phenomenon that we will never forget these events—that they are indelibly imprinted into memory just as photographs are pasted into wedding albums (Brown & Kulik, 1977).

However, after more than a decade of research on so-called "flashbulb" memories, it has been found that these subjective phenomena are not necessarily correct—that one does forget many of the details of these highly memorable events and that these memories are susceptible to the same constructive/schematic distortion processes as are everyday memories. Studies that have examined recollections of the space shuttle disaster, and other salient events, have repeatedly found reconstructive errors. Moreover, it is not only the peripheral details that get altered with time and suggestion, but the gist of the event can become altered as well.

Although researchers of flashbulb memories have tried to make the case that highly salient events get encoded permanently, there are other researchers who have tried to make the case that "amnesia" is common for highly stressful events. In general, this research reveals that, contrary to common depictions in films or in literature (e.g., see Patterson's [1985] fictional account of a Viet Nam veteran's amnesia), in real life, the vast majority of adult survivors of traumatic experiences can usually recall the gist of their frightful experiences if they are asked to do so (e.g., "Do you remember being mugged in the parking lot when you worked at your former job?" "Do you remember being in Auschwitz?" "Do you remember coming under combat fire in the Viet Nam War?"). Many can recall even minute details of these experiences.

For example, therapists experienced in treating Viet Nam veterans report that often the problem with those diagnosed as suffering from post-traumatic stress is not that their memories are repressed but that they cannot be forgotten; they intrude into conscious awareness unexpectedly and/or in response to some auditory stimuli (e.g., a car backfiring). This is not to say that all aspects of traumatic events are retained, because like all memories, they are vulnerable to fragmentation and loss. Additionally, some aspects of the traumatic experience may never have been encoded or stored to begin with, as opposed to having been stored and later splitting off from the rest of the conscious experience. To whatever extent this is true, later failure to recollect is not due to repression or amnesia, but to failure to store the experience in the first place.

Some readers may be perplexed by this argument, so we will spell it out in more detail. At the moment of encountering a traumatic event, it is common for the perceptual system to narrow its focus. There are physiological reasons for *perceptual narrowing* that are adaptive in the sense that they allow the organism to recruit all of its psychic resources to deal with the most immediate threat, a so-called "fight or flight" state. Thus, a combat veteran may remember seeing his wounded buddy lying in a pool of blood on the ground beside him, but may not remember carrying him back to camp amidst a galaxy of gun and mortar fire. In other words, all of the soldier's limited conscious resources are centered (or narrowed) on dealing with the most immediate threat, namely, avoiding the enemy shells whistling around his head. That he may not recall events extraneous to this immediate threat is unsurprising and does not establish that repression is the cause of his subsequent failure to retrieve this experience. Rather, much of the event may never have been stored in the first place because his attention was focused entirely on avoiding shell fire, rather than on the visceral cues associated with carrying his wounded buddy.

Although it is common to read clinical case studies of combat veterans who cannot recall some aspects of a traumatic event (like carrying a wounded buddy back to camp amidst a hail of enemy fire), it is quite rare to read of a veteran who professes to have no memory of having come under enemy fire, and it is rarer still to read of combat veterans who deny all memory of having been in Viet Nam. On those rare occasions, psychosis is a more likely explanation than memory repression.

In short, we are arguing for a distinction between repression and perceptual narrowing, suggesting that the latter leads to a bottleneck in which much of the ambient information never gets encoded into the memory system to begin with and thus can subsequently only be inferred. Translated to the context of sexual abuse, we can ask which aspects of an abuse episode cannot be recalled because they were never encoded in the first place, and which aspects were unrecallable due to repression of what was, in fact, encoded. On the basis of what has been argued above, we believe that, if the abuse victim is past the offset of infantile amnesia, the gist of the abuse may survive, much the way that the veteran's combat experience does, although in both cases aspects surrounding the event may be lost.

All these studies relate to the more general question, Are highly stressful experiences more or less memorable than other types of experiences? This issue has been reviewed elsewhere (Ceci & Bruck, 1993b; Christianson, 1992), and we will not rehash these reviews here, except to note that a fundamental difference of opinion exists among researchers regarding the role of affect or stress in memory. Some data indicate that high levels of stress at the time of an event (e.g., a medical procedure) facilitate memory of the event, whereas others indicate the opposite (see the debate between Goodman, 1991, and Peters, 1991). Findings of a recent study of adults' recall of early memories suggest that neither position may be correct. That is, adults' recall of early memories was unrelated to whether the memories were emotionally positive, negative, or neutral (Howes, Siegel, & Brown, 1993). Interestingly, none of these positions fits with the claim that trauma experiences are repressed.

Perhaps there is a relationship between stress and memory when the events are repetitive (e.g., Terr, 1988a).[9] We know of one developmental study that examined this issue. Preschoolers were subjected to voiding-cysto-urethrograms (VCUGs), involving the insertion of a probe into the child's genitalia, following inflation of the bladder with fluid. (This test is mainly administered to children with chronic urinary tract infections.) It is not only painful, but embarrassing, because after the child's bladder is filled to the point of extreme discomfort, she is encouraged to urinate on the examining table in front of strange medical personnel. Films of children undergoing this procedure vividly demonstrate its aversiveness. Goodman and her colleagues (Goodman, Quas, Batterman-Faunce, Riddlesberger, & Kuhn, 1994) reported that children who have been subjected to multiple VCUGs are no more likely to forget the details of these experiences than are children who received only one VCUG. Although this does not prove that repetitive abuse is no more likely to be repressed than a single abuse experience, it does force us to ask what mechanism would lead to the repression of repetitive sexual abuse but not to the repression of repetitive VCUGs or other aversive procedures.

It should be noted that the claim made by some researchers that repetitive rather than single acts of abuse are more likely to be "forgotten" is not entirely straightforward. In fact, in some studies, it actually appears that victims can recall an abuse experience, although they may not be able to recall the details of each abusive experience. It appears that they may recall the central but not the peripheral, less important details, or they may not be able to recall specific events. But this phenomenon may have

---

[9]However, see footnote 4 for criticism of this claim.

nothing to do with repression; it may reflect more general memory principles. Repeated acts, regardless how stressful, lose their uniqueness, and they become merged and, at times, part of a script.

SUMMARY

In this chapter we have laid out six different theoretical constructs (*forgetting, suppression, repression, dissociation, infantile amnesia,* and *perceptual narrowing*) as possible explanations of how documented events may or may not be recalled at a later point. We then reviewed four surveys on the incidence of repressed memories in women with known or reported histories of abuse, and we attempted to provide some interpretations and additional empirical data. In the final section of this chapter we will attempt to pull together these various strands and come to some tentative conclusions about how likely it is that one can "uncover" repressed memories and about the possible alternate explanations for such phenomena.

First, we return to our distinction between repression and ordinary forgetting. On the basis of over 100 years of basic and applied research in the area of memory, most instances of memory failure can be accounted for by ordinary forgetting processes, and do not require a special mechanism such as repression. Under ordinary circumstances, we should expect that the memory, once rediscovered, would be an imperfect record of what had originally been experienced. That is, normal memory processes are susceptible to fading, shaping, alteration, social construction, and outright loss.

Thus, when an adult purports to have uncovered an early abuse memory that is highly detailed, vivid, and coherent, memory experts are skeptical because of their experience with the fallibility of long-term memory for nonabusive events. They have seen many experiments in which the subject misremembers not only the vivid details of a nonevent but its gist, too. As a result, memory researchers find it difficult to accept the claim that there exists a special category of memories that are impervious to these deleterious forces. Thus, when a recovered memory is highly vivid and detailed, it leaves open the possibility that it is constructed, and it opens the door to claims that the recovered memory may have erroneously been shaped by suggestive therapeutic practices or self-induced attempts at retrieval (e.g., repeated visualizations, self-induced trance states).

In general, there is a growing disillusionment in the cognitive literature with "special mechanisms" invoked to validate dramatic and detailed accounts of an alleged early abuse experience that suddenly erupts into consciousness. In the past, special mechanisms have also been evoked to account for other types of important memories, such as flashbulb memories; but these special mechanisms have not stood up well to empirical scrutiny. The bottom line is that there is no way of scientifically segregating a class of memories and bestowing them with privileged status in terms of their immutability, veracity, and durability. We all forget experiences, positive as well as negative ones. It is physiologically impossible to maintain a conscious record of our complete past. We do not need to posit special repression or dissociative mechanisms to account for this type of forgetting.

Second, on the basis of the manifold reasons given in this chapter, one ought to embrace a healthy suspicion when adults recall events that are alleged to have occurred in the first few years of life. This does not mean that we should deny the possibility that they are real, but rather that we need to be skeptical. When known abuse occurs during the first few years of life, but is never recalled, this does not logically lead to the conclusion that the memory was repressed. Rather, when events occur during this early period, or prior to the offset of infantile amnesia, we would expect these early experiences to be unrecallable, no matter how positive or how negative they were. It may be beyond adults' ability to resurrect the world of the 1- or 2-year-old because the cognitive and neurophysiological architecture that laid down such memories in infancy is so unlike that which guides the adult's retrieval of memories. As Sugar (1992) and others have argued, it may be possible for an adult to resurrect an image from the age of 18 months (e.g., of one's mother standing next to a pool of blood on the floor), but the interpretation given to that image at age 18 months is probably undifferentiated anxiety, whereas the adult interpretation that it was blood associated with the mother's miscarriage is "back-propagated."

Finally, adults' confidence about the validity of their newly found memories should not be used as a gauge of their veracity. A large literature exists on the confidence–accuracy relation or lack thereof (see Bothwell, Deffenbacher, & Brigham, 1987). Suffice it to say that although at times there is a positive relationship where the stronger the feeling of confidence in one's memory, the more likely it is true, overall, the relationship between confidence and accuracy of memory is quite weak. Many inaccurate people will be greatly confident, and many highly accurate people will have very little confidence in the accuracy of their memory. This is ironic because jurors attach great weight to the confidence of witnesses, yet study after study has shown that this is misplaced.

If one adds up the alternative interpretations of "repressed memories" that we have presented in this chapter, it seems clear that the reported inability of adults to recollect childhood abuse experiences at some point in their past is usually not the result of repression, at least not in its strong or "robust" form (Ofshe & Singer, 1993). Rather, most of these instances could be the result of ordinary forgetting, infantile amnesia, suppression, or perceptual narrowing. These considerations lead us to suspect that psychic material retrieved during therapy may have been persistently accessible but simply not dwelt on for long periods of time as a result of a deliberate strategy. However, the most important consideration, which is the focus of the next chapter, is that "repressed" memories of early child-hood abuse may be the result of postevent suggestions that include, but are not limited to, erroneous constructions based on suggestive therapeutic practices or personal retrieval techniques that encourage source misattributions.

14

THE ROLE OF SUGGESTION IN DELAYED RECALL OF CHILD SEXUAL ABUSE

In the last chapter we focused on various explanations for delayed recall of sexual abuse, especially among adults. We suggested that in some cases the "recovered" memory was not repressed but suppressed, forgotten, or never encoded in the first place. In this chapter we focus on the possibility that in some cases of "recovered memories," the abuse never occurred; the "memory" is false. We also bring the child back into focus. Nothing that we say here is meant to imply that we believe that it is impossible for someone to recall a long-forgotten experience. It is not. All of us have had such experiences. We do, however, take issue with the special status that is sometimes accorded to such memories, including the assertion that they are veridical and immutable and that their loss, submersion, or repression is the basis for current psychological symptomatology.

In earlier chapters, we described how a variety of suggestive interviewing techniques can influence children's reports, and how these suggestive interviewing techniques may account for some of the allegations made in some of the case studies. If therapists use these techniques, they may unwittingly induce false memories in their clients. But there are other, more subtle techniques that therapists and other interviewers sometimes use that could seed the growth of false memories, conceivably leading clients to imagine that they participated in fictitious scenarios, particularly in childhood. In this chapter we focus on two related mechanisms, reality monitoring and source monitoring, that provide a hospitable environment for the planting of false memories. Although we redirect our focus in this chapter to children, we nevertheless do provide some data and descriptions that are relevant for assessing uncovered memories in adults.

MONITORING THE SOURCES OF OUR MEMORIES: DEVELOPMENTAL PERSPECTIVES

In this section we discuss the evidence for two related concepts. The first is termed *reality monitoring*, and it refers to one's ability to distinguish reality from fantasy or to distinguish memories of actual events from memories of imagined events. The second concept is termed *source monitoring*: This refers to the ability to keep track of the sources of actual events. We begin our discussion with reality monitoring in children.

Over the last 100 years, researchers have held markedly different views on young children's ability to differentiate fantasy from reality. According to the early pioneers, such as Freud, young children's wish-fulfilling fantasies tainted the accuracy of their reports. Piaget, the most famous of child developmentalists, supported this view by claiming that young children cannot distinguish something that actually happened from a dream about the same event. Piaget (1945/1962) noted that the child's "mind is full of these 'ludistic' (fantasy) tendencies up to the age of seven or eight, which means before that age it is very difficult for him to distinguish the truth" (p. 34).

In the 1970s, this view of young children began to change. A variety of researchers demonstrated that even 3-year-olds could correctly classify real and pretend figures and that they have a firm understanding of the distinction between imagined and real entities. Thus, the predominant view shifted to "children do not confuse fantasy with reality."

Recently, the results of an experiment by Harris, Brown, Marriott, Whittall, and Harmer (1991) have modified these conclusions in important ways. As in previous studies, preschool children showed a firm grasp of the distinction between fantasy and reality, with most correctly stating that imagined ghosts, monsters, and witches were not real. However, when the children were told to imagine that a pretend character was sitting in a box, many of them began to act as though the pretend character was real. For example, in one experiment, half of the children were told that the pretend character in the box was a rabbit and the other half were told that it was a monster. After being told this, all of the children agreed that it was only a pretend character and that the box was, in actuality, empty. The experimenter then said she had to leave the room for a few minutes.

However, when she attempted to leave the room, 4 of the 12 four-year-olds who had been told that there was a pretend monster in the box would not let her leave the room. None of the older (6-year-old) children acted this way. Upon the experimenter's return, almost half of the children in both age groups said that they wondered if perhaps there was an imaginary creature in the box after all. Further questioning uncovered some magical and unrealistic thinking. Although most of the children admitted to pretense before the experimenter's departure, 25% of the youngest children (3 out of 12) now thought that pretend creatures could become real. These data illustrate the fragility of children's fantasy–reality distinctions. When situations and questioning become more intense, a sizable portion of children appear to give up distinctions between what is real and what is only imagined. In this study, despite the fact that the children were repeatedly assured that the creatures were unreal, it seems that the experimental procedure that encouraged them to imagine that there were creatures in the box was mildly suggestive, thus breaking down their shaky differentiations within a short period of time.

These results suggest that when young children with fragile fantasy–reality boundaries are asked to "pretend" about some events, even ones that seem bizarre, they may eventually become confused about what is real and what is pretend, especially when the interviewer fails to bring the child back to reality.

A host of therapeutic procedures and interviewing techniques are suggestive precisely because they induce fantasies, and in this chapter we provide sundry examples. Asking children to visualize a scene and focus on some aspect of it and then to make up some encounter that may not have taken place is one example. One widely heralded technique, the *cognitive interview*, asks children to visualize how a scene might appear from the perspective of a person or an object that is situated elsewhere in the room, thus encouraging the children to use their imagination. Children are encouraged to abandon reality when therapists delve into symbols or dreams or when they ask children to create a journal account of what *could* happen. Also, self-empowerment training, sometimes using ordinary or anatomical dolls as props, is another technique that is occasionally used by therapists with their child clients. These techniques create the risk that fantasies will eventually come to be believed by the child, particularly if the interviewer does not provide a context for reality testing.

For example, in the Old Cutler case, several of the children were asked by their therapists to demonstrate with the dolls or figurines how they had beat up the defendant. The therapist's goal in using this technique was to help the children "regain control of their victimization." For example, the children would be asked, "Show me (with the doll) what you will do to Bobby if you see him again." Later, some children claimed that they had been transported from their day-care center by the defendant (himself between 11 and 13 years old at the time of the alleged event) in a truck, bound in chains. They claimed that they escaped from their chains, beat up their captor, tied him up, called the police, and then jumped out the window and ran several miles back to their day-care center. The suggestive aspect of the therapeutic procedures appears not to have been considered by the therapists, who later gave sworn statements that they actually believed some aspects of the children's bizarre stories.

When the allegations become very bizarre and unrealistic, some experts defend these as enactments of the child's fear, or as fantasies devised as a result of, or in order to cope with, the terror of their abuse. It is equally plausible, however, that these aberrations result from the interviewers' and therapists' failure to draw children back to reality after they had made "fantastic" claims during fantasy play. Consider the following therapy excerpt from the Old Cutler case. Here the therapist engages in fantasy play with one of the children (NP) suspected of having been abused by Bobby Fijnje, by asking him to use magic power and to imagine scenarios in which his father rescues him from the clutches of Bobby:

Therapist: You wanted to slap him really good, huh?

NP: Slap him.

Therapist: Did C— did Bobby go—

NP: (inaudible) Superman.

Therapist: Hey, Superman, can you find me a Bobby doll? . . . Show me what Bobby did to MA?

NP: He crashed.

Therapist: You better get out of there. You're trapped in there with Bobby.

NP: Daddy, help me.

Parent: Okay, I'll come get you out of—

Therapist: Daddy, would you get him out of there with Bobby. He don't want to be in there with Bobby.

Parent: Here, let me help you.

Therapist: That's what dads are for all right. . . . Okay, I can take this back Dad. . . . Come over here, NP, I've got the NP doll. Bring him over here, would you, please. . . . I really appreciate your help here. I really, really do. We're getting our job done. . . . That should take care of this culprit, okay. . . . I need to be able to see real clear, okay. In case somebody asks me a question. Get all of your energy back, huh.

NP: (giggling and laughing)

Therapist: I need for you to show me exactly what Bobby did to you. . . . I think Bobby wants us to keep this secret. That's why what we're doing is so important. . . . Let NP (the doll) talk. What does NP want to say?. . . What does he want to say to Bobby?

NP: Hey, you stupid pickle head.

Therapist: Okay, you can say anything you want to Bobby. What do you want to say? . . . Do you want to say you hurt me?

NP: Hurt me, big toad.

Therapist: You hurt me you big toad. Did you hurt my sister?

NP: Hurt my sister, big stupid.

Therapist: Okay, and I'm not going to let you do that to me ever again?

NP: I'm going to shock (sic: meant to say "sock") you in the pants and then you'll fall down.

Therapist: Remember about asking for help? So, little guys don't have to do it all by themselves. They can ask for help. . . . Yeah, and if something happens to a little guy you can talk to a big guy so you can get some help. You're putting the bad stuff, the silver bullet stuff in here? Right? There you go, right. All right, so far so good. A little magic (sounds of stirring in a jar). Give NP some courage so he could show Dr. Q. what happened. Give NP some courage.

As can be seen, some therapists used the dolls to get children to reenact their alleged victimization or to regain control of the situation. Often, there is a mixture of role-playing, visualization, and fantasy (e.g., magic potions, silver bullets, and spells) in such sessions. The following testimony by defense expert Dr. Moishe Shopper illustrates how one Little Rascals child engaged in fantasy with her therapist, and then expressed fear after lapsing into fantasy:

Dr. Shopper: [The child] then makes allegations that Mr. Bob put hot sauce on her eyes and her tongue. . . . It's hard for me to imagine how a child can have something this painful done to them without it becoming known to the parent. . . . When asked where this happened, she says that she was in outer space, where she was taken there by Ms. Betsy and Mr. Bob in a hot air balloon.

At this point in the session, the child notices a shirt with a painted frog on it and asks the therapist about it. The therapist replies that it is for a little boy by the name of Jason. According to Shopper's testimony, the following occurs:

Dr. Shopper: The child said that "Jason also was in outer space." And when the therapist asked what happens in outer space, the child answers, "Mr. Bob killed the babies in outer space." When the therapist asked, "How do you know that Mr. Bob killed the babies in outer space?," the child replied, "Because I saw them."

When the therapist asks for more information, the child says, "I'm too scared."

Source monitoring is closely related to the concept of reality monitoring. It involves identifying the origins of our memories in order to elucidate or validate them. For example, it might entail remembering in what place or at what time an event occurred; it also might entail identifying the speaker of an utterance and keeping track of who did or said what. As adults, we monitor the sources of our memories continuously and often unconsciously. Whereas *reality monitoring* refers to remembering whether an event was imagined or real, *source monitoring* refers to keeping track of the origins of sources that *did* occur. The concepts of reality and source monitoring are sometimes indistinguishable when we try to remember whether something actually happened to us or whether someone merely told us that something happened to us.

Source monitoring was initially studied in the context of adult memories because adults occasionally misidentify the sources of their recollections. They may, for example, remember someone telling them about an event when in actuality they had read about the event in a newspaper.

Source monitoring confusions can be the basis of suggestibility effects, at least in some situations. For example, if one cannot remember the source of a false detail that had been provided by an interviewer, one could come to believe that it was actually experienced rather than suggested.

Recently, a number of developmental psychologists have begun to examine source monitoring in children. A few studies have shown that young children are more prone than adults to making source confusion errors (e.g., Ackil & Zaragoza, in press; Lindsay, Gonzales, & Eso, 1995). In these studies, children experienced an event (e.g., they might see a short film), then were later reminded of a number of details about the event, some of which did not occur. Later still, when asked to recall the details of the original event, the subjects often could not monitor the source of the information; that is, they reported that some of the nonoccurring details that were provided after the event actually happened during the event, and they reported that they remembered hearing or seeing the nonoccurring event. This effect happens at all ages, but it seems that younger children make disproportionately more of these kinds of errors.

It also appears that these errors are true reflections of confusions; that is, when subjects are warned before their final recall not to believe anything that was said to them after the event because it was not true, they nevertheless continue to make source errors. Thus, if a child knew that the misinformation had its origins in an interviewer's remarks following an event, they would have ignored it when instructed that all postevent interview information was incorrect. That they do not relinquish such misinformation and insist that it was part of the original event suggests that they have truly blended the origins of input into their memories. This type of error is most prominent in preschoolers (Lindsay et al., 1995).

Poole and Lindsay (in press) demonstrated how source monitoring errors may occur through subtle interventions, such as parents' reading a book to their child. In this study, preschoolers played with "Mr. Science" for 16 minutes in a university laboratory. During this time, the child participated in four demonstrations (e.g., lifting cans with pulleys). Four months later, the children's parents were mailed a story book that was specially constructed for each child. It contained a biographical description of their child's visit to Mr. Science. However, not all of the information was accurate; although the story described two of the experiments that the child had seen, it also described two that the child had not seen. Furthermore, each story finished with the following fabricated account of what had happened when it was time to leave the laboratory:

> Mr. Science wiped (child's name) hands and face with a wet-wipe. The cloth got close to (child's name) mouth and tasted really yuckie.

The parents read the story to their children three times.

These young children were very susceptible to source monitoring errors. When later interviewed by the experimenters, they reported that they had participated in demonstrations that, in actuality, had only been mentioned in the stories read to them by their parents. When asked whether Mr. Science put anything "yuckie" in their mouths, more than half of the children inaccurately replied "yes," and many of these children elaborated their "yes" answers. Moreover, inaccurate reports of having something "yuckie" put in their mouths increased on repeated questioning. When asked, "Did Mr. Science put something yuckie in your mouth or did your Mom just read you this in a story," 71% of the children said that it really happened. The children made these claims even though they had been previously warned that some of the things in the story had not happened and they had been trained to say "no" to nonexperienced events. This study demonstrates how subtle suggestions can influence children's inaccurate reporting of nonevents that, if pursued in follow-up questioning by an interviewer who suspected something sexual had occurred, could lead to a sexual interpretation. For example, an interviewer who is only interested in obtaining information consistent with the hypothesis that the child engaged in oral sex might feel affirmed when told by the child that something "yuckie" was put in his mouth, yet this could conceivably have been something that the child picked up from prior interviewers.

We wondered what would happen if preschoolers were asked repeatedly to think about some event, creating mental images each time they did so. Would this result in subsequent source misattributions that lead to the creation of false memories? In a series of recent studies, we have addressed this issue (Ceci, Huffman, Smith, & Loftus, 1994; Ceci, Loftus, Leichtman, & Bruck, 1994). The events that children were asked to think about were actual events that they experienced in their distant past (e.g., an accident that required stitches) and fictitious events that they never experienced (e.g., getting their hand caught in a mousetrap and having to go to the hospital to get it removed). Because repeatedly creating mental images is a pale version of what can transpire in therapies where a variety of techniques are used to encourage the creation of various images, our studies provide a fairly conservative test of the hypothesis that repeatedly thinking about fictional events can lead to false beliefs about their reality.

Each week for 10 to 11 consecutive weeks, preschool children were individually interviewed by a trained adult. The adult showed the child a set of cards, each containing a different event. The child was invited to pick a card, and then the interviewer would read it to the child, ask the child to think about it before replying, and ask if the event ever happened to them. For example, when the child selected the card that read, "Got finger caught in a mousetrap and had to go to the hospital to get the trap off," the interviewer would ask, "Think real hard, and tell me if this ever happened to you. Do you remember going to the hospital with a mousetrap on your finger?"[1] As can be seen, this is a very simple procedure. Each

---

[1]We have conducted four variants of this procedure, each differing slightly. In the most suggestive one, we told children that their parents already told us that the event occurred, and asked them if they can remember it ("Do you remember the time that . . .?"). In the least suggestive procedure, we simply ask repeatedly if the event happened ("Think real hard, did this ever happen to you?").

week, the interviewer simply asked the child to think real hard about each actual and fictitious event, with prompts to visualize each scene ("I want you to think about who was with you. What were they wearing? How did you feel?").

After 10 weeks of thinking about both real and fictitious events, these preschool children were interviewed by a new adult who asked, "Tell me if this ever happened to you: Did you ever get your finger caught in a mousetrap and have to go to the hospital to get the trap off?" Following the child's reply, the interviewer asked for additional details ("Can you tell me more?" "What happened next?"). When the child indicated that she had no additional details, the interviewer asked a number of follow-up questions that were based on the child's answers. For instance, if the child said that she did go to the hospital to get the mousetrap off, the interviewer asked how she got there, who went with her, and what happened at the hospital.

In our first study (Ceci, Crotteau-Huffman, et al., 1994), 58% of the preschool children produced false narratives to at least one of the fictitious events, with 25% of the children producing false narratives to the majority of the fictitious events. What is so surprising to many who have watched videotapes of these children is the elaborateness of their narratives by the final week. These narratives are frequently embellished, with internally coherent accounts of the context and emotions associated with the accident.

Consider Bill, a 4-year-old, reporting his experience with a mousetrap. At the first session, Bill correctly claimed to have no memory of ever having his hand caught in a mousetrap, and stated that he had never been to a hospital before. By the tenth session, however, an elaborate story has evolved:

> My brother Colin was trying to get Blowtorch (an action figurine) from me, and I wouldn't let him take it from me, so he pushed me into the wood pile where the mousetrap was. And then my finger got caught in it. And then we went to the hospital, and my mommy, daddy, and Colin drove me there, to the hospital in our van, because it was far away. And the doctor put a bandage on this finger (indicating).

As can be seen, Bill does not simply give yes/no answers after he has been repeatedly asked to think about a fictitious experience during the previous 9 weeks; rather, he provides a richly detailed, plausible account. In fact, Bill went on to "explain" how his father was in the basement collecting fire wood at the time of the accident, and how he initially went into the basement to ask his father to make his lunch. It is not only that Bill's story (and those of other children in this study) is so detailed, but it is also very believable to adults who do not know the procedures of the experiment. We think that these children are so believable because at least some of them have come to believe these false stories themselves.

There is one bit of evidence to support our statement that at least some of these children had come to believe that they actually experienced these fictitious events. When ABC's news program *20/20* heard about this study, they asked permission to visit our lab to film some of these children. We agreed and called some parents to ask if they would bring their children back for an interview with John Stossel, the *20/20* interviewer. One parent came in with her 4-year-old son and then told us that she and her husband had thought that the experiment was over, and therefore had explained to their son that the story about the mousetrap was fictitious and had never happened. She said that her son initially refused to accept this debriefing, claiming that he remembered it happening when the family lived in their former house (the child was only an infant when they moved from that house). She and her husband continued to explain that the whole story was just in his imagination, that nothing like this had ever happened. Two days later, when the child came into our lab for the *20/20* interview, Stossel asked him if he ever got his finger caught in a mousetrap. This child stated that he remembered this happening, and then proceeded to supply a detailed narrative. When Stossel challenged him, asking if it was not the case that his parents had already explained that this event never happened, the child protested, "But it really did happen. I remember it!" Although this child's insistence, in the presence of his parents, is not proof that he believed what he was saying about this fictitious event, it does suggest that he was not duping the interviewer for any obvious motive, given that the social pressures were all tilted *against* his claiming that he remembered this, and were tilted *toward* agreeing with the interviewer and his mother that the event never took place. In fact, this child's behavior was typical of a small proportion of the children in this mousetrap study. Twenty-seven percent of the children in this study refused to accept our debriefing, insisting that they remembered the fictitious events occurring.

In the next study (Ceci, Loftus, et al., 1994), we repeated the procedures of the mousetrap study with several modifications. First, we now used explicit memory induction procedures, telling the children that the fictitious events actually happened; then we encouraged children to create mental images about the fictional events. The children were asked about four real events and four false events for 11 consecutive weeks. They were given the following instructions:

> I am going to read some things that happened to you when you were little, and I want you to think real hard about each one of them. Try to make a picture of it in your head. What do you think you would have been wearing when it happened? Who would have been with you? How do you think you would have felt? We made this list up by talking to your mother to get her to tell us about some things that happened to you when you were younger. So, after you make a picture

of it in your head, and think real hard about each thing for a minute, I want you to tell me if you can remember it or not, OK? Don't worry if you cannot remember it though.

As in the previous study, with each session children increasingly assented to false events. The increases in false reports are shown in Figure 14.1. For the 12th-week interview, a new interviewer tried to discredit the previous interviewer by telling the children that the previous interviewer had made lots of mistakes: This new interviewer explained that the previous interviewer had told the children that many things had happened to them when they really had not happened. This new interviewer then asked the child which of the events had really happened. Our logic was that if children were just being acquiescent in the previous interviews, they might now correctly deny that the false events had occurred, even though they had previously claimed to have remembered them. On the other hand, if the children had come to truly believe that they experienced the false events, just as Bill had done with John Stossel, they should continue to maintain that the events had occurred even when told that the previous interviewer was wrong. The latter is essentially what happened; although there were a small number of children who now told the new interviewer that the false events had never really occurred, most of the children who had assented to false beliefs in previous interviews continued to hold onto their false statements. And, as was true in many of our other studies, young preschoolers were more prone to these kinds of persistent and false state-

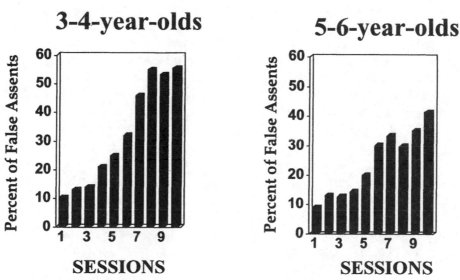

Figure 14.1. Increases in false reports over sessions. Adapted from Ceci, Loftus, Leichtman, & Bruck (1994).

ments than older preschoolers. One hypothesis to account for their difficulty is that there is a confusion among multiple inputs into the memory system. The memory system contains information that is encoded from actual experience, but it also contains information that is encoded from imaginary events. The same neural architecture subserves both functions, thus producing a functional equivalence in the brain. Very young children have particular difficulty separating these sources of familiarity, often mistaking the familiarity of imagined events for real ones.

Thus, preschoolers appear to be vulnerable to source misattributions when they are repeatedly encouraged to think about or visualize events that never occurred. Many of them appear to think that they actually experienced events that they had only imagined. This finding would seem to have relevance for the testimony of a child who has been in a certain type of therapy for a long time, engaging in similar imagery inductions and "memory work" techniques, although clearly the analogy to therapy is imperfect, because of both the nature of the events in question and the techniques used.

In over half of the case studies described in chapter 2 (Old Cutler, Little Rascals, Michaels, Country Walk), children were in counseling for months or even years prior to testifying. Trial testimony and therapy records, where they exist, document repeated imagery inductions, enjoinders to think hard, and repeated encouragement to enact events with props (e.g., dressing a doll as a witch to represent the defendant). Some therapists asked the children to do "homework" or journal writing. These children were encouraged to go home and try to think "very hard" about some of the things that were difficult to talk about. Some therapists played games with the children. For example, one therapist assumed the role of the perpetrator and encouraged the child to assume the role of a policeman. In one session, the therapist touched the genital area of a doll, so that the child could arrest her; the therapist then insisted that she did not do anything, and had the child respond to this remark. This same therapist played another game with another child: According to her trial testimony, she asked him if she should play the "pee game." The child assented and then instructed her to have the dolls (representing the children) pee in the pot and then put it in their mouths. The therapist stated that she did this several times until the child "arrested" her. Several months later, the therapist suggested that they switch roles. Now the child played the "pee game" and the therapist arrested him. According to the therapist, the child was willing to have the dolls pee in the pot and then to have the dolls drink from the pot, but he became very anxious after he was arrested.

There is another element present in many of the day-care cases that could also lead to reality monitoring and source monitoring errors. This involves parents' reading books with abuse themes to their children. These books typically depict situations in which a fantasy character had a "bad" secret that he was afraid to tell. But once he disclosed his bad secret, he felt better. When children had not made disclosures, some therapists gave parents one or more of these books and instructed them to read these to their children.

One story called "Fuzzy the Rabbit" was read to some of the children in the Little Rascals case. The story was about a little rabbit called Fuzzy, who lived with his mother and father in a village of rabbits. The mother and father rabbit had to leave home to find food for the family. During this time Fuzzy was sent to a school for little rabbits. At the school there was one rabbit who was not nice because he

> started[2] telling secrets, things that the little rabbits at school had never heard at home, secret songs, secret touches on their tummies and bottoms, and secret words. Some of the little rabbits thought it was fun at first to have secrets and some didn't know. Then the nice grown-up rabbit did something very bad. He said, "Don't tell your mommy and daddy about the secret or bad things will happen to you."

Fuzzy felt very bad about this because he liked coming home from school and telling his parents about what he had done at school. He had funny feelings inside and began to have problems sleeping. He even began to wonder if he was a bad rabbit. So,

> One night . . . he was thinking about the scary things . . . at school. And the beautiful fairy appeared to him [and] showed him how the pretend grown-up rabbit was really a mean witch . . . who had tried to trick him. . . . The fairy said the way to break the power of the witch and to make him go away was talking . . . to Mommy and Daddy. The fairy sprinkled magic power on Fuzzy. She told Fuzzy . . . he would become stronger and more powerful. Fuzzy went to sleep feeling at peace at last.
>
> The next morning Fuzzy . . . felt very, very powerful. . . . Fuzzy told his mommy and daddy all about the bad things. . . . After he talked to Mommy and Daddy and the other grown-up rabbits, the witch disappeared and Fuzzy felt stronger and more powerful. . . . He found that talking to his mommy and daddy so they would protect and help him was the answer to his problems. So he told them everything about the wicked witch . . . the more he talked, the better he felt. Fuzzy was happy to discover the sound of his voice had made the witch disappear.

We are concerned about this technique on several grounds. First, the results of the Poole and Lindsay (i.e., "Mr. Science") study that we have just described indicate that when suggestions are couched in books that parents read to their children, some of the children may eventually come to believe that the suggested information actually happened to them. How-

---

[2]The story was read at trial by one of the mothers. These excerpts are taken from the trial transcript.

ever, there is an imperfect correlation between the conditions of their study and the conditions under which parents read these books to children suspected of having been abused. In the case studies, the books were intentionally given to the parents so that they could talk to their children about the themes of the book and to encourage the children to think about whether these same things had happened to themselves. Children were asked whether there were any bad people that they knew and whether they had any secrets. And sometimes these books prompted the parents to directly ask their children about abuse.

When one book was unsuccessful in prompting a disclosure, parents were given another "brand" to try. One Little Rascals family had two children in therapy for suspected abuse. After the first assessment session, the therapist gave the mother a book called *Patti the Rabbit* (this was the same story as "Fuzzy the Rabbit"; the former was written for little girls, the latter for little boys) and told her to read it to the girls nightly. The next week, the therapist gave the mother *Tillie the Kitty*. And the third week the therapist read *Boots* to one of the children. The mother was also given *Boots* and was asked to read it to her children. One night soon after, the mother took each child, one at a time, and read them *Patti the Rabbit* and then *Tillie the Kitty*. The children started to make disclosures of abuse that night.

We do not think that the books alone prompted these disclosures, because the children were also visiting their therapists and being questioned by parents and police during the same time period. Perhaps these books served as a catalyst to promote disclosures that were seeded by these other sources. A recent decision by the Supreme Court of Minnesota (*State v. Huss*, 1993) reflects a more extremist view about the potential influences of reading such books to young children. This case was described in the *APA Monitor* (Ewing, 1994, p. 13) as follows:

A recently divorced mother, Ms. Huss, became suspicious concerning the behaviors of her 3-year-old daughter. A medical specialist examined the child and found no medical evidence of abuse. Subsequently, Ms. Huss brought her child to a play therapist who used a number of books about sexual abuse of children, including *It's OK to Tell Secrets*. This book refers to acts of abuse as "yucky secrets." After the book had been read in therapy, Ms. Huss took the book with an accompanying audiotape out of the library. Her daughter subsequently listened to the tape many times and finally disclosed to her mother that she had a "yucky" secret. She told her mother that her father had put his fingers into her vagina and her butt. The child then reported the disclosure to the therapist, who reported the allegation to the authorities. This resulted in a criminal action against the father, Robert Huss, who was convicted of sexual abuse. The appellate court affirmed his conviction. Huss appealed that decision and in October 1993, the state supreme court reversed the conviction, noting that "*Secrets* is a highly suggestive book and . . . its repeated use by the child's mother and therapist combined with the mother's belief that abuse had occurred, may have improperly influenced the child's report of events." The court noted that the child's testimony was contradictory and "even given this contradictory testimony, we might not have been persuaded to reverse [the conviction] absent the repeated used of a highly suggestive book on sexual abuse."

Certainly, our cataloguing of techniques that may promote monitoring errors is a sensitive issue because it raises in some people's minds the possibility that children who are repeatedly exposed to such techniques cannot be believed. Such a conclusion would, we believe, be premature until and unless it can be demonstrated that children are this susceptible to source misattributions about sexual events. And even if they are vulnerable to suggestions about sexual events, it does not mean that their claims are inevitably false, but only that they could be. For example, if therapists simply ask young children to think about certain events that may be beyond the experience and comprehension of children that age, and if the child does come to produce a coherent, logical story, then perhaps the child is in fact faithfully reporting a memory. However, we also believe that the risk of using these techniques could be minimized if therapists gently challenged children to make sure that they understood the need to tell the truth, and repeatedly urged them to check their own memories while engaging in visualization techniques.

The worry is that these safeguards are not always attended to. Asking a child repeatedly to think about the time when he was scared or uncomfortable or to think about whether he was abused is often used in concert with an array of other suggestive techniques (e.g., play therapy). These additional suggestive techniques may provide the details or the script for the child's emerging false memories. Thus, we would not expect most 3-year-olds to have sufficient knowledge to describe oral–genital contacts if they are merely asked to repeatedly think about if someone touched them in a funny way. However, if this request is accompanied by a host of leading questions such as those used in the investigatory interviews that we have reviewed, visually guided imagery may have a profound influence on the accuracy of the children's recall.

A second worry is that therapists and interviewers are often instructed not to challenge the authenticity of children's reports, that doing so will drive the child's emerging disclosure back underground. This is a sensitive issue, too, because frontline workers know from experience that the surest way to get a child to recant a disclosure is to express distrust or disdain. One must take seriously everything the child says. There is, however, a difference between taking a child seriously and believing everything the child says. No parent believes everything their child says, although most of us take our children's statements seriously. One can gently challenge the authenticity of a child's statement without calling into question the child's veracity. For example, one can say to a child who has made a disclosure after suggestive techniques, "OK, now let's talk about what *really* happened, OK? Now you must tell me only about the things that really happened, and not about things that were only pretend."

One expert witness in the Little Rascals case (Dr. Moise Shopper) resoundingly criticized the children's therapists for failing to follow these safeguards. The following are excerpts from the testimony of Dr. Shopper, a child psychiatrist who has devoted much of his professional life to training therapists of young children:

> And the harmful part of the so-called treatment is that there was no attempt to help the child with their reality testing, so that manifestly implausible things, like, "My head was cut off, my arms were cut off," "We were drowned," or "Mr. Bob killed babies in outer space," or "We went for an airplane ride," or "I jumped in and saved so-and-so," these were simply accepted at face value.
>
> And when you accept things at face value, first of all, you are not doing your job as a therapist, but more than that, you do harm to the child because you don't help the child to distinguish between what is possible, what is real, what is not real; what is a fantasy and what is real. And if you accept the child's fantasies as being real, this in the long run becomes very frightening. So a lot of these children got worse in the course of treatment. Their symptoms got worse. They developed more symptoms: more nightmares, more sex play, they became harder to control. And, they did not fare well despite the so-called treatment.
>
> So in answer to your question, these therapists did not do a therapeutic job, but in many ways did the children harm. And it showed up in the sense that many children developed new symptoms and got worse.

MONITORING THE SOURCES OF OUR MEMORIES: ADULT PERSPECTIVES

Although we have emphasized that young children are most prone to making source and reality monitoring errors, this does not imply that children are the only ones to blend real and imagined events. Adults display similar memory problems. For example, in one study, adult subjects experienced an event (they met an Indian woman), and they were also asked to imagine another event (having tea and cookies). Over a period of days, they were asked to review these events in their own minds and to focus on various details. Mentally rehearsing events (especially the perceptual details and the emotions and feelings) made memories of real events more similar to memories of imagined events (Suengas & Johnson, 1988).

On the basis of the adult cognitive literature (see Lindsay & Read, 1994, for a review), distinguishing between what is made up versus what is real is quite difficult to do at a later time. For example, some research by Johnson and her colleagues suggests that adults may be more likely to confuse memories of actual childhood events with imagined childhood events than to confuse memories of actual adult events with imagined adult events (Johnson, Foley, Suengas, & Raye, 1988).

This is exemplified by a recent demonstration by Loftus and her students (Loftus, Feldman, & Dashiell, in press), who attempted to induce false memories in 25 adult subjects of having been lost in a shopping mall when they were young. (According to family members, this event never occurred.) This belief was induced by having a sibling ask them to try to remember the event over the course of the next few weeks. Over this period, approximately 25% of the subjects came to have clearer and more detailed representations of this non-occurring event, which included details concerning how they came to be separated from their parent and how they were finally rescued. As was the case with some of our child subjects, at least one of Loftus's subjects was extremely resistant to the debriefing procedure provided at the end of the experiment, refusing for a while to believe that he had been duped, because his acquired memory seemed so real. Similar studies have been conducted with adults who were led to believe they had been hospitalized at the age of 5 for an ear infection (Hyman, Husband, & Billings, in press). A fifth of these adults succumbed to the suggestions and developed memories of the fictitious event.

This line of studies, along with some other evidence presented later in this chapter, leads us to have a series of concerns about several therapeutic techniques that are used to elicit so-called repressed memories. These concerns are similar to those that we voiced about some interviewing techniques that are used with children.

Some forms of therapy that are popular with suspected survivors of childhood sexual abuse rely on a type of visually guided imagery that could result in source misattributions similar to what was observed with some preschoolers and adults in the studies mentioned above (e.g., Ceci, Huffman, et al., 1994; Ceci, Loftus, et al., 1994; Loftus et al., in press). Self-help books written by experienced clinicians recommend focusing on a childhood theme and generating images around that focal point (e.g., Fredrickson, 1992). Unfortunately, nowhere do these authors acknowledge the risks inherent in the creation of multiple images. In fact, this is dismissed as a problem that can be solved later, after the abuse memory has been recovered, by trying to disentangle mixed images:

> Whether what is remembered around that focal point is made up or
> real is of no concern at the beginning of the process; that can be
> decided at a later date. You need only see what images are in your

mind about the focal point, along with any related body or feeling memories. (p. 109) . . . When the imagery is confusing, you may be mixing images from more than one abusive incident. If you sense that you are doing that, choose only one of the images for now, reminding yourself that you can always work on the contradictory image in another session. (Fredrickson, 1992, p. 114)

In addition to therapists being instructed not to challenge the authenticity of their adult clients' recovered "memories," the clients themselves are urged to resist their own skepticism about the validity of their often hazy, inconsistent memories. Experts have encouraged them to abandon self-doubts, seeing them as evidence that the client is overly sensitive to fairness issues, perhaps a victim of childhood blame:

> Survivors will have a series of realizations about their abuse that they find clear and believable, but rarely do they have a sense of having lived what is being felt or pictured. They call it a memory because the pieces fit into their sense of reality, not because they actually now remember experiencing the abuse. (pp. 96–97) . . . Repressed memories also never feel the same as recall memories. You will not have the sense of having experienced the abuse you are remembering. Expect your repressed memories to have a hazy, dissociated quality to them, even after working with them over an extended period of time. You will gradually come to know that they are real, but not in the same way you remember something that was never repressed. (pp. 99–100) . . . The first thing to check for is if you are more concerned about your memories being made up than real. In other words, you are more worried about being "crazy," making false accusations, and causing your family all kinds of needless trouble than you are about the anguish of being abused as a young child. . . . Having been blamed so often in your family, you can become too sensitive to fairness issues. Like so many survivors, you end up being unfair to yourself in the process. . . . The memories you retrieve seem completely unbelievable and yet, at another level, they feel right. Your dissociation and denial clash with the emotional "fit" of the memory. . . . You may be convinced that your disbelief is a rational questioning of the reality versus unreality of your memories, but it is partially a misguided attempt to repress the memories again. (Fredrickson, 1992, p. 161)[3]

If therapists disseminate such advice, coupled with encouragement to use suggestive techniques, we are concerned that some of their clients could develop elaborate pseudomemories that may not be detected as false by either the client or the professional. One example from the case studies illustrates this danger. In the Country Walk case, Iliana Fuster turned state's evidence and testified that her husband Frank had molested a number of children who were under her care. She also confessed to 12 counts involving molestation of these same children. Recently, however, she re-

[3]From the book *Repressed Memories* by Rene Fredricksen, © 1992. Reprinted by permission of Simon & Schuster, Inc.

tracted her confession and, following this, recanted her retraction! Below we present sections of her sworn statement where she describes how she came to make these allegations during the 2 years that she spent in the Dade county jail prior to her imprisonment. Obviously, we take no stand as to the veracity of her original statement or her retraction of it, or her recantation of her retraction; she obviously presents a grave reliability risk to either side. We present her retraction here solely because it serves to illustrate some of the techniques that we have been discussing in this chapter (e.g., repeated visualization can cause an individual to become unsure whether the visualized material is real or imagined).

> I was in solitary confinement at all times (2 years) . . . I can hardly remember anything . . . they gave me medications . . . they would help me rest, they said, because I wasn't eating properly and I needed to sleep. . . .
>
> I always said that I have nothing to say; that I was innocent . . . and Von Zamft [her attorney] told me that the trial date was coming and . . . he said that I needed to remember something or that I must have something to say. I kept telling him no. And then he thought that I had problems and that I should be seen by a psychologist. And then two psychologists started seeing me . . . they explained to me that I was having problems and that they were there to help me. So they started therapy with me. . . . They diagnosticated that I was having a blackout of events. . . . They came almost every day. And then I started seeing them at nights. . . .
>
> We started talking about the time being in the house in Country Walk. . . I kept saying I was innocent but nobody would listen to me. And they said that I was suffering from a blackout and that those things had happened because the kids said it and the kids don't lie. . . .
>
> They be telling me these stories that the kids were saying about games and stuff happening in the house. [*Note*: Later in her testimony, she claimed that her therapists were getting information about the children's statements from the Bragas.] I would listen to the same things two days, three days, and nights, anytime during the day, on weekends. . . . And you know, before I know it, I was having nightmares. . . . And they said that that was a way of my system remembering what had actually happened.
>
> And then you know, I argued that a little bit, but I got to a point that I was believing that probably those things happened and I just didn't remember because they were so shocking that . . . as a protection I was forgetting about them or putting them in the back of my head. . . .
>
> They told me I had to clear my mind about anything else that was happening. I had to forget that I was in jail and I had to think that I was back in the house. I could actually be in the house. I mean I could

go to any room. They would tell me . . . close your eyes and think you are walking into the room. And I had to give them details of the room first, where the bed was. . . . And then I have to visualize the events the kids were saying and visualized my dreams.

And they said that I was remembering and then after remembering I was going to feel better. And that I needed to help the children and the only way to help them is remembering and backing their word up.

After having the bad dreams, I came to a point that those things really had happened because they convinced me that I was remembering everything through my dreams and I came to realize that maybe those things happened.

But one thing that I always argued with them is how come I didn't have memory of it. And they told me that with time, I will know it. . . . But [now] ten years have gone by and I still don't remember.

[I have no memories] because those things never happened. The big questions that I have had this year is how come I only remember to my nightmares back then, and how come those nightmares are fading, you know to the point that this day I don't have no nightmares?

But the truth of it is that none of these things happened because there's no way that I cannot remember. How come I remember what I was six years old and how come I remember my school? I even remember the bad times I had with Frank. But I don't remember anything with the kids. After getting out of prison, I told myself that maybe the kids would grow up and they will remember too that nothing happened to them. And that maybe if that happened then I'll know what really happened to me.

Of course, this is just one person's memory of psychologists' interviews that took place over 10 years before. In view of her subsequent recantation of part of this statement, it is possible that Iliana's memory of what actually happened is poor or that she is totally confabulating the experience. However, it is possible that the descriptions of the techniques used, her subsequent behaviors, and her psychologists' reactions are accurate but that these behaviors are so atypical as to be noninformative about most other cases. In fact, this type of argument is used to dismiss criticisms of memory recovery therapy in general: That is, it is claimed that very few therapists actually use memory therapy techniques that may be risky (e.g., hypnosis, guided imagery, journal exercises, interpretation of dreams, etc.). To whatever extent this is the case, it would limit any generalizations from this case. However, a recently conducted large-scale survey of the practices of licensed PhD therapists in the United States and Great Britain clearly shows that this dismissive statement is wrong (Poole, Lindsay, Memon, & Bull, in press).

The results of this survey indicated that 25% of the respondents reported a constellation of beliefs and practices indicative of a focus on memory recovery, and that these psychologists reported relatively high rates of memory recovery in their clients. Although 25% is a minority of this population, the researchers concluded that these figures greatly underestimate the number of adults who are being treated by therapists who practice "memory recovery." They estimated that hundreds of thousands of female adult clients have been treated by the members of this highly educated and trained subgroup of therapists. Moreover, this survey did not include therapists who do not have doctoral degrees in psychology. If memory-recovery approaches are more common among less educated mental health professionals, one would estimate that more than 25% of therapists are using such approaches. And these figures do not include the number of therapists who provide treatment to children. Therefore, these numbers do raise some concern about the practices that are being used by at least a substantial minority of therapists in the United States and Great Britain.

Clients are mistaken if they believe that, by virtue of a given therapist's clinical training, research acumen, or knowledge of the sequelae of childhood sexual abuse, that the therapist can distinguish between accurate and inaccurate repressed memories of a client who has been put through relentless suggestive exercises. If a child or adult has been persistently rehearsed with suggestive techniques over long periods of time, there is no way one can be sure that their memory is genuine as opposed to co-constructed. This is particularly the case if the client originally denied the reality of such memories. There is no "Pinocchio Test"; the child's or adult's nose does not grow longer as their reports become less accurate. Until evidence to the contrary can be found, the prudent mental health worker should refrain from urging clients (children and adults) to ignore the telltale signs that their feelings may not be based in reality, and they should refrain from ploughing ahead to unearth evidence of their abuse history without making clear to their clients the reliability risks of such techniques. It is possible that the advice we offer here will be greeted with derision, complaints, and even antipathy by advocates of aggressive memory recovery techniques, who will portray us as part of some putative abuse-denial movement. From our perspective, however, those who prod their clients to assume the reality of ambiguous evidence are risking the mental health of their clients.

The bottom line is that clients should be encouraged to engage in repeated reality testing, and mental health workers should repeatedly test alternate hypotheses when interviewing clients who they believe are uncovering a long-repressed memory. To achieve this goal, therapists might intersperse suggestions that are inconsistent with their hypothesis about the repressed memory and see if the client incorporates these false suggestions into their emerging narrative. If they do, this ought to raise doubts about other aspects of the unfolding report. Clients should not be discouraged from challenging the reality basis of their recollections. To do anything less, given what little we now know, is to court a cognitive as well as emotional disaster.

CONCLUSION

Although we believe that it is possible to make contact with long-forgotten memories during therapy, we also believe that the frequency of such occurrences has probably been exaggerated in the clinical literature. Still, there are undoubtedly some corroborated cases, and we are of the opinion that no good is served by trying to deny the possibility of ever recontacting long-forgotten memories. Whether repression is the best mechanism to explain such a phenomenon remains in doubt, as more prosaic mechanisms seem better able to account for the phenomena. But these alternate mechanisms, unlike repression, involve distortion and forgetting, similar to all forms of remembering.

At the other extreme, we also believe that it is possible to create false memories by using repeated suggestions, visually guided imagery ("think back to a time when you felt uncomfortable . . ."), hypnosis, role-playing ("pretend that I am daddy and you are . . . "), and self-empowerment training ("show me, using the doll to represent you, how you are going to protect yourself the next time you see him . . ."). We do not deny that these techniques may serve important mental health objectives by aiding the client to regain control over his presumed victimization or to bring intrapsychic material to fruition. But based on what we now know, we would be remiss if we failed to point out that such techniques may also serve to increase a client's confidence in his false belief; individuals of all ages may come to believe they have actually experienced what they merely imagined. Although this has not been experimentally demonstrated for the specific case of sexual abuse (because of the ethical impermissibility of trying to convince someone they were molested), a prudent person would assume that similar results would be found in this case, too, given the pervasiveness of the findings from non-sexual-abuse scenarios.

In closing this section on the delayed recovery of memories, we wish to emphasize that this is a very difficult field to work in, and in most cases there is no external verification of these uncovered memories. External verification is the only way to prove the validity of an uncovered memory in therapy, a point also made by the task force reports we mentioned at the outset of this topic. Anyone professing to possess a Pinocchio Test ought to be treated with a large dose of skepticism.

15

AGE DIFFERENCES IN THE RELIABILITY OF REPORTS

Throughout this book we have discussed studies of children's suggestibility without stating any definitive conclusions about age differences. In this chapter, we attempt to summarize these findings. In addition, we examine aspects of suggestibility and memory distortion among adults that may be of importance in understanding some of the case studies.

SUGGESTIVE INTERVIEWS HAVE THE LARGEST IMPACT ON PRESCHOOL CHILDREN

First and foremost, contrary to the claims made by some (e.g., Melton, 1992), there do appear to be significant age differences in suggestibility, with preschool-age children disproportionately more vulnerable to suggestion than either school-age children or adults. This conclusion follows from a synopsis of our previous literature review (Ceci & Bruck, 1993b, Appendix B), where we reported that in approximately 88% of the studies (14 out of 16) that involved comparisons of preschoolers with older children or adults, preschool children were the most suggestible group. Since the date of that publication, new studies on children's suggestibility have been

233

published on a regular basis; these newer data are consistent with the trend that we reported in 1993, with approximately four out of five studies demonstrating significantly greater suggestibility among preschoolers.

Although most researchers would agree with our conclusions regarding age differences in suggestibility, there is still some controversy regarding the boundary conditions for younger children's greater vulnerability. Some argue that suggestibility is diminished or even nonexistent when the act in question concerns a significant action, when the child is a participant (as opposed to a bystander), or when the report is a free narrative, as opposed to a cued or prompted account (e.g., Fivush, 1993; Goodman, Rudy, Bottoms, & Aman, 1990). The strongest claim of this position is that children are not suggestible about personally experienced central actions, especially those that involve their own bodies.

Although it is probably true that children are less prone to suggestions about actions to their own bodies than to neutral, nonbodily acts, the literature clearly does not support the strong view that bodily acts are impervious to distortion. There are numerous demonstrations of how suggestive interviewing procedures can lead children to make inaccurate reports about events involving their own bodies; at times these reports have been tinged with sexual connotations. As noted earlier, young children have made false claims about "silly events" that involved body contact (e.g., "Did the nurse lick your knee? Did she blow in your ear?"), and these false claims persisted in repeated interviewing over a 3-month period (Ornstein, Gordon, & Larus, 1992). Young children falsely reported that a man put something yuckie in their mouths (Poole & Lindsay, in press). Three-year-olds falsely alleged that their pediatrician had inserted a finger or a stick into their genitals (Bruck, Ceci, Francoeur, & Barr, 1995). Preschoolers falsely alleged that some man touched their friends, kissed their friends on the lips, and removed some of the children's clothes (Lepore & Sesco, 1994).

There are other examples that we have not discussed in this book that are provided by research by Goodman and her colleagues. In one study, they reported that 3-year-olds gave false answers 32% of the time to questions such as "Did he touch your private parts," whereas 5-year-olds gave false answers 24% of the time (Goodman et al., 1991). In response to questions such as "How many times did he spank you," 3-year-olds gave false answers 24% of the time, whereas 5-year-olds gave false answers only 3% of the time (Goodman & Aman, 1990). In another study, when 3- and 4-year olds were interviewed about events surrounding an inoculation, there was an error rate of 23% on questions such as "How many times did she kiss you?" and "She touched your bottom didn't she?" (Goodman et al., 1990). That is, many of these children replied "yes" even though these events did not occur. Taking these studies together, one can safely conclude that, compared with older children, young children, and specifically preschoolers, are at a greater risk for suggestion about a wide variety of topics, including those containing potentially sexual themes.

Notwithstanding the above conclusion, it is clear that children—even preschoolers—are capable of accurately recalling much that is forensically relevant. For example, in many of our own studies, children in the control group conditions recalled events flawlessly. This indicates that the absence of suggestive techniques allows even very young preschoolers to provide highly accurate reports, although these may be sparse in the number of details. There are a number of other studies that highlight the strengths of young children's memories (e.g., see Fivush, 1993; Goodman, Batterman-Faunce, & Kenney, 1992, for reviews). What characterizes many such studies is the neutral tone of the interviewer, the limited use of misleading questions (for the most part, if suggestions were used, they were limited to a single occasion), and the absence of the induction of any motive for the child to make a false report. When such conditions are present, it is a common (although not universal) finding that children are much more immune to suggestive influences, particularly about sexual details.

There are three important implications of the studies that focused on the strength of children's reports. The first is that children's inconsistency should not be taken as a marker of their unreliability. Fivush (1993) summarized some data that indicate that children may not provide all elements of an experience during one interview. Additional details may be provided on subsequent interviews, and previously mentioned details may be omitted in subsequent interviews. But remember that this characterization of the child's evolving narrative is based on conversations where there are no suggestive influences. The picture may be different when interviews are repeatedly imbued with suggestions and strong biases.

Second, although children are generally accurate when they are interviewed by a neutral experimenter who asks few leading questions, and when they are not given any motivation to produce distorted reports, there are occasionally a few children who do give bizarre or sexualized answers to some questions. For example, in the Saywitz et al. (1991) study of children's reports of their medical examinations, one child who never had a genital exam falsely reported that the pediatrician had touched her buttocks, and on further questioning claimed that it tickled and that the doctor used a long stick. In a study of children's recalls of their visit to a laboratory (Rudy & Goodman, 1991), one young child claimed that he had seen bones and blood in the research trailer (see Goodman, Taub, et al., 1992, for additional examples). Thus, young children occasionally make spontaneous, strange, and unfounded allegations. However, as Goodman and her colleagues have pointed out, many of these allegations can be understood by sensibly questioning the child and parents further. Often these statistically rare allegations reflect the child's source confusions or anxieties.

One can only imagine what might happen if the rare spontaneous allegations that occurred during experimental interviews were followed up in the same aggressive manner as in some of the case studies. Perhaps participating researchers would have ended up being falsely accused of heinous acts. Conversely, one can imagine that if in the Michaels case the child's initial allegation that "Kelly took my temperature" was investigated in the prudent manner used by Goodman et al. in trying to understand their subjects' bizarre statements, perhaps there would have been no charges.

A third important implication of studies that emphasize the strength of children's memories is that they highlight the conditions under which children should be interviewed if one wishes to obtain reliable reports. Again, when children are interviewed by unbiased, neutral interviewers, when the number of interviews as well as the number of leading questions are kept to a minimum, and when there is the absence of threats, bribes, and peer pressure, children's reports are at considerably less risk for charges of taint.

SUGGESTIVE INTERVIEWS ALSO INFLUENCE THE REPORTS OF OLDER CHILDREN

Although we have concluded that preschool children (those 6 years old and younger) are most at risk for suggestibility, this does not imply that children older than 6 years of age are immune to the effects of suggestive interviews. In some of the studies that we have reviewed in this book, significant suggestibility effects were obtained for children in older age groups. In some studies, 8-year-old, 9-year-old, and even 10-year-old children were found to be significantly more suggestible than adults (Ackil & Zaragoza, in press; Warren & Lane, 1995). Although it could be claimed that these studies have less relevance for the courtroom because children's memories of staged or videotaped events were tested (i.e., the children observed an event), similar findings have been found when children are suggestively interviewed about events in which they themselves participated. For example, we were successful in influencing 7-year-old children's reports of their visit to their pediatrician 1 year previously (Bruck, Ceci, Francoeur, & Barr, 1995). Also, when asked to recall the details of an event that occurred 4 years previously, children between the ages of 7 and 10 were influenced by the atmosphere of accusation created by the experimenters, and came to inaccurately report events even though they had no conscious memory of the original experience (Goodman, Wilson, et al., 1989).

Of course, there are a number of studies that we have described in this book where suggestive influences are negligible in older children, and many studies in which children demonstrate near-perfect accuracy in their recall of events. In the Sam Stone study (Leichtman & Ceci, in press), for example, relatively few of the 6-year-old children made false reports, and in Ceci et al. (1987), 7-year-olds were as accurate as adults. The high levels of accuracy observed in some of these studies may reflect two factors. First, when preschoolers are included in the same study as older children, the task is usually designed to be suitable for the preschool children. As a result, the task may often be too easy for older subjects. It is difficult to create experimental situations that have the same meaning, interest, and difficulty for all age groups.

A second factor is that older children may easily see through the deception in tasks such as Sam Stone, and thus resist suggestion. This does not necessarily mean, however, that older children are impervious to suggestive interviewing procedures. There are a number of well-known cases in which older children did succumb to interviewers' suggestions after initially denying any knowledge of abuse (e.g., Jordan Minnesota, Kern County). It seems that in some cases, children were engaged in highly pressurized interviews; they were told that they could help their (imprisoned) parents after they had been removed from their families or their homes. For example, in the Jordan Minnesota case, Andy Meyers, an 11-year-old child, was removed from the family home and placed across town in an emergency foster placement because his father was suspected of abusing him. He steadfastly denied that his parents had abused him or anyone else. However, after 3 months of almost daily interrogations, he finally told investigators that he had been abused. He claimed that his parents held orgies in the woods and killed babies and then dumped them in a nearby river. His charges, along with those of 39 other children against 24 adults (many of whom were their parents), formed the basis of a long string of indictments that were eventually dropped because of the suggestive manner in which the children had been interviewed. Approximately 9 years after making these charges, Andy described his disclosures to a journalist as follows:

Andy: I finally just said (to investigators) "fine, yeah that happened."

Journalist: Why did you say "yes" that day?

Andy: I have no idea. Probably cause I was just sick of being badgered. I didn't think I was ever going home. I mean, I figured if this is gonna be the way life is, I might as well make it a little more tolerable for myself.

If similar methods were used in our experimental studies, we are of the opinion that we would obtain substantial suggestibility effects in subjects of all ages, including adults. However, this level of deception and coercion would be ethically unacceptable to use in research.

As we have seen in the Macias case, however, older children may at times be suggestible under less coercive circumstances. Jennifer F. was 9 years old when she first testified. And as we have shown, her testimony was inconsistent and influenced by the suggestive questions of the interviewer. Her recantation at age 13, which we quote on the final page of this book, attests to the social influences on her testimony.

MEMORY DISTORTION AND SUGGESTIBILITY EFFECTS IN ADULTS

Although the focus of this book is on children's suggestibility, there is a substantial literature on how adults' reports and memories can be influenced, changed, distorted, or created by a variety of factors, many of which are suggestive in nature. A review of this literature is beyond the scope of this book (the interested reader should consult Lindsay & Read, 1994; Loftus & Wells, 1984; Ross, 1989), but to more completely understand the evolution of allegations in some of the case studies, the behavior of adults needs to be considered briefly.

Suggestive Influences on Adults' Reports: An Example From the Case Histories

Our first point is that in at least one case (Country Walk), an adult appears to have been influenced by highly suggestive and coercive interviewing practices. Country Walk has received wide attention because it is one of the only cases where there seems to have been "hard" evidence that ritualistic abuse occurred. Despite the use of highly suggestive interviewing procedures that produced seemingly bizarre disclosures of ritualistic abuse, the children's reports were later corroborated by Iliana Fuster, wife of the principal defendant, Frank Fuster. She confessed to multiple counts of child molestation and testified against her husband, accusing him of many crimes against the children.

However, as we summarized in the previous chapter, there is some new evidence to suggest that Iliana's own contradictory statements may have been the result of intensive suggestive investigative techniques that some have claimed are best termed "brainwashing" (see Nathan, 1993a, 1993b, for full details).

According to Nathan's well-investigated account, Iliana's lawyer attempted to persuade her to give state's evidence in return for a reduced sentence. Initially, she allegedly repeatedly rebuffed these suggestions. But after she was put into an isolation cell where she was kept naked and put under a suicide watch, she began to claim that she had been abused by her husband; however, she continued to insist that none of the children had been molested by him. Next, Iliana's lawyer hired two psychologists who ran a business called "Behavior Changers." They visited her in prison and conducted relaxation and visualization exercises; during these sessions, they constantly told Iliana that if she confessed, she would receive a lesser sentence, but that if she didn't confess, she would face the horrors of a long prison sentence. After approximately 34 such sessions with the "Behavior Changers" that involved visually guided imagery, trance inductions, and enjoinders to take the state's plea offer, Iliana pleaded guilty to 12 of 14 counts of sexual abuse. At the time, her speech to the court hardly admitted her guilt:

> Judge, I would like you to know that I am pleading guilty not because I feel guilty, but because I think . . . it's the best interest . . . for my own interest and for the children and for the court and all the people that are working on the case. But I am not pleading guilty because I feel guilty . . . I am innocent of all those charges. . . . I'm just pleading guilty to get all this over . . . for my own good. (quote taken from Nathan, 1993a)

With each future deposition, Iliana began to produce more and more reports of ritualistic acts that included the abuse of the children. During these depositions, the psychologists would request brief breaks to help Iliana remember some of these events. We do not know the nature of the techniques used during these breaks and whether they involved suggestions, coercions, partial trance states, or imagery inductions. Subsequently, Iliana has given at least two more statements in which she makes diametrically opposite claims regarding Frank Fuster's innocence. She seemed to sway with the wind, affirming the agenda of the side that questioned her.

Nonetheless, Iliana's treatment by her jailers, attorneys, and psychologists raises questions about the suggestibility of her testimony. Her trial testimony, as we have seen, was produced as she was on the verge of a seemingly psychic breakdown after intervals of isolation and coercive persuasion. If this testimony was false, coupled with the high false-positive rate of the gonorrhea test given to her step-son (see chapter 16), it would tend to cast doubt on the sole "validated" example of ritualistic abuse in a day-care case. On the other hand, if either of her more recent statements is false, the result of her caving into pressures from either side, we can only conclude that this troubled woman is hopelessly unreliable and unable to shed light on this case.

Social Pressures Influence Adults' Beliefs: Examples From the Cases

Although other adults were not faced with these same coercive techniques, there are numerous examples of the types of social pressures in the community that led adults to believe that their children had been abused. The Little Rascals case has a number of examples of how parents came to agree with the prosecution, either because they were at risk for losing their friends in the community who deeply believed in the prosecution or because they were afraid that they themselves might be accused. When the first allegations were made against Bob Kelly, many parents supported the Kellys and continued to send their children to the Little Rascals day-care center. One of the parents, Chris Bean, initially served as Bob Kelly's lawyer. According to Bean, he relinquished this role a few months later, when a police officer and the district attorney told him that the children were naming his own 5-year old son as one of the victims. But there was also social pressure for Bean to stop defending Bob Kelly. As more and more families learned of their children's alleged abuse, the town became divided: There were those who believed something had happened to their children, and there were the "others." The Beans became the "others." Friends stopped talking to them, and they became socially isolated. It almost seemed that having a child suspected of being abused made one part of the "in-group."

It is not that the parents wanted to believe that their children had been abused, but there were many pressures that made it hard for them to reject this belief. The following statement was made by a mother who initially believed that her son had been abused, but later decided that nothing had happened:

Prosecutor: You wanted to believe that your son had been abused?

Mother: Wanted to believe that he was abused? No, you are wording it wrong. It was once you got on this wagon that was going through town, sir, there was no way off. And if you jumped off of it like I did, then believe me, after people saw the way that I was treated, then they didn't want to get off of it and they weren't going to get off of it.

Although it is important not to overstate the extent to which community pressures militated against parent defections, in a number of the case studies there was evidence of fear of being ostracized among parents who contemplated testifying for the defense. Although we have no evidence for the reverse, it is possible that in some cases, witnesses who contemplate testifying for the prosecution might perceive similar pressures.

Retrospective Memories

Another issue concerning the adults in the case studies involves the parents' recollections of their children's behaviors and physical complaints while they attended day care and before any allegations of abuse had been made. A review of the investigators' initial interviews with the parents reveals that most stated that their children seemed to enjoy their day care and were fond of their day-care teachers. The parents did not spontaneously mention any behavioral problems or medical concerns. When available prior to the onset of criminal charges, examinations of the children's medical records revealed that the parents had not expressed any concern to their children's pediatricians about their children's physical or psychological well-being. In the few cases where parents had expressed such concern, either the symptoms were present long before the child had attended day care, or the pediatricians were not concerned about the symptoms.

As the criminal allegations grew, many parents began reporting that they had noticed disturbing behaviors in their children before the allegations were made. They described sleeping difficulties, extreme problems with separation, tantrums, pleas by their children not to go to day care, and especially pleas to be excused from nap time. Other parents recalled physical symptoms that took on significance once the allegations became common. For instance, children had genital rashes and gastrointestinal problems (which were later thought to be due to either stress or poisoning).

There are several interpretations of these reports. The first is that the allegations and the resultant investigations prompted the parents to think more carefully about their children's past behaviors and physical well-being. Consequently, parents may have been able to retrieve significant facts that they had previously overlooked (e.g., nightmares, genital redness, reluctance to attend day care) during the period when the alleged activities occurred. A related interpretation is that the parents always remembered these behaviors, which were regarded as normal before allegations were made, but that they took on special significance in light of their children's allegations. For example, one of the parents in the Michaels case recalled a trip to the shopping mall where her son and one of his female classmates lay on top of each other and wiggled around. At that time, the mothers of these children thought, "Isn't this nice? They are still young enough to be uninhibited." Two years, later, the same mother interpreted this incident as an example of her child's sexual acting-out behaviors.

A completely different interpretation of the parents' reports is that these were accurate depictions of their children's behaviors, but that the parents were incorrect about the timing. That is, the parents recalled aspects of their children's behaviors that occurred after they had made allegations and the series of interviews and examinations had begun. For example, some children in the case studies appear to have developed severe behavioral problems and sexually explicit behaviors only after they were repeatedly interviewed. All three interpretations are possible, and none are atypical. Our memories of the past become molded by our present experiences and expectations.

Adults' Memories of Conversations: The Need for Electronic Recording

The final issue we raise in this section concerns adults' reports of their conversations or interviews with children who made allegations that eventually formed the basis of legal proceedings. One might think that in such important criminal investigations as those described in this book, there would be electronic (video or audio) recordings of the initial interviews, as well as all subsequent interviews, with the children so that the court could hear the earliest versions of the child's stories in the child's own words and examine how the child's story changed over time. Such evidence is crucial to rule out the potential influences of coaching and interrogative suggestion. Although one would excuse such missing data when the allegation was first made to parents, one would hope that it would be normal procedure for the police, social workers, and therapists to have recorded all interviews with the children, if the purpose of the interview could—even remotely—be considered "forensic."

Surprisingly, with the exception of Country Walk, much of this information is not available for the day-care cases. In certain instances, it appears to have been destroyed or missing. In other instances, the interviews were never recorded in the first place. In the Little Rascals case, Bob Kelly, Dawn Wilson, and Betsy Kelly were sent to jail for crimes against children. However, none of the crucial evidence provided by the children was electronically preserved: There are no audio- or videotaped records of the initial interviews with the child witnesses. To our knowledge, with the exception of one audiotape of a child's interview with the district attorney, there are no electronic recordings of the later forensic interviews or of the many therapy sessions with the child witnesses.

There is also scanty information concerning how the children in the Michaels case were initially questioned and how many times they were questioned. There are no electronic copies of the very first interviews conducted at the prosecutor's office in the first week of May 1985 with three of the children and their parents. Importantly, there are no recorded interviews with the child who made the initial allegation. What do exist are 39 recorded interviews with 34 children conducted by the Division of Youth and Family Services over a 2-month period. However, because the recording was instituted after several weeks of interviewing, there are no electronic recordings of these children's initial interviews, nor are there any recordings of the interviews with the parents. In addition, most of the other therapeutic and forensic interviews that were conducted since that time were not recorded.

Some early interviews *were* recorded in the Michaels case, and in some of these the child gave a coherent report of abuse in response to the investigator's neutral questions. However, because we do not have the details of the first interview, it is impossible to evaluate the reliability of these children's statements. If in the first interview the child had been subjected to the same techniques that occurred in some of the later taped interviews, the reliability of his statements would be suspect. Conversely, if the first interview did not contain such techniques, then the accuracy of children's statements would not be contestable. It is thus important and necessary to electronically record the earliest interviews with children, and not simply turn on the video or tape recorder weeks or months later when the children begin to make allegations.

Given the absence of these electronic recordings in some of our case studies, the court was presented with hearsay evidence from parents, investigators, and therapists (which is admissible in many courts dealing with child witnesses). But the court was at times also provided with parents', therapists', and forensic investigators' written summaries of conversations with the child witnesses. That is, these interviewers prepared reports based on their notes or recollections of their meetings with the children. But as we will argue in the rest of this chapter, written summaries are no substitute for electronic recordings of these interviews, particularly in legal proceedings.

Written summaries of unrecorded interviews are subject to a number of distortions, especially if the interviewer is questioning a number of children and parents daily, as happened in the day-care cases. If the investigator has a bias that the child was sexually abused, this can color his interpretations of what the child said or did; it is this interpretation that can appear in the summary in lieu of a factual account of what transpired.

In the Little Rascals case, there appear to be a number of inaccuracies in the police and therapists' reports. As noted in chapter 12, one mother called into question the accuracy of several important details in Officer Brenda Toppin's initial interview with her young son. This mother asserted that in the report her child had referred to his genitals as a "ding-a-ling," whereas she claimed in actuality he never used that word. A second example, taken from this same mother's trial testimony, speaks for itself:

Mother (Mrs. F.): She asked him if he knew what the word sex meant and he said that he was a big boy and he was going to real school next year and of course he knew what sex meant, "Sex is when you color and you stay in the lines." . . .

Attorney: Mrs. F., let me hand you what I have marked for identification as Defendant's Exhibit 107, which is a page . . . reflecting the interview notes from the department of social services with your son; have you had an opportunity to review that previously at my request?

Mother: Yes, I have. . . . There are several things that are just out and out inaccurate. . . . Um, it then says, "When asked when [sic] the word sex meant, he said it means when you take your clothes off." That's an out and out inaccurate statement . . . that particular story of coloring and staying in the lines was repeated the next morning to my family as one of those things I figured I'd remember and embarrass him with when he's twenty years old. Um, that's totally inaccurate.

This interview was not recorded, but later written from notes taken by a participating social worker. It is easy to imagine how such mistakes could innocently occur; the investigator cannot talk to the child and at the same time take verbatim notes of everything the child says. When later reconstructing these reports from notes or memory, the investigator may use his own words or, at times, intrude details from other interviews that had been conducted around the same time. In addition, the investigator's hunch about a case may guide his post-interview summary in such a manner to create "probabilistic reconstructions" by mistakenly inserting antecedents and contextual information.

Another mother in the Little Rascals case was highly critical about the accuracy of the principal therapist's written reports of therapy sessions with her 3-year-old son, James. In one of these reports, the therapist noted that James accurately identified three of the accused day-care workers from a picture that had appeared in the newspaper. However, the mother, who was present during this session, claimed that James could not identify the workers and that the therapist had prompted him with the correct answers. It also seems that one of the defendants in the case was originally indicted on the basis of the therapist's written report of an allegation of this same child that, according to the therapist, was relayed by the mother. On learning of this, James's mother pointed out to the therapist that she had never relayed such information and that the report should be corrected. Although the therapist had allegedly promised to correct it, the indictment was still handed down; it appears to have been based on the therapist's incorrect report of James's statement.

One other disturbing element of James's mother's testimony, and that of some other parents whose children saw the same therapist, is the observation that the therapist did not electronically record the sessions with the children. Nevertheless, this therapist produced transcripts of sessions for the prosecution. These transcripts lead the reader to believe that they were transcribed from audiotape, because they were written in dialogue form with quotation marks around the statements of the participants. If some of these parents were correct that these sessions were not audiotaped, then they were constructed after the therapy sessions ended on the basis of notes made during sessions, supplemented by the therapist's memory. Given the many inaccuracies that one mother noted in this therapist's reports, and on the basis of some data to be presented later in this chapter, these reports cannot be regarded as a faithful record of the events of the therapy sessions. Although a therapist may use them to refresh her memory, they should not be used in criminal investigations. Research shows that such reconstructions present quite serious reliability risks.

In the Little Rascals case, after their children were suspected of having been abused, parents were asked to keep diaries of their conversations with their children. One might think that the conversations recorded in a parent's diary would be accurate. After all, parents, unlike the therapists and forensic investigators, were not interviewing lots of children; they were only dealing with their own child, thus reducing one possible source of contamination. In addition, because parents are familiar with their child's vocabulary and manner of speech, they may be in a better position to accurately record conversations. But it appears that there may be problems with the accuracy of parents' diaries. First, it is impossible for a parent to write down everything that their child says, and one is thus left with entries that reflect what the parent thinks are "significant" events. Second, it was highly unusual for parents to make detailed notes while talking to their children. Rarely did they sit down with their diaries and write down word-for-word their conversations. The entries were made hours and sometimes days after. Here is one parent's account of how these records were kept:

Mother: I wrote down the first conversation with Dave when he was getting ready to take a nap that day. And I think I wrote down something else, I'm not sure. Because I found it rather hard to do it, to go back. You had a conversation with your child and then you talked to your child about something else, and then the child goes to sleep, to go back in there and sit down and try to remember what you had asked your child and what your child had said. I found it hard to do. . . .

Attorney: Did you turn those notes over to the prosecutor or over to the police?

Mother: Yes. Brenda [the police officer] called me several times and wanted the notes, and I hadn't written them yet. And this was several weeks afterwards. And I sat down and wrote down to the best of my recollection what I could remember of just the conversation where he had said that Mr. Bob had stuck his penis in his mouth, and I turned those notes in.

Prosecutor: (reads the following excerpt from the mother's diary:)

"Dave.: It peed right here, momma. *Pointed to cheek.*

Mother: How did it pee right there?

Dave: Mr. Bob put his privates in my mouth.

Mother: What are his privates?

Dave: Mr. Bob put his pee-bug in my mouth. I was bad.

Mother: No, Dave you were not bad. You are a very good boy and I love you.

Dave: Are you mad at me?

Mother: No sweetheart, I am not mad at you.

Dave: Is Daddy mad at me?

Mother: Nobody is mad at you, not Daddy or anybody else.

Dave: Is Rick mad at me?

Mother: No, Rick is not mad at you.

Dave: Is David mad at me?

Mother: No, Dave, nobody is mad at you. We all love you very much."

Does that accurately reflect the conversation you had with your son on April 28th, 1989, that caused you to call Brenda Toppin at the Edenton Police Department?

Mother: I don't know. A lot of this I think I put in here from different conversations when I wrote this up. This isn't the exact conversation that was carrying on. Like I said, I was scared. I did not know that it was all right not to keep notes. I thought that I had to hand these notes in to Brenda Toppin. . . . And I wrote these up several weeks later. And I wrote them all up at the same time and I tried to remember the dates when Brenda had came out there. And I tried to get the dates straight when I wrote the date at the top of them. . . .

Prosecutor: So your testimony is that this is not an accurate account of what Dave told you on April 28—

Mother: Sir, I'm sure that I added some to it. I'm sure that I did. I'm sure that I made it out to be a lot worse than it was. Yes, sir, I am.

Prosecutor: Tell us why you did that, ma'am.

Mother: He (Bob Kelly) was already in jail.

Prosecutor: What did you add to it?

Mother: Well, I'll tell you what, I didn't put down there everything that I had asked him and all the times that he had
denied it. I didn't put all that down there. I didn't put
down there that he had been questioned every day. I
didn't put down there that he had asked to go back to
the day care, that he wanted to go back to the day care.
I didn't put all of that stuff down there. I didn't put any
of it down there.

There are other reasons for requiring electronically preserved interviews with the children. These have to do with the fact that it is crucial
not only to have a record for the "gist" of the conversations (which we
have reason to believe were not accurately preserved in many instances),
but to have a verbatim record of the adult's words and the child's words.
At the very minimum, we need to know all the linguistic details of the
interviews prior to, during, and following the initial allegations. Written
reports that contain statements such as "The child said that Mr. Bob told
them secrets" are meaningless. We need to know whether this was a spontaneous remark, whether this was prompted by an open-ended question
(e.g., "What did Mr. Bob tell you?"), or whether this is merely the interviewer's memory of the gist of a conversation in which the interviewer
asked, "Did Mr. Bob ask you to keep secrets?" and the child reluctantly
may have replied, "Yes." Some summaries of the interviews are written in
such a way as to make one believe that children made spontaneous and
detailed statements about sexual abuse. However, in the few instances
where we have transcripts of some other interviews, it is clear that the
child only responded "yes" or "no" to a barrage of leading questions. But
even if a child does make a spontaneous statement, it is important to know
about the preceding questions and comments by the investigators. For example, was there an "atmosphere of accusation," encouragement to discuss
specific themes, or imagery inductions?

La Fontaine (1994), in her analysis of allegations of ritualistic abuse
claims commissioned by the Department of Health in the United Kingdom,
complained that summaries of interviews frequently neglected to include
important contextual information, such as the number and type of prior
questions:

The nature and content of interviews may be hidden when summaries
are made for a case conference or an affidavit. It was stated in one
affidavit that a little boy had "talked of ghosts" in an interview. The
transcript of the interview showed an hour in which the interviewer
had asked 33 questions on the subject of ghosts, to which the child
had given a few short, and apparently reluctant, answers. (p. 28)

Although some interviewers may defend the accuracy of their own
reports by stating that they remembered the exact wording of their ques-

tions and of the child's answers, there is a substantial literature to document the fact that when adults are asked to recall conversations or passages that they have just heard, their verbatim memory fades within seconds. Subjects tend to extract the meaning, but they forget the form or the exact wording (see Rayner & Pollatsek, 1989, for a review). It may be true that we can remember highly unusual utterances in a conversation, but in a long interview, it is not possible to remember the forms of all of the questions and answers, their context and antecedents, and the emotional tone of the participants.

Proposals for Mandated Video Recording of Child Witness Interviews

Because of these concerns and others, there have recently been some proposals to institute mandated videotaping of interviews with child witnesses (see Child Victim Witness Investigative Pilot Projects, 1994; McGough, 1994). These videotaped interviews could ultimately be used in the courtroom as a substitute or supplement to the child witness's testimony.[1] Proponents of these proposals cite the following advantages. First, children might be spared multiple interviews, because other investigators could review earlier interviews rather than repeating the process. An equally important advantage is that videotapes may provide an important incentive for investigators to carry out proper interviews because they know that they will be scrutinized by the defense team. Another advantage of the use of videotape is that it preserves the evidence of abuse—it provides a record of both the child's verbal and nonverbal behavior during the interviews and subsequent disclosures. This is particularly important when there are long delays between disclosure and trial. Videotapes of the children's interviews are also thought to be useful in convincing non-offending family members that another family member did commit abuse. And finally, videotapes may encourage confessions on the part of the defendant. This is just a brief list of some of the proposed advantages, but it does give a flavor of legal scholars' and policymakers' sensitivity to the issues that we have discussed in the book.

There are also a number of disadvantages that opponents of videotaping proffer. First, some have argued that videotaping may allow the defense an opportunity to exaggerate inconsistencies in the children's statement or to use the videotapes to magnify and distort the existence of "poor" interviewing practices. We have certainly seen this ourselves; some experts go through videotapes of interviews with child witnesses frame by

---

[1]In this chapter, we do not delve into the legal implications of these proposed reforms. The reader should consult McGough's (1994) chapter on this matter.

frame to locate flaws that would not otherwise be detectable. (Of course, the argument goes that prosecution experts could also repeat the same exercise, emphasizing each point where children seem to be responding appropriately to "good" interviewing practices and where children seem to be responding appropriately.) Other arguments against the use of videotape include the concern that the use of electronic recording may inhibit the child. For any researcher, however, who has conducted laboratory studies, this concern is a trivial one. Children quickly acclimate to recording equipment in the interview room, and forget its presence. Furthermore, if the room is set up properly, the video camera can be hidden so that it is undetectable.

So far, we have few data to support the proposed advantages or disadvantages of mandated videotaping of interviews with child witnesses. However, survey data from a pilot project on the taping of investigative interviews suggest that the benefits of videotaping far outweigh the drawbacks (Child Victim Witness Investigative Pilot Projects, 1994). Most of the professionals (law enforcement agents, district attorneys, and social service workers) were enthusiastic about the implementation of videotaping; these professionals expressed the wish to have these procedures continue in the future. As the authors of this report stated, these evaluations are based on professionals' ratings of the pros and cons of videotaping. These data do not indicate the degree to which videotaping itself influences the decisions of the jurors in the courtroom.

Although we believe there are many advantages to videotaping, we also have several concerns. If mandated videotaping were implemented, we would want to make sure that it has the following requirements. The major one concerns when to begin video-taping. It is crucial that the videotaped interviews include the first and all subsequent interviews. Providing a videotape of the session in which the child makes a disclosure is useless unless we know how this disclosure came about, what preceded it, and what succeeded it. Thus, we have a real concern that if a videotape of a child's disclosure is required, previous interviews may go unrecorded or even unreported.

We are also concerned about which types of interviews would be recorded. The research and evaluation advisory panel of the Child Victim Witness Investigative Pilot Projects program recommended that investigative interviews and multidisciplinary interviews be videotaped. But the panel recommended that therapy sessions not be videotaped unless videotaping is done for therapeutic purposes. We feel uneasy about this recommendation. On the one hand, we understand the great burden it would place on many mental health professionals to record all therapy sessions, because in most of their cases abuse is not suspected. But this would be necessary because, as was true in the Old Cutler case, some therapists only began to suspect abuse after many sessions with a child who was brought in for other reasons. Therapists might claim that it is unreasonable to collect months and sometimes years of electronic recordings of sessions when there is little risk of a child making an allegation.

There are two solutions to this problem. The first is one followed by some therapists, who during the first interview tell their clients that they will not be preserving any details of the sessions. If there is any behavior that occurs that might lead to civil or criminal actions, the therapist will not be able to participate. (Of course, because of mandated reporting of abuse, the therapist would have to contact the local agency, but at that point could leave the investigation of the case to other professionals.) The second solution is that as soon as a therapist has any indication that a client will be involved in a criminal or civil suit, she begin to fastidiously preserve all contacts. Of course, one could quibble with the timing of this decision, but there are clearly extremes that could be avoided. For example, in the Little Rascals case, some therapists knew almost from the beginning that their clients were going to be involved in criminal actions. These therapists had contact with law enforcement personnel and with the district attorneys. And yet there is not, to our knowledge, one existing tape of any therapeutic session or, with one exception, of a forensic interview.

One might argue that we are making mountains out of molehills in advocating for the recording of all interviews. Putting aside the very real logistical problems that this recommendation entails, one can ask if it will really matter. Will interviewers be more accurate or careful if they suspect that their behavior will be reviewed? Will this result in some children refusing to disclose if they are aware of the camera or tape recorder? Will juries be influenced by watching the interviews? We do not have good answers to these questions, but there is some fascinating indication that the last question can be answered in the affirmative. In the McMartin case (*State v. Buckey*, 1990), one of the first of the day-care cases in the United States, the jury in the first trial acquitted Raymond Buckey and his mother, Virginia McMartin Buckey, on 52 out of the 65 counts and "hung" on the remaining 13 counts. During a postverdict press conference, many jurors claimed that they believed that some of the children had been abused, but were unable to reach a guilty verdict because of the highly suggestive interviews of these children, which the jurors saw on videotape. According to one of the jurors, "The interviewers asked questions in such a leading manner that we never got the children's stories in their own words." And according to another juror, "Without the tapes, I would have been able to believe the children a little more" (Tranquada, 1990). These statements clearly indicate the large influence that the videotaped interviews did have on these jurors.

SUMMARY

In this chapter we have argued that a thorough review of the literature reveals that there are pronounced age differences in children's suggestibility, with preschoolers most prone to suggestive influences. This conclusion is not limited to children's suggestibility about peripheral, unimportant details. Some studies have demonstrated that children can be led to fabricate entire episodes of an event, whereas other studies demonstrate that children can be led to make false statements about actions to their own bodies that, if these had occurred, could have been quite painful or embarrassing, or else could be interpreted as involving sexual abuse.

This said, it is also important to emphasize that in response to the questions of a neutral, unbiased interviewer, young children can give very accurate reports, although these may contain few details. It is also true that although there are age differences in suggestibility, older children and adults' memories can be tainted by a number of suggestive influences. We emphasize the fallibility of adults' memories of conversations, which underscores the importance of electronically recording forensic interviews, particularly with young children.

In the next chapter, we will consider some of the psychological mechanisms that might account for age-related differences in suggestibility.

16

MECHANISMS THAT MAY ACCOUNT FOR AGE DIFFERENCES IN SUGGESTIBILITY

Although the literature clearly reveals age differences in overall suggestibility, the exact mechanisms that account for this greater distortion in young children's reports are still being debated by researchers. In this chapter, we will provide a brief overview of some of the proposed factors that underlie suggestibility in children and adults but that may be particularly important in accounting for the observed age differences we have discussed in this book.

MEMORY

Some researchers have posited that age differences in suggestibility can be directly linked to age differences in memory. Specifically, children's greater susceptibility to suggestion is viewed as a direct outgrowth of their relatively weaker ability to accurately encode, store, retrieve, and monitor different types of information.

This position is based on a fairly large literature that indicates that a variety of memory skills do improve with age (e.g., see reviews by Kail,

1989; Schneider & Pressley, 1989) and that younger children tend to lose information from storage more rapidly than older children. It is also based on a theoretical position that, in general, suggestibility is related to the strength of one's memory. According to this hypothesis, if information about an event is weakly encoded or if it becomes degraded or lost in storage (which is more likely to be the case with very young children), it will be easier to implant a false suggestion than if the memory was strongly encoded and well-preserved in storage. For example, if the child does not have a clear memory of an event that occurred several years previously at his day-care center, it may be easier to suggest that "bad things" happened to that child than to another child who has a strong memory of the event.

Some researchers have provided support for the proposal that there is a link between suggestibility and memory strength in children (Pezdek & Roe, in press; Warren, Hulse-Trotter, & Tubbs, 1991), but there are other researchers who have argued that there is no consistent relationship between a memory's strength and children's susceptibility to suggestion (Howe, 1991; Zaragoza, 1991). Intuitively, we feel that it makes a great deal of sense to link suggestibility-proneness to the strength of memory. Try suggesting to someone that their birthday is different from what they have been repeatedly told it is. No amount of false suggestions will overwrite the original memory because it is simply too strong, because of years of repetition and reinforcement. On the other hand, it is relatively easy to suggest to someone that their friend's birthday is different from what they were once told. We anticipate that in the coming years there will be increasing evidence for the principle that the weaker the memory, the greater its proneness to being altered or interfered with as a result of erroneous suggestions, even though the current evidence for this principle is ambiguous.

KNOWLEDGE

To a large extent, the ability to encode, store, and retrieve information is directly dependent on the types of knowledge that one possesses. But the amount and structure of one's knowledge about the world can also indirectly influence one's susceptibility to suggestion. Because children have a weaker knowledge base, this may at times account for their greater susceptibility to suggestion. We provide a number of examples of how this mechanism could potentially operate.

Semantic Knowledge

Children differ from adults in the number of facts they have stored in their memories, in their understanding of the structure of events, and in their expectancies about the way the world works. Occasionally, children may have knowledge advantages in certain areas (for example, when they possess greater knowledge about cartoon characters than adults). But generally, knowledge increases as a function of age.

The amount and structure of knowledge can lead to different inferences about witnessed events. Usually, increased knowledge facilitates accurate recall (although not invariably). For example, children's memory for events that transpired during a doctor's visit is related to their knowledge of the types of activities that usually occur in a doctor's office (Ornstein et al., in press), and children's memory for chess positions in a specific game is highly related to their knowledge of chess (Chi, 1978). Another example of this principle is provided by a recent study of preschool children's recall of a fire drill at their day care (Pillemer, Picariello, & Pruett, 1994). In this study, very young preschoolers, but not older ones, erroneously recollected some of the events because of their lack of understanding of the causal structure of the event. For instance, younger children recollected that they first left the building and then heard the fire alarm. This sequencing error was not made by older children, presumably because they understood the procedures of a fire drill.

The relationship of semantic knowledge and memory has important implications for understanding age-related differences in suggestibility. Because of their relatively impoverished knowledge base for many different types of events and experiences, it may be easier to implant suggestions in children than in adults. This may occur when the suggestion is bizarre or incongruent with the adult's knowledge of the world, but is meaningless to the child because of her sparse knowledge of the topic. This may be particularly important in investigations of sexual abuse, where young children have fairly limited sexual knowledge, allowing the incorporation of false suggestions that, because of their implausibility, would be rejected by older children. For example, a parent gave the following testimony about the parent's child at the trial of Kelly Michaels:

> [The child] said that sometimes [the child] stuck a saw or a sword up Kelly's butt and sometimes a knife. . . . She was very polite. She said "thank you."

Scripted Knowledge

Temporally organized, habitual, agent–actor–action routines are referred to as *scripts*. For example, a script for going to a restaurant includes the expectation that the waitress first takes a party to its table, then a menu is used to make a selection, followed by eating the entrée that was ordered, followed by dessert, then the bill is paid. Scripts lead to the automatic generation of expectations, and when these expectations run counter to what actually occurred, the result can be that scripts lead to an erroneous reconstruction of the actual events.

Although scripts develop with age, even very young children possess scripts for familiar events, and these influence the way they reconstruct past events, for instance, by filling in gaps that did not occur (Flannagan & Hess, 1991; Hudson & Nelson, 1986). To confirm this, just imagine any routine activity. For example, suppose that you attend an exercise class every morning that always has the same structure: It begins with 5 minutes of stretching, followed by 5 minutes of light workout to music, then 5 minutes of upper-body exercises, then 5 minutes of lower-body exercises, and finally vigorous aerobic exercise for 10 minutes. After you have endured this same sequence of activities many times (i.e., a script has formed), and you are asked to recall a specific class in which the script was violated (e.g., the lower-body exercises were omitted), it is likely that you would report (inaccurately) the usual routine, because you use your acquired script to guide your recollection. Scripts can be potent reminders for activities, but they also can lead to erroneous filling in of missing or expected activities.

The relationship among age, scripted knowledge, and recall is quite complex. Once children have acquired a script, preschoolers' recall may in fact be more vulnerable to the negative effects of script-based knowledge than that of elementary-school-age children (Hudson & Nelson, 1986). Some research has suggested that preschoolers' vulnerability to scripted information reflects their difficulty distinguishing "special" events from "scripted" events (Farrar & Goodman, 1992). It seems that with age, children become better able to tag unexpected events and to note that they are special; younger children are more likely to incorporate one-time special events into their scripts.

These studies may provide a basis for the observed age-related differences in suggestibility. Younger children may, in part, be more suggestible than older children because they are overly dependent on scripted knowledge and incorporate discrepant or novel events (such as a false suggestion) into their script of the event rather than keeping them tagged as separate events.

However, there are some situations in which one might expect scripted knowledge to have more negative consequences on the recall of older children and adults than on that of younger children. When younger children's scripted knowledge is insufficient or poorer than that of older children, the latter might be expected to make more false inferences about events that were not witnessed but that are part of their scripts. For example, when subjects were erroneously told that the film they were viewing depicted cheaters, sixth-graders and college students tended to report more cheating than did third-graders when the cheating was based on innocent acts such as one student asking another for the time. Younger children's scripts for cheating did not contain the scenario of asking for the time as a pretext for cheating, so their limited "cheating" script made them less prone than older children to the erroneous suggestion (Lindberg, 1991).

Thus, scripted knowledge can exert a potent influence on the susceptibility to suggestion. If an erroneous suggestion is highly congruent with one's script of an event, it should be easier to implant in memory than if it is highly inconsistent with one's script. Because young children's recall at times appears to be more script-driven than older children's and adults', it may be easier to implant script-congruent suggestions in their reports than when recall is less script-driven. As was seen, however, if younger children do not have a script for an event (e.g., a method of cheating), it may be easier to implant suggestions (that are congruent with the script) in older children who do have this knowledge. This is one of those developmentally reverse trajectories where an absence of knowledge actually serves to facilitate younger children's recall.

Although some researchers have emphasized the theoretical importance of knowledge in accounting for suggestibility effects, we believe that this literature should be interpreted with some caution. The reason for this is that if children are persistently interviewed, they may actually acquire facts or scripts about the alleged event, even if they had no previous knowledge of this information prior to the series of interviews. And with the acquisition of knowledge from the interviewing process, children may begin to provide more credible and detailed reports that happen to be inaccurate.

LANGUAGE

Because most of the examples of suggestibility in this book involve the influence of misleading verbal information on children's verbal reports, it seems reasonable to assume that children's level of linguistic comprehension and production skills might influence their suggestibility-proneness (for a full discussion of these issues, see Brennan & Brennan, 1988; Snyder, Nathanson, & Saywitz, 1993; Walker & Warren, in press). When young children are asked to describe events or are asked questions about specific events, their reports may be inaccurate because they fail to understand the question—regardless of whether it is suggestive or not. Similarly, an adult interviewer may incorrectly interpret a child's verbal report as a result of the child's limited linguistic production skills. Children's answers to questions that they have incorrectly understood, in addition to adults' misunderstanding of their limited productions, may be incorporated into future interrogations, further increasing the likelihood of tainted reports. For example, in one study (Goodman & Aman, 1990), some 3-year-old children inaccurately reported that a male experimenter had touched their "private parts." In response to the question "Did he touch your private parts," they answered "yes" even though the experimenter had not. Upon further examination, the experimenters noted that the children simply did not know the meaning of the phrase "private parts." As Goodman and her colleagues noted, if this term had been inappropriately used in an actual case, a misleading conclusion, eventually leading to a potential false allegation, could have occurred (Goodman, Taub, et al., 1992).

SOURCE MONITORING: DISTINGUISHING REALITY FROM FANTASY

We devote little space to this topic in this chapter because we have reviewed the literature in some detail in chapters 13 and 14. To remind the reader, it has been proposed that children's increased suggestibility may be directly related to their relative difficulty in differentiating fantasy from reality, and at a more general level in differentiating actual events from imagined events.

SOCIAL FACTORS

Up to now, our discussion of the potential factors that may account for children's suggestibility has focused on cognitive factors. But since the turn of the century, researchers have also emphasized the importance of social factors in accounting for suggestibility effects in adults and, especially, in children.

In experimental situations, some have argued that suggestibility effects arise out of social pressures: The subject accepts the misleading information to please the experimenter or because the experimenter is trusted. At other times, the pressures may be more subtle, and suggestibility may reflect gap-filling strategies (e.g., McCloskey & Zaragoza, 1985): Subjects accept the misleading information because they have no memory for the original event. Instead of telling the interviewer that they cannot remember or don't know—something that children may do less than adults—they revise or fill in memory gaps to please the interviewer.

On the basis of what we know about the social development of children, it seems clear that social factors should play a large role in the creation of suggestible reports. First, adults (who are the interviewers) have high status in the eyes of young children. Children see adults as omniscient and truthful; rarely do they question adults' statements or actions. On most occasions, children try to comply with the adult norms or what they perceive to be the adult wishes.

This compliant behavior puts the child at risk for suggestion. A child may be very willing to accept the suggestions of an interviewer, no matter how bizarre or incongruent the suggestions, merely because the child trusts the interviewer and wants to please him (see Ceci et al., 1987, for experimental support). Although children may be compliant, it is sometimes with much confusion. Impressions that we derived from listening to some of the existing electronic recordings of children in the case studies, and in similar cases not described in this book, provide a missing dimension undetectable in the written transcripts: There are long pauses in these interviews, children's answers do not come spontaneously, and there is often hesitation and a feeling of confusion as they come to assent to the interviewer's questions. Thus, in contrast with children who have been repeatedly exposed to erroneous suggestions over long periods of time and who, as a result, come to harbor false beliefs that result in spontaneous answers, compliant children's disclosures frequently seem halting and confused.

More constraints exist in child–adult interactions than in adult–adult interactions. When adults engage children in interviews, the interaction usually ends when the adult wants it to end. Children are rarely allowed to end such interactions by saying, "I am not talking about this any more" or "Stop this, you are bothering me" (or "I want my attorney present"). When children are part of an investigative interview, regardless of the coercive nature or unpleasantness of the interview, they are required to continue until the adult decides to terminate. In comparison with adult witnesses, it would be impermissible for children to say, "Stop questioning me, I already told you that I can't remember," or "I already told you that nothing happened." These techniques, which are more permissible and available to adults, have the impact of warding off potential suggestive and coercive questioning methods.

The following example taken from the Country Walk case illustrates the potential impact of suggestive interviewing techniques when the interviewer appears very confident about the accuracy of his hypothesis; in this situation the child, because of his diminished social status, may initially but not finally provide the interviewer with what he wants to hear.

The 6-year-old son, Jaime, of the defendant, Frank Fuster, tested positive for gonorrhea of the throat. This was a major piece of hard evidence for the state. The only problem was that the child had not made any disclosures. Before the test, Jaime was interviewed by the Bragas, who would not accept the child's response that nothing had happened. Jaime stated that Iliana had told him to tell everything, the good and the bad. Nonetheless, he was confronted with the statement that he was not telling everything.

Three months later, Jaime had still not disclosed; he had a final interview with the Bragas. Here, he initially denied any abuse, but after these interviewers insisted that he must not be telling the truth, the child confessed that he had fellated his father, Frank Fuster. Here are some sections of this interview:

J. Braga:	Did they tell you not to tell anybody you had gonorrhea?
Jaime:	Gonorrhea? . . . I didn't know that.
J. Braga:	But you now know?
Jaime:	(inaudible)
L. Braga:	But if they had known, they would have said don't talk about it, don't tell anybody else.
Jaime:	No, never said it. They didn't know.
J. Braga:	Let's go back to talking, I said to you earlier that I know you are not telling me the truth because you said that no one put their penis in your mouth but yet you had the test, the test said you had gonorrhea. If you have gonorrhea, someone put their penis—
Jaime:	I don't remember, maybe they did. I don't remember. Maybe it happened when I was six. I don't remember when I was six. . . .
J. Braga:	You said you don't remember anybody putting their penis in your mouth? Do you think it was your father?
Jaime:	I don't know who did it. . . .
L. Braga:	Let's suppose that it did, okay? Because the doctor said it did, even though you don't remember who did, you think might it have done that to you [sic]. Do you have any idea, even if you don't remember?
Jaime:	I think maybe my dad and maybe somebody else. . . .
J. Braga:	Do you remember the first time your dad did it, did you ask him to stop?
Jaime:	No . . . I don't remember anything about that. I don't want to.
J. Braga:	Do you think if your dad had done it, if you told him to stop, he would have stopped?
Jaime:	I don't remember anything about it. I don't know if I told him to stop. I don't know if I told him, you know like that. I don't remember nothing about it.
L. Braga:	If you did remember about it, would it be hard for you to talk about?
Jaime:	No.
J. Braga:	Would you tell us?
Jaime:	Yes.

After pages and pages of this type of intensive questioning and denial, Jaime finally admitted to many acts that were committed by his father and by Iliana.

But a few months later, in a deposition, the child repeatedly and pointedly denied that he had ever been abused. He told the prosecutors that he had previously confessed only because the Bragas had refused to end the interview until he had made certain claims.

One might think that this was a perfect example of a recantation in the service of self-protection from guilt: that because of the positive medical evidence of gonorrhea of the throat, the child was simply denying the reality of the abuse. Although medical evidence was presented at the trial, it has since been reported by researchers at the Centers for Disease Control that the procedure used for testing gonorrhea in Frank Fuster's son had a false positive error rate of 1 in 3 (Nathan, 1993a). Does this necessarily mean that Fuster's son was telling the truth when he denied being abused by his father? Of course not. But it does reflect the dangers of the unbridled enthusiasm and certitude with which interviewers pursued this child as a result of the positive gonorrhea test?[1]

---

[1]Some interviewers feel that when they have positive evidence of abuse, it justifies any interviewing technique to have the child disclose, as the following excerpt of an expert witness's trial testimony shows:

> A man who worked in a YMCA has confessed to abusing forty-five boys at the YMCA. And it's a nice case in some ways because the man has already confessed, he has told who he has abused. And some of the other kids have talked about seeing other kids being abused. Now, what's interesting in that case is that out of those 45 kids, there are at least 10 of them who are still saying they were not sexually abused. We know they are abused. The defendant said they were abused. . . . Some other kids have reported seeing some of them abused, but they are saying I wasn't abused. What's interesting about it is that the interviewers have a wonderful position. The . . . defendant is not on their shoulder—I mean, not the defendant, but the defense attorney is not there anymore, the guy has already confessed. It is not going to be an ugly battle in court. They know what happened. They can really push gung-ho in interviewing those kids. They can throw caution to . . . away. They can ask leading questions. In some way it's the interviewer's dream come true. You know, there's no defense attorney watching me. I can ask leading questions if I want to. I know what happened. And I need to help this child get it out. If the child doesn't talk about it, it's like a cancer that grows inside of them.

There are a number of concerns about this strategy. The use of these techniques to elicit allegations from the silent children may not necessarily promote accurate recollections. The children may eventually produce reports that are consistent with those of their peers or with the beliefs of the interviewers, but the reports may not reflect their own experiences. In the worst case, such techniques might lead some children (who were abused) to eventually make exaggerated claims and to report additional but nonexistent perpetrators. There is also always the very small chance that the defendant's confession was not accurate and that he named some children whom he did not abuse. Finally, and most critically, there is a need for mental health professionals to be humble about the psychological benefits and risks associated with the aggressive pursuit of disclosures. Although many accept as a tenet of faith the need for disclosure as a prerequisite to healing, this may or may not be the case, and such pursuit may create more problems than it solves.

LYING

This is the first time in this book that we directly address the issue of whether some of the child witnesses' reports were "lies." That is, did the children consciously and deliberately distort the truth with the deliberate goal of deceiving their interviewers? It seems to us that for the most part the children in the case studies and in our experiments did not set out to intentionally deceive their interviewers. Although some may have been aware that their answers were not accurate, we argue that the children's reports reflected their attempts to be compliant rather than to be deceitful. Also, on the basis of the data that we presented in chapter 3, it seems that few of the false reports of abuse can be categorized as deliberate and malicious attempts to distort the truth on the part of the child (Jones & McGraw, 1987). Of course, the line between false statements that occur because of "lying" and those that occur because of "suggestive" practices can at times become blurred. In this section we present a short summary of the literature in the area of children's lies, because it may be relevant to age differences in false reporting when it is thought that the false report is a deliberate lie (for full details the reader should consult Ceci & Bruck, 1993b; Ceci, Leichtman, Putnick, & Nightingale, 1993; McGough, 1994).

Historically, it has been felt that young children were incapable of lying because this act required a level of cognitive sophistication beyond the capability of the young child (e.g., Piaget, 1926). Since the time of Piaget, much progress has been made in understanding the development and definitional features of lying. With advances in our understanding of young children's cognitive sophistication, there is now evidence that even very young children sometimes do lie, with full appreciation of the differing perspectives of their listeners.

We now focus on studies of preschoolers' deception, ignoring whether their behaviors are more appropriately construed as "sabotage," "deceit," "tricking," "politeness," or "tact." Furthermore, we avoid delving into distinctions that have occupied some scholars, such as lying versus telling a lie, and minimal lies versus deception (see Ceci, Leichtman, & Putnick, 1992). Recent research has sought to examine the specific conditions that may foster lying. Five motivations to lie or tell the truth have been studied: (a) avoiding punishment, (b) sustaining a game, (c) keeping a promise (e.g., "it will be our secret"), (d) achieving personal gains (e.g., rewards, being accepted in a group), and (e) avoiding embarrassment. Existing data show that not all motivations produce comparable levels of lying/truth-telling. Below we present a highly abbreviated account of this literature that, although it omits many details, captures the essential findings in this area.

Lying/Truth-Telling to Avoid Punishment

Children will lie about events when the operative motives are sufficiently salient. Mothers report that the most frequent motivation for their 4-year-olds to lie is to avoid punishment (Stouthamer-Loeber, 1987). Michael Lewis and his colleagues did one experiment that vividly demonstrates young children's willingness to lie to avoid punishment. They found that 88% of 3-year-olds who were instructed not to peek at a toy proceeded to peek. When asked if they had peeked, only 38% admitted to it, prompting the investigators to conclude that "thus, we have some evidence . . . that deception strategies are adopted at early ages" (Lewis, Stranger, & Sullivan, 1989, p. 442).

Lying/Truth-Telling to Sustain a Game

Some children can be induced to tell a lie in the context of a game. For example, an adult experimenter pretended to find a watch left behind by the teacher (Ceci et al., 1993). After being shown the watch, the child was told that they were going to play a game of hiding it from the teacher. The child was told the game was a secret and was instructed not to talk to anybody about it. Later, the returning teacher asked the child who had taken her watch. Only 10% of the preschoolers lied to sustain this game (see also Tate & Warren-Leubecker, 1990). However, when the motivational salience of the experimental procedure was increased by having a well-known adult coach the child to tell a lie about playing with a toy, then 35% of 2- to 8-year-olds lied to sustain a secret game (Tate, Warren, & Hess, 1992). It appears that the degree to which children will lie to sustain a game is context-dependent, and that the use of stronger coaching will result in higher rates of deception.

Keeping Promises

There is consistent evidence that children as young as 3 years of age will omit important information about transgressions and accidents if adults ask them to do so (see Pipe & Goodman, 1991, for a recent review). For example, in one study, an adult spilled ink on a pair of gloves the child was wearing, and told the child that she (the adult) would "get into trouble" if anyone found out. Subsequently, 42% of the 5-year-olds claimed not to know who spilled the ink, and 25% maintained ignorance upon repeated questioning 10 days and 2 months later (Wilson & Pipe, 1989). Some of the children in the Clarke-Stewart et al. (1989) study were told by Chester that he would lose his job if his boss learned that he had played with the dolls. Sixty-nine percent of these children kept the secret when they were interviewed by a neutral interviewer. However, they all eventually revealed the secret when asked suggestive questions.[2]

If children will lie to protect a stranger, they should do so even more readily to protect a loved one. Results of one study support this hypothesis (Bottoms, Goodman, Schwartz-Kenney, Sachsenmaier, & Thomas, 1990). When mothers of 3- and 5-year-olds broke a Barbie doll, only 1 of the 49 children mentioned this to an interviewer who asked what happened. Furthermore, when asked specific questions about the event, 5-year-olds did not tell the secret, even when asked leading questions.

Lying/Truth-Telling for Personal Gain

Sometimes children will lie to gain a material reward. Material and psychological rewards do not need to be of a large magnitude to be effective. Children as young as 3 years will engage in sabotage behaviors to gain some reward (e.g., covering up a treasure that is in jeopardy of being discovered by a puppet), but they will not engage in verbal deceit for another year (Leekam, 1992). In one study, over 50% of nursery school subjects lied to obtain a gumball as a prize, by falsely claiming that they had won a game while the interviewer was out of the room (Ceci et al., 1993). Children who had played the game, but who were not offered any prizes for misreporting, accurately reported that they had not won the game, so simple memory failure can be ruled out as an explanation of the other children's erroneous claims.

Lying/Truth-Telling to Avoid Embarrassment

Not all behavior is regulated by external outcomes, rewards, and fears of reprisals. In the context of lies, the most relevant internal regulators are guilt, shame, and pride. Although children younger than the age of 7 (Bussey, 1992; Leekam, 1992) appear to be inferior to older children at inferring some of these self-regulatory states (e.g., appreciating that a sense of pride results from telling the truth), even 4-year-olds distinguish between statements meant to minimize the embarrassment of another ("I like your new hairdo") and those meant to cause distress (Bussey, 1992).

In an effort to study lying to avoid personal embarrassment, Ceci et al. (1993) instructed two parents to kiss their 3-year-olds while bathing them the evening before being interviewed. During an interview in which their parents were absent, the children were told that it was naughty to let someone kiss them when they didn't have any clothes on. They were then asked, "No one ever kissed you when you didn't have any clothes on,

---

[2]Some of these data could also be used to address the issue of the degree to which children withhold the truth when they are threatened.

did they? . . . No one kissed you last night when you were in the bathtub, did they?" These instructions provided a motivation to make "errors of omission" or to withhold information about an event portrayed as taboo, in order to avoid the embarrassment of having done something naughty. Immediately following the child's reply, he or she was told, "But it is OK to be kissed by your mommy or daddy because they know you."

In a different condition, two children who had not been kissed during their baths were told at the start of the interview that parents who loved their children often kissed them and hugged them while they were in the tub. These children were asked, "Your mommy kissed you when she bathed you last night, didn't she?" The purpose of this condition was to provide a motivation to make "errors of commission" (claims that something happened even though it did not) in order to avoid embarrassment.

Initially, both children who were told that it was naughty to allow an adult to kiss them while being bathed replied that they had not been kissed. Later, when a parent interviewed them alone, and asked them if they had been kissed while being bathed, they affirmed that they had, offering specific and accurate details (e.g., "Yes, I think mommy kissed me three times in the tub last night"). Interestingly, the children quickly added a codicil that was nearly a verbatim restatement of the interviewer's assurance: "But its' OK, because I know her." One of the two children who had not been kissed during the evening bath reported that she had been, but reversed her report when interviewed by a parent alone. The results of this case study indicate that children will occasionally consciously distort the truth about events that were allegedly perpetrated to their bodies. Both errors of omission and errors of commission were produced by the strong motives used by these researchers.

Although the results of the above study are very limited because of the small sample size, they do demonstrate an important principle that needs to be considered when evaluating the results of laboratory studies and the statements of child witnesses. It seems to us that researchers who have claimed that children cannot be coached to distort their testimony about bodily events have tilted the odds toward finding truthfulness among preschoolers by implicitly using motives that favor a truthful outcome (e.g., Goodman et al., 1990; Saywitz et al., 1991). That is, there were no motives for the children in these earlier studies to make false disclosures. It might even be claimed that in such studies there were implicit motives to correctly report what happened because to do otherwise (e.g., to claim to have been sexually abused) would bring embarrassment. In other words, if children in these earlier studies were to distort what they had witnessed, and claim to have been sexually touched when they were not, this could be expected to result in embarrassment, thus tilting the motivational structure toward truthful reporting. Contrast this approach with one in which a child is induced to make errors of commission to avoid embarrassment (e.g., "He kissed you because he loves you, didn't he?") or with an approach in which a child is asked to make errors of omission to avoid embarrassment (e.g., "No one ever touched you there, did they?").

In some of our sample cases, the expert witnesses argued that the children would not lie because children lie "to get out of trouble, not to get into trouble." Putting aside the lack of empirical evidence for this claim, some experts seem to have an egocentric perspective of what "out of trouble" refers to. If a child is told, for example, that all his friends have already told, that it is a good thing to tell, and that he will get rewards for telling, and if the child is interviewed until he produces an incriminating statement, one could interpret any resultant disclosure as an attempt to "stay out of trouble."

In summary, the most recent research on lying has attempted to approximate real-life crime contexts by weaving affect and motive into studies of recollection and by using highly familiar contexts such as observing loved ones break toys or being kissed while in the bathtub. Young children will consciously distort their reports of what they witnessed, and they will do so more in response to some motives (e.g., fear of reprisal and avoidance of embarrassment) than to others (to sustain a game, to keep a secret, to gain rewards). Generally, these studies have demonstrated that like adults, children are sensitive to the demand characteristics of a situation, and therefore succumb to a wide range of motives to lie or withhold information.

However, the literature is limited in that the majority of studies of lying have not examined age-related differences because it is difficult to come up with a context that has comparable meaning for the younger and older subjects. So the safest conclusion that can be reached at this point in time is that subjects of all ages will lie when the motives are right. Children may be no different than adults in this regard. Thus, the argument that children are incapable of "lying" should be discounted.

THE INTERACTION OF COGNITIVE AND SOCIAL MECHANISMS

Some researchers have attempted to determine the relative importance of social versus cognitive factors in accounting for suggestibility effects. The results of these studies are inconsistent, and the issue remains unresolved. As we have argued in previous work (Ceci & Bruck, 1993b), it seems that for now we can conclude that although social factors are quite important, they do not appear to fully account for all suggestibility effects. A variety of cognitive factors, specifically memory impairment and source monitoring errors, appear to play important roles in explaining suggestibility effects in children. These conclusions, however, are based almost exclusively on laboratory studies, where children are usually interviewed about an event only one time. Therefore, they tell us little about the time course of the mechanisms underlying suggestibility effects or why reports become increasingly distorted over repeated interviews.

Furthermore, it seems that a focus on whether cognitive or social factors are more important obscures the possibility that both factors interact in producing suggestibility effects. For instance, it is possible that the degree to which social factors play a role has a cognitive basis. When memory traces are weak (or when there is no memory at all for the original event), children may be more compliant and willing to accept suggestions because there is no competing memory trace to challenge the suggestion. On the other hand, when the traces are strong, the child (or adult) is less likely to incorporate misleading suggestions into memory.

In addition to cognitive factors underpinning the effectiveness of social factors, it is also possible for social factors to underpin the effectiveness of cognitive mechanisms in producing suggestibility; that is, a child may attend more to suggestions from an authority figure (a social factor), thus insuring greater encoding (a cognitive factor). But this is a hypothesis in need of data.

Finally, it is possible that a child's report may initially be the result of some social factor, but over time the report may become a part of the child's actual memory. In chapter 10, the "Sam Stone" study was described in which preschool children were given stereotypical knowledge about a clumsy character (Leichtman & Ceci, in press). Children later used this knowledge to reconstruct what Sam Stone *might* have done, telling the interviewer, "Maybe Sam did it," or "It could have been Sam." Upon repeated postevent questioning, however, these children often became more and more convinced that the clumsy events had actually occurred, as opposed to *might* have occurred. In the legal arena, in response to strongly suggestive—even pressurized—interviews, children may initially realize that they are providing the interviewer with an erroneous account in order to please him (a social factor), but after repeated retellings to different interviewers, the erroneous account may become so deeply embedded as to be indistinguishable from an actual memory (a cognitive factor).[3]

Although cognitive as well as social factors may play a role in suggestibility effects, the important question, for which we have no empirical data, is whether there are age-related differences in the interaction of these

---

[3]It is important to bear in mind the myriad ways in which suggestive mechanisms operate. Throughout this chapter we have discussed suggestibility in terms of influencing a child to make errors of commission, that is, to claim that she experienced some event that never transpired. One can ask whether the opposite could also occur: Could a child (or an adult) be influenced through suggestive techniques to make errors of omission? Could one be influenced to claim that nothing happened when in reality something did transpire? Our answer is "yes," and we have provided some examples throughout this book where children, in response to suggestive interviewing techniques, changed their answers from "yes it happened" to "no it didn't happen," or from a shot hurt a lot to

factors. Specifically, do younger children differ from older children and adults in terms of how quickly false reports, which may have been initially motivated by social factors, come to be believed (i.e., a cognitive factor)? Clearly, much more research is needed to gain a complete understanding of the boundary conditions. For now, we must content ourselves with the knowledge that young children are disproportionately more susceptible to suggestive interviews than older children, leaving aside the basic research question, "Why?"

SUMMARY

We have discussed a number of cognitive mechanisms and social factors that might account for the greater suggestibility of young children. Children's suggestibility might be explained by their weaker memory skills, by their smaller knowledge base, by their less developed language skills, and by their fragile reality monitoring skills. Any one or a combination of these cognitive mechanisms might be involved. On the other hand, social factors, particularly children's compliant behavior with adult interviewers, might put them at risk for suggestion. We also considered the role of lying and concluded that although young children do lie under a number of circumstances, these behaviors do not seem to account for most of the phenomena that we report in this book. In the future, we expect that researchers will focus on the interaction of cognitive and social factors in order to understand the time course of suggestibility effects.

---

it hurt only a little or not at all. Having said this, it is important to note that we do not think that the same mechanisms often underlie commission (implantation) and omission (erasure) suggestibility errors. Specifically, omission errors probably rarely reflect cognitive changes (that is, the subject does not usually come to believe that the event never happened), but only reflect social influences (the subject knowingly assents to what the interviewer wants to hear). In part, our reasoning for this claim is based on the literature on "directed" or "motivated" forgetting. In these studies, subjects are pointedly told to forget information that has occurred during a session; at times they are told that the information is wrong or else it is trivial. These instructions do not usually increase forgetting, although on occasion they may do so.

17

ETHICAL AND PROFESSIONAL
ISSUES

In this chapter we discuss certain issues concerning the conduct of professionals who deal with child witnesses. The first part of this chapter focuses on expert witnesses; here we discuss the distinction between what expert witnesses *should* tell the court versus what they *do* tell the court about the reliability of children's reports. The second part of the chapter focuses on the obligations of therapists who treat prospective child witnesses; here, we attempt to bring together some of the issues that have cropped up in various places throughout the book, such as the blending of the roles of therapist, forensic interviewer, and expert witness.

THE ETHICS OF EXPERT TESTIMONY

When a child comes to court to testify, it is often because she is the sole witness to a crime. This is particularly likely to be the situation in sexual abuse cases, where not only is the child the sole witness, but there may be no medical signs of abuse, or circumstantial physical evidence. The difficulty posed by uncorroborated reports of sexual abuse is compounded by the fact that the testimony of young children may at times seem to lack credibility. Because of this, both the prosecution and defense may call physicians, mental health professionals, and social scientists to serve as expert witnesses to either support or discredit the child's testimony. In this section, we discuss the qualifications and roles of mental health professionals and social scientists who serve as expert witnesses in these cases.

According to legal views (see Mason, 1991; McGough, 1994; Myers, 1993), these expert witnesses can be classified into several categories. Although some legal scholars have used three or more classifications (e.g., McGough, 1994), for the purposes of the discussion in this chapter we use a simple two-category distinction.

The first type of expert witness is called on to educate fact finders about the scientific literature relevant to the credibility of child witnesses in general. This type of expert may review various topics, including the literature on age-related differences in suggestibility as well as the literatures on cognitive, emotional, and social development (e.g., for examples, see Myers, 1992). Ordinarily, such experts would not have had direct contact with the child.

The second type of expert, usually a mental health professional, is asked to provide an opinion as to whether or not a particular child's demeanor is consistent with that of having been abused. This expert may formulate her opinion on the basis of therapy or a formal assessment of the child witness. This category of experts may also provide a generic description of the behavioral symptoms associated with sexual abuse. In giving this latter type of testimony, the expert may or may not have had direct contact with the child in question, but may base his testimony primarily on a review of the clinical and scientific literatures, as well as on his clinical experiences with similar children. An example of this type of testimony is the expert who is called on to rehabilitate the credibility of a child witness whose credibility has been attacked during cross-examination by the defense (e.g., for inconsistent, delayed, or recanted reporting). In such a situation, the expert witness for the prosecution explains that although such behaviors are not themselves diagnostic of abuse, it is not unusual for abused children to display some of these same behaviors.

Although it is clear that the research on children's suggestibility discussed in this book has direct implications for the first type of witness, knowledge of this research is equally relevant to the testimony of the second type of expert witness, the mental health professional who offers an opinion or attempts to restore credibility. Such a witness should take into consideration competing hypotheses that could explain why the child in question, or children in general, demonstrates particular symptoms or makes delayed allegations of sexual abuse. One alternative hypothesis to be considered is that the particular child's allegations or symptoms could have resulted from suggestive influences of the sort described in chapters 8 through 14. It is important for this type of expert to consider such an alternative because the same symptoms associated with sexual abuse (delayed reporting, retraction of the allegation, inconsistent accounts, age-inappropriate knowledge of sexual behavior, or sexually graphic play with anatomically correct dolls) have at times been observed in nonabused children who have been exposed to suggestive interviews. Thus, expert testimony related to the diagnosis of child sexual abuse is a complex task, one requiring experience with sexually abused children in addition to knowledge of both the clinical and scientific literatures.

There is one final point about the testimony of expert witnesses. Although most courts disallow expert testimony that speaks directly to the ultimate question of the defendant's guilt or innocence, some courts do permit expert witnesses to testify as to whether they believe the child was abused, whether they are certain that the child's symptom pattern is that of an abused child's, whether there is a high probability that the child was abused, and so forth (see Myers, 1992, 1993). One would think that an expert's opinion that a particular child was abused might have the same psychological effect on jurors as speaking directly to the child's credibility. In fact, as shown by the following example, this distinction leads to confusion even among the legal scholars whom we have consulted about this state of affairs, with one well-known scholar remarking that the courts' thinking on this issue is little more than "wordplay." In *United States v. Azure* (1986), the court held that the expert overstepped his role when he stated that an 11-year-old's story of sexual abuse was credible and he could "see no reason why she was not telling the truth," but the court went on to give examples of testimony that would have had a similar corroborative effect but would be within the bounds of propriety (e.g., by describing patterns of consistency in the stories of actual abuse victims and comparing these with the story of the 11-year-old in question, pointing out their resemblance).

What the Expert Witness on Children's Suggestibility *Should* Tell the Court

We come now to the question that has vexed any social scientist who ever dreamed (or had nightmares) of being called on to serve as an expert witness or to prepare an amicus brief for an appellate court on children's testimony: namely, what does our present state of scientific knowledge permit us to say about the reliability of a child's report? Having acknowledged the complexities of the relevant research, we hold that expert witnesses, regardless of whether they are testifying for the prosecution or for the defense, should cover several points:

1. There are reliable age differences in children's suggestibility, with preschoolers being more vulnerable than older children to a variety of factors that contribute to unreliable reports.
2. Although young children are often accurate reporters, some do make mistakes—particularly when they undergo sugges-

tive interviews; and these errors are not limited to peripheral details, but may include salient events that involve children's own bodies.

3. Measures can be taken to lessen the risk of suggestibility effects. To date, the factors that we know most about concern the nature of the interview itself: its frequency, degree of suggestiveness, and demand characteristics.

- A child's report is less likely to be distorted, for example, after one interview than after several interviews. (The term "interviews" includes any conversations between adults and children about the target event.)

- Interviewers who ask nonleading questions, who do not have a confirmatory bias (i.e., an attachment to a single hypothesis), who do not inculcate a negative stereotype about the defendant, and who do not repeat close-ended, yes/no questions within or across interviews are more likely to obtain accurate reports from children.

- Interviewers who are patient and nonjudgmental, and who do not attempt to create demand characteristics (e.g., by providing subtle rewards for certain responses), are likely to elicit the most accurate reports from young children.

Thus, at one extreme we can have more confidence in a child's spontaneous statements made prior to any attempt by an adult to elicit what they suspect may be the truth. At the other extreme, we are more likely to be concerned when a child has made a statement only after prolonged, repeated, and suggestive interviews.

4. Finally, it is also important that the court appreciate the complexity of the interrelationships among the factors affecting children's report accuracy. As in most areas of social science, effects are rarely as straightforward as one might wish. For example, even though suggestibility effects may be robust, they are not inevitable, nor are they ineluctably large in magnitude, as we show below.

Some studies may show statistically reliable differences between younger and older children's suggestibility even though the vast majority of both the younger and older children do not succumb to suggestions. For example, in one published study (Ceci, Ross, & Toglia, 1987), the suggestibility rate of younger children was 12%, and that of older children was 6%, indicating that neither age group was very suggestible. Yet because of the large sample size and small variance, this small difference was statistically significant. Such "significance" means only that this 6% difference was nonrandom and not the result of sampling error or chance. As a general rule, the expert needs to explain this statistical reasoning to fact find-ers, so that they understand that just because a study reports statistically reliable age differences, this does not mean that each younger child was more vulnerable to suggestions than each older child, or that the gap be-tween the two age groups was necessarily large. Statistical significance im-plies neither of these conclusions.

Results sometimes vary dramatically among studies, and children's be-haviors sometimes vary dramatically within studies. Thus, even in studies with significant suggestibility effects, there are always some children who are highly resistant to suggestion. We have seen this in our own studies, and we have also seen it in transcripts of forensic and therapeutic inter-views. In some cases, no matter how much an interviewer may try to er-roneously suggest that a false event occurred, some children will consis-tently resist and not incorporate the interviewer's suggestion. This aspect needs to be made known to courts. On the other hand, although suggest-ibility effects tend to be most dramatic after prolonged and repeated in-terviewing, some children incorporate suggestions quickly, even after one short interview (e.g., Clarke-Stewart et al., 1989, as reported in Goodman & Clarke-Stewart, 1991; Lepore & Sesco, 1994). This aspect also needs to be made known to courts.

In short, we urge expert witnesses to review the full corpus of relevant scientific work, describing the magnitude of errors, the inconsistencies within and across studies, and the boundary conditions that might limit any generalization from the science to the case at bar. If this seems like a tall order, it is. But there are methods of conveying this message to fact finders that fall short of presenting an exhaustive disquisition of the entire scientific literature. One such method is to explain at the outset of one's testimony that the conclusions to be described are based on a full consid-eration and critical synthesis of all relevant scientific studies, and that although these studies will not be described at the individual level, the expert will be willing to do so if the court so requests. This strategy allows opposing counsel to attempt to impeach the expert's claims by citing studies that may contradict the expert's conclusions, and it allows the expert to show that the studies were part of her analysis, or if they were not, to explain why they were excluded.

Ideal Versus Actual Expert Witnesses: What Experts Have Actually Told the Court

The "model" expert witness who comes forward to testify on issues related to children's suggestibility should be someone who has thoroughly reviewed the pertinent literature and who can present the relevant facts in a balanced manner. This requirement is not an easy one to meet; this research area is developing rapidly and is riddled with a host of complex issues that necessitate a broad understanding of research design, statistics, and theory. This knowledge is easier to come by for those who are part of the research community, with its libraries, graduate students, and professional networks of electronic communication.

Unfortunately, some who serve as expert witnesses do not have this breadth of knowledge. We have reviewed many examples of experts' testimony that appeared to have been based on incomplete and at times dubious knowledge. Nowhere in these experts' testimony is there any hint of the complexities that ought to have tempered their statements to the jury. In the worst cases, the testimony was actually the opposite of what we know to be the best evidence from systematic research. All too often, such an expert appears in court solely because his opinion is consistent with that of the side that hired him, rather than because he is truly knowledgeable about the field. Such testimony can be a disservice to the aims of justice, not to mention to the professions the expert witness represents.

Partisan Experts: Hired Guns, Whores, or Saints?

Problems with expert testimony are endemic to the legal systems of countries whose codes have been derived from British common law. As far back as one can check, there has been a strong suspicion among jurists and laypersons alike that expert witnesses are untrustworthy, going beyond the data to put a "spin" toward the side that hired them:

> Perhaps the testimony which least deserves credit with a jury is that of skilled witnesses. . . . It is often quite surprising to see with what facility, and to what extent, their views can be made to correspond with the wishes and interests of the parties who call them. (Judge John Pitt Taylor, 1858, pp. 65–69, as quoted in Gross, 1991, p. 1115)

These views continue to be expressed by American jurists:

> To put it bluntly, in many professions service as an expert witness is not generally considered honest work. . . . Experts in fields see lawyers as unprincipled manipulators of their disciplines, and lawyers and experts alike see expert witnesses—those members of the learned professions who will consort with lawyers—as whores. (Gross, 1991, p. 1115)

and by British jurists:

> Expert evidence is sometimes given by people whose level of knowledge seems lamentably low. A number of the recent, and best-known scandals show this. . . . How does this come about? In the first place, I think it is because our present system provides no systematic quality control. Broadly speaking, anyone can be an expert witness, provided they have some relevant knowledge, and nothing whatever is done to see that only the best people are used. To be allowed to give expert evidence, witnesses must satisfy the judge that they have some practical experience, or some professional qualifications; but that is all. No min-

imum standards are laid down. The only test is opposing counsel's cross-examination; and, in a jury trial, this may be designed to score clever points, rather than to test whether they (i.e., the experts) are really good at their job. (Spencer, 1992, pp. 216–217)

Some of our own experiences coincide with these jaundiced evaluations of experts. As already mentioned, we receive hundreds of phone calls each year from attorneys requesting our assistance as expert witnesses. Although we rarely agree to serve as experts, sometimes we ask the attorneys to describe the case so that we can help them locate a suitable expert witness. Often, however, after hearing the facts of the case, we have told the attorney that a scientific expert witness is inappropriate because the specific constellation of factors is so vague or so unlike the research as to render the latter irrelevant to their case. Despite our advice that the attorney find an explanation more congruent with the facts, on some occasions we have discovered that an expert was eventually found to provide the desired testimony. Although we understand that attorneys have a responsibility to advocate aggressively for the best interests of their clients, we believe that professionals should only agree to accommodate such partisanship when there is some link between the facts as they are known and the social science research. Unfortunately, this is not always true.

However, even when experts do testify in cases that speak directly to their expertise, they sometimes have difficulty maintaining a neutral stance and presenting the evidence in a scientifically neutral manner. Often this is because there is a strong tendency for counsel on each side to consciously or unconsciously attempt to co-opt experts and to get them to be "team players." Many of these situations begin with the initial telephone conversation, when the attorney reports how absolutely convinced she is of her client's guilt or innocence. Over time, communication with counsel may become closer and warmer. The expert starts behaving as if he were trying to help one side win their courtroom debate rather than educating the fact finder in the most careful, balanced manner possible.

Some experts manage to remain untainted by their personal relationship with the side that hired them, providing a fair and balanced review of the research—until cross-examination! As many who have experienced it know, it sometimes seems as though the primary purpose of cross-examination is not merely to intentionally discredit the expert's testimony, but to demolish the expert's scientific credibility and persona as a decent human being. At this point, some experts forget that they are not the ones on trial; they fall prey to the natural urge to defend their reputation. This can result in putting a "spin" on their testimony or overstating their conclusions in order to help the side that contracted for their services.

In some of the case studies, experts gave testimony about the scientific literature, where they spent a great deal of time describing "facts" that were not supported by systematic research. Several of these experts who testified for the defense and for the prosecution have international reputations for being well versed in the scientific literature. And yet, either because they became swept up in the emotion of the trial or because they had not systematically reviewed the literature, their testimonies were punctuated with inaccuracies and with one-sided accounts of the relevant literature.

Our advice to experts who seriously wish to educate the court is to remain uninvolved in the court proceedings and in the personal lives of the defendants. Experts who plan to review the scientific literature should learn only enough about the case to assure that their testimony is relevant. Learning too much about the case before testifying can bias the expert's review of the literature as well as his demeanor in the courtroom. Although the opposing counsel may not share this view of an expert who plans to assume an educational role, we suggest nevertheless that experts try to act as though they are a friend of the court, ready to impart their knowledge in a neutral manner so that both sides might make of it what they will.[1]

Although the above discussion was aimed at the social scientist who testifies about children's report accuracy from an indirect basis by reviewing the literature, the same points can be made with equal force about mental health professionals who testify about their direct contact with clients or about the behavioral symptoms associated with sexual abuse. We present examples from two cases, both of which were appealed in part because of the testimony of the experts.

In the first case, *State v. Bullock* (1989), a defendant was convicted of sexual abuse of a child. The interviewing techniques and expert testimony of one of the mental health professionals was a central aspect of the defense's case and the defendant's appeal, which was subsequently denied. This case is of importance to our discussion because it reflects the difficulties presented to the court when an expert witness appears biased in her interviewing practices. In this case, a social worker named Dr. Barbara Snow testified that on the basis of her interviews with three boys, she determined that they had been abused and were telling the truth. In writing the dissenting opinion, Justice Stewart stated,

> Indeed, Dr. Snow herself admitted that she used interrogation procedures that were not intended to sift truth from error. She forthrightly

---

[1]We have followed this strategy with some success. That is, we insisted that the attorney who contacted us not describe any but the most global case details, because we wished to educate the jury about the research, unconstrained and unfettered by the attorney's attempts to tailor it to the case at bar. We went into court and reviewed the corpus of research relevant to the global case details (e.g., age of child) and allowed both sides to pick up on whatever aspects of the research they wished to pursue in questioning us. Although this might not always be feasible, when it is, the practice has worked well for us, with both sides agreeing that our testimony was fair and helpful. Importantly, where we have done this, stories got back to us that the judge and jury appreciated this nonpartisan approach, overcoming their initial skepticism when first told that we insisted on being told little or nothing about the case.

admitted she was not a neutral interviewer; rather she was "an ally for the child," "biased," and not a fact collector like the police. . . . She also testified in effect that there was nothing in her methods that served as a standard for determining the truthfulness of the stories she produced by her interrogation. . . . But since she starts an interrogation with the assumption that abuse has occurred, she then proceeds to prove that point. Never before to my knowledge has a court of law allowed an "expert" to testify to such self-fulfilling prophecy in the guise of an expert opinion. Thus whatever expertise Dr. Snow demonstrated has to do with obtaining evidence from children to prove an assumption and not to elicit truthful responses. . . . In short, any claim that scientific principles or Dr. Snow's own expertise and experience validated her conclusions and procedures is devastatingly refuted by her own statement, "I didn't believe any of those kids when they told me it didn't happen" (p. 175).[2] . . . Indeed her "intervention with the children is not from a neutral position," as she is "a child's advocate." (p. 156)

One of the defense experts testified that anyone who interviews a child in such cases must remain neutral and that when Dr. Snow conceded

---

[2]The following testimony by one of the defendant's children provides an example of why one of the justices seemed to consider this expert to be biased:

Attorney: Did she (Barbara Snow) tell you what she meant, if anybody touched you?

Child: Well, I got what she meant.

Attorney: You knew she was talking about sexual touching.

Child: Yes.

Attorney: What did she say to you and what did you say to her after that?

Child: . . . She acted like she already thought that somebody had and I asked her about that and she said no. And, she just kept asking me if somebody had and I told her no. But you know it seemed like she was trying to get me to say yes. She just kept bugging me to say it.

Attorney: Did she tell you some other kids had told her that you have been involved in sexual touching?

Child: Yes.

Attorney: And did she keep asking you over and over and over whether or not these kids were telling the truth and you had been involved in sexual touching?

Child: Yes.

Attorney: Did there come a time when she told you that, if you didn't admit to what had happened . . . did she ever mention at any time, juvenile authorities?

Child: Yes, she said that if I kept lying, that then it would just make a bigger problem and she said something about going to juvenile courts. And she just said it would be better if I just admitted it now. (State v. Bullock, 1989, pp. 170–171)

that she was a child advocate looking for sexual abuse, she missed the forensic mental health standard "by a mile."[3]

A second example of challenged testimony, which did result in a reversal by a higher court, is provided by one of the experts in the Michaels case. Eileen Treacy, an expert for the prosecution, testified that the conduct of the child witnesses was consistent with having been sexually abused. There were three main components to her conclusion. The first was the existence of a child sex abuse syndrome consisting of five phases: engagement, sexual interaction, secrecy, disclosure, and suppression. Treacy was able to interpret children's denials and recantations in terms of the suppression phase, which was taken to be consistent with sexual abuse.

The second component of Treacy's conclusion was a "confounding variable analysis." This apparently self-designed system led her to rule out (in all but one of the cases) all conceivable nonsexual factors (e.g., divorce, birth of a new sibling), including the interrogation process itself, as likely causes for the children's observed behavior.

Finally, this expert compiled a list of 32 behavioral indicators (e.g., sucks thumb, accident prone, excessive bathing, talks about sex a lot, fears men). Two years after the alleged abuse, this list was given to the parents of the child witnesses, and these parents were asked to recall any changes in their children's behaviors during the period of alleged abuse. Treacy believed that when parents noted changes in 5 to 15 of these behaviors in combination with her confounding variable analysis, this suggested the occurrence of sexual abuse. This expert witness summed up her three-tiered model as follows:

> I think it is a sophisticated enough vehicle to disentangle many of the complexities involved in child sexual abuse. That is the reason that I presented it to you.

The appellate court forcefully challenged the testimony of this expert witness, reversing Kelly Michaels's conviction (although not until after she had spent 5 years in prison), in part because this expert was permitted to testify that the system she had used to arrive at her conclusion was rooted in science and was thus a reliable means of determining sexual abuse.[4] This expert's testimony could be viewed as advocacy in the guise of science. The appelate court concluded that "no amount of cross-examination could have undone the harm caused by Treacy's purported validations" and that the impact of erroneously permitting the jury to hear this evidence was "so overwhelming as to require reversal."

---

[3]On appeal, the justices affirmed the original conviction; they argued that the trial counsel's failure to object to the alleged errors (e.g., the testimony of the expert) was a result of a conscious trial strategy. Despite this ruling, some members of the court were critical of Snow's testimony.

[4]"It is clear that the jury could only have understood Treacy's 'consistent with' opinion testimony to mean consistent with the child abuse alleged by the State. . . . Her testimony constituted nothing less than substantive evidence of the defendant's guilt, albeit Treacy's opinion thereof." (Superior Court of New Jersey Appellate Division A-199-88T1, March 26, 1993)

The two cases that we have just reviewed are not unique. Mason (1991) analyzed 122 civil and criminal appellate court cases in which expert witnesses testified about child sexual abuse. She found that experts frequently presented testimony that either was internally inconsistent or was contradicted by other experts. For example, 14 experts cited age-inappropriate knowledge of sex and sexual preoccupations as characteristics of an abused child, whereas 6 experts asserted that naivete and aversion to sexual matters characterized the sexually abused child. Some experts maintained that consistent accounts of events were important indicators of sexual abuse, whereas others maintained the opposite, that sexually abused children are characterized by their inconsistent accounts. Mason also reported that appellate courts tended to take expert testimony at face value; they rarely raised questions about the testimony's acceptance by the scientific community or about the credentials of the mental health professional presenting expert testimony:

> The response of the courts in this study reveals that there is a critical gulf between the scientific community and the judiciary. Judges are not willing and probably not able to critically evaluate the reliability of the testimony offered. (Mason, 1991, p. 205)

These examples of the testimony of mental health professionals support our recommendation that it is critical that experts should have a firm understanding of both the clinical and scientific literature. As we have stated in other parts of this book, there are no diagnostic behavioral indicators of sexual abuse that occur in all or even most abused children but that are simultaneously absent in all nonabused children. Although many experts have claimed that nonsexual symptoms such as sleep disturbances, night tremors, regressive toileting (e.g., urinary accidents, bed wetting), sudden personality shifts, anxiety, and reluctance to go to school are consistent with sexual abuse, these very same nonsexual symptoms are commonly found among many nonabused preschool-age children.

As Mason (1991) has catalogued, some experts have claimed that although these nonsexual childhood problems may not be diagnostic indicators, sexualized behaviors surely are reliable indicators of sexual abuse. But again, the experts who have made these claims appear to have failed to consider the complete literature on children's sexual knowledge and children's sexual play. Some studies have indicated that young sexually abused and nonabused children do not differ in their levels of sexual knowledge (Gordon, Schroeder, & Abrams, 1990). Also, although some expert witnesses have claimed that children's display of precocious sexual behaviors such as masturbation, French kissing, and showing genitals to adults is diagnostic of sexual abuse, a recent survey indicated that young nonabused children also exhibit these behaviors (Friedrich, Grambsch, Broughton, Kuiper, & Beilke, 1991).

Finally, expert witnesses who claim that a child's sexualized behaviors are "consistent with" a diagnosis of sexual abuse should also review for the court the results of a survey of common behaviors found among day-care children (Phipps-Yonas, Yonas, Turner, & Kauper, 1993). According to directors of day-care centers, children commonly play sexual games like "doctor"; a substantial portion of all preschool children display sexual behaviors, including masturbation, fondling, and exhibitionism; and many report genital soreness. As correctly noted by Lamb (1994),

> No specific behavioral syndromes characterize victims of sexual abuse. Sexual abuse involves a wide range of possible behaviors which appear to have widely varying effects on its victims. The absence of any sexualized behavior does not confirm that sexual abuse did not take place any more than the presence of sexualized behavior conclusively demonstrates that sexual abuse occurred. (Lamb, 1994, p. 153)

Another aspect of some expert's testimony that is particularly worrisome is the underlying message that there are subtle signs that allow one to detect the accuracy of children's reports. Some experts, for example, have claimed that one can detect when children have been influenced by suggestible interviewers because they mechanically parrot the words of the interviewer, use adultlike language, exhibit inappropriate affect, and use few perceptual details to embellish their accounts. For example, one of the experts in the Little Rascals case testified as follows:

> What you look for is the child having emotion that is consistent with what they are telling you and also is consistent with their defenses. One reason it's important is that it is not something that you can really coach. . . . You can coach a kid to say certain things, but you can't coach a kid to have the right feelings to go along with it.

There may be instances when the experts are correct in making such claims, but we suspect that those instances include ones where the child has been deliberately coached to provide false testimony, or else has deliberately decided to provide false testimony (i.e., to lie). Under these circumstances, perhaps professionals (and perhaps even nonprofessionals) can detect false reports, because children have not yet learned to use their faces as masks for deception, and they are unrehearsed in contriving false narratives. There is some scientific evidence that professionals can detect outright lies when children are interviewed immediately after lying about an act to protect a loved one (Honts, 1994), but much more work remains to be done before we can be confident about this finding. However, on the basis of the following evidence, it appears that trained adults cannot reliably detect false reports from children who are exposed to repeated suggestive techniques over long periods of time. This is because the effect of such prolonged suggestion may alter some of the children's memory; if they have a false belief, they are not consciously lying, and therefore no form of lie detection ought to identify this.

To examine experts' judgments of children's credibility, we asked them to rate the credibility of some of the subjects in our studies. For example, we showed videotapes of the final interview with the Sam Stone children (see chapter 10) to approximately 1,500 judges, researchers, and mental health professionals who work with children. They were told that all of the children observed Sam Stone's visit to their day-care centers. They were asked to decide which of the events reported by the children actually transpired and then to rate the overall credibility of each child. They were quite inaccurate. Analyses indicated that these experts—who conduct research on the reliability and credibility of children's reports, provide therapy to children suspected of having been abused, or carry out law enforcement interviews with children—generally failed to detect which of the children's claims were accurate and which were inaccurate, despite being confident in their judgments. When these experts were asked to make credibility ratings of individual children, they were also highly inaccurate: The very children who were least accurate were rated as most accurate. Because so many of the children claimed that Sam Stone ripped the book and/or soiled a teddy bear, it is understandable why many of the experts believed that these false events must have transpired (after all, they reasoned, how could so many children report the same thing if it did not happen?).

Similar results were obtained when psychologists who specialize in interviewing children were shown videotapes of the children in the mouse-trap study described in chapter 14 (Ceci, Huffman, et al., 1994; Ceci, Loftus, Leichtman, & Bruck, 1994). Recall that these children had been simply asked to repeatedly think about whether a fictitious or real event had actually happened. Again, professionals had great difficulty detecting which of the events in the children's narratives were real and which were not. One reason for their difficulty may have been that they could not imagine such plausible, internally coherent narratives being fabricated. In addition, the children exhibited none of the tell-tale signs of duping, teasing, or tricking. They seemed sincere, their facial expressions and affect were appropriate, and their narratives were filled with the kind of low-frequency details and contextual embedding that make accounts seem plausible. (This can be seen in the account of the child who described how his hand got caught in a mousetrap, chapter 14.)

One might argue that the content and quality of the children's narrations in laboratory-based studies is quite different from the narratives of children reporting sexual abuse, thus enabling well-trained professionals to reliably differentiate between true and false reports of sexual abuse even if they cannot do so for other types of events. Unfortunately, the existing literature suggests that this is not the case. There is little consistency among professionals' judgments about children making claims of sexual abuse. Two programs of research illustrate this point.

Realmuto et al. (1990) asked a highly trained child psychiatrist to interview abused and nonabused children and then to determine which of them had been sexually abused. Next, videotapes of this psychiatrist's assessments were shown to 14 professionals (pediatricians, psychiatrists, social workers, psychologists, attorneys), each with more than 10 years of experience in the field of child sexual abuse. These professionals were asked to classify the children as either abused or nonabused. Although there was high concordance between the interviewer and these 14 raters in terms of which children they classified as abused and nonabused, the overall rates of accurate classification were low. The interviewing psychiatrist correctly identified only 33% of the abused children and 67% of the nonabused children. The group of professionals correctly classified 23% of the abused children and 85% of the nonabused children.

Horner, Guyer, and Kalter (1993a, 1993b) presented an actual case of alleged sexual abuse of a 3-year-old to mental health specialists. These specialists heard a detailed presentation of the court-appointed clinician's findings, which included parent interviews and videotaped child–parent interaction sequences. The case presentation lasted approximately 2 hours, during which time the participants questioned the clinician who evaluated the child and her family. After the presentation, the specialists estimated the likelihood that sexual molestation had occurred. The range of estimated probabilities of abuse was extreme: Many clinicians were confident that abuse had occurred, and many others were just as confident that abuse had not occurred. The same pattern was obtained when the analyses were restricted to a smaller group of experts who were uniquely qualified to assess child sexual abuse.

Although surprising to some, these results are depressing to all. They suggest that at least for some allegations of child sexual abuse, there is no "Pinocchio Test" that can be used even by the most experienced and qualified experts to definitively ascertain whether or not abuse occurred. Yet despite this limitation, experts continue to go into court and give their opinions with great confidence solely on the basis of the signs and characteristics of sexual abuse and on the basis of the markers of credibility in children. Wise counselors and judges should put these experts' feet to the coals, forcing them to provide scientifically adequate evidence for their interpretations. In light of the research described in these pages (e.g., Ceci, Crotteau-Huffman, et al., 1994; Ceci, Loftus, et al., 1994; Horner et al., 1993a, 1993b; Realmuto et al., 1990), to do otherwise would seem akin to accepting the testimony of a forensic astrologer.

To summarize, we advise those who consult with attorneys, prepare reports for court, or serve as expert witnesses to recognize the limits of their knowledge, skills, and insights; to make clear these limits when consulting or testifying; to be balanced and provide all sides of an issue; and to keep at arm's length from both sides of the case. Scientific experts should advocate for the truth, not for or against a defendant.

Judicial Changes on the Horizon: Making a Bad Situation Worse

On the final day of the Supreme Court's 1992–93 term, the nine justices changed the rules for expert testimony in federal courts by essentially relaxing the standard for its admissibility. The case, *Daubert v. Merrell Dow Pharmaceuticals* (1993), involved a product liability suit brought against Merrell Dow Pharmaceuticals, makers of Bendectin, an antinausea drug prescribed to pregnant women. The plaintiffs were two children (and their parents) who suffered birth defects that they claimed to be the result of the mothers' use of Bendectin during pregnancy. According to eight experts, Bendectin was a teratogenic drug (i.e., it causes birth defects). Their opinion was based on animal studies and on their reanalysis of some published data on human subjects. The case reached the Supreme Court because the trial court and the appeals court gave little weight to these experts' opinion. Adopting the traditional *Frye* test (*Frye v. United States*, 1923) that requires that expert testimony be based on principles that are generally accepted by the relevant scientific community, the lower courts ruled that these experts' analyses were inadmissible because they had not been subjected to scientific scrutiny in peer-reviewed journals.

The Supreme Court overturned this decision, partly on the grounds that the *Frye* test was overly austere in its requirement that expert testimony be in accord with general acceptance within the relevant scientific community. There are times, for example, when new scientific discoveries are known only to a cadre of researchers who work on a specific problem, and are therefore unknown to the broader community of scholars, but are nevertheless valid.

Although refraining from developing a new standard to govern expert testimony, the court ruled that scientific testimony must be supported by appropriate validation of the expert's reasoning or methods. Such validation is to be based on (a) whether the expert's theory or methods have been tested, (b) whether the expert's opinion has been subjected to peer review and publication, (c) whether the potential rate of error in using the method or theory is established, and (d) whether the technique is generally accepted within the relevant scientific community (i.e., the *Frye* test). These grounds were construed as a flexible means of determining whether an expert's testimony "rests on a reliable foundation."

What does this new ruling bode for experts in child sex abuse cases? No one is really sure, and some legal scholars have opined that it will "open up" the courts to evidence that previously has been declared inadmissible because it lacked general acceptance among scientists, whereas others have argued that it will actually bar some previously admissible testimony because it now fails to meet the new validity standard (Stewart, 1993).

Regardless of what happens, one thing seems sure: Judges will increasingly be expected to become "amateur scientists," foisted into the role of determining the validity of expert testimony. It is difficult enough for trained scientists to make such determinations, but it may be asking too much of trial judges to do so. When scientists disagree (as we sometimes do), which side will the trial judge choose? And why will that side be chosen? This ruling may exacerbate an already bad situation.

Proposals for Reform

As should be clear by now, our discussion has been animated by the belief that the current and proposed changes to this system are antithetical to the court's truth-seeking function. Expert evidence is often misused in proceedings that involve children, and the court seems unable (or unwilling) to rectify the situation, as Mason (1991) has pointed out. We present two different proposals for the reform of procedures for calling expert witnesses in trials involving the child witness.

1. Professional Organizations Should Serve as Ethical Gatekeepers

Professional organizations could help resolve some of the problems we have been discussing by making ethics codes for expert witnesses more explicit. Existing codes for expert witnesses of the organizations that represent various constituencies (psychology, social work, pediatrics) tend to be weak and ill-defined—in part because "expert witness" is an ill-defined legal concept. The Federal Rules of Evidence 702 states that if scientific, technical, or other specialized knowledge will assist a fact finder in understanding evidence, a witness may be regarded as an expert by virtue of his or her knowledge, skill, experience, training, or education. This rule construes expertise broadly enough to cover all fields, including emerging areas within fields, and is constrained by two other Federal Rules of Evidence (401 and 403), which specify that the expert testimony must be relevant. Together, these Federal Rules allow virtually anyone who possesses an advanced degree, or who has some clinical experience, to offer expert testimony on children's reliability or credibility, even though the expert may have scant knowledge of the current scientific findings.

To some extent, weak ethics codes also reflect the ascendancy of guild interests. Because no constituency wants to be excluded from activities that involve service to others (at times for financial gain), its representatives ensure that its members' role is not diminished by ethics code language. Ethics codes tend to be explicit about matters that are relatively benign to the group as a whole (e.g., rules for preparing reports, or statements regarding generic conflicts of interest), but vague about matters that could adversely affect the entire membership (e.g., defining precisely what an expert should know in order to testify about children's suggestibility, or what it means to conduct a good interview). Thus, for example, when psychologists look to their own specialty guidelines and general ethics codes for guidance about the credentials or conduct of an expert witness, they find little help other than nonspecific enjoinders to act responsibly, to be informed, and to aspire to the norms that guide a professional toward the highest ideals. Consider some of the sections of the most recent revision of the American Psychological Association code of ethics (American Psychological Association, 1992) relevant to forensic services:

- Psychologists appropriately take into account the ways in which a prior relationship might affect their professional objectivity or opinions and disclose potential conflict to the parties. (Section 705)
- Psychologists who engage in . . . professional activities maintain a reasonable level of awareness of scientific and professional information in their fields. (General Standards 1.5)
- Psychologists rely on scientifically and professionally derived knowledge when making scientific or professional judgments. (General Standards 1.6)
- In addition, psychologists base their forensic work on appropriate knowledge of and competence in the areas underlying such work. (General Standards 7.1)
- In forensic testimony and reports, psychologists . . . describe fairly the bases for their testimony and conclusions [and] whenever necessary to avoid misleading, acknowledge the limits of their data or conclusions. (General Standards 7.4)

However well intended, these statements taken together lend themselves to ambiguous interpretations. For example, can a psychologist testifying about children's suggestibility choose to *either* rely on research knowledge *or* clinical experience? Can a therapist be expected to avoid a conflict of interest and maintain sufficient objectivity to serve as an expert witness when he or she has had extended contact with the child? (Apparently so: Mason's [1991] analysis showed that many expert witnesses who testified in abuse cases were often the child's therapist, and only 13%

of all experts had no prior relationship with the child.) And precisely what does it mean to "maintain a reasonable level of awareness of scientific information"? Reasonable from whose perspective?

Missing from ethics codes and specialty guidelines for expert witnesses (e.g., Committee on Ethical Guidelines, 1991) is language that would specify that an expert is expected to bring to court more than an advanced degree, a supervised internship that had brought them into contact with sexually abused children, or other clinical experience whereby they had occasionally treated sexually abused clients in their practice. An expert testifying on children's suggestibility, and more generally on the credibility of child witnesses, should be intimately familiar with the systematic scholarship on the topic. Although it is not necessary for this expert to be a researcher, he or she needs to be at least a critical consumer of the research literature.

The failure of professional organizations to constitute and then to enforce principled guidelines has serious consequences. First, it can undermine the judicial system's confidence in the capacity of professionals to offer valid testimony. Of more importance, in criminal proceedings where the defendant faces incarceration, or in civil proceedings where the future placement of the child is at stake, the legitimacy of the expert's testimony can be critical to protecting the rights of both the child and the defendant.

A recent development in this area may ultimately spur professional organizations to carefully monitor the conduct of their members. Namely, a number of civil cases are coming to court in which mental health professionals are being sued for questionable practices. In some of these cases, the litigants are parents who claim that they were falsely accused by their adult children of sexual abuse (see chapter 13). They are suing their children's therapists, who, they argue, used incompetent practices that reflected their poor levels of awareness of scientific and professional information in the field. If found guilty, these professionals will not have to bear the full burden of their financial punishment; the settlements will be paid by insurance companies. As already mentioned in chapter 13, one plaintiff has been awarded $500,000. With several other major settlements recently enacted, and others on the horizon, the insurance premiums for mental health professionals could become exorbitant. To head off such law suits in the future, we anticipate that insurance companies may pressure professional organizations to revise and strictly monitor their guidelines requiring their members to adhere to acceptable scientific practices both in and out of the courtroom.

To conclude, enforcement mechanisms are needed to ensure that expert testimony can be evaluated for its scientific merit. Until such mechanisms are openly advertised to all consumers of legal services, enjoinders to "stay informed" will probably do little to ebb the sorts of abuses reported by Mason (1991) and Spencer (1992). Because of their vagueness, professional ethics codes will be implemented more often in the letter than the spirit.

2. The Cornell Proposal

These problems could be remedied if courts developed procedures for inviting nonpartisan experts, much the way that the French system does (see Spencer, 1992). Recently, the Royal Commission on Criminal Justice in Great Britain arrived at a similar recommendation, "embracing a more inquisitorial approach to expert evidence in the pretrial stages of the criminal justice process" (Redmayne, 1994, p. 157).

At Cornell University, we have been trying to launch a national "Amicus Institute" that would provide nonpartisan, not-for-profit opinions and analyses for courts, upon request. Our mechanism for doing this is to invite prominent scholars from North America and Europe to affiliate with the Amicus Institute. These affiliates would be chosen to represent the best scholarship in each of the relevant areas (e.g., child language, memory, emotional development, child welfare, pediatrics, trauma, etc.). In response to a specific request from the court, a database would be searched for the 10 individuals most knowledgeable about the topic. These 10 names, along with their curricula vitae, would be given to the court, and each of the sides in the dispute would be invited to reject 2 names, leaving 6. After examining materials provided by the court, (e.g., depositions, taped interviews, forensic reports), the 6 experts would interactively discuss the case, for example, by using the Cornell satellite video uplink. At the conclusion of this lengthy discussion, in which these experts have had an opportunity to hear each other's concerns and challenge each other's evidence, they would write a summary analysis that would be submitted as an amicus brief to the court. Should the case come to court, one of the permanent members of the Amicus Institute would represent the brief in court for the purposes of cross-examination.

Ultimately, we hope that the use of such a nonpartisan service would reduce the frequency of court appearances, helping attorneys settle outside of court or advising investigative agencies on when and how to proceed with an investigation. This mechanism also has the advantage of providing a nonadversarial, nonpartisan atmosphere in which the opinions of the international scholars can be elicited and critiqued by their own peers before a final analysis of the problem is presented to the court. It may thus avoid the battle of the hired guns, because none of the experts would have been hired by the defense or by the prosecution. Furthermore, the final opinion would reflect that of the full panel, thus promoting a full disclosure and critique of the available data. This is a scientifically superior venue for resolving differences of opinion than the stilted, formalized procedures of the courtroom. An uninformed or biased expert may fool a jury, but he will not fool a panel of other experts.

THERAPISTS IN THE FORENSIC ARENA

Balancing Scientific and Humanitarian Concerns

Therapists face many dilemmas and choices in providing for children who may have been sexually abused. Often the favored treatment may conflict with forensic procedures. Let us take one example: How should a therapist proceed with a child client when there is reason to believe that the child may be asked to testify in a trial about matters that are the subject of therapy (e.g., sexual abuse)? Should a therapist withhold treatment until the forensic interviews are completed and the trial is over?

On humanitarian grounds, many would argue against withholding treatment, particularly considering the slow pace of criminal justice proceedings. In one study of 833 substantiated cases, Tjaden and Thoennes (1992) found that the average length of time between the initial allegation to the time of criminal disposition was 344 days. In both the Little Rascals case and the Michaels case, the figure was triple this estimate: There was a 3-year interval between the first allegation and the guilty verdict!

We do not want to get into the debate over whether the children in the case studies truly required therapy, or benefitted from it when they received it, because these cases are clearly ambiguous and were selected for this very reason. Putting aside these sample cases, however, there are many circumstances in which children suspected of being abused are clearly in need of therapy and could benefit from it. Take the case of a child who has been removed from her home as a result of a report of sexual abuse and has been placed across town in emergency foster care, separated from her family, friends, and school. The child is greatly distressed and in need of immediate counseling. Are we to make this child languish in a strange family, community, and school for weeks, months, or years before providing her with mental health services?

In light of some research findings that children's reports are likely to be more accurate if all nonforensic interviews (which include therapy sessions) concerning the alleged abuse are held to a minimum until after the final forensic interview takes place, when should the mental health professional begin therapy with the child? How can we avoid the twin dangers of, on the one hand, putting the child's emotional needs on hold until after the forensic interviews are completed and, on the other hand, allowing counseling to jeopardize the veracity of the child's forensic report? Although we know of no easy answers, we think there is a middle ground in this dilemma, one that can achieve the interests of justice as well as humanity.

Given the pressing needs of both sides in a criminal dispute to prepare, investigate, and often re-interview, no amount of child-friendly court procedures can totally alleviate some of the problems associated with children's testimony. Yet perhaps there are ways of providing therapeutic support that lessen the likelihood of tainting the child's report. On the basis of what we now know, it would be imprudent to use fantasy inductions, imagery play, and "memory work" during therapy sessions conducted before the completion of forensic interviews. These practices can be saved for after the legal resolution. Prior to it, therapy should be restricted to working on everyday coping strategies that cannot be challenged by the defendant's counsel as creating false memories. This would seem to be a reasonable compromise, one that provides needed mental health support to the child while minimizing potentially suggestive practices.

Although some might argue that it is too restrictive and ultimately damaging to a child's development if therapists were to avoid the use of potentially suggestive techniques, it could also be argued that using such interventions simply constitutes too great a risk to the child's testimonial accuracy. On the one hand, if the defendant is innocent, such techniques could promote and reinforce false allegations. On the other hand, if the defendant is guilty, the use of such techniques may be invoked to discredit the child's testimony, with defense experts arguing that the child's reports are the product of highly suggestive therapeutic practices.

Finally, on the empirical side, we are unaware of any persuasive treatment-outcome validity research indicating that suggestive techniques are necessary in therapy to achieve a positive mental health outcome for children suspected of being abused. Thus, until mental health professionals can demonstrate that these techniques are critical to use prior to the legal resolution of a case, the "costs" of using them would seem to outweigh their presumed benefits. Given this state of knowledge, therapists might consider limiting their interventions to nonsuggestive techniques until their young clients have given sworn statements; such an approach may afford maximal protection for everyone, including the child.

Therapists Should Not Act as Forensic Investigators

In the previous sections, the issue was when treatment should begin for children who are suspected victims of child abuse and who may serve as witnesses in a trial. There are occasions, however, when a disclosure that leads to a legal proceeding actually eventuates during therapy, rather than prior to it. For example, in the Old Cutler case, one child's regressive toilet practices, night tremors, and fearfulness so concerned her parents that they consequently enrolled her in therapy. After several months of therapy, this child made a disclosure of having been sexually abused. In such cases, there is nothing one can do to completely forestall the potential contamination of therapy on the child's recollections. But there are a number of precautions that could be taken in such situations.

The first is that if a child comes to disclose sexual abuse during a therapy session, the therapist should separate herself from the forensic proceedings and should insist that a second professional conduct the evaluation and investigate the allegations of sexual abuse. We take this recommendation one step further. We believe that therapists who are helping children cope with the trauma of sexual abuse should not become involved in the forensic aspects of the case. Of course, mental health professionals are mandated to report suspicions of abuse, but therapists should not attempt to "crack" the case or to discover other aspects of abuse that may be helpful to the courts. In general, they should stay out of the legal arena when the case concerns someone with whom they have a pre-existing therapeutic relationship; in such cases, they should leave forensic activities to another.

Our recommendation reflects our belief that there is a basic incompatibility between the goals of a forensic interviewer and those of a therapist. The primary and sole role of the forensic investigator is to collect the facts of the case. In therapy, however, there is an emphasis on "helping," as opposed to getting the facts; therapists acknowledge that there are multiple depictions of their client's reality that need to be weighed before deciding which approach will be the most therapeutic. Depending on their theoretical orientation and perceived role, therapists may be interested in bringing to fruition intrapsychic conflicts that may or may not be reality-based.

> Of course, there are many possible depictions that will fit for a given client in a given situation. The specific construction is, perhaps, unimportant. What matters is that clients find the solution that they and the therapist construct to be a satisfactory one. (Gingerich, de Shazer, & Weiner-Davis, 1991, p. 21)

Because of these incompatibilities, there are numerous professional guidelines that explicitly state that the forensic and clinical roles should be filled by two different individuals (e.g., American Academy of Child and Adolescent Psychiatry [1988]; the American Psychological Association's "Guidelines for Child Custody Evaluations in Divorce Proceedings," [1994, p. 678]; American Professional Society on the Abuse of Children [1990]).

There is also a second precaution that mental health professionals should take when they do become the recipient of the child's first disclosure, which is then reported to the authorities: The therapist should provide objective descriptions of his therapeutic techniques, describing how the disclosure was elicited. Our concern here goes beyond that noted in chapter 15, where we discussed the importance of providing electronically preserved copies of the sessions of the child's disclosure. It involves the danger that the use of some therapeutic techniques that are intended to help a child interpret a victimization experience (e.g., fantasy play, symbolic interpretation, visualizations), and later regain control over it (e.g., self-empowerment training), may lead to a co-construction of events and feelings that are not entirely reality based. This becomes a problem when the therapist herself testifies as to the reality of such constructions.

In some of our case histories, the roles of therapists and forensic investigators were at times undifferentiated. For example, in the Little Rascals case, a handful of therapists were compensated by the state for evaluating and "treating" the child witnesses. But there seemed to be other motivations for these therapists to become "investigators" for the district attorney's office. According to one mother's testimony, one therapist seemed to have a vested forensic role:

> [The therapist] evidently had been involved in this for a long time, and she was planning on flying in experts and FBI people from everywhere, because she thought this was going to be bigger than the McMartin Preschool case in California. . . . And she wanted to get on this one right away, wanted to go ahead and get all of these expert people in here because she knew there was a lot more to it.

Because of this possible vested role, some therapists in the case studies repeatedly questioned the children and encouraged them to tell their stories. On the basis of their sessions with their child clients, the therapists would report new allegations to the authorities. And they apparently would do this without cautioning the legal authorities about how to interpret these allegations—some of which seemed like pure fantasy. Unfortunately, much of this material fueled the investigations and resulted in additional charges and additional questioning of the children. This problem would not have occurred if the therapists had confined their interpretations of children's narratives to the clinical domain.

When therapists enter the forensic arena, as happened in some of the cases studies, they sacrifice their "help-providing" mission. They construct a setting whose major purpose is to generate disclosures or allegations rather than one that attempts to help the child cope with his experiences or fantasies. According to a prominent child psychoanalyst who was an expert witness for the defense in the Little Rascals case, the therapists did not address therapeutic issues but saw their main role as collecting allegations from the children. This stance, according to the expert, had devastating consequences for these therapists' clients, who sometimes became more and more disturbed over the course of treatment. If this defense expert is correct in his assumptions, then by putting forensic concerns first, these therapists sacrificed their primary professional responsibility to take care of these children's needs.

THE ETHICS OF INTERVIEWING CHILDREN

In closing, we want to underscore a constant undercurrent of this book that has not been made explicit until now: Many of the methods that have been used to interview some of the children in some of the case studies are ethically unacceptable. In fact, some of these interviews are impeachable in courts of law because they not only challenge common sense about the suggestibility of young children, but they violate national codes of interviewing practices that explicitly enjoin professionals to remain open-minded. For example,

> During the interview process, the interviewer must remain open-minded and try not to be influenced by any preconceived ideas. . . . As an interviewer you must remain open, neutral, and objective, and beware of any reactions which could be interpreted as reinforcing certain responses. . . . Avoid leading questions. . . . Never threaten or try to force a reluctant child to talk or continue an interview. (the manual of the National Center for the Prosecution of Child Abuse, p. 473)

Our opinion concerning the ethical unacceptability of some of these interviews is shared by a number of our fellow researchers. The following paragraph was signed by 45 respected researchers in the allied fields of cognitive, developmental, and clinical psychology, as part of an amicus brief in the Michaels case (Bruck & Ceci, 1995). Its message applies to all cases in which interviewers slide into being forensic advocates, more concerned with "getting the goods" than helping the child. Such interviewers have, at times, lapsed into being vigilantes, a strong term for very disturbing behavior.

> The authors of this brief also wish to convey their deep concern over the children in this case. Our concern is that if there were incidents of sexual abuse, the faulty interviewing procedures make it impossible to ever know who the perpetrators were and how the abuse occurred. Thus, poor interviewing procedures make it difficult to detect real abuse. But we have further concerns. And these involve the interviewing techniques which we view as abusive in themselves. After reading a number of these interviews, it is difficult to believe that adults charged with the care and protection of young children would be allowed to use the vocabulary that they used in these interviews, that they would be allowed to interact with the children in such sexually explicit ways, or that they would be allowed to bully and frighten their child witnesses in such a shocking manner. No amount of evidence that sexual abuse had actually occurred could ever justify the

use of these techniques especially with three- and four-year-old children. Above and beyond the great stress, intimidation, and embarrassment that many of the children so obviously suffered during the interviews, we are deeply concerned about the long-lasting harmful effects of persuading children that they have been horribly sexually and physically abused, when in fact there may have been no abuse until the interviews began. The authors of this brief will be permanently disturbed that children were interviewed in such abusive circumstances regardless of the ultimate innocence or guilt of the accused. (signed by 45 social scientists)

18

IN CONCLUSION

In this our final chapter, we attempt to pull together the messages of earlier chapters, focusing on issues that present the greatest challenges and the most serious concerns. Our thesis in this chapter is that only by firmly rooting our behavior in scientifically grounded research can we avoid jeopardizing the truth-seeking goal of the courtroom. It is with this aim in mind that we begin our ending.

SUGGESTIVE INTERVIEWS VERSUS SUGGESTIVE TECHNIQUES

We have argued throughout that children's reporting accuracy can be influenced by a number of different interviewing techniques. Techniques that induce the child to imagine scenarios that might not have occurred, that encourage children to think repeatedly about fictional events, or that provide negative stereotypes that are paired with repeated suggestions can result in a substantial diminution of children's testimonial accuracy. Furthermore, when an interviewer selectively reinforces certain elements of a child's report, or when she induces the child to make a disclosure through the use of peer pressure and through the aggrandizement of her own authority over the child, the interviewer runs the risk of eliciting inaccurate and false reports. Each of these techniques are especially suggestive when they are paired with repeated interviews that occur long after the alleged event.

Although there is scientific evidence that the use of any one of these techniques may usurp the child's memory, we do not conclude that the presence of any one of these techniques in a single forensic or therapeutic interview necessarily renders all of the child's reports suspect *if these are used by a neutral unbiased interviewer in a single interview*. This should not be taken to mean that we endorse the use of suggestive interviewing techniques, because we do not. But we realize how difficult it is, for even the best-trained neutral interviewer, to refrain from using any of the techniques that we have termed suggestive and to conduct an interview in which there is an element of spontaneity and support.

We believe that suggestive techniques exert their greatest toll on testimonial accuracy when they are used by interviewers with a strong *confirmatory bias*: Confirmatory bias is the major mechanism that drives the intensity and number of suggestive techniques used. When an interviewer avoids confirmatory biases by posing and testing alternative hypotheses, the suggestive techniques do not seem to result in serious problems. Although we have no systematic data on this point, only our casual (uncontrolled) observations of the many videotaped interviews we are sent, it does appear that if interviewers remain open to alternative hypotheses, the isolated use of a suggestive technique may not be that deleterious.

A concrete example may help explain why we feel this way. In one case we were sent, an interviewer asked the child why he had said that the defendant was bad: "Is he bad because he takes things that do not belong to him, or because he doesn't share things with others, or is he bad for some other reason?" One could criticize this interviewer for asking the child a set of leading questions, but it is also true that he is providing the child with a number of open-ended choices. Contrast this interviewer's method of questioning with an interviewer who asks, "Is he bad because he touches your private parts," or even worse, "He's bad because he does things to your private parts, doesn't he?" It is only a matter of time before the latter interviewer will elicit information consistent with his bias. If he pursues the child over long periods of time with such single-minded and single-hypothesis questioning, there is a real danger that the child will assent to the interviewer's line of questioning. And, as was shown in chapter 14, children's initial tentative assents have a way of developing over long periods of time into fully embellished details, contained within a coherent narrative structure. When this happens, experts do not seem able to discriminate them from narratives about true events. The children can be very convincing, not only to the experts but to the children themselves, who frequently refuse to accept debriefing about their falsity!

Having said this about the evolution of fictitious events, there are two additional points. First, as we discussed in chapter 7, these same suggestive techniques are very effective when used to elicit reports of actual events. In fact, there are no better tactics to use to reveal all that a child knows about an event than suggestive tactics. They serve to weaken the child's motives to withhold information, to cue the child's fading memories, and to help structure their recollection in a coherent manner. The problem, of course, is that the forensic interviewer does not know whether an event is real or constructed. He may have hunches, but he seldom truly knows, otherwise there would be no need to conduct interviews.

Second, our analysis of the materials of the four day-care cases (Little Rascals, Michaels, Country Walk, and Old Cutler) leads us to conclude that the rash of allegations of these children emerged as a result of highly biased interviews. Whether any of the allegations may be true is another issue. Perhaps, as some of the investigators stated, their techniques were necessary to get the children to tell of the horrors they experienced. What we do know, however, is that the persistent biased interviews created a situation in which we will never know what happened to these children. The interviewers' methods have rendered their testimony doubtful, at best. So to repeat, if the adults who have had access to children in the aftermath of an alleged event engaged in highly suggestive practices over long periods, coupled with a confirmatory bias, a reasonable person can have doubts over whether the children have accurately described their experiences.

THE STRENGTHS OF CHILDREN'S MEMORIES

Parents, researchers, interviewers, and policymakers recognize that children possess considerable strengths. If parents ask their children to recollect a family outing, a trip to Disney World, or a friend's birthday party, some children are able to supply vivid and detailed accounts even after considerable delays. That this book has not been devoted to a description of such strengths was a deliberate choice. As stated in the Preface, we opted to concentrate on children's weaknesses rather than their strengths because their weaknesses are less apparent and less widely understood than are their strengths. Indeed, it is precisely because of their awareness of children's strengths that many of the professionals involved in children's lives fail to fully appreciate their vulnerability to the suggestive techniques we have been describing. Now that we have presented the case for children's weaknesses in some detail, there are several points that we wish to make through our case histories about their strengths.

First, although much of the scientific literature and the examples from the case histories demonstrate how children's reports and memories can be usurped by suggestive interviewing techniques, we are at times surprised by the children's resistance to their interviewers' biases. We are referring to the children in our case histories and not to the children in laboratory experiments. For some of the children in these cases, it took many months of weekly interviews to get them to assent to suggestions that they had been abused. (And even then, some of the children later recanted their disclosures.) Although some mental health professionals would claim that the children's denials were proof of their abuse, we raise the hypothesis that these children's resistance is an indication of how difficult it sometimes is to use suggestive techniques to capture and change the memories and reports of some young children who steadfastly refuse to relinquish their accurate memories. We think that these children's resistance demonstrates that, at times, children are able to clearly differentiate fact from fantasy, that their memories are so reliable that they can ward off attacks to usurp them. Of course, because of a number of other factors, their attempts to maintain accuracy may eventually falter.

Second, there is nothing in the scientific literature that proves that if a child incorrectly remembers one aspect of an event, she will be incorrect about everything else as well. Memory is not traitlike or invariant. It changes in response to many factors, and it is common for children as well as adults to accurately report one detail but not another, particularly if the inaccurate details are neither interesting nor important to the child. For example, there is a very weak correlation between different types of memory (Ceci, 1990), with memory for faces being unrelated to memory for dance steps, which, in turn, is unrelated to memory for prose or memory for digits or memory for colors. Translated to the legal arena, this means that some inconsistency in recall is normal, and no one ought to routinely dismiss testimony just because the child (or adult) cannot recall the answers to every question that a clever attorney can think to ask. Anyone who expects a child to be able to recall the answers to every question that an adult can think to ask does not understand this fundamental aspect of human memory; it is selective.

We selected the case of the Rape at Devil's Dyke (chapter 2) because it illustrates our point that although a young child may not be able to accurately recall many details of an important experience, the same child's report can nevertheless be highly informative. The child in this case testified that she could not remember many things about her abduction and rape, including the perpetrator's age, the color of his trousers, whether the floor of his trunk where she had been stowed was carpeted, whether she had clothes on when she awoke, or whether his car had seat belts. Yet she correctly recalled that his trunk contained a can of WD-40 lubricant, a hammer, and a chisel, and she identified the defendant in a lineup and correctly described his wristwatch, among other things.

THE ROLE OF THE SOCIAL SCIENTIST IN THE FORENSIC ARENA

The question that we raise in this section is one that we have raised throughout this book, namely, have we accumulated a sufficient body of information to be helpful to the court or are we more likely to confuse it? And given the fact that no study perfectly mimics the constellation of variables observed in any particular case, how much weight should fact finders attach to the social science literature? Should experts even go into court to give testimony about the reliability of children's reports, in view of the imperfect nature of our knowledge? And to what degree should mental health professionals factor in the social science research when opining about the reliability of a child's report or the similarity of her behavior with that of an abused child?

We believe that there is a highly consistent literature that *can* inform the court and mental health professionals about certain elements of children's testimony. This research indicates that suggestive interviewing procedures *can* lead young children to give false reports of real-life experiences, including erroneous claims about interactions involving physical contact between an adult and a child. This same research shows that few young children would fabricate detailed claims of bizarre sexual abuse in response to one or two mildly leading questions; it usually takes more than a single false suggestion to get children to adopt false beliefs, and it usually takes a long period of exposure to a biased interviewer.

Although it is true that no scientific study mirrors all of the influences operating in a particular case, this does not necessarily limit the generalizability of this field of study to that case. The major differences between suggestive interviews in laboratory studies and suggestive interviews in actual cases is that the former are generally less intense and contain fewer suggestive elements than the latter. And yet even under these much-reduced circumstances, a number of children can produce highly inaccurate reports. This leads to the conclusion that if experiments were more like real-life cases we would elicit many more false reports from children than we have done to date; thus, our empirical evidence may in some circumstances underestimate the influence of suggestive interviewing techniques.

Although social scientists are increasingly creative in the paradigms that they devise to study components of suggestive interview techniques, we will never carry out studies that perfectly map many of the factors operating in any one case because researchers and their institutional review boards would consider many of the interviewing procedures that have been used with actual child witnesses grossly unethical to experiment with. Because we cannot experiment with them, we must "go by the best available light," meaning that we must base our inferences on the most scientifically rigorous evidence we have available. Thus, even though there is not a single study that reflects all of the variables that were operative in our case studies, we do have scientifically adequate knowledge about many of these. This knowledge leads prudent scientists to conclude that if a study were to include all of the variables that were operative in the case studies, the result would be a large number of erroneous reports by preschoolers.

This said, it is important to underscore the fact that although social science has revealed a great deal about the inner workings of young children's minds, and the methods to elicit these contents, we are still a long way from possessing perfect knowledge, from predicting which children will succumb to suggestions and which will not. In all of the experiments, as well as the case materials that we have reviewed, it is clear that some children are more immune to the biases of their interviewers than are others. And yet, aside from the child's age, we have little consistent empirical data concerning the characteristics that differentiate these immune children from their peers who are more vulnerable to the pressures of a biased interview. Factors such as gender, intelligence level, language skills, and the understanding of the concept of a "lie" do not assist in this identification. Future researchers may find keys to this puzzle through the exploration of personality traits, "theory of mind," and parental socialization practices, but for now, there are no clear answers. The social science researcher at this point can provide strong and consistent data on age-group trends, but not on individual variation within a given age group.

However, there are two other areas where the social science research can present some evidence, and yet this evidence seems to go unheeded by a number of members of the mental health and legal professions. An example of the first area is the professional "lore" that children refuse to disclose their abuse because they have been threatened by their perpetrators. For example, such a claim was made in four of the case studies. The following example is illustrative:

Attorney: Did they (the children), to the best of your knowledge, allege and then recant sexual abuse at any time?

Therapist: Yes.

Attorney: Do you have an opinion as to why that would be, and why?

Therapist: They were both afraid that their parents would be killed or that they would be killed.

Attorney: Do you have an opinion as to why (the children) may have delayed alleging the sexual abuse from the time it occurred?

Therapist: They were afraid they would be killed or their parents would be killed or their sister would be killed.

The intent of this type of testimony, which was provided by a number of experts in our sample cases, was to explain to the jury why the child did not disclose and why it may have been necessary to badger a child after she had repeatedly denied being abused.

However, there is little empirical basis to this claim. Recall that in chapter 3 we pointed out that the likelihood of disclosure was unrelated to claims of threats by the offender. When the offender used aggressive methods to gain the child's silence, children were equally likely to tell about the abuse immediately following the event or to never disclose the abuse at all. Moreover, two thirds of children who were threatened not to tell nevertheless did disclose the details of their victimization. Thus, threatened children appeared to disclose as often as children who were not threatened, and therefore denial of abuse ought not inevitably to lead to the conclusion that a child is keeping his abuse secret. Furthermore, Peter's studies (see chapter 11, footnote 1) showed that although children in a laboratory experiment would not disclose a crime to their parents if the perpetrator was present, they were quite likely to do so as soon as the perpetrator was absent.

A second example of where the social science research has been ignored by mental health professionals and the courts concerns the validity of allegations of satanic or ritualistic abuse (e.g., cult activities that include witchcraft or animal sacrifice; organized rings of adults specializing in child pornography). Three of the day-care cases that we described in this book (Little Rascals, Country Walk, and Old Cutler), as well as many other cases that have come to the courts, are characterized by these types of allegations. And yet, as we have discussed, there is no compelling evidence to support these claims, both in our cases and in the others that have been investigated. As a result of the mounting empirical evidence that there is no basis for such allegations, perhaps they will subside in the courtroom. But we are not sure whether the total number of allegations outside of the courtroom will subside. Those professionals who believe that such acts are common may continue to spread these biases in their interviews with children. And although these cases may not come to court, children's minds and lives may be permanently distorted because of an interviewer's stalwart beliefs about satanic or ritualistic abuse. Being aware of the scientific data will help prevent miscarriages of justice to both defendants and the young child who is the object of relentless digging by a misguided interviewer.

In summary, there is always some risk when generalizing from scientific studies to real-world cases because the two contexts are usually not perfectly analogous. Scientists believe, however, that the best basis for generalization is to extrapolate from the corpus of research, with a special focus on those studies that come closest to matching the constellation of variables that operate in the particular case before the court—even if the match is less than perfect. The alternative to basing predictions on these nearest scientific relatives to the case at bar is to eschew insights, predictions, or hypotheses gained from systematic, controlled studies in lieu of anecdotes, personal opinions, and ideological views about children's gullibility or innocence. When these take precedence over scientifically derived conclusions, we have substituted heat for light.

ENDING AT THE BEGINNING . . .

We began this book with a description of the Circle Girls' testimony in the Salem witch trials. Perhaps it is fitting that we end there, too. Are America's children pawns in a modern witch hunt, propelled by vigilante interviewers, hell-bent on extracting evidence at any cost? There are those who would say, "No." According to these commentators, although there are egregious examples of miscarriages of justice that result from poor interviewing, the parallels with Salem are ill-wrought.

Some have based their arguments on speculations about the causes of those sad days in 1692 when, according to one account, crazed villagers, driven by mind-altering corn spores, did crazy things. We believe that this is a misinterpretation of those times and people. They were not crazy, and their behaviors were quite reasonable, given their cultural beliefs and the political/economic motives that prevailed (see Gemmill, 1924; Nevins, 1892; Seth, 1969). In fact, villagers often engaged in reasonable precautions to avoid false convictions. For instance, it was commonly believed that being stared at by a witch could put the person gazed upon under a spell or into a fainting fit. To preclude obvious examples of feigning and lying, the Salem elders sometimes blindfolded child witnesses as a protection against their false fainting and fits. They seem to have reasoned that if a child who was blindfolded still fainted when gazed upon by a defendant, this was superior evidence. Such precautions were not the behavior of crazed, psychotic individuals, but of reasoned human beings, no different from those of us today.

Recently, Myers (1995) asserted that parallels with Salem are ill-wrought because the witch trials do not resemble the modern child-protective system:

> Although Salem is a powerful image, the comparison of modern child protection to Salem, Massachusetts in 1692 is misleading. In Salem, all of the accused "witches" were innocent. Today, many who are accused of child abuse are guilty. In Salem, children were one hundred

percent inaccurate. Today, children are often completely accurate. Playing the Salem card distorts reality and fuels irrational fears.

To attempt to dismiss any parallel between *some* modern trials and the Salem trials is to deny the obvious. Myers (1995) created a "red herring" by trying to force this parallel to one between Salem's treatment of child witnesses during the witch trials in 1692 and modern child protective services investigations. The correct focus should be on the parallel between the Salem trials and some modern trials that shared a similar pattern of strongly suggestive interviews extending over long intervals.

One cannot simply dismiss the earlier period by noting that the children's testimony was flawed (i.e., defendants were innocent) and then, without any external corroboration, asserting that the modern period is different because some, many, or most of the defendants are guilty. In both instances, a jury decided that the defendants were guilty, and crucial testimony was given by children who in all of the Salem cases as well as in *some* of the modern ones were exposed to relentlessly suggestive interviewing, confirmatory bias, and negative stereotypes. Although it is certainly not the case that all trials today resemble the ones in Salem, some certainly do. To attempt to gainsay this parallel is to miss an important historical lesson. One wonders if a future generation will look back on the final years of this millennium with the same sense of fascination and revulsion that we now look back at Salem.

We hope for the sake of the children who testify in modern cases that resemble Salem that their testimony is accurate because, if the decade succeeding Salem is any measure, they might be expected to suffer severe misgivings if they later realize that their testimony was inaccurate. Some of the girls who testified in Salem had the horrible realization, many years afterward, that they had been deluded when they testified and that they were responsible for sending innocent individuals to their graves. Such a realization was profoundly upsetting. Ann Putnam, one of the Circle Girls in Salem who subsequently realized the erroneous basis of her testimony, made the following public confession 14 years later:

> I desire to be humbled before God for that sad and humbling providence that befell my father's family in the year 1692: that I, then being in my childhood, should by such a providence of God, be made an instrument for the accusing of several persons of a grievous crime, whereby their lives were taken away from them, whom now I have just grounds and good reason to believe they were innocent persons; and that it was a great delusion of Satan that deceived me in that sad time, whereby I justly fear that I have been instrumental, with others, though ignorantly and unwitting, to bring upon myself and this land the guilt of innocent blood; though what was said or done by me against any person I can truly say and uprightly say before God and man, I did it

not out of anger, malice or ill-will to any person, for I had no such thing against them, but what I did was done ignorantly, being deluded of Satan. . . . I desire to lie in the dust, and to be humbled for it, in that I was the cause, with others, of so sad a calamity to them and their families. (from the Witchcraft Papers, State House, Boston, cited in Nevins, 1892, p. 250)

It is eerie to compare Ann Putnam's confession with that of Jennifer F., the modern 9-year-old whose testimony proved critical to Frederico Macias's conviction and death sentence. Four years after her testimony (and 2 weeks before Macias was scheduled to be executed by a lethal injection), Jennifer F. made the following statement:

When I first saw Fred with red stuff on his shirt, I didn't think it was that important. At first, I didn't really know if it was blood or chili. Later, when I saw Fred had a gun or a knife, it caught my attention, and I thought that it must be blood. Because different people asked me so many different questions about what I saw, I became confused. I thought I might have seen something that would be helpful to the police. I didn't realize that it would become so important. I thought they wanted me to be certain, so I said I was certain even though I wasn't. Originally, I think I told the police just what I saw. But the more questions I was asked, the more confused I became. I answered questions I wasn't certain about because I wanted to help the adults. (subscribed and sworn before Regina Jarius, notary, on August 13th, 1988, El Paso County, Texas)

REFERENCES

Ackerman, B. (1983). Speaker bias in children's evaluation of the external consistency of statements. *Journal of Experimental Child Psychology, 35*, 111–127.

Ackil, J. A. & Zaragoza, M. (in press). Developmental differences in eyewitness suggestibility and memory for source. *Journal of Experimental Child Psychology.*

Alloy, L. B., & Tabachnik, N. (1984). Assessment of covariation by humans and animals: The joint influence of prior expectations and current situational information. *Psychological Review, 91*, 112–149.

Alpert, J. L., Brown, L. S., & Cortois, C. A. (in press). Symptomatic clients and memories of childhood abuse: What the trauma literature tells us. *American Psychologist.*

American Academy of Child and Adolescent Psychiatry. (1988). Guidelines for the clinical evaluation of child and adolescent sexual abuse. *Journal of the American Academy of Child and Adolescent Psychiatry, 27*, 655–657.

American Humane Association. (1988). Highlights of official child neglect and abuse reporting, 1986. Denver, CO: Author.

American Professional Society on the Abuse of Children (APSAC). (1990). *Guidelines for psychosocial evaluation of suspected sexual abuse in young children.* Unpublished manuscript.

American Psychiatric Association. (1994). *Diagnostic and statistical manual of mental disorders* (4th ed.). Washington, DC: Author.

American Psychological Association. (1992). Ethical principles of psychologists and code of conduct. *American Psychologist, 47*, 1597–1611.

American Psychological Association. (1994). Guidelines for child custody evaluations in divorce proceedings. *American Psychologist, 49*, 677–680.

Anderson, D. (1990, February 27). Handcuffed to history. *New York Times*, p. B-9.

Andrews, J. A. (1964). The evidence of children. *Criminal Law Review, 64*, 769–777.

August, R. L., & Forman, B. D. (1989). A comparison of sexually abused and nonsexually abused children's behavioral responses to anatomically correct dolls. *Child Psychiatry and Human Development, 20*, 39–47.

Baddeley, A. D. (1990). *Human memory: Theory and practice.* Boston: Allyn & Bacon.

Bartlett. F. C. (1932). *Remembering: A study in experimental and social psychology.* Cambridge: Cambridge University Press.

Bass, E., & Davis, L. (1990). *The courage to heal: A guide for women survivors of child sexual abuse.* New York: Harper & Row.

Batterman-Faunce, J. M., & Goodman, G. S. (Ed.). (1993). *Effects of context on the accuracy and suggestibility of the child witness*. New York: Guilford Press.

Bauer, P. J., Hertsgaard, L. A., & Dow, G. A. (1994). After 8 months have passed: Long-term recall of events by 1- to 2-year-old children. *Memory, 2*, 353–382.

Beitchman, J. H., Zucker, K. J., Hood, J. E., DaCosta, G. A., & Akman, D. (1991). A review of the short-term effects of child sexual abuse. *Child Abuse & Neglect, 15*, 537–556.

Belli, R. F. (1989). Influences of misleading postevent information: Misinformation interference and acceptance. *Journal of Experimental Psychology: General, 118*, 72–85.

Belli, R. F., Windschitl, P., McCarthy, T., & Winfrey, S. (1992). Detecting memory impairment with a modified test procedure: Manipulating retention interval with centrally presented event items. *Journal of Experimental Psychology: Learning, Memory, and Cognition, 18*, 356–367.

Benedek, E., & Schetky, D. (1985). Allegations of sexual abuse in child custody and visitation disputes. In E. Benedek & D. Schetky (Eds.), *Emerging issues in chld psychiatry and the law* (pp. 145–156). New York: Brunner/Mazel.

Berry, K., & Skinner, L. G. (1993). Anatomically detailed dolls and the evaluations of child sexual abuse allegations: Psychometric considerations. *Law and Human Behavior, 17*, 399–422.

Besharov, D. (1991). Child abuse and neglect reporting and investigation: Policy guidelines for decision making. *Child & Youth Services, 15*, 35–50.

Bikel, O. (1991, May 7) Innocence lost. *Frontline* (Show No. 918).

Bikel, O. (1993a, July 20). Innocence lost—The verdict (Part 1). *Frontline* (Show No.1120).

Bikel, O. (1993b, July 21). Innocence lost—The verdict (Part 2). *Frontline* (Show No. 1121).

Binet, A. (1900). *La suggestibilité*. Paris: Schleicher Frères.

Boat, B., & Everson, M. (1988). The use of anatomical dolls among professionals in sexual abuse evaluations. *Child Abuse & Neglect, 12*, 171–186.

Boat, B., Everson, M., & Holland, J. (1990). Maternal perceptions of nonabused young children's behaviors after the children's exposure to anatomical dolls. *Child Welfare, 64*, 389–399.

Bothwell, R. K., Deffenbacher, K. A., & Brigham, J. C. (1987). Correlation of eyewitness accuracy and confidence: Optimality hypothesis revisited. *Journal of Applied Psychology, 72*, 691–695.

Bottoms, B., Goodman, G., Schwartz-Kenney, B., Sachsenmaier, T., & Thomas, S. (1990, March). *Keeping secrets: Implications for children's testimony*. Paper presented at the biennial meeting of the American Psychology and Law Society, Williamsburg, VA.

Brainerd, C., & Reyna, V. (1994). *Mere memory testing creates false memories in children*. Manuscript submitted for publication.

Brainerd, C., Reyna, V., & Brandes E. (1994). *Are children's false memories more persistent than their true memories?* Manuscript submitted for publication.

Brainerd, C., Reyna, V. F., Howe, M. L., & Kingma, J. (1990). The development of forgetting and reminiscence. *Monographs of the Society for Research on Child Development, 55*(3–4 Serial No. 222).

Brehm, S. S., & Smith, T. W. (1986). Social psychological approaches to psychotherapy and behavior change. In S. L. Garfield & A. Bergin (Eds.), *Handbook of psychotherapy and behavior change* (3rd ed., pp. 69–116). New York: Wiley.

Brennan, M., & Brennan, R. E. (1988). *Strange language.* Wagga Wagga, New South Wales, Australia: Riverina Murry Institute of Higher Education.

Briere, J., & Conte, J. (1993). Self-reported amnesia for abuse in adults molested as children. *Journal of Traumatic Stress, 6,* 21–31.

Brown, A., & Kulik, J. (1977). Flashbulb memories. *Cognition, 5,* 73–99.

Brozan, N. (1984, September 18). Witness says she fears "child predator" network. *New York Times,* p. A-21.

Bruck, M., & Ceci, S. J. (1995). Brief on behalf of amicus developmental, social, and psychological researchers, social scientists, and scholars. *Psychology, Public Policy and the Law, 1,* 1–51.

Bruck, M., Ceci, S. J., & Francoeur, E. (1995, March). *Anatomically detailed dolls do not facilitate preschoolers' reports of touching.* Paper presented at the Society for Research on Child Development, Indianapolis, Indiana.

Bruck, M., Ceci, S. J., Francoeur, E., & Barr. R. J. (1995). "I hardly cried when I got my shot!": Influencing children's reports about a visit to their pediatrician. *Child Development, 66,* 193–208.

Bruck, M., Ceci, S. J., Francoeur, E., & Renick, A. (1995). Anatomically detailed dolls do not faciltate preschoolers' reports of a pediatric examination involving genital touching. *Journal of Experimental Psychology: Applied, 1,* 95–109.

Burgess, A. H. (Ed.). (1984). *Child pornography and sex rings.* Lexington, MA: Lexington Books.

Burtt, H. E. (1948). *Applied psychology.* Englewood Cliffs, NJ: Prentice-Hall.

Bussey, K. (1992). Children's lying and truthfulness: Implications for children's testimony. In S. J. Ceci, M. Leichtman, & M. Putnick (Eds.), *Cognitive and social factors in preschoolers' deception* (pp. 89–110). Hillsdale, NJ: Erlbaum.

Campis, L. B., Hebden-Curtis, J., & DeMaso, R. (1993). Developmental differences in detection and disclosure of sexual abuse. *Journal of American Academy of Child and Adolescent Psychiatry, 32,* 920–924.

Cassel, W. S., & Bjorklund, D. F. (in press). Developmental patterns of eyewitness memory, forgetting, and suggestibility: An ecologically based short-term longitudinal study. *Law and Human Behavior.*

Ceci, S. J. (1990). *On intelligence . . . more or less: A bio-ecological treatise on intellectual development.* Englewood Cliffs, NJ: Prentice-Hall.

Ceci, S. J. (1994). Cognitive and social factors in children's testimony. In B. Sales & G. Vandenbos (Eds.), *Psychology in litigation and legislation: Master lectures* (pp.14–54). Washington, DC: American Psychological Association.

Ceci, S. J., & Bronfenbrenner, U. (1991). On the demise of everyday memory: The rumors of my death are greatly exaggerated. *American Psychologist, 46,* 27–31.

Ceci, S. J., & Bruck, M. (1993a). Children's recollections: Translating research into policy. *SRCD Social Policy Reports, 7,* No. 3.

Ceci, S. J., & Bruck, M. (1993b). The suggestibility of the child witness: A historical review and synthesis. *Psychological Bulletin, 113,* 403–439.

Ceci, S. J., Caves, R., & Howe, M. J. (1981). Children's long term memory for information incongruent with their knowledge. *British Journal of Psychology, 72,* 443–450.

Ceci, S. J., Crotteau-Huffman, M., Smith, E., & Loftus, E. W. (1994). Repeatedly thinking about non-events. *Consciousness & Cognition, 3,* 388–407.

Ceci, S. J., Leichtman, M. D., & Bruck, M. (1995). The suggestibility of children's eyewitness reports: Methodological issues. In F. Weinert & W. Schneider (Eds.), *Memory development: State of the art and future directions* (pp. 323–347). Englewood Cliffs, NJ: Erlbaum.

Ceci, S. J., Leichtman, M., & Putnick, M. (1992). *Cognitive and social factors in early deception.* Hillsdale, NJ: Erlbaum.

Ceci, S. J., Leichtman, M., Putnick, M., & Nightingale, N. (1993). Age differences in suggestibility. In D. Cicchetti & S. Toth (Eds.), *Child abuse, child development, and social policy* (pp. 117–137). Norwood, NJ: Ablex.

Ceci, S. J., Leichtman, M., & White, T. (in press). Interviewing preschoolers: Remembrance of things planted. In D. P. Peters (Ed.), *The child witness in context: Cognitive, social, and legal perspectives.* The Netherlands: Kluwer.

Ceci, S. J., & Loftus, E. F. (1994). "Memory work": A royal road to false memories? *Applied Cognitive Psychology, 8,* 351–364.

Ceci, S. J., Loftus, E. F., Leichtman, M., & Bruck, M. (1994). The role of source misattributions in the creation of false beliefs among preschoolers. *International Journal of Clinical and Experimental Hypnosis, 62,* 304–320.

Ceci, S. J., Ross, D., & Toglia, M. (1987). Age differences in suggestibility: Psychological implications. *Journal of Experimental Psychology: General, 117,* 38–49.

Ceci, S. J., Toglia, M., & Ross, D. (1990). The suggestibility of preschoolers' recollections: Historical perpectives on current problems. In R. Fivush & J. Hudson (Eds.), *Knowing and remembering in young children* (pp.285–300). New York: Cambridge University Press.

Chadbourn, J. (1978). *Wigmore on evidence.* Boston: Little, Brown.

Chapman, L. J. (1967). Illusory correlation in observational report. *Journal of Verbal Learning and Verbal Behavior, 6,* 151–155.

Chi, M. (1978). Knowledge structures and memory development. In R. S. Siegler (Ed.), *Children's thinking: What develops?* (pp. 73–96). Hillsdale, NJ: Erlbaum.

Child Victim Witness Investigative Pilot Projects. (1994, July). *Research and evaluation final report.* California Attorney General's Office, Sacramento, California.

Christianson, S.-A. (1992). Emotional stress and eyewitness memory: A critical review. *Psychological Bulletin, 112,* 284–309.

Chu, J. A., & Dill, D. L. (1990). Dissociative symptoms in relation to childhood physical and sexual abuse. *American Journal of Psychiatry, 147,* 887–892.

Clarke-Stewart, A., Thompson, W., & Lepore, S. (1989, May). *Manipulating children's interpretations through interrogation.* Paper presented at the biennial meeting of the Society for Research on Child Development, Kansas City, MO.

Cohen, R. L. (1975). *Children's testimony and hearsay evidence* (Law Reform Commission of Canada, Report on Evidence). Ottawa, Canada: Information Canada.

Cohen, R. L., & Harnick, M. A. (1980). The susceptibility of child witnesses to suggestion. *Law & Human Behavior, 4,* 201–210.

Cohn, D. S. (1991). Anatomical doll play of preschoolers referred for sexual abuse and those not referred. *Child Abuse & Neglect, 15,* 455–466.

Committe on Ethical Guidelines for Forensic Psychologists. (1991). Specialty guidelines for forensic psychologists. *Law and Human Behavior, 15,* 655–665.

Conte, J. R., Sorenson, E., Fogarty, L., & Rosa, J. D. (1991). Evaluating children's reports of sexual abuse: Results from a survey of professionals. *American Journal of Orthopsychiatry, 78,* 428–437.

Coy v. Iowa., 108 S. Ct. 2798 (1988).

Crocker, C. (1981). Judgment of covariation by social perceivers. *Psychological Bulletin, 90,* 272–292.

Cunningham, J. L. (1988a). Contributions to the history of psychology: L. French historical views on the acceptability of evidence regarding child sexual abuse. *Psychological Reports, 63,* 343–353.

Cunningham, J. L. (1988b). Contributions to the history of psychology: XLVI. The pioneer work of Alfred Binet on children as eyewitnesses. *Psychological Reports, 62,* 271–277.

Daubert v. Merrell Dow Pharmaceuticals, Inc., 113 S. Ct. 2789 (1993).

Dawes, R. (1992, Spring). The importance of alternative hypothesis and hypothetical counterfactuals in general social science. *General Psychologist,* pp. 2–7.

DeLoache, J. S., & Marzolf, D. P. (in press). The use of dolls to interview young children: Issues of symbolic representation. *Journal of Experimental Child Psychology.*

Edmiston, S. (1990, November). A twenty-nine-year-old California woman charges her father with a 20-year-old murder. *Glamour,* pp. 228–285.

Elliott, R. (1993). Expert testimony about eyewitness identification: A critique. *Law and Human Behavior, 17*, 423–437.

Ervin-Tripp, S. (1978). Wait for me, Roller-Skate. In S. Ervin-Tripp & C. Mitchell-Kernan (Eds.), *Child discourse* (pp. 165–188). San Diego, CA: Academic Press.

Ethical principles of psychologists and code of conduct. (1992). *American Psychologist, 47*, 1597–1611.

Everson, M., & Boat, B. (1989). False allegations of sexual abuse by children and adolescents. *Journal of the American Academy of Child and Adolescent Psychiatry, 28*, 230–235.

Everson, M., & Boat, B. (1990). Sexualized doll play among young children: Implications for the use of anatomical dolls in sexual abuse evaluations. *Journal of the American Academy of Child and Adolescent Psychiatry, 29*, 736–742.

Everson, M. D., & Boat, B. (1994). Putting the anatomical doll controversy in perspective: An examination of the major uses and criticisms of the dolls in child sexual abuse evaluations. *Child Abuse & Neglect, 18*, 113–129.

Ewing, C. P. (1994, January). Psychological harm can be prosecuted. *APA Monitor*, p. 13.

Faigman, D. L.(1989). Notes: The battered woman syndrome and self-defense: A legal and empirical dissent. In S. L. Johann & F. Osanta (Eds.), *Representing battered women who kill* (pp. 333–362). Springfield, IL: Charles C Thomas.

Faller, K. C. (1984). Is the child victim of sexual abuse telling the truth? *Child Abuse & Neglect, 8*, 473–481.

Faller, K. (1991). Possible explanations for child sexual abuse allegations in divorce. *American Journal of Orthopsychiatry, 61*, 86–91.

Farrar, M. J, & Goodman, G. S. (1992). Developmental changes in event memory. *Child Development, 63*, 173–187.

Femina, D. D., Yeager, C. A., & Lewis, D. O. (1990). Child abuse: Adolescent records vs. adult recall. *Child Abuse & Neglect, 14*, 227–231.

Finkelhor, D. (1994). The international epidemiology of child sexual abuse. *Child Abuse & Neglect, 18*, 409–417.

Finkelhor, D., Hotaling, G., Lewis, I. A., & Smith, C. (1990). Sexual abuse in a national survey of adult men and women: Prevalence, characteristics and risk factors. *Child Abuse & Neglect, 14*, 19–28.

Finkelhor, D., Williams, L. M., & Burns, N. (1988). *Nursery crimes: Sexual abuse in day care*. Newbury Park, CA: Sage.

Fisher, F. (1994, November 20). Daughter's memories lead to arrests in grissly killing. *Chicago Sun-Times*.

Fivush, R. (1993). Developmental perspectives on autobiographical recall. In G. S. Goodman & B. Bottoms (Eds.), *Child victims and child witnesses: Understanding and improving testimony* (pp. 1–24). New York: Guilford Press.

Fivush, R., Hamond, N. R., Harsch, N., Singer, N., & Wolf, A. (1991). Content and consistency in young children's autobiographical recall. *Discourse Processes, 14*, 373–388.

Flannagan, D., & Hess, T. (1991, April). *Developmental differences in children's abilities to utilize scripts in promoting their recall for scenes*. Paper presented at the biennial meeting of the Society for Research in Child Development, Seattle, WA.

Flin, R. (1993). Hearing and testing children's evidence. In G. S. Goodman & B. L. Bottoms (Eds.), *Child victims and child witnesses: Understanding and improving testimony* (pp. 279–300). New York: Guilford Press.

Foley, M. A., & Johnson, M. K. (1985). Confusions between memories for performed and imagined actions. *Child Development, 56,* 1145–1155.

Foley, M. A., Johnson, M. K., & Raye, C. L. (1983). Age-related confusion between memories for thoughts and memories for speech. *Child Development, 54,* 51–60.

Fredrickson, R. (1992). *Repressed memories: A journey to recovery from sexual abuse.* New York: Parkside Books/Simon & Schuster.

Friedrich, W. N., Grambsch, P., Broughton, D., Kuiper, J., & Beilke, R. L. (1991). Normative sexual behaviour in children. *Pediatrics, 88,* 456–464.

Frye v. United States, 293 F. 1013 (D.C. Cir. 1923).

Gabriel, R. M. (1985). Anatomically correct dolls in the diagnosis of sexual abuse of children. *Journal of the Melanie Klein Society, 3,* 45–50.

Gardner, D. S. (1933). The perception and memory of witnesses. *Cornell Law Quarterly, 18,* 391–409.

Garvey, C. (1984). *Children's talk.* Cambridge, MA: Harvard University Press.

Geiselman, R., Saywitz, K., & Bornstein, G. (1990). *Effects of cognitive interviewing, practice, and interview style on children's recall performance.* Unpublished manuscript.

Gelman, R., Meck, E., & Merkin, S. (1986). Young children's numerical competence. *Cognitive Development, 1,* 1–29.

Gemmill, W. N. (1924). *The Salem witch trials: A chapter of New England history.* Chicago, IL: McClurg.

Giannelli, P. C. (1980). *The admissibility of novel scientific evidence*: Frye v. United States, *a half-century later*. 80 Column. L. Rev. 1197–1250.

Gingerich, W. L., de Shazer, S., & Weiner-Davis, M. (1991). Constructing change: A research view of interviewing. In E. Lipchik (Ed.), *Interviewing* (pp. 21–32). Rockville, MD: Aspen.

Glaser, D., & Collins, C. (1989). The response of young, non-sexually abused children to anatomically correct dolls. *Journal of Child Psychology and Psychiatry, 30,* 547–560.

Godden, D. R., & Baddeley, A. D. (1975). Context-dependent memory in two natural environments: On land and underwater. *British Journal of Psychology, 66,* 325–331.

Goodman, G. (1984). Children's testimony in historical perspective. *Journal of Social Issues, 40,* 9–31.

Goodman, G. S. (1991). Commentary: On stress and accuracy in research on children's testimony. In J. Doris (Eds.), *The suggestibility of children's recollections* (pp. 77–82). Washington, DC: American Psychological Association.

Goodman, G. S. (1993). Understanding and improving children's testimony. *Children Today, 22,* 13–15.

Goodman, G., & Aman, C. (1990). Children's use of anatomically detailed dolls to recount an event. *Child Development, 61,* 1859–1871.

Goodman, G. S., Batterman-Faunce, J. M., & Kenney, R. (1992). Optimizing children's testimony: Research and social policy issues concerning allegations of child sexual abuse. In D. Cicchetti & S. Toth (Eds.), *Child abuse, child development, and social policy.* Norwood, NJ: Ablex.

Goodman, G., Bottoms, B., Herscovici, B., & Shaver, P. (1989). Determinants of the child victim's perceived credibility. In S. J. Ceci, D. F. Ross, & M. P. Toglia (Eds.), *Perspectives on children's testimony* (pp. 1–22). New York: Springer-Verlag.

Goodman, G. S., Bottoms, B. L., Schwartz-Kenney, B., & Rudy, L. (1991). Children's testimony about a stressful event: Improving children's reports. *Journal of Narrative and Life History, 1,* 69–99.

Goodman, G. S., & Clarke-Stewart, A. (1991). Suggestibility in children's testimony: Implications for child sexual abuse investigations. In J. L. Doris (Eds.), *The suggestibility of children's recollections* (pp. 92–105). Washington, DC: American Psychological Association.

Goodman, G. S., Rudy, L., Bottoms, B., & Aman, C. (1990). Children's concerns and memory: Issues of ecological validity in the study of children's eyewitness testimony. In R. Fivush & J. Hudson (Eds.), *Knowing and remembering in young children* (pp. 249–284). New York: Cambridge University Press.

Goodman, G., Qin, J., Bottoms, B., & Shaver, P. (1994). *Characteristics of allegations of ritualistic child abuse* (Final report to National Center on Child Abuse and Neglect, Washington, DC).

Goodman G. S., Quas J. A., Batterman-Faunce J. M., Riddlesberger, M. M., & Kuhn, J. (1994). Predictors of accurate and inaccurate memories of traumatic events experienced in childhood. *Consciousness & Cognition, 3,* 269–294.

Goodman, G. S., Taub, E. P., Jones, D. P. H., England, P., Port, L. K., Rudy, L., & Prado, L. (1992). *Monographs of the Society for Research in Child Development, 57*(5, Serial No. 229).

Goodman, G. S., Wilson, M. E., Hazan, C., & Reed, R. S. (1989, April). Children's testimony nearly four years after an event. Paper presented at the annual meeting of the Eastern Psychological Association, Boston, MA.

Gordon, B., Ornstein, P. A., Clubb, P. A., Nida, R. E., & Baker-Ward, L. E. (1991, October). *Visiting the pediatrician: Long term retention and forgetting.* Paper presented at the annual meeting of the Psychonomic Society, San Francisco, CA.

Gordon, B., Ornstein, P. A., Nida, R., Follmer, A., Creshaw, C., & Albert, G. (1993). Does the use of dolls facilitate children's memory of visits to the doctor? *Applied Cognitive Psychology, 7*, 459–474.

Gordon, B. N., Schroeder, C. S., & Abrams, M. (1990). Children's knowledge of sexuality: A comparison of sexually abused and nonabused children. *American Journal of Orthopsychiatry, 60*, 250–257.

Gray, E. (1993). *Unequal justice: The prosecution of child sexual abuse.* New York: MacMillan.

Gross, S. R. (1991). Expert evidence. *Wisconsin Law Review, 1991*, 1113–1231.

Gudjonsson, G. (1986). The relationship between interrogative suggestibility and acquiescence: Empirical findings and theoretical implications. *Personality and Individual Differences, 7*, 195–199.

Hale, M. (1980). *Human science and social order: Hugo Münsterberg and the origins of applied psychology.* Philadelphia: Temple University Press.

Haney, C. (1980). Psychology and legal change: On the limits of a factual jurisprudence. *Law & Human Behavior, 4*, 147–199.

Harris, P., Brown, E., Marriott, C., Whittall, S., & Harmer, S. (1991). Monsters, ghosts and witches: Testing the limits of the fantasy–reality distinction in young children. *British Journal of Developmental Psychology, 9*, 105–123.

Harvard Law Review Notes. (1985). The testimony of child sex abuse victims in sex abuse prosecutions: Two legislative innovations. *Harvard Law Review, 98*, 806–827.

Hastie, R. (1981). Schematic principles in human memory. In E. T. Higgins, C. P. Herman, & M. P. Zanna (Eds.), *Social cognition: The Ontario Symposium* (Vol. 1, pp. 39–88). Hillsdale, NJ: Erlbaum.

Herbert, C. P., Grams, G. D., & Goranson, S. E. (1987). *The use of anatomically detailed dolls in an investigative interview: A preliminary study of "non-abused" children.* Unpublished manuscript.

Herman, J., L., & Schatzow, E. (1987). Recovery and verification of memories of childhood sexual trauma. *Psychoanalytic Psychology, 4*, 1–14.

Hollingsworth, J. (1986). *Unspeakable acts.* New York: Congdon & Weed.

Holmes, D. S. (1994). Is there evidence for repression? Doubtful. *Harvard Mental Health Letter, 10*, 4–6.

Honts, C. R. (1994). Credibility assessment with children: Scientific and legal issues in 1994. *North Dakota Law Review, 70*, 879–903.

Horner, T. M., Guyer, M., J., & Kalter, N. M. (1993a). The biases of child sexual abuse experts: Believing is seeing. *Bulletin of the American Academy of Psychiatry and Law, 21*, 281–292.

Horner, T. M., Guyer, M., J., & Kalter, N. M. (1993b). Clinical expertise and the assessment of child sexual abuse. *Journal of the American Academy of Child and Adolescent Psychiatry, 32*, 925–931.

Horsnell, M. (1990a, November 16). Girl describes how she was abducted then left for dead. *The London Times*.

Horsnell, M. (1990b, December 14). Girl's sex attacker jailed for life for attempted murder. *The London Times*, p. 3.

Howe, M. L. (1991). Misleading children's story recall: Reminiscence of the facts. *Developmental Psychology, 27*, 746–762.

Howe, M. L., & Courage, M. L. (1993). On resolving the enigma of infantile amnesia. *Psychological Bulletin, 113*, 305–326.

Howes, M., Siegel, M., & Brown, F. (1993). Early childhood memories: Accuracy and affect. *Cognition, 47*, 95–119.

Hudson, J. A. (1990). Constructive processing in children's event memory. *Developmental Psychology, 26*, 180–187.

Hudson, J., & Nelson, K. (1986). Repeated encounters of a similar kind: Effects of familiarity on children's autobiographical memory. *Cognitive Development, 1*, 253–271.

Hughes, M., & Grieve, R. (1980). On asking children bizarre questions. *First Language, 1*, 149–160.

Hurlock, E. (1930). Suggestibility in children. *Journal of Genetic Psychology, 37*, 59–74.

Hyman, I. E. , Husband, T., & Billings, F. (in press). False memories of childhood experiences. *Applied Cognitive Psychology*.

Jampole, L., & Weber, M. K. (1987). An assessment of the behavior of sexually abused and nonsexually abused children with anatomically correct dolls. *Child Abuse & Neglect, 11*, 187–192.

Johnson, M. K., Foley, M. A., Suengas, A. G., & Raye, C. L. (1988). Phenomenal characteristics of memories for perceived and imagined autobiographical events. *Journal of Experimental Psychology: General, 117*, 371–376.

Johnson, M. K., Hashtroudi, S., & Lindsay, D. S. (1993). Source monitoring. *Psychological Bulletin, 144*, 3–28.

Jones, D., & McGraw, J. M. (1987). Reliable and fictitious accounts of sexual abuse in children. *Journal of Interpersonal Violence, 2*, 27–45.

Jussim, L. (1986). Self-fulfilling prophecies: A theorectical and integrative review. *Psychological Review, 93*, 429–445.

Kail, R. V. (1989). *The development of memory in children* (2nd ed.). New York: Freeman.

Kalichman, S. C. (1993). *Mandated reporting of suspecting child abuse: Ethics, law, and policy*. Washington DC: American Psychological Association.

Kandel, M., & Kandel, E. (1994, May). Flights of memory. *Discover*, pp. 32–38.

Kayne, N. T., & Alloy, L. B. (1988). Clinician and patient as aberrant actuaries: Expectation-based distortions in assessment of covariation. In L. Y. Abramson (Ed.), *Social cognition and clinical psychology: A synthesis*. New York: Guilford Press.

Kelley, S. J., Brant, R., & Waterman, J. (1993). Sexual abuse of children in day care centers. *Child Abuse & Neglect, 17*, 71–89.

Kendall-Tackett, K. (1991, April). *Professionals' standards of "normal" behavior with anatomical dolls and factors that influence these standards.* Paper presented at the meeting of the Society for Research in Child Development, Seattle, WA.

Kendall-Tackett, K. A., & Watson, M. W. (1992). Use of anatomical dolls by Boston-area professionals. *Child Abuse & Neglect, 16*, 423–428.

Kendall-Tackett, K. A., Williams, L. M., & Finkelhor, D. (1993). Impact of sexual abuse on children: A review and synthesis of recent empirical studies. *Psychological Bulletin, 113*, 164–180.

Kenyon-Jump, R., Burnette, M., & Robertson, M. (1991). Comparison of behaviors of suspected sexually abused and nonsexually abused preschool children using anatomical dolls. *Journal of Psychopathology and Behavioral Assessment, 13*, 225–240.

King, M., & Yuille, J. (1987). Suggestibility and the child witness. In S. J. Ceci, D. Ross, & M. Toglia (Eds.), *Children's eyewitness memory* (pp. 24–35). New York: Springer-Verlag.

Klatzky, R. L. (1980). *Human memory: Structures and processes.* San Francisco: Freeman.

Koocher, G. P., Goodman, G. S., White, S., Friedrich, W. N., Sivan, A. B., & Reynolds, C. R. (in press). Psychological science and the use of anatomically detailed dolls in child sexual abuse assessments. *Psychological Bulletin.*

La Fontaine, J. S. (1994). *The extent and nature of organised and ritual abuse: Research findings.* London: Department of Health, HMSO.

Lamb, M. E. (1994). The investigation of child sexual abuse: An interdisciplinary consensus statement. *Expert Evidence, 2*, 151–163.

Lamb. M. E., Hershkowitz, I., Sternberg, K. J., Esplin, P. W., Hovav, M., Manor, T., & Yudilevitch, L. (in press). Effects of investigative utterance types on Israeli children's responses. *International Journal of Behavioral Development.*

Landy, F. J. (1992). Hugo Münsterberg: Victim or visionary? *Journal of Applied Psychology, 77*, 787–802.

Langer, L. L. (1991). *Holocaust testimonies: The ruins of memory.* New Haven, CT: Yale University Press.

Lanning, K. (1991). Ritual abuse: A law enforcement perspective. *Child Abuse & Neglect, 15*, 171–173.

LeDoux, J. E. (1994, June). Emotion, memory, and the brain. *Scientific American, 270*, 50–55.

Leekam, S. (1992). Believing and deceiving: Steps to becoming a good liar. In S. J. Ceci, M. DeSimone, & M. Putnick (Eds.), *Social and cognitive factors in preschool deception* (pp. 47–62). Hillsdale, NJ: Erlbaum.

Leichtman, M. D. (1994). Long term memory in infancy and early childhood. Unpublished doctoral dissertation, Cornell University, Ithaca, NY.

Leichtman, M. D., & Ceci, S. J. (in press). The effects of stereotypes and suggestions on preschoolers' reports. *Developmental Psychology.*

Leippe, M., Manion, A., & Romanczyk, A. (1992). Eyewitness persuasion: How and how well do factfinders judge the accuracy of adults' and children's memory reports? *Journal of Personality and Social Psychology, 163,* 181–187.

Leippe, M., & Romanczyk, A. (1987). Children on the witness stand: A communication/persuasion analysis of jurors' reactions to child witnesses. In S. J. Ceci, M. P. Toglia, & D. F. Ross (Eds.), *Children's eyewitness memory* (pp. 155–177). New York: Springer-Verlag.

Leippe, M., & Romanczyk, A. (1989). Reactions to child (versus adult) eyewitnesses. *Law and Human Behavior, 13,* 102–132.

Lepore, S. J., & Sesco, B. (1994). Distorting children's reports and interpretations of events through suggestion. *Applied Psychology, 79,* 108–120.

Lewis, M., Stranger, C., & Sullivan, M. (1989). Deception in three-year-olds. *Developmental Psychology, 25,* 439–443.

Lindberg, M. (1991). A taxonomy of suggestibility and eyewitness memory: Age, memory process, and focus of analysis. In J. L. Doris (Eds.), *The suggestibility of children's recollections* (pp. 47–55). Washington, DC: American Psychological Association.

Lindsay, D. S. (1990). Misleading suggestions can impair eyewitnesses' ability to remember event details. *Journal of Experimental Child Psychology, 52,* 297–318.

Lindsay. D. S., Gonzales, V., & Eso, K. (1995). Aware and unaware uses of memories of postevent suggestions. In Zaragoza, M. S., Graham, J. R., Gordon, C. N., Hirschman, R., & Ben-Porath, Y. (Eds.), *Memory and testimony in the child witness* (pp. 86–108). Newbury Park, CA: Sage.

Lindsay, D. S., Johnson, M. K., & Kwon, P. (1991). Developmental changes in memory source monitoring. *Journal of Experimental Child Psychology, 52,* 297–318.

Lindsay, D. S., & Read, J. D (1994). Psychotherapy and memories of childhood sexual abuse: A cognitive perspective. *Applied Cognitive Psychology, 8,* 281–338.

Lipmann, O. (1911). Pedagogical psychology of report. *Journal of Educational Psychology, 2,* 253–260.

Lipovsky, J. A., Tidwell, R., Crisp, J., Kilpatrick, D. G., Saunders, B. E., & Dawson, V. L. (1992). Child witnesses in criminal court. *Law and Human Behavior, 16,* 635–650.

Loftus, E. F. (1979). *Eyewitness testimony.* Cambridge, MA: Harvard University Press.

Loftus, E. F. (1986). Ten years in the life of an expert witness. *Law and Human Behavior, 10,* 241–263.

Loftus, E. F. (1992). When a lie becomes memory's truth: Memory distortion after exposure to misinformation. *Current Directions in Psychological Science, 4,* 121–123.

Loftus, E. F., Feldman, J., & Dashiell, R. (in press). The reality of illusory memories. In D. L. Schacter, J. T. Coyle, G. D. Fischbach, M. M. Mesulam, & L. E Sullivan (Eds.), *Memory distortion: How minds, brains, and societies reconstruct the past.* Cambridge, MA: Harvard University Press.

Loftus, E. F., Miller, D. G., & Burns, H. J. (1978). Semantic integration of verbal information into a visual memory. *Journal of Experimental Psychology: Human Learning and Memory, 4,* 19–31.

Loftus, E. F., Polansky, S., & Fullilove, M. T. (1994). Memories of childhood sexual abuse: Remembering and repressing. *Psychology of Women Quarterly, 18,* 67–84.

Loftus, E., & Wells, G. (1984). *Eyewitness testimony: Psychological perspectives.* New York: Cambridge University Press.

Loh, W. D. (1981). Psychological research: Past and present. *Michigan Law Review, 79,* 659–707.

Luus, C. A. E., Wells, G., & Turtle, J. (in press). Child eyewitnesses: Seeing is believing. *Journal of Applied Psychology.*

MacLean, H. (1993). *Once upon a time.* New York: HarperCollins.

Manshel, L. (1990). *Nap time.* New York: Kensington.

Marin, B., Holmes, D., Guth, M., & Kovac, P. (1979). The potential of children as eyewitnesses: A comparison of children and adults on eyewitness tasks. *Law and Human Behaviour, 3,* 295–306.

Martin, K. M., & Aggleton, J. P. (1993). Contextual effects on the ability of divers to use decompression tables. *Applied Cognitive Psychology, 7,* 311–316.

Maryland v. Craig, 110 S. Ct. 3157 (1990).

Mason, M. A. (1991, Winter). A judicial dilemma: Expert witness testimony in child sexual abuse cases. *Journal of Psychiatry and Law,* 185–219.

McCloskey, M. M., & Egeth, H. (1983). Eyewitness identification: What can a psychologist tell a jury? *American Psychologist, 38,* 550–563.

McCloskey, M., & Zaragoza, M. (1985). Misleading postevent information and memory for events: Arguments and evidence against the memory impairment hypothesis. *Journal of Experimental Psychology: General, 114,* 1–16.

McConnell, T. R. (1963). Suggestibility in children as a function of chronological age. *Journal of Abnormal and Social Psychology, 67,* 286–289.

McGough, L. (1994). *Fragile voices: The child witness in American courts.* New Haven, CT: Yale University Press.

McGough, L. S., & Warren, A. R. (1994). The all-important investigative interview. *Juvenile and Family Court Journal, 45,* 13–29.

McIver, W., Wakefield, H., & Underwager, R. (1989). Behavior of abused and non-abused children in interviews with anatomically correct dolls. *Issues in Child Abuse Accusations, 1,* 39–48.

Melton, G. B. (1985). Sexually abused children and the legal system: Some policy recommendations. *American Journal of Family Therapy, 13,* 61–67.

Melton, G. (1992). Children as partners for justice: Next steps for developmentalists. *Monographs of the Society for Research in Child Development, 57*(Serial No. 229), 153–159.

Messerschmidt, R. (1933). The suggestibility of boys and girls between the ages of six and sixteen. *Journal of Genetic Psychology, 43,* 422–437.

Mian, M., Wehrspann, W., Klajner-Diamond, H., LeBaron, D., & Winder, C. (1986). Review of 125 children 6 years of age and under who were sexually abused. *Child Abuse & Neglect, 10,* 223–229.

Miller, A. (1953). *The crucible: A play in four acts.* New York: Bantam Books

Montoya, J. (1992). On truth and shielding in child abuse trials. *Hastings Law Journal, 43,* 1259–1319.

Montoya, J. (1993). *When fragile voices intersect with a fragile process: Pretrial interrogation of child witnesses.* Unpublished monograph, University of San Diego School of Law.

Moore, C. (1907). Yellow psychology. *Law Notes, 11,* 125–127.

Moore, C. (1908). Psychology and the courts. *Law Notes, 11,* 186–187.

Morgan, E. M., & Maguire, J. M. (1937). *Looking backward and forward at evidence.* 50 Harv. L. Rev. 909–36.

Moston, S., & Engelberg, T. (1992). The effects of social support on children's eyewitness testimony. *Applied Cognitive Psychology, 6,* 61–75

Münsterberg, H. (1907a, April). Nothing but the truth. *McClure's Magazine,* pp. 26–29.

Münsterberg, H. (1907b). Yellow psychology: Dr. Munsterberg replies to Mr. Moore. *Law Notes, 11,* 145–146.

Münsterberg, H. (1908). *On the witness stand.* New York: Doubleday & Page.

Myers, J. E. B. (1987a). *Evidence in child abuse and neglect cases* (Vol. 1). New York: Wiley Law.

Myers, J. E. B. (1987b). *Evidence in child abuse and neglect cases* (Vol. 2). New York: Wiley Law.

Myers, J. E. B. (1992). *Legal issues in child abuse and neglect.* Newbury Park, CA: Sage.

Myers, J. E. B. (1993). Expert testimony regarding child sexual abuse. *Child Abuse and Neglect, 17,* 175–185.

Myers, J. E. B. (1994). The literature of the backlash. In J. E. B. Myers (Ed.), The backlash: Child protection under fire (pp. 86–103). Thousand Oaks, CA: Sage.

Myers, J. E. B. (1995). New era of skepticism regarding children's credibility. *Psychology, Public Policy, and Law, 1,* 387–398.

Myers, J. E. B. (in press). Expert testimony in child sexual abuse cases. In *American Professional Society on the Abuse of Children handbook on child maltreatment.*

Nathan, D. (1993a). Revisiting Country Walk. *Issues in Child Abuse Accusations, 5,* 1–11.

Nathan, D. (1993b). Reno reconsidered. *New Times, 7*(46), 10–37.

National Center on Child Abuse and Neglect. (1988). *Study of national incidence and prevalence of child abuse and neglect: 1988*. Gaithersburg, MD: U.S. Department of Health and Human Services.

National Center on Child Abuse and Neglect. (1993). *National Child Abuse and Neglect Data System, 1991: Summary data component*. Gaithersburg, MD: U.S. Department of Health and Human Services.

Neisser, U. (1982). *Memory observed: Remembering in natural contexts*. San Francisco: Freeman.

Neisser, U., & Harsch, N. (1992). Phantom flashbulbs: False recollections of hearing the news about Challenger. In E. Winograd & U. Neisser (Eds.), *Affect and accuracy in recall: Studies of "flashbulb" memories*. New York: Cambridge University Press.

Nelson, K. (1988). The ontogeny of memory for real events. In U. Neisser & E. Wonograd (Eds.), *Remembering reconsidered: Ecological and traditional approaches to memory* (pp. 244–276). New York: Cambridge University Press.

Nelson, K. (1993). The psychological and social origins of autobiographical memory. *Psychological Science, 4*, 7–14.

Nelson, K., & Gruendel, J. (1979). At morning it's lunchtime: A scriptal view of children's dialogues. *Discourse Processes, 2*, 73–94.

Nevins, W. S. (1892). *Witchcraft in Salem Village*. Salem, MA: Salem Observer Press.

Ofshe, R. J., & Singer, M. T. (1993). *Recovered memory therapies and robust repression: A collective error*. Unpublished manuscript, University of California, Berkeley.

Ofshe, R., & Watters, E. (1993, March/April). Making monsters. *Society*, 4–16.

Oldenberg, D. (1991, June 20). Dark memories: Adults confront their childhood abuse. *Washington Post*, p. D5.

Ornstein, P. (1991). Commentary: Putting interviewing in context. In J. L. Doris (Eds.), *The suggestibility of children's recollections* (pp. 147–152). Washington, DC: American Psychological Association.

Ornstein, P., Gordon, B. N., & Larus, D. (1992). Children's memory for a personally experienced event: Implications for testimony. *Applied Cognitive Psychology, 6*, 49–60.

Ornstein, P. A., Shapiro, L. R., Clubb, P. A., & Follmer, A. (in press). The influence of prior knowledge on children's memory for salient medical experiences. In N. Stein, P. A. Ornstein, C. J. Brainerd, & B. Tversky (Eds.), *Memory for everyday and emotional events*. Hillsdale, NJ: Erlbaum.

Otis, M. (1924). A study of suggestibility in children. *Archives of Psychology, 11*, 5–108.

Paradise, J., Rostain, A., & Nathanson, M. (1988). Substantiation of sexual abuse charges when parents dispute custody or visitation. *Pediatrics, 81*, 835–838.

Patterson, R. N. (1985). *Private screening*. New York: Ballantine Books.

Pear, T., & Wyatt, S. (1914). The testimony of normal and mentally defective children. *British Journal of Psychology, 3,* 388–419.

Pendergrast, M. (1994). *Victims of memory: Incest accusations and shattered lives.* Hinesburg, VT: Upper Access Books.

Peters, D. P. (1990, March). Confrontational stress and lying. Paper presented at the biennial meeting of the American Psychology/Law Society, Williamsburg, VA.

Peters, D. P. (1991). Commentary: Response to Goodman. In J. L. Doris (Ed.), *The suggestibility of children's recollections* (pp. 86–91). Washington, DC: American Psychological Association.

Peters, D. P., Wyatt, G. E., & Finkelhor, D. (1986). Prevalence. In D. Finkelhor (Ed.), *A sourcebook on child sexual abuse* (pp. 15–59). Beverly Hills, CA: Sage.

Pettit, F., Fegan, M., & Howie, P. (1990. September). *Interviewer effects on children's testimony.* Paper presented at the International Congress on Child Abuse and Neglect, Hamburg, Germany.

Pezdek, K., & Roe, C. (in press). The effect of memory trace strength on suggestibility. *Journal of Experimental Child Psychology.*

Phipps-Yonas, S., Yonas, A., Turner, M., and Kauper, M. (1993). Sexuality in early childhood. *Center for Urban and Regional Affairs Reporter, 23*(2), 1–5.

Piaget, J. (1926). *The language and thought of the child.* London: Routledge, Kegan Paul.

Piaget, J. (1962). *Play, dreams, and imitation in childhood* (C. Cattegno & F. M. Hodgsen, Trans.). New York: W.W. Norton. (Original work published 1945)

Pillemer, D. B., Picariello, M. L., & Pruett, J. C. (1994). Very long-term memories of a salient event. *Applied Cognitive Psychology, 8,* 95–106.

Pillemer, D. B., & White, S. H. (1989). Childhood events recalled by children and adults. In H. W. Reese (Ed.), *Advances in child development and behavior* (Vol. 21, pp. 297–340). San Diego, CA: Academic Press.

Pipe, M. E., & Goodman, G. S. (1991). Elements of secrecy: Implications for children's testimony. *Behavioral Sciences and the Law, 9,* 33–41.

Poole, D. A., & Lindsay, D. S. (in press). Interviewing preschoolers: Effects of nonsuggestive techniques, parental coaching and leading questions on reports of nonexperienced events. *Journal of Experimental Child Psychology.*

Poole, D. A., Lindsay, D.S., Memon, A., & Bull, R. (in press). Psychotherapy and the recovery of memories of childhood sexual abuse: U.S. and British practitioners' opinions, practices and experiences. *Journal of Consulting & Clinical Practice.*

Poole, D., & White, L. (1991). Effects of question repetition on the eyewitness testimony of children and adults. *Developmental Psychology, 27,* 975–986.

Poole, D., & White, L. (1993). Two years later: Effects of question repetition and retention interval on the eyewitness testimony of children and adults. *Developmental Psychology, 29,* 844–853.

Poole, D., & White, L. (1995). Tell me again and again: Stability and change in the repeated testimonies of children and adults. In M. S. Zaragoza, J. R. Graham, C. N. Gordon, R. Hirschman, & Y. Ben Porath (Eds.), *Memory and testimony in the child witness* (pp. 24–43). Newbury Park, CA: Sage.

Powers, P., Andriks, J. L., & Loftus, E. F. (1979). Eyewitness accounts of females and males. *Journal of Applied Psychology, 64,* 339–347.

Pynoos, R. S., & Nader, K. (1989). Children's memory and proximity to violence. *Journal of the American Academy of Child and Adolescent Psychiatry, 28,* 236–241.

R. v. Russell Bishop. The Law Courts, Lewes Crown Court, UK (1990).

R. v. Wallwork, 42 Cr. App. R. 153 (1958).

Rabinowitz, D. (1990, May). Out of the mouth of babes and into a jail cell. *Harper's Magazine,* pp. 52–63.

Rayner, K., & Pollatsek, A. (1989). *The psychology of reading.* Englewood Cliffs, NJ: Prentice-Hall.

Read, B., & Cherry, L. (1978). Preschool children's productions of directive forms. *Discourse Processes, 1,* 233–245.

Realmuto, G., Jensen, J., & Wescoe, S. (1990). Specificity and sensitivity of sexually anatomically correct dolls in substantiating abuse: A pilot study. *Journal of the American Academy of Child and Adolescent Psychiatry, 29,* 743–746.

Realmuto, G., & Wescoe, S. (1992). Agreement among professionals about a child's sexual abuse status: Interviews with sexually anatomically correct dolls as indicators of abuse. *Child Abuse & Neglect, 16,* 719–725.

Redmayne, M. (1994). The Royal Commission's proposals on expert evidence: A critique. *Expert Evidence, 2,* 157–163.

Rice, S. A. (1929). Interviewer bias as a contagion. *American Journal of Sociology, 35,* 421–423.

Romaine, S. (1984). *The language of children and adolescents.* Cambridge, MA: Basil Blackwell.

Rose, S., & Blank, M. (1974). The potency of context in children's cognition: An illustration through conservation. *Child Development, 45,* 499–502.

Rosenthal, R. (1985). From unconscious experimenter bias to teacher expectancy effects. In J. B. Dusek (Ed.), *Teacher expectancies* (pp. 37–134). Hillsdale, NJ: Erlbaum.

Rosenthal, R., & Rubin, D. B. (1978). Interpersonal expectancy effects: The first 345 studies. *Behavioral and Brain Sciences, 3,* 377–386.

Ross, D., Dunning, D., Toglia, M., & Ceci, S. J. (1990). The child in the eyes of the jury: Assessing mock jurors' perceptions of the child witness. *Law and Human Behavior, 14,* 5–23.

Ross, M. (1989). Relation of implicit theories to the construction of personal histories. *Psychological Review, 96,* 341–357.

Rudy, L., & Goodman, G. S. (1991). Effects of participation on children's reports: Implications for children's testimony. *Developmental Psychology, 27,* 527–538.

Salter, A. C. (1992). Response to the "Abuse of the Child Sexual Abuse Accomodation Syndrome." *Journal of Child Sexual Abuse, 1,* 173–177.

San Diego County Grand Jury (1994, June 1). *Analysis of child molestation issues* (Report No. 7).

Sas, L. D., Hurley, P., Hatch, A., Malla, S., & Dick, T. (1993). *A longitudinal study of the social and psychological adjustment of child witnesses referred to the child witness project.* London: Child Witness Project, London Family Court Clinic, Inc.

Sauer, M. (1993, August 29). Decade of accusations. *San Diego Union Tribune,* pp. D1–D3.

Sauzier, M. (1989). Disclosure of child sexual abuse: For better or for worse. *Treatment of Victims of Sexual Abuse, 12,* 455–469.

Saywitz, K., Goodman, G., Nicholas, G., & Moan, S. (1991). Children's memory for genital exam: Implications for child sexual abuse. *Journal of Consulting and Clinical Psychology, 59,* 682–691.

Schneider, W., & Pressley, M. (1989). *Memory development between 2 and 20.* New York: Springer-Verlag.

Seth, R. (1969). *Children against witches.* New York: Taplinger.

Sgroi, S. M. (1982). *Handbook of clinical intervention in child sexual abuse.* Lexington, MA: Lexington Books.

Sherman, I. (1925). The suggestibility of normal and mentally defective children. *Comparative Psychology Monographs, 2.*

Siegel, J. M., Sorenson, S. B., Golding, J. M., Burnam, M. A., & Stein, J. A. (1987). The prevalence of childhood sexual assault: The Los Angeles epidemiologic catchment area project. *American Journal of Epidemiology, 126,* 1141–1153.

Siegal, M., Waters, L., & Dinwiddy, L. (1988). Misleading children: Causal attributions for inconsistency under repeated questioning. *Journal of Experimental Child Psychology, 45,* 438–456.

Sivan, A. B., Schor, D. P., Koeppl, G. K., & Noble, L. D. (1988). Interaction of normal children with anatomical dolls. *Child Abuse & Neglect, 12,* 295–304.

Small, W. S. (1896). Suggestibility of children. *Pedagogical Seminary, 13,* 176–220.

Snyder, L. S., Nathanson, R., & Saywitz, K. (1993). Children in court: The role of discourse processing and production. *Topics in Language Disorders, 13,* 39–58.

Sonnenschein, S., & Whitehurst, G. (1980). The development of communication: When a bad model makes a good teacher. *Journal of Experimental Child Psychology, 3,* 371–390.

Sorensen, T., & Snow, B. (1991). How children tell: The process of disclosure of child sexual abuse. *Child Welfare, 70,* 3–15.

Spence, D. P. (1994). Narrative truth and putative child abuse. *International Journal of Clinical and Experimental Hypnosis, 42*, 289–303.

Spencer, J. R. (1992). Court experts and expert witnesses. In R. W. Rideout & B. Hepple (Eds.), *Current legal problems* (Vol. 45, pp. 214–236). London: Oxford University Press.

State v. Buckey, Superior Court, Los Angeles County, California, #A750900 (1990).

State v. Bullock, 791 P.2d 155 (Utah 1989).

State v. Fijnje, 11th Judicial Circuit Court, Dade Country, Florida, #89-43952 (1991).

State v. Francisco Fuster, 11th Judicial Circuit Court, Dade Country, Florida, #84-19728 (1985).

State v. Frederico Martinez Macias, 168th Judicial District Court, El Paso County, Texas, #41270-168 (1984).

State v. Geyman, 729 P.2d 475 (Montana, 1986).

State v. Huss, 506 N.W. 2d 290 (1993).

State v. Kathryn Dawn Wilson, Superior Criminal Court, Perquimans County, North Carolina, #92-CRS-4296-4306; 92-CRS-4309-4312 (1992-1993).

State v. Michael (W. Va., 1893).

State v. Michaels, Superior Court, Essex County, New Jersey (1988).

State v. Michaels, 264 N.J. Super 579, 625 A.D. 2d 489 (N.J. Super Ad, 1993).

State v. Michaels. 136 N.J. 299, 642 A.2d 1372 (N.J., 1994).

State v. Morasco, § 571 (Utah, 1912).

State v. Robert Fulton Kelly, Jr., Superior Criminal Court, Pitt County, North Carolina, #91-CRS-4250-4363 (1991–1992).

Stern, W. (1910). Abstracts of lectures on the psychology of testimony and on the study of individuality. *American Journal of Psychology, 21*, 270–282.

Stewart, D. O. (1993, November). Supreme Court report: A new test. *American Bar Association Journal*, pp. 48–51.

Stouthamer-Loeber, M. (1987). *Mothers' perceptions of children's lying and its relationship to behavior problems.* Paper presented at the biennial meeting of the Society for Research in Child Development, Baltimore, MD.

Suengas, A. G., & Johnson, M. K. (1988). Qualitative effects of rehearsal on memories for perceived and imagined events. *Journal of Experimental Psychology: General, 103*, 377–389.

Sugar, M. (1992). Toddlers' traumatic memories. *Infant Mental Health Journal, 13*, 245–251.

Summit, R. C. (1983). The child sexual abuse accommodation syndrome. *Child Abuse & Neglect, 7*, 177–193.

Tate, C., Warren, A., & Hess, T. (1992). Adults' liability for children's "lie-ability": Can adults coach children to lie successfully? In S. J. Ceci, M. D. Leichtman,

& M. E. Putnick (Eds.), *Cognitive and social factors in early deception* (pp. 69–87). New York: Macmillan.

Tate, C. S., & Warren-Leubecker, A. R. (1990, March). Can young children lie convincingly if coached by adults? In S. J. Ceci (chair), *Do children lie? Narrowing the uncertainties*. Symposium conducted at the biennial meeting of the American Psychology/Law Society, Williamsburg, VA.

Terr, L. (1988a). Anatomically correct dolls: Should they be used as a basis for expert testimony? *Journal of the American Academy of Child and Adolescent Psychiatry, 27,* 254–257.

Terr, L. (1988b). What happens to early memories of trauma? A study of twenty children under age five at the time of documented traumatic events. *Journal of the American Academy of Child and Adolescent Psychiatry, 27,* 96–104.

Terr, L. (1994). *Unchained memories.* New York: Basic Books.

Thoennes, N., & Tjaden, P.G. (1990). The extent, nature and validity of sexual abuse allegations in custody/visitation disputes. *Child Abuse and Neglect, 14,* 151–163.

Tjaden, P. G., & Thoennes, N. (1992). Predictors of legal intervention in child maltreatment cases. *Child Abuse & Neglect, 16,* 807–821.

Tobey, A., & Goodman, G. S. (1992). Children's eyewitness memory: Effects of participation and forensic context. *Child Abuse & Neglect, 16,* 779–796.

Tranquada, J. (1990, January). Mistakes marred case from the start, jurors say. *Orange County Register,* p. 1.

United States v. Azure, 801 F.2d 336 (8th Cir. 1986).

U.S. Department of Health and Human Services. (1988). *Study findings: Study of national incidence and prevalence of child abuse and neglect.* Bethesda, MD: Westat.

U.S. Department of Health and Human Services, National Center on Child Abuse and Neglect. (1993, April). *Child maltreatment 1991: Reports from the states to the National Center on Child Abuse and Neglect.* Washington, DC: U.S. Government Printing Office.

U.S. Department of Health and Human Services, National Center on Child Abuse and Neglect. (1994, April). *Child maltreatment 1992: Reports from the states to the National Center on Child Abuse and Neglect.* Washington, DC: U.S. Government Printing Office.

Usher, J. A., & Neisser, U. (1993). Childhood amnesia and the beginnings of memory for four early life events. *Journal of Experimental Psychology, 122,* 155–165.

Vaillant, G. E. (1977). *Adaptation to life.* Boston: Little, Brown.

Van der Kolk, B. A. (in press). Disorders of extreme stress. In D. Cicchetti & S. Toth (Eds.), *The 8th Annual Rochester Symposium on Developmental Psychopathology: The effects of trauma on the developmental process.* New York: Academic Press.

Van der Kolk, B. A., & Van der Hart, O. (1991). The intrusive past: The flexibility of memory and the engraving of trauma. *American Imago, 48,* 425–454.

Varendonck, J. (1911). Les témoignages d'enfants dans un procès retentissant. *Archives de Psychologie, 11,* 129–171.

Veitch, V., & Gentile, C. (1992). Psychological assessment of sexually abused children. In W. O'Donohue & J. Geer (Eds.), *The sexual abuse of children: Clinical issues* (Vol. 2, pp. 143–187). Hillsdale, NJ: Erlbaum.

Wagenaar, V. A., & Groeneweg, J. (1990). The memory of concentration camp survivors. *Applied Cognitive Psychology, 4,* 77–87.

Walker, A. G., & Warren, A. R. (in press). The language of the child abuse interview: Asking the questions, understanding the answers. In T. Ney (Ed.), *Allegations in child sexual abuse, assessment and case management.* New York: Brunner/Mazel.

Warren, A. R., Hulse-Trotter, K., & Tubbs, E. (1991). Inducing resistance to suggestibility in children. *Law and Human Behavior, 15,* 273–285.

Warren, A. R., & Lane, P. (1995). The effects of timing and type of questioning on eyewitness accuracy and suggestibility. In M. Zaragoza, J. R. Graham, G. C. Hall, R. Hirschman, & Y. S. Ben Porath (Eds.), *Memory and testimony in the child witness* (pp. 44–60). Newbury Park, CA: Sage.

Weihofen, H. (1965). *Testimonial competence and credibility.* 34 Geo. Wash. L. Rev. 53–91.

Wells, G. L., Turtle, J., & Luus, C. A. E. (1989). The perceived credibility of child eyewitnesses. In S. J. Ceci, M. P. Toglia, & D. F. Ross (Eds.), *Children's eyewitness memory* (pp. 23–46). New York: Springer-Verlag.

Wexler, R. (1992). *Wounded innocents.* New York: Prometheus Books.

Whipple, G. M. (1909). The observer as reporter: A survey of the "psychology of testimony." *Psychological Bulletin, 6,* 153–170.

Whipple, G. M. (1911). The psychology of testimony. *Psychological Bulletin, 8,* 307–309.

Whipple, G. M. (1912). Psychology of testimony and report. *Psychological Bulletin, 9,* 264–269.

Whipple, G. M. (1913). Psychology of testimony and report. *Psychological Bulletin, 10,* 264–268.

Whitcomb, D. (1992). *When the child is a victim* (2nd ed.). Washington, DC: National Institute of Justice.

White, S., Strom, G., Santili, G., & Halpin, B. M. (1986). Interviewing young sexual abuse victims with anatomically correct dolls. *Child Abuse & Neglect, 10,* 519–530.

Wigmore, J. H. (1909). Professor Muensterberg and the psychology of testimony. *Illinois Law Review, 3,* 399–445.

Wigmore, J. (1940). *Wigmore on evidence* § 509 at 601 (3rd. Ed.); Wigmore is paraphrasing C. J. Campbell, in Hughes v. R. Co., 65 Michigan 10, 31 N.W. 605 (1887).

Williams, L. M. (1994). Recall of childhood trauma: A prospective study of women's memories of child sexual abuse. *Journal of Consulting and Clinical Psychology, 62,* 1167–1176.

Wilson, J. C., & Pipe, M. E. (1989). The effects of cues on young children's recall of real events. *New Zealand Journal of Psychology, 18,* 65–70.

Wolfner, G., Faust, D., & Dawes, R. (1993). The use of anatomical dolls in sexual abuse evaluations: The state of the science. *Applied and Preventative Psychology, 2,* 1–11.

Wyatt, G. E. (1985). The sexual abuse of Afro-American and white American women in childhood. *Child Abuse & Neglect, 9,* 507–519.

Yates, J. L., & Nasby, W. (1993). Dissociation, affect, and network models of memory: An integrative proposal. *Journal of Traumatic Stress, 6,* 305–326.

Zaragoza, M. (1991). Preschool children's susceptibility to memory impairment. In J. L. Doris (Eds.), *The suggestibility of children's recollections* (pp. 27–39). Washington, DC: American Psychological Association.

Zaragoza, M. S., & Lane, S. (1994). Source misattributions and the suggestibility of eyewitness memory. *Journal of Experimental Psychology: Learning, Memory, and Cognition, 20,* 934–945.

Zechmeister, E. B., & Nyberg, S. E. (1982). *Human memory: An introduction to research and theory.* Monterey, CA: Brooks/Cole.

AUTHOR INDEX

Loh, W. D., 49, 52
Luus, C. A. E., 63, 64

MacLean, H., 189
Maguire, J. M., 49
Malla, S., 30
Manion, A., 64
Manor, T., 82
Manshel, L., xiv
Marin, B., 57, 60
Marriott, C., 212
Martin, K. M., 43
Maryland v. Craig, 65, 66n
Marzolf, D. P., 172
Mason, M. A., 162, 172, 270, 279, 284, 285, 287
McCarthy, T., 110
McCloskey, M. M., 64, 258
McConnell, T. R., 55
McGough, L., 36, 48, 50, 65, 66, 82, 145n, 162, 248, 262, 270
McGraw, J. M., 31, 32, 33, 84n, 262
McIver, W., 165
Meck, E., 79
Melton, G. B., 83, 233
Memon, A., 230
Merkin, S., 79
Messerschmidt, R., 55
Mian, M., 30, 34
Miller, A., 9
Miller, D. G., 110
Moan, S., 69, 170, 174, 235, 265
Montoya, J., 66
Moore, C., 50, 51
Morgan, E. M., 49
Moston, S., 151
Münsterberg, H., 50, 51
Myers, J. E. B., x, 8, 270, 271, 302–3

Nader, K., 147
Nasby, W., 196
Nathan, D., xiv, 238, 239, 261
Nathanson, M., 32
Nathanson, R., 257
National Center on Child Abuse and Neglect, 23, 29, 32, 36
Neisser, U., 46, 193, 197
Nelson, K., 58, 78, 83, 198, 256
Nevins, W. S., 302, 304
Nicholas, G., 69, 170, 174, 235, 265
Nida, R. E., 72, 170
Nightingale, N., 262, 263, 264

Noble, L. D., 167
Nyberg, S. E., 41

Ofshe, R., 194, 209
Oldenberg, D., 190
Ornstein, P., 71, 72, 73, 170, 234, 255
Otis, M., 55, 59

Paradise, J., 32
Patterson, R. N., 205
Pear, T., 52
Pendergrast, M., 195n
Peters, D. P., 23, 57, 145n, 207
Pettit, F., 90, 147, 159
Pezdek, K., 254
Phipps-Yonas, S., 280
Piaget, J., 201, 212, 262
Picariello, M. L., 255
Pillemer, D. B., 77, 255
Pipe, M. E., 263
Polansky, S., 202, 203
Pollatsek, A., 248
Poole, D. A., 108, 119, 217, 230, 234
Powers, P., 44
Pressley, M., 41, 254
Pruett, J. C., 255
Putnick, M., 262, 263, 264
Pynoos, R. S., 147

Qin, J., 28
Quas, J. A., 207

R. v. Russell Bishop, 17
R. v. Wallwork, 65
Rabinowitz, D., xiv
Raye, C. L., 58, 227
Rayner, K., 248
Read, B., 78
Read, J. D., 201n, 227, 238
Realmuto, G., 165, 282
Redmayne, M., 287
Reed, R. S., 141
Renick, A., 172, 177, 178
Reyna, V., 42, 120
Reynolds, C. R., 161, 164, 185n
Rice, S. A., 87–88
Riddlesberger, M. M., 207
Robertson, M., 165
Roe, C., 254
Romaine, S., 78
Romanczyk, A., 63, 64
Rosa, J. D., 162

SUBJECT INDEX

Electronic recording of child witnesses
(*continued*)
  proposals for mandating, 248–50
Escalona, Francisco "Frank" Fuster. *See*
    Fuster, Frank (accused in
    Country Walk case)
Ethics
  in forensic context for therapists,
      288–93
  of interviewing children, 292–93
Expert witnesses, 269–70
  ability of, to detect lying, 280–82
  partisan, 274–76, 279–83
    in Michaels case, 278–79
    in *State v. Bullock*, 34n, 276–78
  testimony of, 64, 66, 299–302. *See
      also* Expert witnesses, partisan
  judicial changes affecting,
      xii–xiii, 283–84
  reforms proposed for, 284–88
  types of, 270–71

False allegations. *See also* Lying, by
    children
  causes of, 33, 133–34, 262
  studies about, 30–33
False memories, 60, 211–12, 232
  studies about, 218–22
  and suggestive questioning, 225–26
False narratives. *See* False allegations;
    false memories
Federal Rules of Evidence, 36, 65, 284
Flashbulb memories, 205–6
Forgetting, 192–93
Frye test, applied to expert witnesses,
    283–84

Guided imagery, use of, in therapy, 222,
    227–29, 232, 239

Infantile amnesia, 197–201
Interviewer bias, 34n, 80–82, 87–89,
    93–94
  defined, 79–80
  effects of, on children's accuracy,
      89–93
  examples of, 94–105, 155–59
  reasons for, 82–84
Interviews. *See also names of specific case
    studies*; Reinterviewing;
    Suggestive questioning
  with children

as conversations, 77–79, 258–59
ethics of, 292–93
forensic, 79–85
reforms affecting, xii–xiii,
    248–50, 283–84
defined, 76
repeated questioning across. *See*
    Reinterviewing
repeated questioning within, 119–21
  in case studies, 121–25

Lipmann, O., suggestibility studies of,
    57–58
Little Rascals case, 9–11, 39, 146
  accusatorial atmosphere in, 141–43,
      153–54, 247
  and books with abuse themes,
      222–25
  interviews in, 72–73, 96–98, 150–51
    with anatomically detailed dolls,
        96, 175–77, 181–83, 215–16
    in court, 103–4
    inaccuracy of notes taken during,
        243–47
  interviewer bias in, 94–96
  repeated questioning during,
      112–15, 121
  peer pressure in, 150–51, 240
  ritualistic abuse alleged in, 26–27,
      301
  stereotype induction in, 134–35
  therapists in, 96–98, 288, 291
    criticized, 226
Lying, by children, 262–66. *See also* False
    allegations
  expert witnesses' ability to detect,
      280–82

Macias, Frederico "Fred." *See* Macias case
Macias case, 17–18, 39, 45, 304
  recantation of witness in, 238, 304
  suggestive questioning in, 123–25
McMartin preschool case, 27, 250
Memories, 40–41. *See also* False
    memories; Memory system;
    Recall
  acquired, 219–21, 227
  children's, 39, 83–85, 235, 297–98
  concepts of, 208–10
    dissociation, 196–97
    forgetting, 192–93
    infantile amnesia, 197–201

repression, 194–96, 210. *See also*
Source monitoring studies
about, 201–4
suppression, 194
effects of stressful events on, 205–8
flashbulb, 205–6
and perceptual narrowing, 206–8
recovered. *See* Recall
retrospective, 240–41
and scripted knowledge, 43, 255–57
strength of, and suggestibility,
253–54
through postevent rehearsal,
200–201
Memory system. *See also* Memories
encoding, 41–42, 221–22
retrieval, 42–44
storage, 42
Michaels case, 11–13, 27, 278, 288
accusatorial (conspiratorial)
atmosphere in, 143
amicus brief filed in, 292–93
interviews in, 73, 133, 144–45
with anatomically detailed dolls,
178–80
by authority figures, 152–53
electronic recording of, 242–43
interviewer bias in, 99–103,
155–59
peer pressure in, 149–50
repeated questioning during,
115–18, 121–22
stereotype induction during,
135–36
retrospective memories in, 241
Moore, C., 50–51
Münsterberg, Hugo, 50–51

Old Cutler case, 13–14, 39, 289–90
accusatorial atmosphere in, 141
interviews in
with anatomically detailed dolls,
163, 213–15
suggestive questioning in, 118–19
ritualistic abuse alleged in, 26–27,
301
therapist's testimony in, 300–301

Peer pressure, 240
in suggestive questioning, 146–52
Perceptual narrowing, 206–8
Piaget, Jean, 200–201, 212

Postevent rehearsal, 200–201

R. v. Russell Bishop, 16, 17, 298
Reality monitoring, 212–16, 226–28,
230–32
defined, 212
errors in, 222–26
Recall. *See also* Memories; Memory
system
children's, 39
of events involving bodily
touching, 68–74
delayed, of sexual abuse, 187–90
controversy concerning, 190–91
effect of stress on, 205–8
Recovered memories. *See* Recall
Reinterviewing
with anatomically detailed dolls,
177–78
in case studies, 111–19
effects of, 108–11, 237
reasons for, 80–81, 107–8
Repeated questioning
across interviews. *See* Reinterviewing
within interviews, 119–21
in case studies, 121–25
Repressed memories, 194–96, 210
studies about, 201–4
Retrospective memories, 240–41
Ritualistic abuse
analysis of, 247–48
lack of evidence about, 26–29, 94,
98–99, 301

Salem Witch Trials, 8–9, 48, 83, 302–4
Sam Stone study (suggestive
questioning), 129–34, 267,
281
Satanic cults. *See* Ritualistic abuse
Scripted knowledge, and suggestibility,
43, 255–57
Selective reinforcement, 144–45
Semantic knowledge, and suggestibility,
254–55
Sexually abused children. *See* Child
sexual abuse; Child witnesses
Source monitoring, 226–28, 230–32
defined, 212
errors in, 216–18, 222–26
Spontaneous disclosure. *See* Disclosure
State v. Buckey (McMartin preschool
case), 27, 250

ABOUT THE AUTHORS

Stephen J. Ceci is the Helen L. Carr Professor of Psychology at Cornell University. His honors include an NIH Research Career Scientist award and a Senior Fullbright–Hayes fellowship. Maggie Bruck is an associate professor of Psychology and of Pediatrics at McGill University. Her honors include two consecutive career development awards from the National Health Research Development program of Canada. Both authors have conducted research and published extensively in the fields of developmental, social, and cognitive psychology. Between them, Ceci and Bruck have published over 300 scholarly articles, chapters, and books. Both serve on a number of editorial boards of scientific journals. Their collaboration on the issues of the reliability of children's testimony has produced a number of research studies, as well as reports and briefs to various judges and courts. Their amicus brief presented by the Committee of Concerned Social Scientists for the case of *New Jersey v. Margaret Kelly Michaels* was quoted by the Court in its decision. Their work has been widely acclaimed. In 1994, they were awarded the Robert Chin Prize by the Society for the Psychological Study of Social Issues for the best article dealing with child abuse. This same article was also named one of the 20 outstanding articles in *Child Psychiatry and Child Development.*